INTERNATIONAL LAW

International Law

Second Edition

ANDERS HENRIKSEN

OXFORD
UNIVERSITY PRESS

Great Clarendon Street, Oxford, OX2 6DP,
United Kingdom

Oxford University Press is a department of the University of Oxford.
It furthers the University's objective of excellence in research, scholarship,
and education by publishing worldwide. Oxford is a registered trade mark of
Oxford University Press in the UK and in certain other countries

First edition 2017

Impression: 1

Public sector information reproduced under Open Government Licence v3.0
(http://www.nationalarchives.gov.uk/doc/open-government-licence/open-government-licence.htm)

Published in the United States of America by Oxford University Press
198 Madison Avenue, New York, NY 10016, United States of America

British Library Cataloguing in Publication Data

Data available

Library of Congress Control Number: 2019937812

ISBN 978-0-19-882872-3

Printed in Great Britain by
Bell & Bain Ltd., Glasgow

Preface

This book introduces law students and legal practitioners to the basic purposes and principles of public international law. It is first and foremost intended for undergraduate law students who study public international law for the first time. The overarching aim is to enhance the understanding of international law by presenting and exploring that part of the lawyer's legal toolbox that contains the answers that are needed to resolve questions involving two or more sovereign states. The ambition has been to compile a textbook that would appeal to students and universities across continental Europe in non-common law jurisdictions.

This book offers a fairly pragmatic approach to international law and it deliberately refrains from offering a highly theoretical account of the law. In fact, one of its core ambitions is to highlight the occasional tension between, on the one hand, stability and order and, on the other, certain notions of 'justice'. Where possible, the book has sought to illustrate the points made through brief presentations of cases.

The book combines presentations and discussion of both general topics of public international law (such as its history, structures, sources, subjects, jurisdiction, immunity and state responsibility) as well as many of its specialized sub-disciplines (including the law of the sea, human rights law, environmental law, economic law, dispute settlement, the regulation of the international use of force, the law of armed conflict and international criminal law). For pedagogical purposes, all chapters contain a brief introductory list of the central issues covered in the chapter, a concluding summary, some suggestions for further reading and a range of questions for discussions.

Public international law is a field prone to constant rapid developments and, while every effort has been made to ensure the book is as up to date as possible at the time of publication, the law has been stated as I believe it should be stated as of mid-November 2018.

I wish to thank those who have assisted me in preparing this second edition. First, I wish to thank Liana Green of Oxford University Press for her very professional and dedicated job at securing the completion of this edition. I would also like to thank the anonymous reviewers for useful comments and suggestions and those at our law faculty here at the University of Copenhagen who made valuable comments on individual chapters along the way. So, thank you Yoshi Tanaka, Jens Elo Rytter, Amnon Lev and Beatriz Martinez Romera. Finally, I want to thank Caisa for providing me with love and patience.

Anders Henriksen
University of Copenhagen, Denmark
November 2018

New to this Edition

This edition includes the following new material:

- a new section on the current challenges to international law (Chapter 1)
- new discussion of the legality of cyber operations, including the 2017 *Tallinn Manual* (Chapters 5, 13 and 14)
- treatment of the regulation of coercion that falls below the threshold for constituting a use of force under the UN Charter (Chapters 5 and 13)
- a new section on shared state responsibility (Chapter 7)
- a new section on diplomatic protection (Chapter 7)
- additional coverage of the regulation of piracy (Chapter 8)
- a further section on the international protection of refugees (Chapter 9)
- a new section on the legality of using force to deter chemical warfare (Chapter 13)
- a new section on the regulation of belligerent occupation (Chapter 14)
- new case law, such as *Maritime Delimitation in the Indian Ocean (Somalia v Kenya)* [2017]

Guide to the Book

International Law is written with the student in mind. Its user-friendly style will ensure you gain a sound understanding of the subject area and a range of supporting features throughout will help you to consider the latest debates and reflect upon the issues at hand.

This guide shows you how to use those features so that you can get the most out of your studies.

CENTRAL ISSUES

mines the system of   3. The chapter analyse
tion that has emerged   scope of the most impo
econd World War.   conventions and the app
he mechanisms for the   rights conventions in ti

Central issues

Central issues boxes highlight the key issues and introduce you to the key principles within the topics covered and the critical areas of debate to consider as you read each chapter.

Summary

al society has its own legal sources and the di
it of departure in article 38 of the ICJ Statute.
ernational law can be divided into those of a pri
While treaties, customary international law and

Summaries

Chapter summaries provide an overview of the topics covered in each chapter, allowing you to review the essential concepts and points discussed.

Recommended reading

ces in general, see Hugh Thirlway, *The Sources of*
ress, 2014); Jean d'Aspremont, *Formalism and the*
on the Ascertainment of Legal Rules (Oxford Univers
Statute, see Alain Pellet, 'Article 38' in Andreas Zim

Recommended reading

At the end of each chapter is a list of recommended further reading, carefully selected to help supplement your knowledge and develop your understanding of key topics.

Questions for discussion

of Westphalia perceived as a crucial turning point
ic international law?

Questions for discussion

Questions at the end of each chapter allow you to test your understanding of the topics covered. You will find guidance on how to answer these questions on the accompanying Online Resources.

Outline Contents

Detailed Contents

Table of Cases

Table of Legislation

1
Foundations and structure of international law

CENTRAL ISSUES

1. This chapter introduces the reader to the subject of public international law and provides an overview of its most important elements.

2. It contains a brief historical overview of the development of modern international law from the late Middle Ages until the present.

3. It also introduces the various structures within international law, consisting of the international law of coexistence and the international law of cooperation.

4. The chapter discusses the issue of enforcement in international law and touches upon the tension between notions of justice and stability that is a consequence of the state-centric configuration of international law.

1.1 Introduction

Public international law deals with legal issues of concern to more than one state. It is traditionally defined as the system of law that regulates the interrelationship of sovereign states and their rights and duties to one another. But to that must be added a host of other actors, most notably international organizations and individuals that may also possess rights and/or obligations under international law. Public international law is not the same as 'private international law', which consists of national laws dealing with conflicts of law and establishes rules for the treatment of cases that involve a foreign element.[1]

Like all law, international law reflects the society to which it applies. So as international society becomes ever more specialized and intertwined, so does international law. In 2006, the American Society of International Law (ASIL) identified 100 ways international law shapes and affects our lives and the world in which we live.[2] The

---

[1] In this book, the term 'international law' refers to public international law.
[2] American Society of International Law, 'International Law: 100 Ways It Shapes Our Lives' (2006) https://www.asil.org/resources/100Ways (accessed 15 October 2018).

issues highlighted by ASIL included, of course, many of the fundamental topics of concern to international society that we shall explore in this book, such as the creation of states, jurisdiction, state immunity, the peaceful settlement of disputes, the prevention and regulation of armed conflict, the governing of the seas and oceans etc., but they also covered a lot of the more mundane aspects of our lives. In fact, international regulation is everywhere around us, such as in the cars we drive, the phone calls we make, the food we eat, the wine we drink, the clothes we wear, the movies we watch, the medicine we use and so on and so forth. Indeed, the preparation, production and shipping of the very book you hold in your hands were subject to a host of international legal instruments.[3]

One of the consequences of the seemingly ever-expanding reach of international law has been the gradual development of a myriad sub-disciplines, such as the international law of the sea, international human rights law, international environmental law, international economic law, the laws of armed conflict etc. As we shall see throughout this book, these sub-disciplines often have their own distinct institutions and occasionally also adjudicatory bodies.[4] Another characteristic of contemporary international law is that legal issues formerly dealt with exclusively within one of the sub-disciplines are increasingly scrutinized in several of them. For instance, while up until a few decades ago it was sufficient for experts on the international regulation of armed conflicts to be familiar with the law and developments within the laws of war—a branch of international law particularly created for the purposes of regulating armed conflict—this no longer suffices. The expansive reach of human rights law and the establishment of a range of international criminal tribunals mean that genuine expertise on how armed conflicts are regulated internationally also requires extensive knowledge of human rights law and international criminal law.

Despite its increasing practical relevance, though, as we shall see throughout this book, international law remains a system of law that is very different from the national legal systems most lawyers are familiar with. Most notably, unlike in a domestic legal system, there is neither a legislative nor an executive branch in the international legal system. Similarly, although a number of international courts have been created over the years, there is no mandatory and well-established procedure for the settlement of legal disputes. In general, as we shall return to later in this chapter, international law remains a decentralized legal system in which it is primarily up to the legal subjects themselves to create, interpret and enforce the law.

We begin this introductory chapter in Section 1.2 with a brief historical overview of international law before Section 1.3 presents the international legal system consisting of different structures of legal rules and principles. Subsequently, Section 1.4 discusses the basis of international legal obligation and Section 1.5 offers a brief overview of the

---

[3] In the event that you consider copying and distributing the book, you may also find it useful to know that international law contains instruments that seek to protect intellectual property and copyright.

[4] On so-called 'fragmentation' of international law, see, inter alia, Jan Klabbers, Anne Peters and Geir Ulfstein, *The Constitutionalization of International Law* (Oxford University Press, 2009). See also ILC, 'Fragmentation of International Law: Difficulties Arising from the Diversification and Expansion of International Law' (13 April 2006), UN Doc. A/CN.4/L.682, para. 492.

relationship between international law and national law. Section 1.6 deals with the issue of enforcement. Section 1.7 contains some remarks about the alleged inadequacies of international law and the tension between notions of justice and order that is so prevalent within the international legal system.

1.2 A brief history of international law

1.2.1 Early modern international law

Cultures and communities have traded and interacted for millennia and there are numerous historical records of the creation of more or less formal practices and mutual expectations that may be considered to be early traces of what we today call international law.[5] Whatever their preferences, cultures and traditions, political communities have felt a need for international rules and principles and the certainty and predictability they bring to their international relations.[6] But since international law as we know it today was invented in Europe, this is also where our brief overview of its history should begin. Europe in the *late Middle Ages* (15th and 16th centuries) was characterized by both multiple levels of different allegiances and rights and obligations as well as the universal political and religious forces of, respectively, the Holy Roman Empire and the Catholic Church. By providing the spiritual authority of the Western world, the Pope in particular was able to exert considerable influence over the various princes, emperors and kings who governed their territories. But the networks of knights and merchants were of a transnational nature and the populations at the time often felt a closer sense of allegiance to such communities than to their fellow 'nationals'. It was also a time when ideas about the normative structure of the world were dominated by theories of natural law originally developed in the classical eras. Natural law contained an all-embracing set of ideas about natural and social life in the universe and, though primarily focused on the individual and his or her relations to the world, it also applied to states by virtue of the fact that rulers were also individuals and therefore subject to it. Next to natural law (*jus naturale*) was *jus gentium*—a law of people/nations and hence inferior to natural law, at times simply perceived as being derived from the latter. While an elaborate international legal structure did not yet exist, legal obligations and contracts were nevertheless created in day-to-day relations of the communities at the time, leading to numerous agreements on issues such as the treatment of merchants, maritime traders and diplomatic envoys and the conduct of war and the exchange and ransoming of prisoners of war.

---

[5] For a historical overview, see Wilhelm G. Grewe, *The Epochs of International Law* (rev edn, De Gruyter, 2010); Stephen C. Neff, *Justice Among Nations: A History of International Law* (Harvard University Press, 2014); and Bardo Fassbender and Anne Peters (eds), *The Oxford Handbook of the History of International Law* (Oxford University Press, 2012).

[6] See also Alexander Orakhelashvili, 'The Idea of European International Law' (2006) 17 *European Journal of International Law* 315.

The period was also the dawn of colonialism, and the early confrontations between Spanish explorers and native Indian populations and kingdoms in the New World posed a particular challenge to the philosophers and legal scholars of the time. In a series of famous lectures from 1532—*De Indis et De Iure Belli Relectiones*—the Spanish Dominican professor Francisco de Vitoria (1483–1546) concluded that the native populations of the New World were part of the society of the human race and that the acts of the Spanish conquistadores were thus governed by natural law. Vitoria rejected the claim that the Spanish could justify their conquests of the new areas based on notions of 'discovery' (it is, after all, hard to discover something that the locals have already 'found') or by grant of the Pope. To Vitoria, like all other wars, the waging of war against the natives of the New World had to be 'just' and the acts of the Spanish could only be justified on the basis of alleged local resistance to the activities of the Christian missionaries and opposition to the free passage and trading policies of the Spaniards.[7]

It is, however, not until the *17th and 18th centuries*, that we begin to see the contours of a modern international legal system. For one thing, a much clearer distinction was introduced between *jus naturale* and *jus gentium* and it is from the latter that international law as we know it would subsequently develop as a distinct discipline. A leading figure in this period was the Spanish Jesuit Francisco Suárez (1548–1617), who in 1612 published his important work *A Treatise on Laws and God the Lawgiver*. Suárez was succeeded by the, arguably, most famous international lawyer of all time, the Dutchman Hugo Grotius (1583–1645), whose major contributions to the development of international law include *The Freedom of the Seas* and *On the Law of War and Peace* published in, respectively, 1609 and 1625. Among other things, Grotius was instrumental in applying natural law to the conduct of international relations and developing the law of nations to make it a practical tool for regulating a variety of areas of international relations. Another influential figure was Emmerich de Vattel (1714–1767), whose *Law of Nations* from 1758 contains useful legal guidance for practitioners of international law.

1.2.2 **Peace of Westphalia**

The international legal system that we recognize today is generally tied to the emergence and consolidation of nation states in Europe. The 'birth' of the international state system is usually traced back to the 1648 Peace of Westphalia that brought an end to the Thirty Years War that had ravaged continental Europe. In the peace treaties of Westphalia, consisting of the Peace of Munster and the Treaties of Munster and Osnabruck, the major European powers sought to establish a semblance of order and structure in an otherwise anarchical and disorderly European world. The idea was to reduce the powers of transnational forces, like empire and religion, and instead compartmentalize territory and individuals into sovereign states. In turn, over time, this established the state as the primary source of authority, paving the way for an increasing sense of allegiance among citizens to their respective states of nationality.

---

[7] See also Matthew Craven, 'Colonialism and Domination' in Fassbender and Peters (n 5) 863–869.

By seeking to create an international order derived from agreed rules and limits and basing it on a multiplicity of 'states' of equal legal importance, Westphalia was a decisive turning point, and what had initially merely been conceived of as a concept of order for war-torn continental Europe spread to the rest of the world and to this day remains a key building block of international law. Before the Peace of Westphalia, the French lawyer Jean Bodin (1530–1596) had already conceptualized the all-important notion of state sovereignty that—as we shall see in Section 1.4—is vital to understanding the purposes and functions of international law. Bodin was influenced by the chaos and turmoil of the raging wars of religion in France and he felt the need for a system that contained a clear and unquestionable source of authority. In his *Six Livres de la République*, published in 1576, he developed the theory of a 'sovereign' possessing 'absolute and indivisible' power answerable only to God. The sovereign would be above the law and could both create and break the law at his own discretion. In a sense, the sovereign stood above society and was bound by no one. Bodin's hugely influential thoughts were later supplemented by the equally important conceptions of sovereignty developed by Thomas Hobbes (1588–1679) and John Locke (1632–1704).

1.2.3 **The 19th century and the era of positivism**

The 19th century was dominated by a full-on assault on the idea that acts of states could be judged according to whether or not they conformed to transcendent ideals of fairness or divine will. In international law, this was the era of 'positivism', the primary tenet of which was that the only true source of law was state will. Consequently, positivism attached primary importance to state consent, whether expressed explicitly in the form of a treaty or implicitly by customary practices adhered to by states due to a belief that the practice was legally binding. According to the 'consensual theory', unless a state has consented to be bound by a rule, no international legal obligation exists and the state remains entitled to act as it pleases. Unlike natural law, then, positive law does not envisage a universal legal system, but rather one that is fragmented and in which states are bound by different legal obligations. As Chapter 2 illustrates, positivism and the consensual theory remain fundamental influences on the theory of international legal sources.

Positivism owed much of its appeal as a theory of international law to the emergence of formal institutions of international law, including the 1865 International Telegraph Union and the 1874 Universal Postal Union. It was also during this period that the first multilateral treaties regulating armed conflict were concluded. In 1856, for example, the *Declaration of Paris* set legal limits to the capture of private property at sea and the 1868 Declaration of St Petersburg banned the use of explosive bullets and stipulated that the only permissible aim of war is to defeat the armed forces of the enemy. Of even greater importance were the two Hague Conferences in 1899 and 1907 that led to the adoption of conventions on, respectively, the conduct of war and a permanent Court of Arbitration. The latter half of the century also saw a peak in colonialism in Asia and, in particular, Africa. Although most of the states in South America gained independence from their European colonizers in the first half of the 19th century, at the 1884–1885

Berlin Conference the major European powers gathered to discuss the criteria for the partition of Africa ('the Scramble for Africa')[8] and, at the outbreak of the First World War in 1914, 90 per cent of Africa was under European control.[9]

1.2.4 The interwar period

The destruction and carnage of the First World War dominated events in the interwar period. The primary development was the creation in 1919 of the League of Nations—an organization tasked with maintaining world peace. While the League did not prohibit war, it required states to submit potential destabilizing disputes to one of a number of settlement mechanisms and to desist from resorting to war until a certain period had elapsed following the decision by that mechanism.[10] Efforts to outlaw war were not attempted until 1928 when the *Treaty of Paris* (also known as the Kellogg–Briand Pact) obliged parties to refrain from going to war as a means of settling their international controversies and as an instrument of national policy.[11] A major achievement in the period was the successful establishment of the Permanent Court of International Justice (PCIJ) based in The Hague in the Netherlands. Although the Court did not have compulsory jurisdiction, it did build a substantial body of case law and was the forerunner to the present day International Court of Justice (ICJ).

1.2.5 The period after the end of the Second World War

The period immediately after the Second War World was a time of major achievements in international law. For one thing, one of the ways in which the world (or, more correctly, the victorious states in that war) reacted to the atrocities of the Nazis was to prosecute top German officials for international crimes before a war crimes tribunal in Nuremberg, thereby setting an important precedent in international criminal law.[12] More importantly, the League of Nations was replaced by the United Nations (UN), which was entrusted with the maintenance of international peace and security. The UN is built on solid 'Westphalian' principles and based on respect for the principle of equal rights and self-determination of peoples and on the sovereign equality of all its member states.[13] The founding treaty of the UN—the Charter of the United Nations—introduced a ban on the use of force and gave a collective organ—the

---

[8] Craven (n 7) 879–887.

[9] For studies of colonialism and international law, see the major works by Anthony Anghie, *Imperialism, Sovereignty and the Making of International Law* (Cambridge University Press, 2004); Martti Koskenniemi, *The Gentle Civilizer of Nations: The Rise and Fall of International Law 1870–1960* (Cambridge University Press, 2011).

[10] Covenant of the League of Nations (adopted 28 June 1919, entered into force 10 January 1920), art. 12.

[11] Treaty Between the United States and Other Powers Providing for the Renunciation of War as an Instrument of National Policy (adopted 27 August 1928, entered into force 24 July 1929) 94 LNTS 57 (Kellogg–Briand Pact).

[12] Major Japanese war criminals prosecuted before an international military tribunal in Tokyo. See Chapter 15.

[13] See, respectively, Charter of the United Nations (adopted 26 June 1945, entered into force 24 October 1945), arts 1(2) and 2(1).

Security Council—the competence to maintain international peace and security and, to that end, if necessary, to authorize forceful measures.[14] From then on, the maintenance of peace and the conduct of war were to be a collective effort. In practice, however, from the outset the activities of the UN were marred by the outbreak of the Cold War and the struggle between the Great Powers of the East and West. Consequently, the Security Council remained by and large inactive throughout the Cold War. It was not until after the collapse of communism and the successful UN-sanctioned ousting of Iraq from Kuwait in 1991 that the collective security system in the UN began to live, to some extent, up to its promises.

The UN Charter also established a General Assembly where all member states are represented. Although the Assembly only has a consultative role, it offers an organizational structure where all states—including those of marginal importance—can voice their opinions and raise their concerns. The Assembly has also been instrumental in the promotion of a wide range of goals of global interest. One of the best examples is the important role it played in the decolonialization process. When the UN was created, almost one-third of the world's population lived in territories which were in some way dependent on a colonial power. In 1960, the Assembly adopted a landmark declaration on the granting of independence to colonies that affirmed the right of all people to self-determination and proclaimed that colonialism should be brought to a speedy and unconditional end.[15] Today, 80 former colonies have gained their independence. The Assembly has also helped advance the development of international law. In 1946, it established the International Law Commission (ILC) whose primary purpose is to promote the 'progressive development of international law and its codification'.[16] With the creation of the UN, the current ICJ also replaced the PCIJ and gradually assumed an increasingly important role.

The UN serves as an umbrella structure for a number of important international organizations. A 1944 conference at Bretton Woods in the United States created the most important international organizations for the regulation of trade and monetary policy: the International Monetary Fund (IMF), the International Bank for Reconstruction and Development (the 'World Bank') and the General Agreement on Tariffs and Trade (GATT). While the GATT was created to liberalize world trade by reducing tariffs and other barriers to trade, the IMF was established to ensure exchange stability and to make resources available to states with balance of payments difficulties. To supplement the IMF, the World Bank provides loans to developing countries. In 1995, the World Trade Organization (WTO) replaced the old GATT system.[17] The creation of the UN and its various 'sister organizations' illustrates that states often seek to pursue common goals by creating international organizations.

---

[14] Peaceful settlement of disputes is discussed in Chapter 12. The regulation of the use of force is the subject of Chapter 13.

[15] Declaration on the Granting of Independence to Colonial Countries and Peoples, GA Res. 1514 (XV) (14 December 1960), UN Doc. A/RES/1514(XV).

[16] Statute of the International Law Commission, GA Res. 174 (II) (21 November 1947), UN Doc. A/RES/174(II), art. 1. For an overview, see Alan Boyle and Christine Chinkin, *The Making of International Law* (Oxford University Press, 2007) 171–183.

[17] International economic law is covered in Chapter 11.

Membership of these organizations varies according to purpose and region. An important regional organization is the North Atlantic Treaty Organization (NATO), whose members agree to offer each other mutual defence in the event of an attack by an external actor. NATO was created in 1949 to counter the threat from the Soviet Union but it remains of vital importance. Institutional cooperation has been particularly strong in Europe, where the European Union (EU) stands out as an impressive example of what ambitious states can accomplish. Like the UN, the impetus for the creation of what later became the EU was the motivation to avoid large-scale conflict. In 1951, six European states established the European Coal and Steel Community and a common market for coal and steel.[18] In 1957, the same states adopted the Treaty of Rome that created the European Economic Community (EEC) consisting of an economic common market and a customs union.[19] By 1993, the EEC had developed into a single market. The 1992 Maastricht Treaty created the European Union[20] and the 1999 Treaty of Amsterdam brought the members of the Union even closer together. On 1 May 2004, the EU was expanded with ten new member states, thus bringing the total membership to 25.[21] Today it stands at 28.[22] The EU consists of a number of important institutions, including the European Council, the Council of the European Union, the European Parliament, the European Commission and the Court of Justice of the European Union (CJEU). Some of these may adopt legally binding instruments or render binding decisions.

Mention should also be made of the 1949 Council of Europe, created to strengthen intergovernmental and inter-parliamentary cooperation.[23] In 1950, the Council adopted the European Convention on Human Rights (ECHR), which remains the central instrument for the protection of human rights in Europe. The Convention established the European Court of Human Rights (ECtHR) in Strasbourg, France, which deals with complaints from both states and individual citizens and which renders binding decisions.

Important regional organizations have also been created outside Europe. In the Americas, for example, the 1948 Organization of American States (OAS) was established to create a peaceful order and to promote solidarity and collaboration and to defend the sovereignty, territorial integrity and independence of its members. It has 35 member states and consists of, among other things, a General Assembly and an Inter-American Commission on Human Rights (IACHR). In Africa, the 2001

---

[18] The states were Belgium, France, Germany, Italy, Luxembourg and the Netherlands.

[19] In 1973, Denmark, Ireland and the UK joined the EEC. Greece joined in 1981 and Portugal and Spain in 1986.

[20] In a referendum on 2 June 1992, a narrow majority of Danish voters rejected the Maastricht Treaty. In a subsequent referendum on 18 May 1993, a majority of Danish voters accepted Danish ratification of the Maastricht Treaty on the basis of an agreement entered into in Edinburgh according to which Denmark was granted four exceptions to the Treaty (EU citizenship, participation in the economic and monetary union, defence, and justice and home affairs).

[21] The new states were Cyprus, the Czech Republic, Estonia, Hungary, Latvia, Lithuania, Malta, Poland, Slovakia and Slovenia. Austria, Finland and Sweden had joined in 1995.

[22] In 2007, Bulgaria and Romania were admitted to the EU. Croatia joined in 2013.

[23] Statute of the Council of Europe (adopted 5 May 1949, entered into force 3 August 1949), ETS No. 1. See also the overview in Chapter 12.

African Union (AU) grew out of the 1963 Organisation of African Unity and works to ensure a prosperous and secure African continent.[24] It has 54 member states and its most important organs include an Assembly, an Executive Council, a Pan-African Parliament and a Court of Justice.

1.2.6 The present

For the most part, the post-Second World War events described in the previous section were driven by the West, which used its dominance in world affairs to create a rules-based international order that would be less prone to the sort of economic protection-ism and authoritarianism that led the world into the chaos and mass slaughter of the Second World War. In fact, most of the international institutions we know today were set up to create a world order based on Western values, most notably open and free economic markets, increasing respect for individual rights and institutional coop-eration. However, the Western-driven 'liberal international legal order' now shows signs of break-up. In part, this is because the international system—in the words of the UN Secretary-General—has become more 'multipolar'.[25] Global transformations in economic power have seen the emergence of a range of 'emerging' and/or more assertive non-Western powers, most notably China, and a comparatively diminishing influence and power of the West. Russia's unlawful annexation of Crimea in 2014 and China's policy of land-grab in the South China Sea seem to illustrate that the world may be witnessing not just increasing interstate competition but also profound disa-greements about the means whereby states may pursue their interests. The increasing international competition means that major states seem increasingly unable to reach agreement on ambitious collaborative efforts to create new legally binding global agreements on important contemporary issues and instead opt for less ambitious non-binding global political agreements or legally binding regional agreements with like-minded states. As we shall see in Chapter 11, for example, the so-called 'BRICS' countries (Brazil, Russia, India, China and South Africa) have set up a range of new financial institutions that may be potential rivals to the traditional global institutions, such as the IMF and the World Bank.

In the West, a number of states are at present experiencing somewhat of a popular 'backlash' against some of the values and institutions that underpin the post-Second World War liberal international legal order. Around Europe, core institutions like those in the EU and the European Court of Human Rights in Strasbourg are ever more frequently criticized for making unwarranted encroachments on national sov-ereignty, in particular in sensitive areas such as social security, asylum and migration and national security. In June 2016, the British people decided to leave the EU, and by

---

[24] See Constitutive Act of the African Union (adopted 11 July 2000, entered into force 26 May 2001), OAU Doc. CAB/LEG/23.15.

[25] UN Secretary-General, 'Securing Our Common Future: An Agenda for Disarmament', 24 May 2018, pp. 3–4. Available at: https://www.un.org/disarmament/publications/more/securing-our-common-future/ (accessed 11 September 2018).

October 2018 the British government was still trying to come to some sort of agreement with representatives of the EU on the UK–EU relationship after the UK leaves the Union in March 2019. In the United States, President Trump has pulled the US out of the ambitious *Trans-Pacific Partnership Agreement* (TPPA) and started a trade war with the EU and China after introducing tariffs on steel and aluminium. Trump has also made the US leave the UN Human Rights Council, the Joint Comprehensive Plan of Action (JCPOA) ('Iran Nuclear Deal') and the 2015 Paris Climate Agreement, and voiced his support for political leaders in Europe critical of the EU.

1.3 The structures of international law

1.3.1 Introduction–a society of sovereign nation states

The international legal system consists of different structures of rules reflecting the historical evolution of the law and the political order and configuration of the world.[26] Since the 1648 Peace of Westphalia, the centre of the international system has been the sovereign state, and international society is first and foremost a society of individual national states. The conception of the state as a (national) sovereign helps explain the primary purpose of international law.[27] International law is best conceived of from the standpoint of national law and as a response to a lawyer's need for legal rules and principles to complement those found in national legal systems. National law is adequate to deal with the majority of legal disputes that merely involve the relationship between citizens of a sovereign state or between the citizens and the state. But mutual respect for sovereignty dictates that national law is ill-suited to a situation where the interests of more than one sovereign state collide. Thus, whenever a lawyer encounters an issue of interest to more than one state, it is in international law the legal answer is found. In essence, then, international law serves as a supplement to national law—as a residual legal system—the scope of which cannot be determined independently of national law. Only when an issue is of interest to more than one national sovereign will international law enter the picture. The *scope* of international law is thereby determined by the inadequacy of national law. The *content* of international law, and thus the concrete answers to the questions that cannot be answered in national law, on the other hand, must be found in international law.

The two ways in which an issue becomes of interest to more than one state define the two substantive structures of international law. The first is where two or more states may have colliding interests in the substance of the issue. Here, the mere fact

---

[26] See also the approach of the so-called 'English School' in the international relations theory, inter alia, the seminal works of Hedley Bull, *The Anarchical Society: A Study of Order in World Politics* (Palgrave Macmillan, 1977). See also Wolfgang Friedmann, *The Changing Structure of International Law* (Stevens & Son, 1964) and the more recent account of the structures of international law in Ole Spiermann, *International Legal Argument in the Permanent Court of International Justice* (Cambridge University Press, 2005) ch. 2.

[27] The following approach is taken from Spiermann (n 26).

that international society is composed of a multitude of sovereign states with different interests is sufficient to make the issue international. The second way an issue becomes of interest to more than one state is when the involved states have agreed in a treaty to turn the issue (that would otherwise have been dealt with by national law) into one of an international character. In practice, therefore, a matter may become an issue for international law either due to its *content* or due to its *form*. While the former is governed by what is called 'the international law of coexistence', the latter is dealt with under 'the international law of cooperation'.[28]

1.3.2 **The international law of coexistence**

The international law of coexistence—at times referred to as 'general international law'—contains the legal answers to questions that are inherently of interest to more than one state and required to separate the powers of the sovereign states and thereby uphold peaceful coexistence. Thus, it is here the lawyer finds the classic topics of international law where states may have colliding interests, such as delimitation of—and title to—territory, the criteria for statehood and the recognition of new states and governments, jurisdiction and immunity, the use of force, the conduct of armed hostilities and neutrality in times of armed conflict. Also included are the fundamental principles of treaty law and the secondary legal principles on state responsibility. As a legal structure, the international law of coexistence is primarily *horizontal* in the sense that it is mainly concerned with the manner in which sovereign states interact with—and between—each other. It is less preoccupied with how sovereign authority is constituted or exercised in relation to the citizens within the state. As we shall see below, such issues are matters for international law because states have decided to make them the object of a treaty, in which case they are part of the international law of cooperation. It is also important to note that the international law of coexistence is similarly not concerned with binding states closer together in some sort of international 'community'. It merely seeks to ensure that states can pursue their different and separate interests (whatever they may be) in a way that respects the sovereignty and rights of other states. As a fundamental structure of international law, then, the international law of coexistence is relatively stable and not subject to much change. There is, however, an inherent vagueness to the *content* of this part of international law and easily recognizable rules are rare. In fact, there has always been an element of 'law-creation' in the process of resolving issues in which the interests of two or more states collide.

1.3.3 **The international law of cooperation**

The second substantive structure of international law is the international law of cooperation and it is here one finds the legal answers to issues that are not inherently of interest to two or more states but which have nevertheless been turned into matters of international concern through the adoption of a treaty. The reason why the issues are of an

---

[28] Ibid, 49–50, 69–70.

international character (and thus ill-suited to be dealt with by national law) is because treaties are international agreements governed by international law. As an international legal structure, the international law of cooperation is much 'younger' than the international law of coexistence. As the overview in Section 1.2.5 illustrated, in the period immediately after the end of the Second World War states began to create organizations that were given competence to deal with issues that had until that time been considered to be of an entirely national interest.[29] The result was the emergence of a new structure of international law involved in the promotion of a variety of 'societal' goals. International law thereby began to be concerned with the manner in which sovereign authority was exercised within individual states. Topics covered by the international law of cooperation include international human rights law, the majority of international environmental law and international economic law. EU law is a particularly good example of a legal regime solidly situated in the international law of cooperation.

Unlike the international law of coexistence, the international law of cooperation is 'optional' in the sense that states decide for themselves if they want to turn a matter previously dealt with by national law into a matter of international law. The consensual character of this part of international law helps explain the pace—or rather the lack thereof—with which international society deals with wider societal goals, such as the reduction of poverty or curbing climate change. Tackling such issues often requires legally binding agreements by states—something that is often hard to achieve.

1.4 The basis of international obligation

The question of why states are bound to observe international law has dominated international legal theory for centuries.[30] As the historical overview has illustrated, the theoretical debate has traditionally been dominated by proponents of natural law and positivism. While the former derives the binding force of international law from the claim that dictates of nature require certain behaviour of states, the latter bases international obligation on the consent of states (the 'consensual theory'). International legal theory has struggled to reconcile state sovereignty with international obligation.[31] If a state is truly sovereign and the legal subject of no one, how can it be bound by international law? To uphold the binding character of international law seems to imply the negation of sovereignty. It would therefore appear that *either* the state is sovereign, and hence not bound by international law, *or* it is bound by international law, and thus not sovereign.

---

[29] Friedmann (n 26) 61–71. See also Wolfgang Friedmann, 'The Changing Dimensions of International Law' (1962) 62 *Columbia Law Review* 1147.

[30] See also Oscar Schachter, 'Towards a Theory of International Obligation' (1967–1968) 8 *Virginia Journal of International Law* 300.

[31] A classic discussion is H. L. A. Hart, *The Concept of Law* (Clarendon Press, 1961) 220–226. For a critical account, see Martti Koskenniemi, *From Apology to Utopia: The Structure of International Legal Argument* (Cambridge University Press, 1989); David Kennedy, 'Theses about International Law Discourse' (1980) 23 *German Yearbook of International Law* 353.

As we saw in the previous section, however, there need not be an irreconcilable tension between sovereignty and international legal obligations. Indeed, if one looks outside the law for the answer to the question of why international law is binding, things become less complicated.[32] The existence of a plurality of sovereign states justifies the binding character of international law. It is not, in other words, a matter of choosing between upholding either state sovereignty or international legal obligations but, rather, of perceiving international legal obligations as a logical consequence of sovereignty.[33] Just as domestic societies must impose limits on how individuals can exercise their liberties, if liberty for all is to be respected, it is only by limiting the manner in which sovereign states may exercise their sovereignty that international society can ensure respect for the sovereignty of all states. The peaceful coexistence of sovereign states requires the existence of a number of basic rules that dictate how states may behave and may not behave in their mutual relations. And even sovereign states are bound by the basic rules of the society of which they form part.

In practice, of course, all states accept that they are members of a *society of states* and that they benefit from the rules required for maintaining peaceful coexistence within the society they form. They also participate in the working of the rules of the system. This, of course, does not mean that states may not disagree about the content of the law or that individual states may not decide to occasionally violate the law. Although Louis Henkin was right when he famously noted that 'almost all nations observe almost all principles of international law and almost all of their obligations almost all the time',[34] breaches of international law are not hard to find. But states never question that they are bound by international law. Thus, if a state is accused of torturing its citizens, it does not argue that the prohibition against torture is not binding upon it. Instead, it argues that the allegations of torture are incorrect or that it was somehow justified in violating the prohibition. When Russia intervened in Ukraine and annexed Crimea in 2014, it did not claim that it was not bound by international law, including the prohibition on the use of force, but instead that its acts fell outside those prescribed by international law. By justifying its actions with international legal arguments, Russia in reality affirmed the existence of the international legal system.

1.5 The relationship between international law and national law

A few points must be noted about the relationship between international law and national law. First of all, as we shall see throughout this book, *international law asserts its own supremacy over national law*. A state cannot justify a breach of its international legal obligations by arguing that compliance would be at variance with its national

---

[32] See also Spiermann (n 26) 44.
[33] Ibid, 45–47.
[34] Louis Henkin, *How Nations Behave* (Columbia University Press, 1979) 47.

law.[35] International law is not, however, generally preoccupied with *how* a state lives up to its international obligations and it usually leaves it to each state to determine how it will implement its international commitments. What are of interest are actual breaches of international legal obligations in the form of concrete results that follow from acts or omissions. But there are exceptions and member states of the EU may, for example, be under obligations to implement certain EU regulations and directives in their domestic legal systems in a specific manner.[36] A number of conventions in international criminal law also require state parties to take effective domestic measures to ensure that certain prescribed acts constitute offences under national law and allow states to establish jurisdiction over those offences.[37]

A second point relates to the manner in which *international law is applied in national legal systems by the legislature and national courts*. National implementation and concrete application of international law is a constitutional issue that varies from state to state. Most presentations begin the analysis with the two different approaches that have dominated legal theory: monism and dualism. *Monism* holds that international law and national law essentially form a single legal order or a set of mutually intertwined legal orders that are presumed to be coherent. The monist approach therefore also holds that international law can be applied directly in the national legal system of states and that the international norm prevails in the case of conflict. The best known exponent of monism was Hans Kelsen (1881–1973), who argued that international law and national law form a single legal system because they both derive their validity from the same ultimate source, the *Grundnorm*.[38] *Dualism*, on the other hand, holds that international law and national law are two separate legal systems that operate independently. While international law primarily regulates the relationship between states, national law governs the relationship between citizens or the citizens and the state. Following a dualistic approach, neither of the two legal systems creates rules for the other, and if international law is applied domestically it is because it is 'translated' into the national legal system, in most cases through the adoption of national legislation. In practice, though, neither monism nor dualism can explain the many ways in which international law is applied by national legislatures and courts. In part, this is due to the post-1945 growth in treaties that concern issues that were traditionally dealt with solely under national law (the international law of cooperation). As a result, the theoretical debate has moved away from the dichotomy between monism/dualism and instead turned to pluralism.[39]

As already noted, the extent to which international law is integrated into a national legal system depends on the constitutional approach of the state in question. In

---

[35] See also Vienna Convention on the Law of Treaties (adopted 23 May 1969, entered into force 27 January 1980), 1155 UNTS 331, art. 27.

[36] For a classic case, see Case 6/64 *Costa v ENEL* [1964] ECR 585.

[37] See Chapter 15.

[38] Hans Kelsen, *General Theory of Law and State* (Harvard University Press, 1945) 564.

[39] James Crawford, *Brownlie's Principles of Public International Law* (8th edn, Oxford University Press, 2012) 50. See also Giorgia Gaja, 'Dualism—A Review' in Janne Nijman and André Nollkaemper (eds), *New Perspectives on the Divide Between National and International Law* (Cambridge University Press, 2007) 52–53.

general, however, since it is in customary international law that one finds the answers required to separate the powers of sovereign states (the international law of coexistence), national courts are more willing to apply norms derived from customary international law than treaty-based norms. National courts are usually well aware that disputes inherently involving the interests of more than one state must be answered by international—and not national—law. Both civil law and common law jurisdictions therefore apply customary international law directly in their legal systems and often stipulate that it takes precedence over domestic legislation.[40] Since treaties often govern issues that are not inherently of an international nature, they will not necessarily be applied in a national legal system. But in return for tight parliamentary control over the ratification of treaties, some civil law states in Europe accept treaties on an equal footing with national legislation.[41] Other civil law states, however, including the Nordic states, adopt a more 'dualistic' approach that requires a treaty to be formally *incorporated* into national law before it is given direct effect.[42] Incorporation of treaties usually takes one of two forms. The treaty is either incorporated into national law by a short statute with the treaty as an annex or through a more thorough reformulation and interpretation in new—or an amendment to existing—legislation. Incorporation is also a requirement in the common law system in England.[43] In the United States, there is no requirement of incorporation and the decisive issue is the extent to which the national court deems the treaty to be 'self-executing'.[44] In practice, though, national courts will usually try to avoid a breach of an international obligation and, to that end, seek to interpret national legislation in accordance with the content of an international obligation. Courts generally assume that the national legislature did not intend to violate obligations under international law.

1.6 The issue of enforcement of international law

As noted in the introduction, one of the ways in which the international legal system differs from a national legal setting is in its lack of an international police force and a mandatory judicial system that can enforce the law. When it comes to complaint

---

[40] For an overview of selected jurisdictions, see Crawford (n 39) 88–93. See also Eileen Denza, 'The Relationship between International and National Law' in Malcolm D. Evans (ed.), *International Law* (4th edn, Oxford University Press, 2014) 418–425. For an overview of relevant practice from Sweden, see Michael Bogdan, 'Application of Public International Law by Swedish Courts' (1994) 63 *Nordic Journal of International Law* 3, 4–6. For Denmark, see the analysis in Ole Spiermann, *Moderne Folkeret* (3rd edn, Jurist—og Økonomforbundets Forlag, 2006) 156–161. For Norway, see Morten Ruud and Geir Ulfstein, *Innføring i Folkerett* (4th edn, Universitetsforlaget, 2011). For the UK and the US, see respectively, Crawford (n 39) 67–71, 80–82.

[41] See the overview of selected jurisdictions in Crawford (n 39) 93–102.

[42] Incorporation is generally required in the Nordic states; see for Sweden: Bogdan (n 40) 611 and also NJA 2004.225 H. For Denmark, see UfR 2006.770 H and UfR 1986.898 H and the overview in Ole Spiermann (n 40) 151–154. For Norway, see NR 1997.580 H and NR 2000.1811 H.

[43] See the overview in Crawford (n 39) 63–65.

[44] For the—complicated—US practice, see Crawford (n 39) 77–80. See also the American Law Institute, *Restatement (Third) of the Foreign Relations Law of the United States* (1987) ch. 2.

mechanisms, however, significant progress has been made since the Second World War. As we shall see throughout the book, most notably in Chapter 12, a number of courts and tribunals with competence to hear complaints and decide disputes about alleged breaches of international law do exist. The most notable example is The Hague-based ICJ that deals with interstate complaints. Other examples include the Permanent Court of Arbitration (PCA), the International Tribunal for the Law of the Sea (ITLOS) and the Dispute Settlement Body (DSB) within the WTO system. The UN has also created a range of monitoring bodies and committees with varying mandates to entertain complaints in the realm of human rights law. In Europe, legal adjudication is particularly strong and both the CJEU and the ECtHR are competent to issue binding decisions on matters that may potentially constitute violations of the relevant treaties.

The picture is less promising when it comes to 'policing' and actual *enforcement* of breaches of international law. In some cases, as we shall examine in more detail in Chapters 12 and 13, an aggrieved state may try to seek redress before the UN Security Council, but enforcement by the Security Council is rare. Also, the Security Council's role is not to enforce international law but rather to uphold international peace and security, so the Council is obviously more influenced by political and strategic considerations than by law. If the Council *does* decide to take action it has a wide range of options available to it, culminating in the competence to authorize the use of force to uphold or restore the peace. At times, the Council will seek to uphold peace and security—and by implication also help enforce violations of international law—by imposing a variety of forms of sanctions. Mention should also be made of the practice of establishing peacekeeping operations in the form of deployment of UN personnel to an area of dispute in an attempt to uphold international peace and security and in many cases to prevent further violations of international law. As we shall see in Chapter 15, the Council may also establish criminal tribunals tasked with prosecuting serious international crimes. Collective action to help enforce international law may also take place outside the framework of the UN, including in regional organizations. One of those institutions is the EU, which has created an elaborate system for enforcing various forms of breaches of EU law. At the time of writing (autumn 2018), for example, EU institutions were considering how to sanction Hungary for violating the EU Charter of Fundamental Rights over legislation that criminalizes people aiding asylum seekers. The EU also imposed sanctions on Russia following its unlawful annexation of Crimea.

In most cases, however, an aggrieved state is left with no choice but to adopt its own measures in response to another state's violation of international law. International law is thus first and foremost a system of 'self-help'. Measures of self-help may take a number of forms that take account of the reciprocal nature of many parts of international law. For one thing, as Chapter 3 will demonstrate, if the violation of international law relates to a breach of a treaty obligation, the aggrieved state will often be allowed to respond by suspending its own performance of the treaty. Also, Chapter 7 discusses how the principles of state responsibility generally allow a state to respond to another state's breach of international law by employing proportionate and non-forceful 'countermeasures' and breaching its international legal obligations towards the delinquent state. A state may, furthermore, respond to a breach of international law by adopting measures of 'retorsion' that are unfriendly—but lawful—acts, such as halting foreign aid, suspending trade, severing non-legally-binding agreements, cancelling state visits or downgrading or even breaking off diplomatic contact.

When discussing the limited means of enforcing violations of international law it should be noted that states generally honour their legal obligations towards each other. They do so for a number of reasons.[45] For one thing, there is a strong element of reciprocity in the international legal system and states are well aware of the long-term benefits to everyone of a well-functioning international legal system where promises are kept and agreements are honoured. In addition, like most individuals, states generally care about their reputation and they will often go to great lengths to be seen as respectable and law-abiding members of the international society. In fact, one of the implications of increasing global interconnection is the rising cost of acquiring a reputation for being unreliable and untrustworthy.[46] Also, to reap the benefits of an international organization, participating states are generally expected to abide by the established norms, practices and institutions.

1.7 The alleged inadequacy of international law in the 21st century

One of the recurring criticisms of international law is that the existing state-centric configuration of the international legal system is outdated and at times counterproductive to creating a more fair and just world. For example, respect for state sovereignty sometimes stands in the way of benevolent efforts to alleviate the suffering of a distressed civilian population. Likewise, the consensual character of treaty-making makes much needed progress on issue, of global concern—such as the eradication of poverty, fair trade agreements or combating climate change—hard to achieve.[47] While there is no denying the occasional tension between the state-centric system and 'justice' (whatever that is), one should remember that the construction of a legal system around sovereign states was never motivated by a desire to create a more just and equitable world as such. It was instead led by a desire to find an organizing principle for upholding international order and stability. It was, in other words, less about justice

---

[45] There is a growing literature on state compliance with international law: see, among others, the classic work by Thomas M. Franck, *The Power of Legitimacy Among Nations* (Oxford University Press, 1990). See also Andrew Guzman, *How International Law Works: A Rational Choice Theory* (Oxford University Press, 2008) 33–71. A critical view is found in Jack L. Goldsmith and Eric Posner, *The Limits of International Law* (Oxford University Press, 2006).

[46] On reputation, see Rachel Brewster, 'Unpacking the State's Reputation' (2009) 50 *Harvard International Law Journal* 231; Abram Chayes and Antonia H. Chayes, *The New Sovereignty: Compliance with International Regulatory Agreements* (Harvard University Press, 1995) 273.

[47] A well-known critique of the classic approach to state sovereignty and an endorsement of a world of global networks, is Anne-Marie Slaughter, *A New World Order* (Princeton University Press, 2004).

than it was about order. In fact, while it sounds harsh, it is a misconception to assume that the primary purpose of international law is to create a more just world. As we shall see throughout this book, when balancing notions of 'justice' and stability and order, international law often prioritizes the latter. As discussed in Section 1.3, international law is primarily preoccupied with finding the answers that are required to separate the powers of the sovereign states and to ensure the maintenance of order and stability.

In practice, of course, order may also be a value in itself, and those who argue for less respect for state sovereignty should remind themselves that it is often hard to realize broader societal goals in a society without order and stability. Indeed, when considered through a lens of stability, the many unwarranted inroads into state sovereignty in recent years—whether in the form of Russian interferences in Ukraine or Western-led 'humanitarian interventions' without UN backing—constitute one of the most serious threats to international society. Critics of the state-centric configuration of the world also tend to under-appreciate the fact that the current system, however 'unjust' it may appear to be, ensures a level of global representation by far surpassing that offered by possible alternatives—including, of course, that offered by the various 'anti-globalization' movements who proclaim to speak on behalf of an ill-defined 'global community'.

The 'Westphalian' configuration of international society is not, of course, the only conceivable way of structuring international society. Indeed, as the brief historical overview in Section 1.2 illustrated, when seen from a wider historical perspective the emergence of sovereign states is a fairly recent phenomenon. It was not inevitable that states were to assume the primary role in the international system and it cannot be ruled out that future generations may want to rethink the current configuration of the world and decide that the world should instead be structured around, say, ethnic or religious lines or by a 'world government'. At present, however, the state system remains alive and well, and states seem destined to remain the principal international legal actors for the foreseeable future. While states frequently disagree about whether or not the existing system should be more responsive to a variety of more or less pertinent 'global issues', there are currently no serious attempts to replace the state-centric system with something else. Despite its weaknesses, there is an overall recognition that the existing system is the best option on offer.

Summary

Public international law is the legal system that deals with issues of concern to more than one state. It consists of different structures that reflect historical legal evolution and the principles and political configuration of the world. The most fundamental principle is the one that constitutes the nation state as the most important legal actor in the international system. The international law of coexistence—or general international law—contains the answers required to separate the powers of sovereign states. The international law of cooperation provides the legal answers to issues that have been turned into matters of international concern pursuant to the adoption of a treaty. The existence of a plurality of sovereign states provides the theoretical justifications for the binding character of international law. A state cannot justify a breach of its international legal obligations with the claim that it would breach its national laws if it were to comply. The application of international law in national law is governed by the constitutional principles of each state and thus varies substantially. In practice, however, most states will apply customary international law domestically. Treaty-based obligations, on the other hand, often require incorporation. Enforcement of international law remains a challenge but it is not totally absent. In addition, non-legal incentives often move states towards compliance with their international obligations. While there is an undeniable tension between the existing state-centric system and wider notions of 'justice', the current configuration of the international legal system was not motivated by a desire to create a more just and equitable world or to facilitate the realization of wider 'community' goals but instead to find an organizing principle that could uphold international order and stability in world affairs.

Recommended reading

For classic works on the history of international law, see Arthur Nussbaum, *A Concise History of the Law of Nations* (Macmillan, 1947); Wilhelm G. Grewe, *The Epochs of International Law* (De Gruyter, 2010).

More recent contributions include Stephen C. Neff, *Justice Among Nations: A History of International Law* (Harvard University Press, 2014); Alexander Orakhelashvili, 'The Idea of European International Law' (2006) 17 *European Journal of International Law* 315; Bardo Fassbender and Anne Peters (eds), *The Oxford Handbook of the History of International Law* (Oxford University Press, 2012).

For the structures and purposes of international law, see the seminal work by Hedley Bull, *The Anarchical Society: A Study of Order in World Politics* (Palgrave Macmillan, 1977); Wolfgang Friedmann, *The Changing Structure of International Law* (Stevens & Son, 1964). An excellent and more recent account is available in Ole Spiermann, *International Legal Argument in the Permanent Court of International Justice* (Cambridge University Press, 2005) ch. 2.

For a classic discussion of the basis of legal obligation, see H. L. A. Hart, *The Concept of Law* (Clarendon Press, 1961) 220–226.

There is a rich literature on state compliance with international law, see, inter alia, the classic work by Thomas M. Franck, *The Power of Legitimacy Among Nations* (Oxford University Press, 1990). Other works include Andrew Guzman, *How International Law Works: A Rational Choice Theory* (Oxford University Press, 2008) 33–71; Christian Reus-Smit, 'Politics and the International Legal Obligation' (2003) 9 *European Journal of International Relations* 591. For a critical view, see Jack L. Goldsmith and Eric Posner, *The Limits of International Law* (Oxford University Press, 2006).

Questions for discussion

1. Why was the Peace of Westphalia perceived as a crucial turning point in the history and development of public international law?

2. What is the difference between natural law and legal positivism? Do you see any reflections of the two theories in contemporary debates on public international law?

3. How would you describe the relationship between international law and national law in the legal system of your state?

4. Why does the conception of a national sovereign help to explain the role and primary purposes of international law?

5. What is the difference between the international law of coexistence and the international law of cooperation? Why is the law of coexistence a more stable structure?

6. Where do you see a (potential) tension between order and justice in international law?

7. Can you think of any way that international society can be structured other than around states? And what consequences might an alternative configuration have?

2

Sources of international law

CENTRAL ISSUES

1. This chapter discusses the legal sources in international law and takes its point of departure in article 38 of the Statute of the International Court of Justice.

2. It discusses the primary sources of international law: treaties, customary international law and general principles.

3. It also provides an overview of the secondary sources of international law as well as a description of unilateral statements.

4. The chapter lists legal sources of a higher normative value and discusses the issue of so-called soft law and the legal value of, among other things, resolutions and declarations from the United Nations General Assembly.

2.1 Introduction

Sources of law determine the rules of legal society and, like national legal societies, the international legal society has its own set of rules. Thus, when we look for the content of international law, we consult the sources of international law. In practice, sources of international law are the argumentative tools available to the international lawyer. It is in the sources of international law that one finds the legal answers to the questions that cannot be found in national law. In domestic law, the identification of relevant legal sources is rarely a problem and there is traditionally a very definite method of ascertaining the law in any given subject matter. In most constituencies, the domestic lawyer will simply consult parliamentary legislation as well as potentially relevant court cases in order to find the law. This method also reflects the hierarchical nature of the domestic legal order. In international law, however, the lack of a universal legislature and a system of courts with compulsory jurisdiction often makes the task of uncovering the law more difficult. Furthermore, since international law is a decentralized legal system, legal obligations may derive from more than one particular source.

Legal sources enable legal subjects to distinguish between legal norms and those of a 'merely' political, moral or ethical nature. The International Court of Justice (ICJ) has stressed the difference between law and politics on a number of occasions. In the *South West Africa* cases, the Court stated:

> Throughout this case it has been suggested, directly or indirectly, that humanitarian considerations are sufficient in themselves to generate legal rights and obligations, and that the Court can and should proceed accordingly. The Court does not think so. It is a court of law, and can take account of moral principles only in so far as these are given a sufficient expression in legal form. Law exists, it is said, to serve a social need; but precisely for that reason it can do so only through and within the limits of its own discipline. Otherwise, it is not a legal service that would be rendered.[1]

The concept of a legal source is tied to the theories about the basis and structure of international law discussed in Chapter 1. So while proponents of natural law find sources of international law in what they consider to be elementary dictates of justice, positivists will look for evidence of state consent. The modern theory of sources as reflected in article 38 of the ICJ Statute is based on positivist theory. Thus, whether expressed *explicitly* in a treaty or more *tacitly* in an international custom accepted as law or in a general principle already recognized by states, all international legal obligations are considered to be derived from the consent of the state. This book adopts a more pragmatic approach to legal theory. Not all answers in international law can be found in freely undertaken obligations and it is a fallacy to assume that states can only be bound by obligations they have consented to. States are always bound by those behavioural rules that are required for the maintenance of peaceful coexistence in the society of which they form part.

We begin in Section 2.2 with article 38 of the ICJ Statute. Section 2.3 discusses treaties, Section 2.4 covers customary international law and Section 2.5 turns to general principles of international law. Attention then shifts to the two additional sources listed in article 38. Section 2.6 discusses judicial decisions and Section 2.7 examines academic contributions. Section 2.8 discusses unilateral statements before Section 2.9 looks at the hierarchy of sources in international law. Section 2.10 discusses non-binding instruments and so-called 'soft law'.

2.2 Article 38 of the Statute of the International Court of Justice

The classical attempt at listing the sources of international law is found in article 38 of the ICJ Statute:

1. The Court, whose function is to decide in accordance with international law such disputes as are submitted to it, shall apply:

   a. international conventions, whether general or particular, establishing rules expressly recognized by the contesting states;

   b. international custom, as evidence of a general practice accepted as law;

---

[1] *South West Africa, Second Phase (Ethiopia and Liberia v South Africa)*, Judgment [1966] ICJ Rep 6, paras 49–50. See also *Barcelona Traction, Light and Power Co., Ltd (Belgium v Spain)*, Judgment [1970] ICJ Rep 3, para. 89.

   c. the general principles of law recognized by civilized nations;

   d. subject to the provisions of Article 59, judicial decisions and the teachings of the most highly qualified publicists of the various nations, as subsidiary means for the determination of rules of law.

2. This provision shall not prejudice the power of the Court to decide a case *ex aequo et bono*, if the parties agree thereto.

Although article 38 is purely directed to the Court, it is considered of *general* relevance.

The ICJ essentially continues the work of the 1922 Permanent Court of International Justice (PCIJ) and article 38 is therefore almost identical to the corresponding article in the statute of its predecessor. Thus, the preparatory works for the ICJ date back to the drafting process of the PCIJ in 1920. Of particular relevance is the work carried out by an Advisory Committee of Jurists that was created to formulate a first draft for the original court.[2]

It has been the subject of much academic debate whether or not the list of sources in article 38 is exhaustive.[3] In practice, the ICJ has relied on sources not mentioned in the article—most notably unilateral statements. Article 38 distinguishes between primary and secondary sources of law. While the former is constituted by conventions (treaties), customary law and general principles, the latter refers to judicial decisions and scholarly contributions. The first three sources are law *creating* because they create (new) rights and obligations whereas the latter two are law *identifying* since they merely apply or clarify the content of existing law.

2.3 Conventions (treaties) as a legal source

The adoption of a convention—or a 'treaty'—is the most direct way for states to create rights and obligations under international law and it is the only instrument available to two or more states that want to enter into a formal legal relationship. The most important legal sources within a given area of international law are therefore often treaty-based. The legal basis of treaty-based obligations is state consent and a treaty only creates legal obligations for the consenting states. So while it is a mistake to assume that all international legal obligations derive from state consent, in treaty law consent *is* decisive. The effect of a treaty is expressed in the principle *pacta sunt servanda* according to which states are bound to honour their treaty-based obligations.

As we shall examine in more detail in Chapter 3, treaties come in many forms and the title of the instrument is immaterial. A treaty concluded by two states—a *bilateral* treaty—often governs a particular issue of mutual interest, such as the construction of joint infrastructure, and resembles a contract. Treaties between larger groups of states—*multilateral* treaties—often have general application and possess 'law-making'

---

[2] For a historical background, see Ole Spiermann, 'Historical Introduction' in Zimmermann and others (eds), *The Statute of the International Court: A Commentary* (2nd edn, Oxford University Press, 2012) 47–71. On the PCIJ, see also the same author in *International Legal Argument in the Permanent Court of International Justice: The Rise of the International Judiciary* (Cambridge University Press, 2005).

[3] See Hugh Thirlway, *The Sources of International Law* (Oxford University Press, 2014) 19–30.

features. When a treaty establishes an international organization it is referred to as a 'constituent treaty'.[4] Some constituent treaties create international organizations with the competence to adopt legally binding instruments. The Charter of the United Nations, for example, gives the Security Council the competence to adopt resolutions binding on all members of the UN.[5] Within the EU, the European Parliament and the Council of the European Union can adopt binding 'EU legislation'. A state that becomes party to the constituent treaty consents to be bound by any subsequent legal instruments adopted pursuant thereto. Since the instruments in question derive their binding character from the constituent treaty, they are 'treaty-based' and not an independent legal source.

2.4 Custom as a source of international law

2.4.1 Introduction

Often in societies, the way things have always been done becomes the way that things *must* be done. Indeed, to some extent all law begins with custom.[6] The absence of an international 'law-maker' has made custom a particularly important source of international law and many well-known legal principles and rules are derived from common usage and interstate practice. Furthermore, while the exact content of customary law may not be as detailed as treaty law, it is based on the everyday interaction of states and therefore has the ability to adapt to changing circumstances. As a legal source, however, custom is controversial and volumes have been written on its theoretical complexities.[7]

International customary law arises when a particular way of behaving is: (1) followed as a general practice among states; and (2) accepted by those states as legally binding. Thus, there is both an *objective* element (state practice) and a *subjective* element (the belief that the practice is legally binding). One of the challenges is to identify the point in time when behaviour—the custom—ceases to be optional and becomes legally required.

A customary rule binds *all* states (unless a state persistently objects, on which see Section 2.4.2) including a state that has not taken part in the formation of the practice, such as a newly emerged state. Customary legal norms need not be universal in scope, though. In *Right of Passage over Indian Territory*, the ICJ stated that 'long continued practice between two States accepted by them as regulating their relations' can form the basis of mutual rights and obligations between those states.[8] Customary international law may also develop *regionally* between a particular group of states. Thus,

---

[4] On international organizations as subjects of international law, see Chapter 4.
[5] See more in Chapter 13.
[6] David J. Bederman, *Custom as a Source of Law* (Cambridge University Press, 2010).
[7] See, e.g., Jorg Kammerhofer, *Uncertainty in International Law: A Kelsian Perspective* (Routledge, 2011) 59–86.
[8] *Case concerning Right of Passage over Indian Territory (Portugal v India)*, Merits [1960] ICJ Rep 6, 39.

in the *Asylum Case*, Colombia claimed that a Latin American custom existed which granted safe conduct from its embassy in Lima, Peru, for a political opponent of the Peruvian government. Although the ICJ denied the existence in customary law of that particular entitlement, it implicitly acknowledged that the practice could potentially constitute a local custom binding (only) on the regional states.[9] In Europe, democratic governance may qualify as an example of regional customary international law.[10]

2.4.2 **The objective element—state practice**

Before a specific pattern of state behaviour becomes legally binding, it must be 'the way things are done'. In most cases, this requires *consistent repetition of a particular behaviour*, meaning that for a considerable period of time states have acted in a certain (identical) manner when confronted with the same facts. This, of course, raises the question of what counts as acts of a state. In theory, all state acts may be taken into consideration: both physical acts—such as the conduct of military operations, the seizure of foreign vessels etc.—and verbal acts—like diplomatic statements, press releases, official manuals and statements in international organizations. But verbal acts must be public, and internal documents and memoranda do not qualify as state practice.[11] Resolutions and declarations by international organizations constitute the sum of individual acts by the participating states and may therefore also be relevant.

Conceptually, state practice can be divided into three elements: consistency, duration and generality. The element of *consistency* requires that practice be reasonably uniform. In *Right of Passage over Indian Territory*, the Court found that a '*constant and uniform practice*' on the part of the rulers of India of allowing free passage to Portuguese individuals, civil officials and goods constituted practice for the purposes of creating customary international law.[12] In *Nicaragua*, however, the Court stated that it is not to be expected that states have acted 'with complete consistency'. As long as the conduct is *generally* consistent with the rule, and inconsistent conduct is by and large treated as a breach of the rule rather than an indicator of the recognition of a new rule, the conduct may suffice.[13] Thus, minor departures from a collective uniformity may be acceptable. In *Jurisdictional Immunities of the State*, the Court used the term 'settled practice'.[14]

---

[9] *Colombian–Peruvian Asylum Case*, Judgment [1950] ICJ Rep 266, 277–278.

[10] Steven Wheatley, 'Democracy in International Law: A European Perspective' (2002) 51 *International and Comparative Law Quarterly* 225, 234.

[11] See also ILC, 'Guiding Principles applicable to unilateral declarations of States capable of creating legal obligations' (2006), UN Doc. A/61/10, principle 5 (ILC Guiding Principles).

[12] The same was not the case, however, with regard to the passage of armed forces, armed police and arms and ammunition which had always required the permission of the local authorities: (n 5) para. 43. See also *The Case of the SS Lotus (France v Turkey)*, Judgment, 1927, PCIJ, Series A, No. 10, 26–30.

[13] *Military and Paramilitary Activities in and against Nicaragua (Nicaragua v United States)*, Merits [1986] ICJ Rep 14, para. 186. But see *Asylum Case* (n 9) 277 and *Fisheries Case (UK v Norway)*, Judgment [1951] ICJ Rep 116, 131.

[14] *Jurisdictional Immunities of the State (Germany v Italy: Greece intervening)*, Judgment [2012] ICJ Rep 99, para. 55.

As for *duration*, practice generally evolves slowly and gradually over time, often through years of repeated behaviour. But as the ICJ stated in the *North Sea Continental Shelf Cases*, 'the passage of only a short period of time is not necessarily, in itself, a bar to the formation of a new rule of customary law'.[15] Consistency and generality (see below) are therefore usually considered to be of greater importance than mere duration. Indeed, in situations of rapid change, state practice may be formed in a very short time potentially paving the way for the creation of so-called 'instant custom'.[16] The international reaction to the terrorist attacks on the United States on 9/11 may be an example of instant custom. As we shall see in Chapter 13, the overwhelming response to the attacks indicated that states were suddenly willing to accept that armed attacks under article 51 of the UN Charter could be perpetrated by a non-state actor.

The third and potentially most difficult element of the identification of practice relates to the *generality* of the practice and the question of how widespread participation in the practice must be. While unanimity is not required, practice should include the majority of states. In the *North Sea Continental Shelf Cases*, the ICJ stated that the practice by states 'whose interests are specially affected' is particularly relevant.[17] The task is therefore not simply to determine how many states participate in a given practice, but *which* states. A state may avoid being bound by an emerging customary rule by *persistently objecting* to the practice.[18] The law therefore protects a state from the imposition by a majority of other states of new obligations upon it while simultaneously allowing that same majority to progressively develop the law without having to wait for acceptance of it by every state involved. In the *Fisheries Case*, the ICJ noted that the emergence of a potential ten-mile rule for the closing line of bays would 'be inapplicable as against Norway inasmuch as she has always opposed any attempt to apply it to the Norwegian coast'.[19] In a similar vein, in the *Asylum Case* the ICJ noted that an alleged Latin American practice of diplomatic asylum could not be binding on Peru because it had explicitly repudiated the practice in question.[20] The persistent objector rule only applies, however, in relation to new and *emerging* customary rules. Once a rule has come into existence, it can no longer be objected to. New states are also bound by existing customary law. Lastly, the persistent objector rule does not apply to peremptory norms/*jus cogens* (see Section 2.9).

2.4.3 The subjective requirement—*opinio juris*

State practice, however general and representative, only creates a legally binding custom when it is accepted as law—the so-called requirement of *opinio juris sive*

---

[15] *North Sea Continental Shelf Cases*, Merits [1969] ICJ Rep 3, para. 74.

[16] Bin Cheng, 'United Nations Resolutions on Outer Space: "Instant" International Customary Law?' (1965) 5 *Indian Journal of International Law* 23. See also Michael Scharf, *Customary International Law in Times of Fundamental Change* (Cambridge University Press, 2013).

[17] *North Sea Continental Shelf Cases* (n 15) para. 74.

[18] See also Jonathan I. Charney, 'The Persistent Objector Rule and the Development of Customary International Law' (1985) 56 *British Yearbook of International Law* 1.

[19] *Fisheries Case* (n 13) 131.

[20] *Asylum Case* (n 9) 277–278.

necessitatis. The purpose of the subjective requirement is to differentiate between acts motivated by a desire to honour—or create—a legal obligation and those that are not. The subjective element is controversial and there is no denying the theoretical difficulties in the requirement that a state must participate in a practice believing it to be legally required. How does one ascertain what states believe to be the law? States rarely explain why they act or refrain from acting as they do. Also, since practice has to start somewhere, it seems odd to insist that a state that begins to depart from an existing custom acts in the belief that the new behaviour is legally mandated.

According to the International Law Association, the existence of sufficient general and representative state practice (the objective element) is *usually* sufficient to create a binding custom, and evidence of *opinio juris* is usually only looked for if there is reason to believe that a particular behaviour stems from non-legal motivations.[21] If no general and representative practice exists, however, a state initiating a new practice cannot realistically be said to have a belief in its legality. There is, in other words, a distinction between behaviour at a time when a particular rule begins to be formed (where it cannot be a requirement that the states believe their behaviour is permitted or required by law) and behaviour at a time when it has already been established (where such a belief is presumed to exist).[22]

The subjective requirement is particularly relevant where circumstances indicate that a given practice stems from motivations that are unrelated to law. Thus, if conduct is ambiguous, proving *opinio juris* is a requirement. In the *Lotus* case, the PCIJ did not find that an alleged practice was based on a conscious decision on the part of states that they were under a duty to abstain from prosecutions not falling within that practice.[23] And in the *Asylum Case*, the ICJ found that the practice in question had been so 'much influenced by considerations of political expediency' that it was not possible to discern a usage that was 'accepted as law'.[24] Indeed, according to the Court, rather than any feeling of legal obligation, the practice in question was motivated by 'extra-legal factors', such as good-neighbour relations.[25]

The subjective element is important when a state acts contrary to an existing customary rule. While breaches of an existing custom may lead to the formation of new custom, much will depend on the justification offered. In *Nicaragua*, the ICJ noted that if a state defends its breach of a rule of customary international law 'by appealing to exceptions or justifications contained within the rule itself', its attitude will actually confirm and not weaken the rule.[26] Indeed, even repeated breaches of customary norms will not do away with the binding nature of the latter as long as *opinio juris* of their normative status continues to exist.[27]

---

[21] International Law Association, 'Final Report of the Committee, Statement of Principles Applicable to the Formation of General Customary International Law' (London Conference 2000), part III, para. 16. For a similar approach, see Maurice Mendelson, 'The Subjective Element in Customary International Law' (1996) 66 *British Yearbook of International Law* 177, 204–207.

[22] International Law Association (n 21) part III, para. 16.   [23] *Lotus* (n 12) 28.

[24] *Asylum Case* (n 9) 277.   [25] Ibid, 286; *Jurisdictional Immunities* (n 14) 55.

[26] *Nicaragua* (n 13) para. 186.

[27] See also Rosalyn Higgins, *Problems & Process: International Law and How We Use it* (Oxford University Press, 1994) 20–22.

We saw earlier that a customary rule is binding on all states, including those that have not taken part in the formation of the practice, unless a state persistently objects. But while it is not generally necessary to prove that a state has given its consent to a rule of customary international law, proof that it *has* consented will usually suffice.[28] To that end, it is important to remember that customary law can also arise between a limited set of states.

2.4.4 **The relationship between custom and treaty law**

When a treaty codifies customary international law, the parties to the treaty will be bound by the treaty as well as customary international law while non-parties are only bound by the latter. In practice, of course, all states are under the same substantial obligation. The ICJ confirmed the potential existence of such 'parallel obligations' in *Nicaragua*, where it stated that the use of interstate force is regulated in both the UN Charter as well as in customary international law and that the two norms retained a separate existence.[29] Treaty-based obligation may also be identical to obligations in customary international law if the treaty has a 'crystallizing' effect whereby its content develops into customary law. In *The Wall*, for example, the ICJ indicated that the provisions of the 1907 Hague Regulations had *over time* developed into customary law.[30] When a treaty contains elements of both codification of existing customary law and progressive developments, non-parties are only bound by the former. If, however, state practice develops along the lines of the progressive parts of the treaty, the latter may also become binding as customary international law on the states that are not parties to the treaty.

When the content of a treaty-based and a custom-based obligation are identical, the two sources will complement and reinforce each other. If the content of the two obligations are not exactly identical, a potential conflict can often be avoided through interpretation.[31] But if conflicting content cannot be reconciled, the question arises which of the two sources prevails. As we shall see in Section 2.9, if one of the two norms has a peremptory/*jus cogens* character, it prevails. It is more uncertain how a conflict is resolved in other situations. Since the adoption of a treaty is a deliberate act of law-creation, the treaty normally prevails over custom between the parties to the treaty. The situation is less clear when the customary norm has developed *subsequent* to the inconsistent treaty-based rule. In many instances, the conflict will be governed by the principle of *lex posterior* whereby that which is later in time prevails. A more pragmatic approach is to let the subsequent customary norm modify the content of the treaty-based rule. If there is a conflict between a norm of a general and one of a more detailed character, the *lex specialis* principle stipulates that the latter prevails.

---

[28] See also International Law Association (n 21) part III, para. 18.

[29] *Nicaragua* (n 13) para. 179.

[30] *Legal Consequences of the Construction of a Wall in the Occupied Palestinian Territory*, Advisory Opinion [2004] ICJ Rep 136, para. 89.

[31] See also ILC, 'Conclusions of the Study Group on the Fragmentation of International Law: Difficulties Arising from the Diversification and Expansion of International Law' (2006), UN Doc. A/61/10, paras 2 and 4.

2.5 General principles as a source of law

The third source in article 38 is that of 'general principles of law recognized by civilized nations'. Although the ICJ rarely refers to general principles, such principles are never far from the minds of the judges. Indeed, it is often in 'general principles' that the lawyer finds the legal answers that cannot be found in domestic law. General principles of law were inserted into article 38 because the drafters of the PCIJ Statute were concerned that treaties and custom were insufficient to provide all the legal answers needed. General principles of international law would prevent the Court being unable to decide a dispute due to a shortage of applicable law—so-called *non liquet*.[32] General principles were thus primarily intended as 'gap fillers' that only needed to be consulted when a dispute could not be resolved on the basis of a treaty or customary international law. The phrase 'recognized by civilized nations' is meant to illustrate that the general principles are limited to those common to developed national legal systems as a means to prevent arbitrariness on the part of the judges.[33] Today, the reference to 'civilized nations' is devoid of meaning.

The most relevant 'general principle of international law' is *equity*. In *Diversion of Water from the Meuse*, Judge Hudson of the PCIJ stated that 'principles of equity have long been considered to constitute a part of international law'[34] and that the Court 'has some freedom to consider principles of equity as part of the international law which it must apply'.[35] The ICJ has also made many references to equity, most notably in cases concerning maritime delimitations.[36] According to the Court, it relies on equity as a logical and integral part of the application of law and only as a mean to influence the application of substantive legal rules. Thus, it is unrelated to more overarching considerations of 'justice'.[37] In *Maritime Delimitation in the Black Sea*, it reiterated that the role of equity in delimitation cases is 'to achieve a delimitation that is equitable' not 'an equal apportionment of maritime areas'.[38]

International law also contains a general principle of *good faith* that stipulates that states must act honestly in the fulfilment of their international obligations. The ICJ referred to the principle in the *Nuclear Tests Cases*.[39] Another general principle is

[32] For the historical background, see Bin Cheng, *General Principles of Law as Applied by International Courts and Tribunals* (Cambridge University Press, 1953) 1–26.

[33] See also PCIJ, Advisory Committee of Jurists, 'Procés-Verbaux of the Proceedings of the Advisory Committee, June 16th–July 24th with annexes' (Van Langenhuysen Brothers, 1920) 310, 318. See also Cheng, *General Principles* (n 32) 19–25.

[34] *Diversion of Water from the Meuse*, Individual Opinion by Mr Hudson, 1937, PCIJ, Series A/B, No. 70, 76.

[35] Ibid, 77.   [36] See also Section 8.3.9.

[37] *North Sea Continental Shelf Cases* (n 15) para. 88. See also *Continental Shelf (Libyan Arab Jamahiriya v Malta)*, Judgment [1985] ICJ Rep 1, para. 45; *Fisheries Jurisdiction (UK v Iceland)*, Merits [1974] ICJ Rep 3, para. 78; *Land and Maritime Boundary (Cameroon v Nigeria: Equatorial Guinea intervening)*, Judgment [2002] ICJ Rep 303, para. 294; *Continental Shelf (Tunisia v Libyan Arab Jamahiriya)*, Judgment [1982] ICJ Rep 18, para. 71.

[38] *Maritime Delimitation in the Black Sea (Romania v Ukraine)*, Judgment [2009] ICJ Rep 61, para. 111.

[39] For almost identical cases, see *Nuclear Tests Case (New Zealand v France)*, Judgment [1974] ICJ Rep 457, para. 49 and *Nuclear Tests Case (Australia v France)* [1974] ICJ Rep 253, para. 46.

that international agreements are binding—also known as *pacta sunt servanda*. In *Nicaragua*, the Court also referred to the rules in Common article 3 to the four 1949 Geneva Conventions as constituting 'a minimum yardstick' that reflect *elementary considerations of humanity*.[40] It also referred to 'elementary considerations of humanity' in its advisory opinion on the *Legality of the Threat or Use of Nuclear Weapons*.[41] In *Corfu Channel*, the ICJ made reference to a number of principles that could be candidates for general principles of international law. The Court found that Albania had violated a principle of *the freedom of maritime communication* as well as 'every State's obligation not to allow knowingly its territory to be used for acts contrary to the rights of other States'.[42] In international environmental law, the latter principle is known as the *no harm* principle.[43] Related to this principle is a principle of *due diligence* whereby a state must seek to prevent activities on its own territory from causing significant damage in another state.[44] International rules on procedure and evidence are often based on legal principles derived from national law. In *Genocide*, the ICJ referred to a general principle of *res judicata* according to which a decision is final and binding on the parties.[45] The principle ensures that litigation comes to an end at a certain point. In *Corfu Channel*, the Court also relied on circumstantial evidence and noted that such 'evidence is admitted in all systems of law'.[46]

2.6 Judicial decisions

Judicial decisions are a subsidiary source of law. This is also reflected in the reference in article 38(1)(d) to article 59 of the Statute according to which the ICJ's decisions are only binding on the parties to the case. Judicial decisions may, however, carry substantial interpretative weight and, as the principal judicial organ of the UN, the ICJ's decisions and advisory opinions—as well as those of its predecessor the PCIJ— are particularly important contributions. In practice, of course, there may be a thin line between those instances where the Court merely *identifies* rather than *develops* the law. For example, a we shall see in Chapter 3, in *Genocide Reservations* the Court adopted a new approach to treaty reservations.[47] The ICJ is not bound by its earlier decisions but it strives to maintain judicial consistency and usually makes reference

---

[40] *Nicaragua* (n 13) para. 218.

[41] *Legality of the Threat or Use of Nuclear Weapons*, Advisory Opinion [1996] ICJ Rep 226, para. 79. See also *The Wall* (n 30) para. 157.

[42] *Corfu Channel (UK v Albania)*, Merits [1949] ICJ Rep 4, 22. See also *Nuclear Weapons* (n 41) para. 29.

[43] *Trail Smelter (United States v Canada)* (1938 and 1941) III RIAA 1905. See the discussion in Section 10.4.2.

[44] See the discussion in Section 10.4.2.

[45] *Application of the Convention on the Prevention and Punishment of the Crime of Genocide (Bosnia and Herzegovina v Serbia and Montenegro)*, Judgment [2007] ICJ Rep 43, paras 115–116.

[46] *Corfu Channel* (n 42) 18.

[47] *Reservations to the Convention on Genocide*, Advisory Opinion [1951] ICJ Rep 15.

to its case law. At times, the Court's earlier decisions even constitute the natural point of departure for the analysis, as was the case in *Cameroon v Nigeria* where the Court simply referred to its earlier case law and noted that the 'real question is whether, in this case, there is cause not to follow the reasoning and conclusions of earlier cases'.[48]

The judgments ('awards') from international courts of arbitration also contain important contributions. Prominent examples include the *Alabama Claims* arbitration,[49] the *Island of Palmas* case[50] and the *Trail Smelter* case.[51] A more recent award that could well have an important impact on international law is the award by a court of arbitration in July 2016 in the *South China Sea Arbitration*.[52] Decisions by those international courts and tribunals with specialized subject-matter competence are also of substantial interpretative value. Here, reference should primarily be made to the most noteworthy judgments and decisions from the 1946 International Military Tribunal (IMT) at Nuremberg[53] and the International Criminal Tribunal for the former Yugoslavia (ICTY).[54] Judgments and decisions from the International Criminal Court (ICC) as well as from the WTO's Dispute Settlement Body (DSB) and the International Tribunal for the Law of the Sea (ITLOS) may also have substantial influence. Relevant specialized regional international courts include the European Court of Human Rights (ECtHR) and the Court of Justice of the European Union (CJEU). The Iran–US Claims Tribunal, set up after the 1979 revolution in Iran, has rendered many noteworthy decisions, in particular on issues relating to investment protection and the legal effects of expropriation of foreign property.[55] Finally, depending on the circumstances, decisions by national courts, in particular those of courts of last instance, such as supreme courts and constitutional courts, may also be of relevance. Noticeable examples include the Canadian Supreme Court's 1998 opinion about the province of Quebec's right to self-determination[56] and the District Court of Jerusalem's judgment in the case against Adolph Eichmann.[57] Municipal decisions may additionally constitute state practice for the purposes of identifying customary international law.[58]

---

[48] *Land and Maritime Boundary between Cameroon and Nigeria*, Preliminary Objections [1998] ICJ Rep 275, para. 28.

[49] *Alabama claims of the United States of America against Great Britain* (1872) XXIX RIAA 125.

[50] *Island of Palmas (Netherlands v United States)* (1928) II RIAA 829.

[51] *Trail Smelter* (n 43) 1965.

[52] *The Republic of the Philippines and the People's Republic of China*, Award, PCA Case No. 2013-19, 12 July 2016.

[53] See, inter alia, *Judgment of the Nuremberg International Military Tribunal 1946* (1947) 41 *American Journal of International Law* 172.

[54] Arguably the most important of the decisions is the Appeals Chamber decision in *Tadić*, see *Tadić*, Decision on the Defence Motion for Interlocutory Appeal on Jurisdiction, ICTY-94-1 (2 October 1995).

[55] For a thorough account, see George H. Aldrich, *The Jurisprudence of the Iran–United States Claims Tribunal* (Oxford University Press, 1996).

[56] *Reference re Secession of Quebec* (1998) 2 SCR 217. See the discussion in Section 4.2.5.

[57] *Attorney General v Adolph Eichmann*, District Court of Jerusalem, Criminal Case No. 40/61. See also Chapters 5 and 15.

[58] See, in particular, *Jurisdictional Immunities* (n 14) para. 64.

2.7 Scholarly contributions and the ILC

Of the sources listed in article 38(1), 'the teachings of the most highly qualified publicists of the various nations' is the least important. While writers and thinkers like Suaréz, Grotius and Vattel have historically influenced the development of international law, academics today play a much less significant role. Although some courts refer to academic analysis,[59] the ICJ rarely makes any references to specific academics.[60] Academic interpretations and commentaries may, of course, influence practitioners or those who develop international law, especially if the author(s) of the contribution is/are highly esteemed academics or if the institution has a special role to play.[61] An example of the latter is the commentaries to the 1949 I-IV Geneva Conventions by the International Committee of the Red Cross (ICRC).[62] New and updated commentaries began to be published by the ICRC in 2016.[63] As we shall return to in Chapter 4, the ICRC plays a special role in international law. Another example of an academic contribution that may well prove to have a noteworthy impact on the development of international law is the *2017 Tallinn Manual 2.0 on the International Law Applicable to Cyber Operations*, which was drafted by a large group of international law experts.[64]

The contributions of the *International Law Commission* (ILC) play a special role in international law. As noted in Chapter 1, the ILC was established in 1947 with the primary purpose of promoting the progressive development of international law and its codification. The composition of the Commission is intended to be representative of all the principal legal systems of the world and the members sit in their individual capacities. Among other things, the Commission selects topics and makes proposals for draft conventions and codifications. Usually, once a topic has been chosen for consideration, a working group will be formed and a Special Rapporteur will be appointed who will produce a series of reports that may contain concrete proposals. In turn, these may lead to the adoption of important conventions. When that is the case, the Commission's draft articles and commentaries thereon serve as valuable interpretive tools.[65] The ILC has been instrumental in the adoption of important treaties, such as on the law of the sea, diplomatic and consular relations, human rights, and on treaty law itself.

---

[59] Michael Wood, 'Teachings of the Most Highly Qualified Publicists (Art. 38(1) ICJ Statute)' in Rüdiger Wolfrum (ed.), *Max Planck Encyclopedia of Public International Law* (Oxford University Press, 2010) para. 14.

[60] For an exception, see *Nottebohm (Second Phase) (Liechtenstein v Guatemala)*, Judgment [1955] ICJ Rep 4, 22; *Lotus* (n 12) 26.

[61] See also Jean d'Aspremont, *Formalism and the Sources of International Law: A Theory on the Ascertainment of Legal Rules* (Oxford University Press, 2011) 209–211.

[62] See, inter alia, Jean S. Pictet, *Commentary to the III Geneva Convention Relative to the Treatment of Prisoners of War* (ICRC, 1960).

[63] By October 2018, the ICRC had published new commentaries to the I and II 1949 Geneva Conventions.

[64] Michael N. Schmitt (ed.), *The Tallinn Manual 2.0 on the International Law Applicable to Cyber Operations* (Cambridge University Press, 2017).

[65] For practical examples of the ILC's contribution to codification and progressive development of the law, see Alan Boyle and Christine Chinkin, *The Making of International Law* (Oxford University Press, 2007) 183–200.

2.8 Unilateral statements

Case law from both the PCIJ and the ICJ shows that unilateral statements by state representatives can create obligations under international law. Importantly, there would not seem to be any requirements of form and both oral and written statements may qualify.[66] Like treaties, binding unilateral declarations can be issued by heads of state, heads of government and ministers for foreign affairs. In *Eastern Greenland*, the PCIJ interpreted a declaration issued by a Norwegian foreign minister—the so-called 'Ihlen Declaration'—as a statement that was legally binding on Norway. In the course of a bilateral Danish–Norwegian dialogue on the status of Eastern Greenland, the Foreign Minister of Norway (Mr Ihlen) referred to Danish claims to the whole of Greenland and stated that his country 'would not make any difficulties in the settlement of this question'.[67] When Norway later contested Danish sovereignty over the area, the Court found the earlier statement 'unconditional and definitive' and therefore binding on Norway.[68] In the *Nuclear Tests Cases*, the ICJ concluded that a series of clearly unilateral public statements by, among others, the French president were legally binding on France.[69] The cases concerned French atmospheric nuclear tests in the South Pacific that caused radioactive fall-out in, among other places, New Zealand and Australia. The Court found that official French statements testified to an intention to be legally bound to cease atmospheric tests.[70] According to the Court, 'nothing in the nature of a *quid pro quo*, nor any subsequent acceptance of the declaration, nor even any reply or reaction from other States, is required' for a unilateral statement to be legally binding.[71]

It will often be difficult to determine if a state intends to bind itself *legally* when it makes a particular statement. Weight must be given first and foremost to the text of the declaration, together with the context and the circumstances in which it was formulated.[72] A unilateral declaration should, however, only be considered binding if it is stated in clear and specific terms.[73] In the *Nuclear Tests Cases*, the ICJ stressed that a 'restrictive interpretation' is called for when states make 'statements by which their freedom of action is to be limited'.[74]

---

[66] *Nuclear Tests Case (New Zealand v France)* (n 39) para. 48; *Nuclear Tests Case (Australia v France)* (n 39) para. 45. See also *Temple of Preah Vihear (Cambodia v Thailand)*, Preliminary Objections [1961] ICJ Rep 17, 31.

[67] *Legal Status of Eastern Greenland (Denmark v Norway)*, Judgment, 1933, PCIJ, Series A/B, No. 53, para. 58.

[68] Ibid, paras 195, 201.

[69] *Nuclear Tests Case (New Zealand v France)* and *Nuclear Tests Case (Australia v France)* (n 39).

[70] *Nuclear Tests Case (New Zealand v France)* (n 39) paras 51–53 and *Nuclear Tests Case (Australia v France)* (n 39) paras 49–51.

[71] *Nuclear Tests Case (New Zealand v France)* (n 39) para. 46 and *Nuclear Tests Case (Australia v France)* (n 39) para. 43. See *Nuclear Tests Case (Australia v France)*, Dissenting Opinion of Judge de Castro (n 39) 374–375. For a critique of the Court's reasoning in the *Nuclear Tests Cases*, see Alfred P. Rubin, 'The International Legal Effects of Unilateral Declarations' (1977) 71 *American Journal of International Law* 1.

[72] See also ILC Guiding Principles (n 11) principle 7. See also *Frontier Dispute (Burkina Faso v Republic of Mali)*, Judgment [1986] ICJ Rep 554 paras 39–40.

[73] ILC Guiding Principles (n 11) principle 7.

[74] *Nuclear Tests Case (Australia v France)* (n 39) para. 47. See also the debate in Thomas Franck, 'Word Made Law: The Decision of the ICJ in the *Nuclear Test Cases*' (1975) 69 *American Journal of International Law* 612, 617.

2.9 Hierarchy of sources

One of the characteristics of a national legal system is a hierarchy of legal norms. National systems are vertical in the sense that constitutional norms have a higher legal status than legislation and administrative regulation. The international legal system, on the other hand, is by and large a horizontal legal order.[75] Apart from the distinction between primary and secondary sources of law in article 38 of the ICJ Statute, all legal sources generally carry the same normative weight. Usually, conflicts between sources are therefore not resolved by granting one of the sources a higher normative value than the other but by determining which of the conflicting norms prevails in the particular case. For example, as we saw earlier, cases of conflict between treaties and customary international law are usually—but not always—resolved by giving priority to a treaty-based rule because the adoption of a treaty can be seen as a more deliberate act of law-creation than the creation of customary law.

In practice, however, all legal systems have norms that are considered to be of greater importance than others, and international law is no exception. In fact, there are at least three exceptions to the general presumption of normative equality. The first relates to the concept of peremptory norms—also known as *jus cogens*—that are assigned a superior value than other norms. As we shall return to in Chapter 3, article 53 of the Vienna Convention on the Law of Treaties (VCLT) stipulates that a treaty is void if it 'conflicts with a peremptory norm of general international law'.[76] According to article 53, a *jus cogens* norm is one that is 'accepted and recognized by the international community of States as a whole as a norm from which no derogation is permitted and which can be modified only by a subsequent norm of general international law having the same character'. Thus, since the prohibition against genocide is a norm of *jus cogens* (see below) an agreement between state A and state B on the extermination of a particular ethnic group would be invalid and void. As a legal concept, *jus cogens* is not free from theoretical difficulties[77] but international courts have increasingly accepted its existence. In *Armed Activities*, the ICJ referred to the prohibition of genocide as a peremptory norm of general international law[78] and in *Obligation to Extradite or Prosecute*, it stated that the prohibition against torture is not only part of customary international law but also 'has become a peremptory norm (*jus cogens*)'.[79] Aside from the ban on genocide and torture, it is not clear what norms possess a *jus cogens* character. The ILC

---

[75] A classic work on the issue of hierarchy in international law is Prosper Weil, 'Towards Relative Normativity in International Law?' (1983) 77 *American Journal of International Law* 413.

[76] See also VCLT art. 64. An early contribution is Alfred von Verdross, 'Forbidden Treaties in International Law: Comments on Professor Garner's Report on "The Law of Treaties"' (1937) 31 *American Journal of International Law* 571. A unilateral declaration that conflicts with a peremptory norm of general international law is similarly void, see the ILC Guiding Principles (n 11) para. 8, and VCLT art. 53.

[77] For a debate see, **inter alia**, Alexander Orakhelashvili, *Peremptory Norms in International Law* (Oxford University Press, 2006). See also Thirlway (n 3) 154–163. A critical position is found in Weil (n 75).

[78] *Armed Activities on the Territory of the Congo (New Application: 2002) (Democratic Republic of the Congo v Rwanda)*, Jurisdiction and Admissibility [2006] ICJ Rep 6, para. 64.

[79] *Questions relating to the Obligation to Prosecute or Extradite (Belgium v Senegal)*, Judgment [2012] ICJ Rep 422, para. 99. See also *Prosecutor v Anto Furundžija*, Judgment, ICTY-95-17/1 (20 December 1998) para. 153.

has stated that the concept refers to 'those substantive rules of conduct that prohibit what has come to be seen as intolerable because of the threat it presents to the survival of States and their peoples and the most basic human values'.[80] Aside from the prohibition against torture and genocide, likely *jus cogens* norms include the ban on slavery, the prohibition of aggression, the ban on crimes against humanity and grave breaches of the laws of armed conflict, the prohibition of piracy, the right to self-determination and the prohibition of apartheid and other forms of gross racial discrimination.[81] The ILC has explicitly decided against trying to make a list.[82]

The second exemption to the normative equality of international legal norms is obligations *erga omnes*. Such obligations are normatively superior in the sense that they are not merely owed to another state but to the 'international community as a whole'. They are therefore also referred to as 'communitarian norms'. Thus, the higher normative weight of these norms is visible in their special procedural feature. As we shall return to in Chapter 7, unlike a breach of other legal obligations, a breach of an *erga omnes* norm/obligation can be invoked by any state and not just by a state that is the immediate beneficiary of the obligation. The ICJ made reference to the concept of *erga omnes* in the *Barcelona Traction* case where it did not find that Belgium had legal standing on behalf of shareholders in Belgium of a Canadian company in a case against Spain. To the Court,

> an essential distinction should be drawn between the obligations of a State towards the international community as a whole, and those arising vis-à-vis another State in the field of diplomatic protection. By their very nature the former are the concern of all States. In view of the importance of the rights involved, all States can be held to have a legal interest in their protection; they are obligations *erga omnes*.[83]

Since the prohibition against genocide is not just a *jus cogens* norm (see above) but also one of an *erga omnes* nature, all states are deemed to have a legal interest in ensuring the fulfilment of that prohibition and thus entitled to invoke it. Interestingly, *erga omnes* obligations are referred to with increasing frequency in international environmental law.[84] Conceptually, there are many similarities between *jus cogens* and *erga omnes* and the two categories of norms are more or less the same. To be clear, then, although there is overlap between the norms that are labelled as, respectively, *jus cogens* and *erga omnes*, they serve different purposes. While the former category refers to substantive obligations that cannot be derogated from, the latter is a procedural designation of a set of obligations that all states can invoke.

The third and final category of international legal norms with a higher value is *obligations under the UN Charter*. Article 103 of the Charter stipulates that obligations

---

[80] Draft Articles on the Responsibility of States for Internationally Wrongful Acts, with commentaries, *Yearbook of the International Law Commission*, 2001, vol. II, Part Two, p. 112.

[81] For a tentative list, see ILC, 'Fragmentation of International Law' (n 31) para. 374. See also the discussion in Section 3.7.

[82] ILC, Draft Articles on the Law of Treaties, with commentaries, *Yearbook of the International Law Commission*, 1966, vol. II, p. 187 and p. 248, para. 3.

[83] *Barcelona Traction* (n 1) para. 33. But see also *SS Wimbledon*, 1923, PCIJ, Series A, No. 1, 33.

[84] See Section 10.6.

under the Charter prevail if they conflict with obligations under any other international agreement. Since article 25 of the Charter obliges members states to accept and carry out resolutions of the Security Council that have been adopted under Chapter VII of the Charter, the practical effect of article 103 is that states must comply with the Council's resolutions even if it means that they thereby violate other international legal commitments.[85] The primacy of Security Council resolutions is not absolute, however, and the Council cannot oblige states to disregard norms of a *jus cogens*/peremptory character. This was also the conclusion reached by the Court of First Instance of the EU in the *Kadi* case concerning the EU's incorporation of obligations under the sanctions regime in Security Council Resolution 1267.[86] In a controversial 2008 judgment in the same case, the CJEU held that *all* measures adopted by the Union—including those implementing resolutions adopted by the Security Council—must be compatible with fundamental rights.[87] It would seem, therefore, that among the three categories of norms in international law that are deemed to be of a higher status than the more general legal norms, obligations under the UN Charter are the least important.

2.10 Non-binding commitments and the concept of 'soft law' instruments

When states make use of the legal sources we have examined so far in this chapter they create an expectation of behaviour (a norm) that is binding under international law. It is not uncommon, however, for states to create expectations of behaviour that are merely supposed to be politically—and not legally—binding. The creation of political instruments tends to be a much faster and more flexible way to come to an agreement than to adopt legally binding instruments. While a violation of a non-legally binding instrument cannot result in any legal consequences, the political price associated with violating political agreements may still be very high.

The determination of whether an instrument is legally binding or a mere political pledge generally revolves around the intention of the parties. Did the parties intend the instrument to be legally binding or not? As we shall return to in Chapter 3, making that determination may at times be difficult. When a legally non-binding instrument begins to play a role in the creation of international law, it can be referred to as 'soft law'.[88] The term 'soft law' is used in contrast to 'hard law', which describes the legally

---

[85] For the competences of the Security Council, see also Chapter 13.

[86] Case T-315/01 *Kadi v Council and Commission* [2005] ECR II-3659, paras 224–226.

[87] Cases C-402/05 P and C-415/05 P *Kadi and Al Barakaat International Foundation v Council and Commission* [2008] ECR I-6351, paras 281ff. See also Juliane Kokott and Christoph Sobotta, 'The *Kadi* Case—Constitutional Core Values and International Law—Finding the Balance?' (2012) 23 *European Journal of International Law* 1015–1024. See also ECtHR, *Nada v Switzerland*, App. no. 10593/08, 12 September 2012, paras 171, 176 and 212. However, in neither of the cases did the Courts question the prima facie normative priority of the resolutions in question.

[88] See Daniel Thurer, 'Soft Law' in Rüdiger Wolfrum (ed.), *Max Planck Encyclopedia of Public International Law* (Oxford University Press, 2009).

binding sources. So whether a rule or norm is referred to as 'hard' or 'soft' relates to its normative character (is it legally binding or not?) and not to the precision of the norm (is it formulated in vague language?).

There is often some confusion about the concept of 'soft law' and the role it plays in international law. To be clear, 'soft law' instruments are not *in themselves* legally binding under international law and they do not constitute independent sources of law. Thus, a state cannot be found in violation of international law because it has breached a 'soft law' instrument.[89] 'Soft law' instruments may nevertheless be legally relevant when they assist in the formation or interpretation of one of the recognized legal sources, most notably customary international law. 'Soft law' documents may be evidence of state practice or *opinio juris* and *on that basis* become relevant to the creation of (binding) international law.

Soft law instruments come in different shapes and forms and they are prevalent within many fields of international law. For example, as we shall return to in Chapter 10, this is the case in international environmental law where some of the most cited instruments, including the 1972 Stockholm Declaration and the 1992 Rio Declaration, are non-binding 'soft law' documents. There are also many 'soft law' instruments in international human rights law, the most notable example being the 1948 Universal Declaration of Human Rights. While the Declaration is often referred to as one of the foundational human rights documents it is merely a political document. The 'soft law' category includes a wide range of instruments adopted by various international organizations, agencies and committees that do not have the competence to adopt legally binding instruments. A particularly important type of soft law instrument is that of *resolutions and declarations adopted by the United Nations General Assembly.* Unlike the UN Security Council, the Assembly only holds recommendatory powers and is not competent to adopt legally binding resolutions and declarations. In practice, however, the resolutions and decisions by the Assembly can have a noticeable impact on the formation of customary international law as both a reflection of state practice as well as *opinio juris.* This was also noted by the ICJ in *Nuclear Weapons,* where the Court stated that such resolutions 'even if they are not binding, may sometimes have normative value. They can, in certain circumstances, provide evidence important for establishing the existence of a rule or the emergence of an *opinio juris.*'[90] Examples of important General Assembly resolutions include the 1960 Declaration on the Granting of Independence to Colonial Countries and Peoples,[91] the 1963 Legal Principles Governing the Activities of States in the Exploration and Use of Outer

---

[89] Law is inherently binary and a specific obligation is either legally binding or it is not. There is no such thing as a 'partially' binding legal obligation and no instruments can be 'a little bit' legally binding. Theoretically, then, since instruments that are not legally binding do not constitute 'law', one could argue that it is contradictory to describe some law as 'soft'. See also Jan Klabbers, *The Concept of Treaty in International Law* (Kluwer, 1996) 13; Jan Klabbers, 'The Redundancy of Soft Law' (1996) 65 *Nordic Journal of International Law* 167. See, however, also Richard R. Baxter, 'International Law in "Her Infinite Variety"' (1980) 29 *International and Comparative Law Quarterly* 549, 563.

[90] See also *Nuclear Weapons* (n 41) 70 and the extensive reliance on General Assembly instruments in *Nicaragua* (n 13).

[91] GA Res. 1514 (XV) (14 December 1960), UN Doc. A/RES/1514(XV).

Space[92] and the 1970 Declaration on Friendly Relations.[93] To reiterate, although such declarations and resolutions cannot create a legally binding obligation in their own right, they are relevant to the formation of international law because they can assist in the 'crystallization' of customary law. In particular, this will be the case if the instrument in question is adopted with broad or even universal support.

Summary

The international legal society has its own legal sources and the discussion therefore takes its natural point of departure in article 38 of the ICJ Statute. According to that article, sources of international law can be divided into those of a primary and those of a secondary nature. While treaties, customary international law and general principles constitute the primary and undoubtedly most important legal sources, judicial decisions and scholarly contributions are listed as merely secondary sources of law. Article 38 is not exhaustive, however, and international legal answers may be found elsewhere too, most notably in unilateral statements by states. While the sources of international law are generally considered to possess the same normative value, exceptions do exist. Examples include norms of a peremptory character (*jus cogens*), *erga omnes* obligations and those legal obligations that derive from the UN Charter. 'Soft law' refers to commitments undertaken by states that are not legally binding. Depending on the circumstances, soft law commitments may pave the way for the creation of customary international law and thus hard law norms.

Recommended reading

For more on legal sources in general, see Hugh Thirlway, *The Sources of International Law* (Oxford University Press, 2014); Jean d'Aspremont, *Formalism and the Sources of International Law: A Theory on the Ascertainment of Legal Rules* (Oxford University Press, 2011).

On article 38 of the ICJ Statute, see Alain Pellet, 'Article 38' in Andreas Zimmermann and others (eds), *The Statute of the International Court of Justice: A Commentary* (2nd edn, Oxford University Press, 2012) and Ole Spiermann, 'Historical Introduction' in the same work.

On the PCIJ, see Ole Spiermann, *International Legal Argument in the Permanent Court of International Justice: The Rise of the International Judiciary* (Cambridge University Press, 2005).

For customary international law, see David J. Bederman, *Custom as a Source of Law* (Cambridge University Press, 2010) and the three reports by Michael Wood for the ILC on identification of customary international law, in particular 'Third Report on identification of customary international law' (ILC, 2015), UN Doc. A/CN.4/682. See also Maurice Mendelson, 'The Subjective Element in Customary International Law' (1996) 66 *British Yearbook of International Law* 177.

For *jus cogens* and peremptory norms, see Alfred von Verdross, 'Forbidden Treaties in International Law: Comments on Professor Garner's Report on "The Law of Treaties"' (1937) 31

---

92 GA Res. 1962 (XVIII) (13 December 1963), UN Doc. A/RES/1962(XVIII).
93 GA Res. 2625 (XXV) (24 October 1970), UN Doc. A/RES/2625(XXV).

American Journal of International Law 571; Alexander Orakhelashvili, *Peremptory Norms in International Law* (Oxford University Press, 2006).

On hierarchies in international law as such, see Prosper Weil, 'Towards Relative Normativity in International Law?' (1983) 77 *American Journal of International Law* 413.

For soft law, see Alan Boyle, 'Soft Law in International Law-Making' in Malcolm D. Evans (ed.), *International Law* (4th edn, Oxford University Press, 2014); Jan Klabbers, 'The Redundancy of Soft Law' (1996) 65 *Nordic Journal of International Law* 167.

Questions for discussion

1. Why is the theory of sources tied to more basic theories about international law and the basis of legal obligation?

2. What are the theoretical difficulties associated with the requirement of *opinio juris* as part of the formation of customary international law?

3. Where should one look for the practice of states for the purposes of the formation of customary international law?

4. What is the difference between primary and secondary sources of international law? What are the primary and secondary legal sources in the national legal system in your country?

5. In some cases, a conflict of norms may exist between the different sources of international law. Can you provide some examples of how international law tries to resolve such conflicts?

6. Is a 'soft law' instrument legally binding?

7. What is the legal significance of a soft law instrument?

3
The law of treaties

CENTRAL ISSUES

1. This chapter examines the international law of treaties as reflected in the 1969 Vienna Convention on the Law of Treaties.

2. It discusses the treaty as a legal concept and provides an overview of the rules on who can conclude treaties, how consent to be bound by a treaty is expressed, the rules on entry into force, treaty reservations, the interpretation of treaties, amendments and modifications, the invalidity of treaties and the termination of and withdrawal from treaties.

3. For the most part, the international law of treaties resembles domestic rules for the creation and operation of contracts.

4. The most contentious issues in the law of treaties relate to the subject of reservations and treaty interpretation.

3.1 Introduction

Like other societies, the society of states needs rules that govern the agreements entered into by its legal subjects. No society can function properly if its subjects are in constant disagreement on the application and interpretation of their agreements. Not surprisingly, then, the law of treaties is one of the oldest areas of public international law and it is part and parcel of the international law of coexistence, without which stability and predictability would be difficult to maintain.

The primary rules in the law of treaties are found in the 1969 Vienna Convention on the Law of Treaties (VCLT) that was adopted by the UN Conference on the Law of Treaties in May 1969 and entered into force in January 1980. The draft articles of the VCLT were prepared by successive Special Rapporteurs of the International Law Commission (ILC). Since the VCLT seeks to codify customary practices, it generally reflects customary international law. In fact, there has yet to be a case where the International Court of Justice (ICJ) has found that the content of a particular provision in the VCLT does *not* reflect customary law.[1]

---

[1] Anthony Aust, *Modern Treaty Law and Practice* (3rd edn, Cambridge University Press, 2013) 11.

The VCLT applies to *all* types of written treaties between states. It therefore governs treaties as diverse as a bilateral agreement to construct infrastructure and a multi-lateral document such as the UN Charter. In practice, however, as this chapter will illustrate, the concrete application of the VCLT may differ depending on the type of treaty. Like domestic contract law, the international law of treaties is not concerned with the material content of the instrument itself; that is a matter for the parties to the particular treaty.

The overview begins in Section 3.2 with the treaty as a legal concept. Section 3.3 examines who possesses the authority to conclude treaties, Section 3.4 deals with treaties between states and international organizations and Section 3.5 discusses the various forms of consenting to be bound by a treaty. Section 3.6 covers entry into force and obligations in the so-called 'interim period'. Section 3.7 discusses validity/invalidity. The complicated issue of reservations is discussed in Section 3.8 and treaty interpretation in Section 3.9. The chapter concludes in Sections 3.10 and 3.11 with, respectively, an overview of amendments and modifications, and termination and withdrawal from treaties.

3.2 The treaty as a concept under international law

A treaty is an *international agreement governed by international law concluded by two or more international subjects with treaty-making capacity*. The adoption of a treaty reflects a will among two or more international subjects to apply international law as a means of regulating their interests. The vast majority of treaties are concluded by two or more states and interstate treaties regulate an increasing array of international relations. As we saw in Chapter 2, one can meaningfully distinguish between *bilateral* treaties (concluded by two states) and *multilateral* treaties (between larger groups of states). As noted, the VCLT only applies to *written* treaties concluded between states.[2] While *international organizations* can also be parties to a treaty governed by international law, the treaty will not be governed by the VCLT but by the 1986 Vienna Convention on the Law of Treaties between International Organizations or between States and International Organizations. It is important to note that a state may sometimes enter into an agreement under national law. In that case, the agreement will be governed by domestic as opposed to international law.

The legal basis of a treaty obligation is state *consent*. No one can force a sovereign state to enter into a legally binding agreement and a treaty only creates legal obligations for the parties. This is reflected in article 34 of the VCLT. So while state A and state B are free to enter into a treaty that governs their mutual relations, they cannot conclude a treaty that creates rights or obligations for state C unless the latter consents. When a state has consented to be bound by a treaty and has become a party, it must comply with the terms. This is reflected in the principle of *pacta sunt servanda*. Thus, article

---

[2] Vienna Convention on the Law of Treaties (adopted 23 May 1969, entered into force 27 January 1980), 1155 UNTS 331, art. 2(1)(a).

26 of the VCLT states that a treaty in force 'is binding upon the parties to it and must be performed by them in good faith'. As noted in Chapter 2, both the *pacta sunt servanda* principle and the principle of good faith are considered general principles of international law. Article 27 specifies that a state party may not invoke its national laws as justification for a failure to perform a treaty-based obligation.[3] Hence, a state is obliged to comply with such a treaty-based obligation even if doing so requires breaching its national laws.

Even though the VCLT only applies to written treaties (between states), *oral* agreements are also 'treaties' for the purposes of international law. Article 3 of the VCLT explicitly stipulates that the fact that the Convention only applies to written treaties does not affect the legal force of other agreements. In *Great Belt*, a telephone conversation between the prime ministers of Finland and Denmark brought an end to a dispute between the two states concerning Denmark's decision to construct a bridge across 'Storebælt' (Great Belt).[4]

The *title of the written instrument* is immaterial and everything from 'minutes', 'protocols', 'exchanges of notes', 'memoranda of understanding' to 'covenants', 'charters' and 'conventions' may qualify as a treaty.[5] As long as the instrument in question testifies to an *intention* to create rights and obligations under international law it is a treaty. As we saw in Chapter 2, states often adopt instruments that are not intended to be legally binding[6] and it is only when a political pledge is accompanied by a desire to create rights and obligations under international law that a treaty has been created. In practice, of course, it may be difficult to determine if an agreement is intended to be legally binding and states have an unfortunate tendency to be reluctant to explicitly specify if that is the case.[7] What is decisive is the intention of the parties.[8] In some cases, the instrument may help determine what the parties intended. In practice, both the *terminology* and the *form* of the instrument may provide guidance. A lack of precision in the wording and the use of very general and vague terms may indicate a lack of intention to create a legally binding commitment. Terms such as 'will' and 'ought' usually signal that the parties do not intend to make a binding commitment, whereas words like 'shall', 'rights', 'oblige' or 'must' indicate the opposite. Guidance may also be sought from the circumstances surrounding the conclusion of the

---

[3] But see the exception in art. 46.

[4] See *Passage Through the Great Belt (Finland v Denmark)*, Application Instituting Proceedings, General List No. 86 [1991] ICJ Rep 1 and the subsequent Order [1992] ICJ Rep 348.

[5] *Aegean Sea Continental Shelf (Greece v Turkey)*, Judgment [1978] ICJ Rep 3, para. 96; *Maritime Delimitation and Territorial Questions between Qatar and Bahrain (Qatar v Bahrain)*, Jurisdiction and Admissibility, Judgment [1994] ICJ Rep 112, para. 23.

[6] Anthony Aust, 'The Theory and Practice of Informal International Instruments' (1986) 35 *International and Comparative Law Quarterly* 787. But see the scepticism voiced by Jan Klabbers, *The Concept of Treaty in International Law* (Kluwer, 1996) and the critique of the British practice of concluding apparently non-binding memoranda of understanding in John H. McNeill, 'International Agreements: Recent US–UK Practice Concerning the Memorandum of Understanding' (1994) 68 *American Journal of International Law* 821. For a reply, see Aust, *Modern Treaty Law and Practice* (n 1) 46–49.

[7] Oscar Schachter, 'The Twilight Existence of Nonbinding International Agreements' (1997) 71 *American Journal of International Law* 296, 297.

[8] *Aegean Sea Continental Shelf* (n 5) para. 96. See also Aust, *Modern Treaty Law and Practice* (n 1) 29–35.

instrument as well as the manner in which it is dealt with subsequent to its conclusion. If, for example, the instrument is submitted to a national parliament in accordance with domestic procedures for the conclusion of treaties, it indicates an intention to create a legally binding commitment. The decision by the executive branch in the United States not to submit the December 2015 Paris Agreement on climate change for approval before the US Senate as required for treaties by the US Constitution thus indicates that the US government does not believe that the agreement constitutes a legally binding agreement under international law. Article 102 of the UN Charter specifies that treaties and international agreements entered into by a member of the UN shall be registered with the UN Secretariat. Registration indicates a belief among the parties that they have entered into a legally binding instrument.[9]

Case law from the ICJ shows that it does not take much for an agreement to be considered legally binding. In the *Aegean Sea Continental Shelf* case, for example, the Court did not rule out that a press communiqué without signatures or initials could be considered a legally binding treaty.[10] In *Case Concerning Maritime Delimitation and Territorial Questions between Qatar and Bahrain*, the Court concluded that minutes from a meeting enumerated the 'commitments to which the Parties have consented'. It therefore created rights and obligations in international law.[11] In *Maritime Delimitation in the Indian Ocean*, the Court concluded that a Memorandum of Understanding (MoU) between Kenya and Somalia was a treaty under international law. The Court noted that the document recorded the two parties' agreement on certain points governed by international law; that it included a provision regarding entry into force of the MoU; that Kenya had requested its registration under article 102 of the UN Charter; and that Somalia did not protest that registration until almost five years thereafter.[12]

3.3 The authority to conclude a treaty

All states possess the legal capacity to conclude treaties[13] but not all representatives of a state are considered competent to conclude a treaty on behalf of a state. The issue of 'representation' is dealt with in article 7 of the VCLT, which refers to the concept of 'full powers'. In practical terms, a 'full power' is a document that authorizes a state representative to negotiate and conclude a treaty on behalf of the state. Hence, a representative who produces a document with an authority to negotiate and conclude a treaty on behalf of the state will be so authorized. In *Maritime Delimitation in the Indian Ocean*, for example, the Prime Minister of the Transitional Federal Government of Somalia had 'authorized and empowered' the

---

[9] *Maritime Delimitation and Territorial Questions between Qatar and Bahrain* (n 5) para. 29.

[10] *Aegean Sea Continental Shelf* (n 5) para. 96.

[11] *Maritime Delimitation and Territorial Questions between Qatar and Bahrain* (n 5) paras 25, 30.

[12] *Maritime Delimitation in the Indian Ocean (Somalia v Kenya)*, Preliminary Objections, Judgment, 2 February 2017, para. 42.

[13] VCLT art. 6.

Somali Minister for National Planning and International Cooperation to sign an MoU with the Minister for Foreign Affairs of Kenya.[14] But not all state representatives need to produce 'full powers'. According to article 7(2)(a) of the VCLT, by virtue of their functions heads of state, heads of government and ministers for foreign affairs may perform *all acts* that relate to the conclusion of a treaty on behalf of a state without presenting full powers. Their prominent positions mean that other states can rely on their ability to act on behalf of the state. Thus, in *Eastern Greenland* the Permanent Court of International Justice (PCIJ) concluded that the unilateral statement by the Norwegian Minister of Foreign Affairs was binding on Norway even though the minister was allegedly not competent under Norwegian law to bind Norway in the matter in question.[15] A more limited authority to represent a home state rests on heads of diplomatic missions[16] and representatives accredited by a state to an international conference or an international organization.[17] Depending on the circumstances, these individuals may participate in *the adoption of a text* of a treaty without full powers.

According to article 46(1) of the VCLT, a state may not invoke the fact that its consent to be bound by a treaty has been expressed in violation of its *national laws* as invalidating its consent unless the violation of national law was manifest and concerned a national rule of fundamental importance. Under article 46(2), the *violation of internal law* must be 'manifest' in the sense that it is objectively evident to any state conducting itself in the matter in accordance with normal practice and good faith. The threshold is high, and in *Land and Maritime Boundary between Cameroon and Nigeria* the ICJ concluded that states are not obliged 'to keep themselves informed of legislative and constitutional developments in other States which are or may become important for the international relations of these States'.[18] In *Maritime Delimitation in the Indian Ocean*, the Court concluded that there was no reason to suppose that Kenya could have been aware that a signature of a Somali minister on an MoU may not have been sufficient under Somali law to express consent to a binding international agreement.[19] If a person with no authority to conclude a treaty has nevertheless done so, the state may decide to avail itself of the opportunity to disavow the act of the person in question by subsequently endorsing the act and thereby establishing its consent to be bound.[20] The state will be held to have done so by implication if it invokes the provisions of the treaty or otherwise acts in such a way as to appear to treat the act in question as effective.[21]

---

[14] *Maritime Delimitation in the Indian Ocean* (n 12) para. 43.

[15] *Legal Status of Eastern Greenland (Denmark v Norway)*, Judgment, 1933, PCIJ, Series A/B, No. 53. See also *Maritime Delimitation and Territorial Questions between Qatar and Bahrain* (n 5) paras 26–27.

[16] VCLT art. 7(2)(b).

[17] Ibid, art. 7(2)(c).

[18] *Land and Maritime Boundary between Cameroon and Nigeria (Cameroon v Nigeria; Equatorial Guinea intervening)*, Judgment [2002] ICJ Rep 303, para. 266.

[19] *Maritime Delimitation in the Indian Ocean* (n 12) para. 49.

[20] VCLT art. 8.

[21] ILC, Draft Articles on the Law of Treaties, with commentaries, *Yearbook of the International Law Commission*, 1966, vol. II, pp. 187, 194.

3.4 Treaties between states and international organizations

Depending on the circumstances, international organizations also have treaty-making powers.[22] For example, both the UN and the EU have concluded a number of treaties covering a wide variety of issues. The *Vienna Convention on the Law of Treaties between International Organizations or between States and International Organizations* was adopted in 1986 to regulate treaty relations of international organizations. At the time of writing, however, it has not yet entered into force. When drafting the articles, the ILC used the 1969 VCLT as the basis for the new convention on international organizations and simply proceeded from article to article in order to determine when modifications were called for. Thus, with a few exceptions, the 1986 Convention is identical to the 1969 Convention. The UN is a party to the 1986 Convention.

3.5 Consent to be bound

In order for a state to become legally bound by a treaty, it must consent to it. According to article 11 of the VCLT, consent may be expressed by a signature, an exchange of the instruments, ratification, acceptance, approval or accession 'or by any other means if so agreed'.[23] Hence, the VCLT is fairly flexible and leaves it to the parties to the treaty to determine the means by which the required consent may be expressed. In *Maritime Delimitation in the Indian Ocean*, for example, Kenya and Somalia had signed an MoU that contained a provision that expressly stated that it entered into force upon signature.[24] Today, there is a widespread practice of simply expressing consent by signature—also known as a *definitive* signature.[25] Article 15 of the VCLT permits consent by *accession*, where a state gives its consent to be bound by a treaty already negotiated and signed by other states, often after the treaty has entered into force, in the following circumstances:

(a) if the treaty provides for it;

(b) if it is otherwise established that the negotiating parties were agreed that it should be possible; or

(c) if all the parties have subsequently agreed that a state may express its consent by such means.

Accession is primarily relevant in relation to multilateral treaties, such as human rights conventions, that gradually seek to expand the number of participating states.

---

[22] See *Certain Expenses of the United Nations (Article 17, paragraph 2, of the Charter)*, Advisory Opinion [1962] ICJ Rep 151, 168 and *Legality of the Use of Nuclear Weapons in Times of Armed Conflict*, Advisory Opinion [1996] ICJ Rep 66, para. 19.

[23] See also VCLT arts 12–16.   [24] *Maritime Delimitation in the Indian Ocean* (n 12) paras 37, 47.

[25] George Korontzis, 'Making the Treaty' in Duncan B. Hollis (ed.), *The Oxford Guide to Treaties* (Oxford University Press, 2012) 196.

An important distinction is that between signature and *ratification*. In some circumstances, and very often with regard to multilateral treaties, consent to be bound by a treaty requires not only a signature by the potential state party in question, but also a *subsequent confirmation* by the state that it intends to be bound by the treaty.[26] The purpose of ratification is to allow the signing state a period of time before it gives its binding consent. Often the state may need the approval of its national parliament (more rarely, it may seek approval of the general public through a referendum), or to enact the necessary legislation to give domestic effect to the treaty.[27] Well-known examples of treaties subject to ratification were the 1992 Treaty on the European Union (Maastricht Treaty) and the 2007 EU Treaty of Lisbon. Indeed, the VCLT itself is subject to ratification.[28] When subsequent ratification is required, the (initial) signature is not (yet) confirmation that the state intends to be bound by the treaty. For example, the United States has signed the 1989 UN Convention on the Rights of the Child but not yet ratified it. As we return to later, however, the mere signing of a treaty that must be ratified triggers an obligation to refrain from acts that would defeat the object and purpose of the treaty.

According to article 14 of the VCLT, ratification is required if:

(a) it is specified in the treaty itself;

(b) it is otherwise established that the negotiating parties agreed that it was needed;

(c) the representative who signed the treaty did so subject to ratification; or

(d) it appeared from the full powers of the representative or it was expressed during the negotiation that that was the intention of the state.

If it is not specified or otherwise manifest that ratification is needed, there is a presumption that ratification is *not* required.[29]

3.6 Entry into force—obligations in the interim period

When a state has given its consent to be bound by a treaty, it has shown its intention to undertake the legal obligations it contains. In practice, however, it is not legally bound by the treaty until the treaty enters into force. According to article 24 of the VCLT, a treaty enters into force 'in such manner and upon such date as it may provide or as the negotiating states may agree'. In the case of simple *bilateral* agreements, the treaty may enter into force when both parties sign the agreement. But it is not unusual for a substantial amount of time to pass before a *multilateral* treaty enters into force. The VCLT itself did not enter into force until more than ten years after it was adopted.[30] If the treaty does not specify when it enters into force, it will generally enter into force as soon as consent has been established for *all* the negotiating states. A treaty that has

---

[26] VCLT art. 14.   [27] For an exact definition, see VCLT art. 2(1)(b).   [28] VCLT art. 82.
[29] Aust, *Modern Treaty Law and Practice* (n 1) 96.
[30] Art. 84 states that the Convention enters into force on the 30th day following the date of deposit of the 35th instrument of ratification or accession.

not yet entered into force cannot create any legal obligations for the contracting states. But good faith requires that a state is not entirely free to act as it pleases when it has given its consent to be bound or expressed an initial intention to be bound but needs to give subsequent confirmation—known as 'the interim period'. Article 18 of the VCLT specifies that states must refrain from acts which would 'defeat the object and purpose' of the treaty when (a) it has signed the treaty but not yet ratified it, until it has made its intention clear not to become a party to the treaty; or (b) it has expressed its consent to be bound by the treaty, pending the entry into force of the treaty (and provided the entry into force is not unduly delayed). Whether an act 'defeats the object and purpose' of a treaty must be determined on a case-by-case basis. The provision is easier to apply to treaties of a contractual nature than to more general law-making treaties. As a point of departure, however, it will probably only be in those cases where a state's behaviour in relation to a treaty appears to be 'unwarranted and condemnable' and potentially motivated by bad intentions that it will be found to violate its interim obligations.[31]

3.7 Validity

All legal systems have rules concerning the validity—and invalidity—of their legal instruments, and international law is no exception. Since the legal basis of a treaty obligation is the consent of the state party, most of the grounds for invalidity relate to defects in the consent given by a state. Thus, with the exception of treaties in violation of *jus cogens*, the underlying rationale of a claim of invalidity will be that consent would not have been given had it not been for the circumstance in question.[32] The rules on invalidity are found in articles 46–53 and 64 of the VCLT, and they illustrate that it is very difficult to successfully raise a claim of invalidity. In fact, predictability, stability and mutual trust dictate that once agreed and entered into, even seemingly 'unequal' or 'unreasonable' treaties must be considered valid and legally binding.[33]

The first ground of invalidity has been noted previously in the chapter. Thus, according to article 46 of the VCLT a state can invoke the fact that its consent to be bound by a treaty was expressed in violation of its internal law. It requires, however, that the violation was 'manifest and concerned a rule of its internal law of fundamental importance'.[34] In practice this will mean that 'it would be objectively evident to any State conducting itself in the matter in accordance with normal practice and in good faith'.[35] Article 46 must be distinguished from article 27 whereby a state may not invoke its internal law as a justification for not fulfilling a treaty-based obligation.

---

[31] Jan Klabbers, 'How to Defeat a Treaty's Object and Purpose Pending Entry into Force: Toward Manifest Intent' (2001) 34 *Vanderbilt Journal of Transnational Law* 283, 330.

[32] See also Jan Klabbers, 'The Validity and Invalidity of Treaties' in Hollis (n 25) 557.

[33] On 'unequal' treaties, see Matthew Craven, 'What Happened to Unequal Treaties? The Continuities of Informal Empire' (2005) 74 *Nordic Journal of International Law* 335.

[34] VCLT art. 46(1).   [35] Ibid, art. 46(2).

Article 48 addresses *error* in the formation of treaties and stipulates that error can only be invoked if it 'relates to a fact or situation which was assumed to ... exist at the time when the treaty was concluded' and if it 'formed an essential basis' of the consent expressed. In addition, under article 48(2), error cannot be invoked by a state if the latter contributed by its own conduct to the error or the circumstances were such that the state should have noticed 'a possible error'. Importantly, political miscalculations are different from errors and international law assumes that state representatives can make reasonable judgements of their own actions.

Article 49 specifies that a state can invoke *fraud* as invalidating consent if it has been misled or 'induced to conclude a treaty'. In a somewhat similar vein, article 50 specifies that *corruption of a representative of a state* may be a ground for invoking invalidity. Article 51 concerns *coercion* and stipulates that an expression of consent shall be without legal effect if it has been procured 'through acts or threats' directed against a state representative. A more relevant provision is article 52, according to which a 'treaty is void if its conclusion has been *procured by the threat or use of force in violation of ... the Charter of the United Nations*'. The rule raises a number of questions, including the validity of peace treaties concluded after a use of force of doubtful legality under the UN Charter. Since some measure of coercion and pressure is endemic in international relations and negotiations, it is of some importance that the article only concerns military force.[36]

The most relevant of the provisions on potential invalidity is article 53 concerning peremptory norms/*jus cogens*. As we saw in Chapter 2, article 53 specifies that a treaty is void if it 'conflicts with a peremptory norm of general international law'.[37] Such norms are those that have been 'accepted and recognized by the international community of States as a whole as a norm from which no derogation is permitted and which can be modified only by a subsequent norm of general international law having the same character'. Article 53 differs from the other articles on invalidity in that it is the only one that focuses on the *content* of the treaty in question and thereby tries to limit the contractual freedom of the states. While there is little agreement on which norms are of a *jus cogens* character, the category seems to include the prohibition against torture and genocide, the ban on slavery, the prohibition of aggression, the ban on crimes against humanity, the prohibition of piracy, the right to self-determination and the prohibition of apartheid and other forms of gross racial discrimination.[38] Article 53 should be read in conjunction with article 64 according to which an existing treaty becomes void and terminates if it conflicts with an emerging (new) peremptory norm. In contrast to article 53, the latter article concerns cases where a treaty was valid when concluded but subsequently becomes void due to the establishment of a new rule of *jus cogens*. An example would be a treaty previously intended to regulate the slave trade.

---

[36] Klabbers, 'The Validity and Invalidity of Treaties' (n 32) 569–570.

[37] A unilateral declaration that conflicts with a peremptory norm of general international law is similarly void, see ILC, 'Guiding Principles applicable to unilateral declarations of States capable of creating legal obligations' (2006), UN Doc. A/61/10 (ILC Guiding Principles) and VCLT art. 53.

[38] See also Chapter 2.

3.8 **Reservations**

International law may allow a state to take account of national political, social or cultural attitudes by becoming a party to a multilateral treaty without accepting all of its provisions and obligations.[39] Unilateral statements whereby a state may exclude or modify the legal effect of one or more provisions of a treaty in its application to the state are termed 'reservations'.[40] The rules governing reservations are among the most detailed and complicated in the field of the law of treaties.[41]

It is important to distinguish between 'reservations' and 'interpretative declarations'. Unlike a reservation, an *interpretative declaration* (which is not mentioned in the VCLT) does *not* seek to modify the treaty obligation but merely to *specify* or *clarify* the meaning or scope the declaring state attaches to the obligation in question. Hence, the purpose of such a declaration is to communicate to other parties what the declaring state understands the existing obligation to be. Often, the purpose of an interpretative declaration is to ensure an interpretation of a treaty provision that is consistent with the domestic law of the state in question. The declaration may constitute an element that must be taken into account in interpreting the treaty in accordance with the general rules of treaty interpretation (see Section 3.9).[42] It is also important not to confuse reservations with derogations. As we shall explore further in Chapter 9, some human rights treaties contain provisions that authorize a state to 'derogate'—and thus not to apply certain provisions in the treat—in times of emergency or a similar period of national crisis. A derogation is *not* the same as a reservation.

The concrete rules on treaty reservations owe much to *Genocide Reservations*, where the ICJ in 1951 issued an advisory opinion on reservations to the 1948 Genocide Convention. Until then, reservations had to be accepted by *all* the contracting parties, but in its opinion the ICJ adopted a new and more flexible approach that subsequently found its way into the VCLT.[43] Thus, reservations are now generally acceptable if they are compatible with 'the object and purpose' of the treaty in question.[44] State practice is rich with examples of state reservations and reservations of relatively minor significance are particularly prevalent in relation to human rights conventions, such as the UN Covenant on Civil and Political Rights. Denmark, for example, has a reservation to the Covenant's right for juvenile offenders to be segregated from adults and accorded treatment appropriate to their age and legal status. Sweden and Norway have made a similar reservation, and Sweden also has a reservation to the obligation to prohibit propaganda for war.[45] Among the more well-known examples

---

[39] For an overview, see Aust, *Modern Treaty Law and Practice* (n 1) 114–144.

[40] For a definition, see VCLT art. 2(1)(d).

[41] For an overview, see Edward T. Swaine, 'Treaty Reservations' in Hollis (n 25) 277–301. In practice, of course, given their 'contractual' nature, reservations cannot be made to bilateral treaties.

[42] See also ILC, 'Guide to Practice on Reservations to Treaties' (2011), UN Doc. A/66/10, para. 4.7.1.

[43] *Reservations to the Convention on Genocide*, Advisory Opinion [1951] ICJ Rep 15, 21–22.

[44] Ibid, 24.

[45] For an overview of reservations to the Covenant, see https://treaties.un.org/pages/ViewDetails. aspx?src=TREATY&mtdsg_no=IV-4&chapter=4&clang=_en.

of treaty reservations are the Danish 'opt-outs' to the 1992 Maastricht Treaty on the establishment of the EU. In a May 1992 referendum, a narrow majority of Danish voters rejected the Maastricht Treaty. Since the Treaty had to be ratified by all member states, a solution to the 'Danish problem' was found at the Edinburgh Summit in December 1992, where the member states agreed to allow Denmark to 'opt out' of certain aspects of the Treaty.[46] In a subsequent referendum in May 1993, a majority of Danish voters accepted Danish ratification of the Treaty with the four 'opt-outs'. In essence, the opt-outs were treaty reservations that meant that Denmark would not be bound by certain provisions of the Treaty.[47]

Reservations to treaties are not always permitted. According to article 19 of the VCLT, reservations are excluded in three circumstances. First, reservations cannot be made if the treaty expressly stipulates that reservations are not permitted. Article 120 of the Rome Statute of the International Criminal Court, for example, specifies that no reservations may be made to the Statute. Secondly, some treaties provide that only certain reservations to the treaty can be made. The third exception holds that a reservation cannot be made if it violates the object and purpose of a treaty. In such cases, the reservation will be null and void and without legal effect regardless of whether or not other states have objected to it.[48] According to the ILC, the object and purpose of a treaty is compromised if the reservation 'affects an essential element of the treaty that is necessary to its general tenour, in such a way that the reservation impairs the raison d'être of the treaty'.[49] It may be difficult to identify the object and purpose of a treaty, in particular as these have a tendency to become more elaborate and complex. However, both the title and a preamble of a treaty may offer some guidance.[50] As noted earlier, many states have made minor reservations to human rights conventions and it may be hard to draw the line between permissible and impermissible reservations to human rights conventions. A concrete example is the reservation by the United States to the obligation in the Covenant not to impose the death penalty for crimes committed by persons under 18 years of age.[51]

Articles 20 and 21 of the VCLT deal with the important issues regarding acceptance/objection to reservations and the legal effects of reservations. As a main rule, and as a natural consequence of the consensual nature of the law of treaties, a reservation will not become effective in relation to another contracting state unless that state has accepted it—either explicitly or implicitly. In short, if a state proposes a reservation the other states may accept or object to the reservation. If a state has not objected within 12 months, it is deemed to have accepted it.[52] Article 20 initially stipulates that

---

[46] European Council, 'Denmark and the Treaty on European Union', Edinburgh, 11 and 12 December 1992, 92/C 348/01.

[47] The reservations related to the third stage of Economic and Monetary Union and the introduction of the common currency (the euro), common defence policies, cooperation in the fields of justice and home affairs and provisions relating to EU citizenship.

[48] See also ILC, 'Guide to Practice on Reservations to Treaties' (n 42) paras 4.5.1–4.5.2.

[49] Ibid, para. 3.1.5.

[50] See also Jan Klabbers, 'Some Problems Regarding the Object and Purpose of Treaties' (1997) 8 *Finnish Yearbook of International Law* 138, 156–158.

[51] See reservations by the United States in link in n 45.   [52] VCLT art. 20(5).

acceptance is not required if the reservation is *expressly* authorized by the treaty.[53] If, however, it appears from the limited number of participating states and the object and purpose of the treaty that it is meant to apply in its entirety to all parties, reservation requires the consent of *all* those parties.[54] Unless otherwise provided, a reservation to a treaty that is a constituent instrument of an international organization requires the acceptance of the competent organ of that organization.[55]

If nothing is provided in the treaty, reservations are governed by the following principles.

(a) If a state accepts a reservation by another state they will be parties to the same treaty.[56]

(b) If a state objects to another state's reservation the treaty will not enter into force between the two states *if* the objecting state expresses a definite intention for that to be the case.[57]

(c) A state's reservation is effective when at least one other contracting state has accepted it.[58]

With regard to the *legal effects* of reservations and objections, article 21 of the VCLT stipulates that a reservation modifies the provisions of the treaty for the reserving and the other state.[59] It does not, however, modify the provisions for the other parties *inter se.*[60] As a result of the Danish reservations to the Maastricht Treaty, then, while Denmark is not bound by the 'reserved' parts of the treaty, the other non-reserving states are bound vis-à-vis each other. If an objecting state has not expressly opposed the entry into force of the treaty between itself and the reserving state, the provisions to which the reservation relates do not apply between the two states.[61]

In practical terms, then, a state can react to another state's reservation in three ways: (1) it can accept the reservation, in which event the treaty will enter into force between the two states with the reservation in force; (2) it can object to the reservation and express an intention that the treaty as a whole should not enter into force between the states—if that is the case, the treaty will not govern the two states' relations; or (3) it can object to the reservation but refrain from expressing an intention that the treaty as a whole should not enter into force between the two states. Then the treaty will enter into force between the two states with the reservation in force. In practice, therefore, the legal effect of options (1) and (3) is the same, and the choices for an objecting state are therefore not very favourable. Unless it wants the treaty *as a whole* not to govern the relations between itself and the reserving state, it will make no material difference if it accepts or objects to a reservation.

If a reservation violates a treaty's object and purpose, the reserving state cannot rely on it in its treaty relations with other parties. In practice, then, there would only appear to be two possible outcomes.[62] The first is that the invalidity of the

---

[53] Ibid, art. 20(1).   [54] Ibid, art. 20(2).   [55] Ibid, art. 20(3).   [56] Ibid, art. 20(4)(a).
[57] Ibid, art. 20(4)(b).   [58] Ibid, art. 20(4)(c).   [59] Ibid, art. 21(1).   [60] Ibid, art. 21(2).
[61] Ibid, art. 21(3).
[62] See also Ryan Goodman, 'Human Rights Treaties, Invalid Reservations, and State Consent' (2002) 96 *American Journal of International Law* 531.

reservation nullifies the instrument *as a whole* whereby the (reserving) state is no longer considered a party to the agreement at all. While this approach preserves the integrity of the treaty regime in question, it is a drastic step that the involved states themselves may not desire. The second option is to essentially ignore the reservation and conclude that the (reserving) state remains bound by the treaty, including the provision(s) to which the reservation related. However, this so-called 'severance' option goes against the principle that a state is only bound by the treaty obligations it consents to. While the latter approach has been supported by, among others, the European Court of Human Rights (ECtHR),[63] the Human Rights Committee[64] and the Nordic states,[65] the ILC has suggested a more moderate solution.[66] It introduces a *presumption* of severability according to which the reserving state will be considered a contracting state without 'the benefit of the reservation' unless it 'has expressed a contrary intention or such an intention is otherwise established'.[67] Thus, unless the state makes it manifest that it will *only* be a party to the treaty if it can benefit from the invalid reservation, it will be presumed to be a full party without benefitting from the reservation.

According to article 19 of the VCLT, a reservation must be made by a state 'when signing, ratifying, accepting, approving or acceding to a treaty', and there is no mention of a right to make a reservation after the treaty in question has been ratified. A reservation subsequent to ratification cannot therefore be effective unless it is accepted by the other contracting parties.

It has been debated whether a state that is not satisfied with an existing treaty obligation can withdraw from the treaty in order to 're-accede' with a reservation that excludes the unwanted obligation.[68] One solution would be to just let the issue be dealt with on a case-by-case basis by the other contracting parties. A state that wishes to become 'un-bound' by a treaty obligation will, of course, continue to be bound by the content of the obligation if it has become binding as a matter of customary international law.

---

[63] *Belios v Switzerland*, App. no. 10328/83, 29 April 1998, para. 60. See also *Loizidou v Turkey*, App. no. 15318/89, Preliminary Objections, 23 March 1995.

[64] Human Rights Committee, 'General Comment No. 24: General Comment on Issues Relating to Reservations Made Upon Ratification or Accession to the Covenant or the Optional Protocols thereto, or in Relation to Declarations under Article 41 of the Covenant' (4 November 1994), UN Doc. CCPR/C/21/Rev.1/Add.6, para. 18.

[65] See the overview in Jan Klabbers, 'Accepting the Unacceptable? A Nordic Approach to Reservations to Multilateral Treaties' (2000) 69 *Nordic Journal of International Law* 179.

[66] See the critique in Hugh Thirlway, *The Sources of International Law* (Oxford University Press, 2014) 38–44; Aust, *Modern Treaty Law and Practice* (n 1) 131; Klabbers, 'Accepting the Unacceptable?' (n 65) 190.

[67] ILC, 'Guide to Practice on Reservations to Treaties' (n 45) para. 4.5.3. See also Goodman (n 62) 555–559.

[68] Aust, *Modern Treaty Law and Practice* (n 1) 141–142. See also Glenn McGrory, 'Reservations of Virtue? Lessons from Trinidad and Tobago's Reservation to the First Optional Protocol' (2001) 23 *Human Rights Quarterly* 769, 812; Laurence R. Helfer, 'Not Fully Committed? Reservations, Risk, and Treaty Design' (2006) 32 *Yale Journal of International Law* 367, 373. This would not be possible if the reservation violates the treaty's object and purpose

3.9 Interpretation

Most disputes in international law concern interpretation of treaties, and treaty interpretation is therefore one of the most important skills of any international lawyer. The relevant principles of treaty interpretation are found in articles 31 and 32 of the VCLT, which reflect customary international law.[69] As always, it is the intention of the parties that is the key. Article 31(1) articulates the general rule that a 'treaty shall be interpreted in good faith in accordance with the ordinary meaning to be given to the terms of the treaty in their context and in the light of its object and purpose'. Thus, the interpreter must consider three elements: the *text*, its *context* and the *object and purpose* of the treaty as desired by the parties. *All* elements are relevant and none is afforded a greater weight than the others.[70] While it is generally fair to assume that the ordinary meaning of a word or term is what was intended by the parties to the treaty,[71] the text is only the natural starting point for the interpretation. Thus, if the wording of a treaty is clear but its application would lead to an unreasonable result, the other elements must be included. In practice, it is usually only possible to grasp the 'ordinary meaning' of a text by considering its context and the overall object and purpose of the treaty. In order to determine, for example, what is meant by the terms 'force' or 'armed attack' in articles 2(4) and article 51 of the UN Charter, the interpreter must take account of both the structure of the Charter as well as the Charter's purposes as set out in the preamble and the opening articles. According to article 31(4), a 'special meaning' must be given to a term in a treaty provision if 'it is established that the parties so intended'.

According to article 31(2), the 'context' includes not only the treaty's preamble but also annexes as well as agreements and instruments made by the parties *in connection with the conclusion of the treaty*. Article 31(3)(a) and (b) permits consideration of agreements and practice established *subsequent* to the adoption of the treaty.[72] This makes sense since the manner in which a treaty is actually applied by the parties is a good indication of what they believe the treaty to mean. Indeed, if subsequent practice is sufficiently clear and either expressly or tacitly accepted by all parties, it can take precedence over an otherwise fairly clear wording of the text in a treaty. For example, in *Namibia*, the ICJ found that although article 27(3) of the UN Charter stipulates that decisions by the Security Council on non-procedural matters must be made by an 'affirmative' vote of nine of its members including the 'concurring votes' of the five permanent members, subsequent practice confirmed that the term 'concurring'

---

[69] *Territorial Dispute (Libyan Arab Jamahiriya v Chad)*, Judgment [1994] ICJ Rep 6, para. 41; *Oil Platforms (Islamic Republic of Iran v United States)*, Preliminary Objections [1996] ICJ Rep 803, para. 23; *Kasikili/Sedudu Island (Botswana v Namibia)* [1999] ICJ Rep 1045, para. 18; *LaGrand (Germany v United States)* [2001] ICJ Rep 466, paras 99–101. See also ECtHR, *Golder v UK*, App. no. 4451/70, 21 February 1975, para. 29. See also Ulf Lindefalk, *On the Interpretation of Treaties* (Springer, 2010) 7.

[70] See also ILC, Draft Articles on the Law of Treaties, with commentaries, *Yearbook of the International Law Commission*, 1966, vol. II, pp. 187, 219, para. 8; Richard Gardiner, *Treaty Interpretation* (Oxford University Press, 2008) ch. 5.

[71] See also *LaGrand* (n 69) para. 77.   [72] VCLT art. 31(3)(a) and (b).

should simply be interpreted as 'not objecting'.[73] *Namibia* illustrates that it may be difficult to determine if subsequent practice should be conceived of as an interpretation or an outright amendment of a provision.[74] In *Hassan v UK*, the ECtHR found that subsequent practice of the parties 'could be taken as establishing their agreement not only as regards interpretation but even to modify the text' of the European Convention on Human Rights (ECHR).[75] The Court found that the detention of individuals on the basis of the Third and Fourth 1949 Geneva Conventions in the course of an international armed conflict would appear to be prima facie inconsistent with the right to liberty under article 5 of the ECHR unless the detaining state has made a valid derogation from its obligations under that article. It also concluded, however, that subsequent state practice showed that the lack of a formal derogation should not prevent the Court from taking account of the Geneva Conventions when interpreting and applying article 5.[76]

Article 31(3)(c) of the VCLT specifies that, together with the context, treaty interpretation shall take account of 'any relevant rules of international law applicable in the relations between the parties'. Thus, the treaty must be considered in the wider context of international law.[77] In *Hassan v UK* mentioned above, the ECtHR found that the interpretation of a human rights provision should take account of the existence of international humanitarian law. The grounds for permitting deprivation of liberty set out in article 5 of the ECHR should therefore be 'accommodated ... with the taking of prisoners of war and the detention of civilians who pose a risk to security under the Third and Fourth Geneva Conventions'.[78]

Article 32 of the VCLT concerns the status of the preparatory works to a treaty (*travaux préparatoires*), such as preliminary drafts of the treaty, records from conferences and explanatory statements. Such material is explicitly listed as a 'supplementary means of interpretation' and is only to be consulted 'in order to confirm the meaning resulting from the application of article 31, or to determine the meaning when the interpretation according to article 31' either leaves the meaning ambiguous or obscure, or will lead to a 'result which is manifestly absurd or unreasonable'.[79] In practice, however, the preparatory work will usually be consulted if it has anything meaningful to add about the intention of the parties to a treaty.

If a treaty is drafted in more than one language, it may give rise to a host of interpretative issues.[80] According to article 33 of the VCLT, if a 'treaty has been authenticated in two or more languages' 'the text is equally authoritative in each

---

[73] *Legal Consequences for States of the Continued Presence of South Africa in Namibia (South West Africa) notwithstanding Security Council Resolution 276 (1970)*, Advisory Opinion [1971] ICJ Rep 16, para. 22.

[74] See also Gardiner (n 70) 243–245. See also ECtHR, *Soering v UK*, App. no. 14038/88, 7 July 1989, paras 103–104 and *Öcalan v Turkey*, App. no. 46221/99, 12 March 2003, paras 162–165.

[75] *Hassan v UK*, App. no. 29750/09, 16 September 2014, para. 101.   [76] Ibid, paras 101–103.

[77] On this, see ILC, 'Fragmentation of International Law: Difficulties Arising from the Diversification and Expansion of International Law', Report of the Study Group of the International Law Commission (13 April 2006), UN Doc. A/CN.4/L.682, 206–244. See also Gardiner (n 70) ch. 7.

[78] *Hassan v UK* (n 75) paras 102–104. See also WTO, *United States—Import Prohibition of Certain Shrimp and Shrimp Products* (12 October 1998) WT/DS58/AB/R, paras 126–134 and—somewhat controversially—*Oil Platforms (Iran v United States)*, Merits [2003] ICJ Rep 161, para. 41.

[79] *LaGrand* (n 69) para. 104.   [80] See, e.g., *LaGrand* (n 69) 99–109.

language' unless otherwise specified or agreed. The problem is sometimes overcome by a stipulation in the treaty that one of the languages will prevail in the case of inconsistency.

Although articles 31–33 of the VCLT are intended to govern the interpretation of all types of treaties, how much weight the interpreter assigns to, respectively, the text, context and object and purpose of a treaty often depends on the character of the treaty. Thus, while treaties of a contractual/reciprocal character may dictate an interpretative approach that centres around state consent and the intention of the parties involved, treaties of a more 'law-making' character may call for a teleological approach that places more emphasis on the treaty's stated object and purpose. A *constitutive treaty*, that establishes an international institution and specifies the functions and competences of that institution, is generally considered to be of a 'special nature' that calls less for interpretation in accordance with the intention of the parties that created the institution than an interpretation that stresses 'effectiveness' ('functionality'). In *Reparations*, the ICJ concluded that the UN possesses those competences that are required for it to effectively discharge the functions entrusted to it by the member states.[81] In practice, it falls to the international organization itself to interpret the extent of its own powers.[82] In *Legality of the Use of Nuclear Weapons in Times of Armed Conflict*, the Court found that the World Health Organization (WHO) did not have the competence to request an advisory opinion on whether the use of nuclear weapons was lawful.[83] The constituent treaties of the EU are routinely interpreted by the Court of Justice of the European Union in a manner in which their purpose and 'effectiveness' are stressed. In the seminal 1963 case of *Van Gend en Loos*, the (then) European Court of Justice stated that the Treaty establishing the European Economic Community was 'more than an agreement which merely creates mutual obligations between the contracting states … [It] constitutes a new legal order of international law' and should be interpreted accordingly.[84] *Human rights conventions* are also generally interpreted less according to the original intention of the parties and more in order to ensure the effective, real and concrete protection of the individuals who find themselves under the jurisdiction of the states in question. As we shall return to in Chapter 9, the ECtHR has, for example, adopted what is referred to as 'dynamic' interpretation and it has repeatedly stressed that the Convention is a 'living instrument' that must be interpreted in the 'light of present-day conditions' and not 'solely in accordance with the intentions of their authors at the adoption of the treaty'.[85] A similar approach is visible in the practice of other human rights bodies.[86]

---

[81] *Reparations for injuries suffered in the service of the United Nations*, Advisory Opinion [1949] ICJ Rep 174, 179–180. See also *Certain Expenses* (n 22) 157.

[82] *Certain Expenses* (n 22) 168.

[83] *Nuclear Weapons* (n 22) para. 19. See also *LaGrand* (n 69) para. 102.

[84] Cases 26–62 *Van Gend en Loos* [1963] ECR 1, 12.

[85] See, among others, *Tyrer v UK*, App. no. 5856/72, 25 April 1978, para. 31; *Loizidou v Turkey*, App. no. 15318/89, 23 March 1995, para. 71.

[86] See Human Rights Committee, 'General Comment No. 6: The Right to Life' (30 April 1982), UN Doc. HRI/Gen/1/Rev.7, paras 4–5; *19 Tradesmen v Colombia*, 5 July 2004, Inter-AmCtHR, Series C, No. 109 (2004), para. 173.

3.10 Amendments and modifications

As time passes and conditions and/or political sentiments change, parties to a treaty may feel the need to alter some of the provisions. As we have just seen, subsequent practice in the application of a treaty can have the practical effect of modifying the content of the treaty if it has been consented to by the parties. Under article 39 of the VCLT, a treaty may also be formally *amended* by the specific agreement of the parties—often termed 'protocols'. For example, over the years the ECHR has been supplemented by a large number of protocols.[87] In practice, many treaties, and most multilateral treaties, will contain provisions on amendments. Article 108 of the UN Charter, for example, states that the Charter can be amended and come into force for all members when the amendments have been adopted (and ratified) by two-thirds of the members of the General Assembly, including the five permanent members. Thus, an amendment may even bind states that have voted against it. If there are no such provisions, the usual consent-centred formalities on the conclusion and coming into effect of treaties applies. A proposed amendment should generally be notified to all contracting states.[88] Regardless of any amendment, article 41 of the VCLT states that two or more parties to a multilateral treaty may conclude an agreement *modifying* the treaty between them. It does require, however, that such a possibility is either provided for in the treaty or the modification in question is not prohibited by the treaty and does not affect the other parties' rights or obligations or relate to a provision derogation from which is incompatible with the effective execution of the object and purpose of the treaty as a whole.

When it is particularly obvious to parties that their treaty-based commitments need to take account of subsequent developments, they may decide to adopt a so-called 'framework' convention. Unlike other treaties, a framework convention does not seek to exhaustively regulate a given topic but instead to establish an organizational structure that will be competent to develop the substantive regulation. Framework conventions are particularly prevalent within international environmental law where a well-known example is the 1992 UN Framework Convention on Climate Change (UNFCCC).[89] While the Convention itself only contains few substantive provisions, it establishes a Conference of the Parties (COP) that is tasked with adopting the measures required to reach the objectives of the Convention.

3.11 Termination and withdrawal

A treaty may come to an end and terminate if its purpose has been fulfilled or if it is clear that it is limited in time and that time has passed. Articles 54 and 57 of the VCLT state that a treaty also terminates in accordance with a provision in the treaty or by the consent of all the parties thereto. In January 2003, North Korea famously announced

---

[87] For an overview, see Council of Europe, 'Search on Treaties' at http://conventions.coe.int/Treaty/Commun/ListeTraites.asp?MA=3&CM=7&CL=ENG (accessed 25 October 2018).
[88] VCLT art. 39(2).   [89] See more in Chapter 11.

that it was withdrawing from the Nuclear Non-Proliferation Treaty (NPT) in accordance with article X, paragraph 1 of the NPT, which provides that a party can withdraw from the treaty 'if it decides that extraordinary events, related to the subject matter of this Treaty, have jeopardized the supreme interests of its country'. In other situations, article 56 of the VCLT specifies that a state may only denounce or withdraw from a treaty where the parties intended to permit such a possibility or where the right may be implied by the nature of the treaty. In such cases, a party must give no less than 12 months' notice of its intention to denounce or withdraw from the treaty.

A state may also terminate a bilateral treaty if the other state materially breaches its obligations under the treaty. Under article 60(3) of the VCLT, a *'material breach'* consists of a repudiation of the treaty not permitted by the VCLT or the violation of a provision that is essential to accomplishing the object and purpose of the treaty. In cases of a material breach of a multilateral treaty, article 60(2) specifies that the other parties may, inter alia, unanimously decide to suspend the operation of the treaty in whole or in part or to terminate it either in relations between themselves and the defaulting state or as between all the parties.

In a limited range of situations, international law also permits a state to terminate or suspend its treaty-based obligations for a number of exceptional circumstances. First of all, under article 61 of the VCLT, a state may terminate or withdraw from a treaty if, due to the 'permanent disappearance or destruction of an object indispensable for the execution of the treaty', it becomes impossible for a state to perform the treaty-based obligation. Only a permanent impossibility will be relevant. Secondly, according to article 62, the same may apply in cases of *a fundamental change of circumstances* (*rebus sic stantibus*). The exception is narrow, however, and it may only be invoked if the change was unforeseen at the time the treaty was concluded and the existence of the now changed circumstances 'constituted an essential basis of the consent of the parties to be bound by the treaty' and the 'effect of the change is radically to transform the extent of the obligations still to be performed'. In addition, a state may not invoke its own conduct. In *Gabčíkovo-Nagymaros Project*, the ICJ did not find that changes in environmental knowledge and awareness radically affected the obligations of the parties.[90] According to the ICJ, the provisions for the termination and suspension of the operation of treaties in articles 60–62 of the VCLT reflect customary international law.[91] The consequences of the termination or suspension of a treaty are listed in articles 70–72.

Summary

Like other societies, the society of states has rules and principles that govern the agreements entered into by its legal subjects, and the law of treaties is one of the oldest and most important areas of public international law. The primary rules in the area of the law of treaties are found in the 1969 VCLT, which, for the most part at least, reflects customary

---

[90] *Gabčíkovo-Nagymaros Project (Hungary v Slovakia)*, Judgment [1997] ICJ Rep 7, para. 104.
[91] Ibid, para. 46.

international law. The 1969 Convention regulates the conclusion and entry into force of treaties, the application and interpretation of treaties, the validity and termination of treaties and the withdrawal from treaties, and is intended to be applied to *all* types of treaties whether bilateral or multilateral. For the most part, the rules resemble domestic rules for the creation and operation of contracts and, as with national contract law, the law of treaties is not concerned with the material content of the instrument itself. While the majority of the rules and principles are uncontroversial, issues relating to treaty reservations and the interpretation of treaties remain contentious and therefore fairly complex.

Recommended reading

For a thorough contribution, see Duncan B. Hollis (ed.), *The Oxford Guide to Treaties* (Oxford University Press, 2012).

A classic work on the law of treaties is Lord McNair, *The Law of Treaties* (Oxford University Press, 1986). See also Richard R. Baxter, 'International Law in "Her Infinite Variety"' (1980) 29 *International and Comparative Law Quarterly* 549; Oscar Schachter, 'The Twilight Existence of Nonbinding International Agreements' (1977) 71 *American Journal of International Law* 296; Jan Klabbers, *The Concept of Treaty in International Law* (Kluwer, 1996). More recent works include Anthony Aust, *Modern Treaty Law and Practice* (3rd edn, Cambridge University Press, 2013) and the same author in 'The Theory and Practice of Informal International Instruments' (1986) 35 *International and Comparative Law Quarterly* 787. See also Hugh Thirlway, *The Sources of International Law* (Oxford University Press, 2014) ch. 2.

For other contributions to the literature on reservations, see William A. Schabas, 'Reservations to Human Rights Treaties: Time of Innovation and Reform' (1994) 32 *Canadian Yearbook of International Law* 39; Ryan Goodman, 'Human Rights Treaties, Invalid Reservations, and State Consent' (2002) 96 *American Journal of International Law* 531.

For a thorough work on treaty interpretation, see Richard Gardiner, *Treaty Interpretation* (Oxford University Press, 2008) and Ulf Lindefalk, *On the Interpretation of Treaties* (Springer, 2010).

Questions for discussion

1. In what ways does the interpretation of constituent treaties and human rights treaties differ from a more traditional approach to interpretation?

2. What is the meaning of *pacta sunt servanda* and how does the principle manifest itself in the law of treaties?

3. How should one determine if an agreement is a treaty governed by international law or is merely a political pledge?

4. It is often the case that a treaty does not enter into force after a certain amount of time has passed. While a consenting state cannot be bound by a treaty that has yet to enter into force, it is not entirely free to act as it pleases. Why is that? From where is such an 'obligation' derived?

5. Can you provide some examples of when it is important to identify the object and purpose of a treaty?

4

The actors in the international legal system

CENTRAL ISSUES

1. This chapter introduces the various actors in the international legal system that possess rights, powers and obligations in international law.

2. It presents statehood and the criteria for the creation of new states, and discusses the (limited) legal significance of recognition.

3. The chapter also discusses the modes by which a state can acquire title to new territory and provides an overview of the main issues of state succession and state extinction.

4. The chapter presents an overview of the legal personality of non-state actors, most notably international organizations and individuals.

4.1 Introduction

We saw in Chapter 1 that international society is first and foremost a society of individual sovereign states. But while states remain centre stage, they are by no means the only actors in international law. In fact, one of the consequences of the post-1945 expansion of international law into areas that had up until then been of limited international interest has been the increasing legal importance of a variety of non-state actors, most notably international organizations and individuals. The answer to the question of who international law actually applies to is often found in the concept of 'legal subjectivity' or 'legal personality'.[1] The subjects of international law are those to whom the international legal system gives the capacity to hold rights, powers and obligations. Importantly, though, legal subjectivity/personality is relative. As the International Court of Justice (ICJ) stated in *Reparations*, legal subjects 'are not necessarily identical in their nature or in the extent of their rights,

---

[1] See Roland Portmann, *Legal Personality in International Law* (Cambridge University Press, 2010) and Astrid Kjeldgaard-Pedersen, *The International Legal Personality of the Individual* (Oxford University Press, 2018).

and their nature depends upon the needs of the community'.[2] The principal features of international legal personality include the capacity to bring claims in respect of breaches of international law, the capacity to conclude treaties and the enjoyment of privileges and immunities from the exercise of national jurisdiction. While states have all these capacities, other actors only possess the rights and obligations given to them.[3] Non-state actors thus derive their legal personality from states. In *Unilateral Declaration of Independence in Respect of Kosovo*, the ICJ noted that it is not uncommon for the Security Council to make demands on actors other than states and international organizations and that it would require a case-by-case evaluation to determine 'for whom the Security Council intended to create legal obligations'.[4]

This chapter presents the different actors in the international legal system. It begins in Section 4.2 with an analysis of the state. Sections 4.3 and 4.4 provide a brief overview of the legal personality of, respectively, international organizations and individuals. Section 4.5 discusses other actors with some form of legal personality.

4.2 The state

4.2.1 Introduction

States are by far the most important international legal actors and the only actors that can create international law. One of the major developments of the 20th century was the emergence of a large number of new states. From around 50 states at the beginning of the century to about 75 immediately after the Second World War, the number of states skyrocketed with the decolonialization process in the 1960s and 1970s. By October 2018, the number of states registered as members of the UN stood at 193.[5] The most recent additions to the club of states were South Sudan (2011) and Montenegro (2006). In 2012, Palestine was given status as a 'non-member observer state'[6] by the UN General Assembly. This section concerns the state as a legal actor in international law. First, we discuss the (limited) role played by recognition (Section 4.2.2) before we examine the criteria for statehood in the 1933 Montevideo Convention (Section 4.2.3). Attention then turns to the question of illegality in the creation of a state (Section 4.2.4), the relationship between the right to self-determination and statehood (Section 4.2.5), acquisition of new territory (Section 4.2.6), state succession (Section 4.2.7) and finally state extinction (Section 4.2.8).

---

[2] *Reparations for Injuries Suffered in the Service of the United Nations*, Advisory Opinion [1949] ICJ Rep 174, 178.

[3] See also James Crawford, *The Creation of States in International Law* (2nd edn, Oxford University Press, 2006) 28–29.

[4] *Accordance with International Law of the Unilateral Declaration of Independence in Respect of Kosovo*, Advisory Opinion [2010] ICJ Rep 403, paras 116–117.

[5] See http://www.un.org/en/member-states/ (accessed 20 October 2018).

[6] GA Res. 67/19 (4 December 2012), UN Doc. A/RES/67/19, para. 2.

4.2.2 **Recognition**

The special status afforded to states makes it all the more important to identify the rules and principles that govern the creation of states. It is therefore somewhat unfortunate that the issue is fraught with contention. This is primarily due to diverging opinions about the role played by recognition by other states. Here, it is important to initially distinguish between recognition of *a state* and of *a government*. They are essentially two different issues. Since it is the state that is the legal entity under international law and the government (merely) represents and acts on behalf of the state, there are greater practical effects associated with a lack of recognition of a state than a government. Not recognizing a government is not the same as not recognizing the state. The widespread lack of recognition of the Taleban regime as the government of Afghanistan in the 1990s, for example, did not mean that there was a lack of recognition that Afghanistan constituted a state.[7]

Traditionally, the doctrinal debate about the effects of recognition of states has been dominated by two competing approaches. The *declaratory* view holds that the creation of states is primarily a matter of law and the fulfilment of legal criteria. Thus, as soon as an entity can be said to satisfy a number of predetermined requirements, it will be a state under international law. Under this approach, the important criterion is essentially the entity's *effectiveness*.[8] In contrast, the *constitutive* view holds that recognition by other states is a precondition for statehood. So, unless an entity that appears to bear all the hallmarks of a 'state' is recognized as such by other states, it does not qualify as a state under international law.[9] The emergence of the constitutive view was tied to the rise of positivism and the pre-eminence of state consent in the 19th century. It subsequently served as a useful tool for the established (primarily Western) states to deny 'non-civilized' nations inclusion in the society of nations.[10]

In its practical application, the constitutive approach to recognition is highly problematic. For one thing, there is the issue of the relativism inherent in the constitutive position. If a state only exists in relation to another state that has recognized its existence, it would seem that absolute existence is not possible. That seems hard to accept. Another difficulty relates to the question of quantity. If recognition is indeed required, how many states must recognize an entity for it to become a 'state'? Also, is the recognition of some states more important than that of other states?

Contemporary international law is generally based on the declaratory approach. According to article 3 of the 1933 Montevideo Convention on the Rights and Duties

---

[7] For more on recognition of governments, see Stefan Talmon, *Recognition of Governments in International Law: With Particular Reference to Governments in Exile* (Oxford University Press, 2001).

[8] Crawford (n 3) 4–6.

[9] A pragmatic version of the constitutive view was proposed by Sir Hersch Lauterpacht who noted that *someone* has to ascertain if/when an emerging community fulfils the requirements for statehood and, in the absence of an impartial international organ, that task must be fulfilled by states. To him, the valid objection was not against the constitutive view as such, but instead that states treat recognition as a matter of policy and not of legal duty. See Sir Hersch Lauterpacht, *Recognition in International Law* (Cambridge University Press, 1947) 55.

[10] Crawford (n 3) 13–16.

of States, the 'political existence of the State is independent of recognition by other States'.[11] This is also supported by practice. In a 1920 advisory opinion on the legal status of the Aaland Islands, an International Committee of Jurists stated that the recognition by a number of states of a new state of Finland did not in itself 'suffice to show that Finland, from this time onwards, became a sovereign state'. Instead, the Committee relied on the 'conditions required for the formation of a sovereign State'.[12] In similar vein, a 1991 legal opinion by an Arbitration Commission on the situation regarding the disintegration of Yugoslavia noted that 'the existence or disappearance of the state is a question of fact' and 'that the effects of recognition by other states are purely declaratory'.[13] It also bears noting that non-recognized states are routinely the object of legal claims by non-recognizing states. An example is Israel, which is repeatedly accused of violating international law by the same Arab states that refuse to recognize Israel's existence as a state.

Several points must be noted, however. First, as we shall return to in Section 4.2.4, it seems that the principle that legal rights cannot arise from wrongful conduct (*ex injuria jus non oritur*) may sometimes lead to a denial of statehood to entities that seem to fulfil the formal criteria. Secondly, rejecting the constitutive theory does not mean that acts of recognition are entirely irrelevant. Such acts have evidentiary value because they reflect that other states believe that an entity fulfils the conditions for statehood. Here, a reference should be made to the significance of UN membership. Since membership is only open to states,[14] membership acceptance will effectively resolve the question of statehood under international law.[15] As already noted, Palestine has been granted membership as a 'non-member observer State', and it would therefore now seem that it can be referred to as a 'state'.[16] UN membership is not, however, a *requirement* for statehood. Switzerland did not join the UN until 2002. A third point to note about recognition is its practical importance in interstate relations. Often, recognition is a precondition for the establishment of bilateral relations, including the initiation of diplomatic and treaty relations. In that regard, it is worth noting that, as we shall return to in Chapter 6, states are not obliged to have diplomatic relations with each other, and that nothing precludes a state from conditioning its recognition of an emerging state and the initiation of bilateral relations on conditions that are stricter than those found in the Montevideo Convention (see Section 4.2.3). This is illustrated by the recognition policies of the United States and the European Community (EC),

---

[11] Montevideo Convention on the Rights and Duties of States (adopted 26 December 1933, entered into force 26 December 1934), 165 LNTS 19, art. 3.

[12] International Committee of Jurists, 'Report of the International Committee of Jurists entrusted by the Council of the League of Nations with the task of giving an advisory opinion upon the legal aspects of the Aaland Islands Question', League of Nations Official Journal, Special Supplement No. 3, October 1920, 8.

[13] See the Arbitration Commission of the Peace Conference on Yugoslavia, Opinion No. 1 (20 November 1991). See also Opinion Nos 8 and 10 (both 4 July 1992).

[14] Charter of the United Nations (adopted 26 May 1945, entered into force 24 October 1945), art. 4(1).

[15] On recognition and the practice of the UN, see John Dugard, *Recognition and the United Nations* (Grotius, 1987).

[16] GA Res. 67/19 (n 6). See also Report by the Secretary-General, 'Status of Palestine in the United Nations' (2013), UN Doc. A/67/738; UN Office of Legal Affairs, 'Issues related to General Assembly resolution 67/19

as it then was, in relation to the new states that emerged after the disintegration of the Soviet Union and Yugoslavia.[17] In addition to the traditional criteria for statehood, the US and the EC conditioned their recognition of the new states on their adherence to democracy and the rule of law, including the commitments in the Conference on Security and Co-operation in Europe's 1975 Helsinki Act and the 1990 Charter of Paris for a New Europe.[18] The US and the EC thereby used the political act of recognition as an incentive for the emerging states to commit to policies that served the interests of the potentially recognizing actors.

4.2.3 **The Montevideo criteria**

The 1933 Montevideo Convention on the Rights and Duties of States contains the most authoritative and accepted criteria/requirements for statehood. According to the Convention's article 1, a 'state' must possess the following:

(a) a permanent population;

(b) a defined territory;

(c) a government; and

(d) a capacity to enter into relations with other states.

The criteria are founded on notions of effectiveness.

The first requirement—the existence of a *permanent population*—simply means that *someone* has made the territory its home. The population in question need not have a certain size; for example, small island states like Tuvalu and Nauru only have populations of, respectively, around 10,000 and 11,000 inhabitants. In Europe, 'microstates' include Liechtenstein and San Marino. Since a population must be 'permanent', it is not clear if a population composed entirely of nomadic tribes suffices. In *Western Sahara*, the ICJ simply concluded that nomadic people 'possessed rights, including some rights relating to the lands through which they migrated'.[19]

The second requirement is that of a *defined territory*. There is no minimum size, and entities with tiny landmasses can fulfil the requirement. As we have just seen, small states such as Tuvalu and San Marino are 'states' under international law. In addition, the entity's boundaries need not be precisely demarcated and settled.[20] As long as the authorities control a consistent area of undisputed territory, an entity is likely to fulfil the requirement of defined territory. The lack of a definite territorial delineation of parts of

---

on the status of Palestine in the United Nations' (21 December 2012). On 2 January 2015, Palestine acceded to the Rome Statute of the International Criminal Court.

[17] Sean D. Murphy, 'Democratic Legitimacy and the Recognition of States and Governments' (1999) 48 *International and Comparative Law Quarterly* 545.

[18] See 'Testimony by Ralph Johnson, Deputy Assistant Secretary of State for European and Canadian Affairs, 17 Oct 1991' (1991) 2(3) *Foreign Policy Bulletin* 42; the European Community, 'Declaration on the Guidelines on the Recognition of New States in Eastern Europe and in the Soviet Union' (16 December 1991).

[19] *Western Sahara*, Advisory Opinion [1975] ICJ Rep 12, para. 152.

[20] See also *Monastery of Saint-Naoum*, Advisory Opinion, 1924, PCIJ, Series B, No. 9.

Israel, for example, did not prevent its acceptance as a state by a majority of states. In a similar vein, the political uncertainties about the exact location of a potential territorial border between Israel and Palestine are not decisive to the issue of Palestinian statehood.

The third requirement is that the entity must have a *government*. Someone must exercise control over the territory and be able to run its affairs and ensure that it can comply with its international obligations. In its 1920 advisory opinion on the Aaland Islands, the International Committee of Jurists did not find that Finland fulfilled the conditions for statehood until 'a stable political organisation had been created and until the public authorities had become strong enough to assert themselves throughout the territories of the State without the assistance of foreign troops'.[21] The form of the government is immaterial and it is not a requirement that the government be democratically elected or otherwise can be said to govern according to the wishes of the population of the territory. The decisive issue is its effectiveness: is the government in question able to exercise its authority over the territory? As for the level of effectiveness, there would seem to be a distinction between, on the one hand, situations where the entity attempts to secede from within an existing state structure, in which case the secession will often be contested, and, on the other, instances where the claim to statehood flows from a grant of independence to the territory by a former sovereign. While the requirement of effectiveness is applied strictly in the former situation, the standard appears to be less stringent in the second.[22] It should also be noted that the government in question does not necessarily need to be able to exercise its authority throughout the entire territory. Importantly, the requirement of an effective government ceases to be relevant once a state *has been* established. Somalia is a good illustration. Although Somalia has essentially been without an effective government for decades, no one disputes that it remains a state for the purposes of international law. Similar considerations apply to the situation in Yemen. The fact that Yemen is embroiled in a civil war that has effectively prevented the government from exerting its authority does not mean that Yemen has ceased to exist as a state.

The last of the four Montevideo requirements is that an entity must have the *capacity to enter into relations with other states*. What is important is *legal* rather than political or economic independence. In short, to be a state an entity must have the ability to act without legal interference from other states.[23] Importantly, commitments and obligations undertaken or imposed under international law are not an impediment to statehood. As Judge Anzilotti stated in *Austro-German Customs Union*, the conception of independence has:

> nothing to do with a State's subordination to international law or with the numerous and constantly increasing States of *de facto* dependence which characterize the relation of one country to other countries … As long as … restrictions do not place the State under the legal authority of another State, the former remains an independent State however extensive and burdensome those obligations may be.[24]

---

[21] See *Aaland Islands* (n 12) 9.   [22] Crawford (n 3) 56–60.

[23] See also *Island of Palmas (Netherlands v United States)* (1928) II RIAA 829, 838 and the discussion in Crawford (n 3) 62–89.

[24] *Customs Regime Between Germany and Austria*, Individual Opinion by M. Anzilotti, 1931, PCIJ, Series A/B, No. 41, 58.

It is often the lack of legal independence that prevents an otherwise 'state-like' entity from qualifying as a state. Scotland, for example, has a permanent population, a defined territory and extensive home rule through a parliament in Edinburgh. It is still, however, formally part of the UK with the UK Parliament in London retaining important powers.[25] In a referendum in September 2014, a majority of the population of Scotland decided *not* to seek formal independence from the UK. A somewhat similar situation is that of Greenland. Despite the existence of a permanent population in Greenland, a clearly defined territory and widespread self-rule, Greenland remains part of the Kingdom of Denmark with important competences, including substantial treaty-making authority, vested in Copenhagen.[26]

Temporary interference with an established state's independence and ability to enter into relations with other states—for example, belligerent occupation such as Iraq's unlawful occupation of Kuwait in 1990–1991—does not alter statehood.[27]

4.2.4 Illegality in the creation of a 'state'

Despite the conclusions in the previous section, there have been a few instances where an entity that would appear to fulfil the four requirements in the Montevideo Convention has been met with such widespread rejection by the international society that one cannot reasonably argue that the entity qualifies as a state for the purposes of international law. Although, as we shall see, state practice is not entirely consistent, it seems that an entity may be denied statehood if it has been created in flagrant violation of basic norms of international law, potentially of a *jus cogens* nature.[28] Practice would thereby seem to confirm the *ex injuria jus non oritur* principle according to which no legal rights can arise from wrongful conduct.

Two cases are generally said to support this conclusion. The first concerns Rhodesia, the creation of which *violated the local population's right of self-determination*.[29] On 11 November 1965, a white minority government issued a declaration of independence in the British colony of (South) Rhodesia, but even though the entity appeared to fulfil the formal criteria for statehood it was met with overall rejection of its claim to statehood, including from both the UN General Assembly and the UN Security Council. In a series of resolutions, the Security Council called upon all states to refrain from recognizing the 'illegal racist minority regime' and explicitly referred to the new government as an 'illegal authority'.[30] The second case is the Turkish Republic of Northern Cyprus (TRNC), which was established *through the unlawful use of force*. The TRNC was established in 1974 by Turkish forces in the northern part of Cyprus following the ousting of the president of Cyprus. To date, only Turkey has recognized the TRNC.

---

[25] See Scotland Act 1998 and Scotland Act 2012.
[26] See Act of Greenland Self-Government (Act no. 473 of 12 June 2009).
[27] Crawford (n 3) 73–74.   [28] Ibid, 99–107.
[29] Ibid, 128–131. For more on the right to self-determination, see Section 4.2.5.
[30] See, respectively, SC Res. 216 (12 November 1965), UN Doc. S/RES/216 and SC Res. 217 (20 November 1965), UN Doc. S/RES/217.

As already noted, however, state practice is not entirely consistent with the *ex injuria jus non oritur* principle. Despite the TRNC case, the circumstances surrounding the creation of Bangladesh seem to illustrate that the use of unlawful force may not always be an insurmountable obstacle to achieving statehood. In 1971, after massive internal tension and disturbances, India invaded what was then part of Pakistan (East Pakistan) and paved the way for the subsequent creation—and international recognition—of an independent Bangladeshi state. Why were the TRNC and Bangladesh treated differently? Aside from pure real politics, it may have played a role that the population in the seceding territory in Pakistan had been subjected to massive human rights violations at the hands of the Pakistanis. The two cases could also indicate that while a territorial entity created through the use of illegal force in violation of the right to self-determination of the population of the territory is unlikely to be accepted as a state, the result may be different if the unlawful force is used in order to further the realization of the self-determination of a population.[31]

4.2.5 **The right to self-determination**

One of the most debated issues in international law relates to the relationship between the right to self-determination and statehood.[32] The right to self-determination stipulates that all peoples have a right to freely determine their political status and pursue their economic, social and cultural development, but while the right was touched upon prior to 1945,[33] it did not emerge as a fundamental principle of international law until the decolonization process after the end of the Second World War.[34] Today, the right is found in a number of important legal documents, including article 1 of the UN Charter[35] and resolutions from the General Assembly.[36] It is also mentioned in the first part of article 1 in the 1966 UN Covenant on Human Rights.[37] In the *East Timor* case, the ICJ stated that the right to self-determination is an essential principle of international law that has an *erga omnes* character.[38] The most controversial aspect of the right to self-determination concerns the extent to which it gives a section of a

---

[31] See also the discussion in Crawford (n 3) 134–146.

[32] See generally Antonio Cassese, *Self-Determination of Peoples* (Cambridge University Press, 1995).

[33] See *Aaland Islands* (n 12) 5–6.

[34] See also Matthew Craven, 'Statehood, Self-Determination, and Recognition' in Malcolm D. Evans (ed.), *International Law* (4th edn, Oxford University Press, 2014) 226–227.

[35] See also UN Charter art. 73.

[36] See, inter alia, GA Res. 2625 (XXV) Declaration concerning Friendly Relations (24 October 1970), UN Doc. A/25/2625.

[37] See art. 1 in both the International Covenant on Civil and Political Rights (adopted 16 December 1966, entered into force 23 March 1976), 999 UNTS 171 (ICCPR) and the International Covenant on Economic, Social and Cultural Rights (adopted 16 December 1966, entered into force 3 January 1976), 993 UNTS 3 (ICESCR).

[38] *Case Concerning East Timor (Portugal v Australia)* [1995] ICJ Rep 90, para. 29. See also *Legal Consequences for States of the Continued Presence of South Africa in Namibia (South West Africa) Notwithstanding Security Council Resolution 276 (1970)*, Advisory Opinion [1971] ICJ Rep 16, 31; *Legal Consequences of the Construction of a Wall in Palestinian Territory*, Advisory Opinion [2004] ICJ Rep 136, para. 88.

population a right to secede from an existing state in the absence of acceptance by the government of the 'mother-state'. In the 1920 Aaland Island's advisory opinion, the International Committee of Jurists stated that international law does not 'recognise the right for national groups, as such, to separate themselves from the State of which they form part by the simple expression of a wish'.[39] But this was before 1945, and in the decolonialization process in the 1960s and 1970s a large number of former colonies successfully relied on the right to self-determination in order to acquire their own independent states. A key document was the 1960 General Assembly Declaration on the Granting of Independence to Colonial Countries and Peoples.[40] The relationship between the right to self-determination and statehood resurfaced after the end of the Cold War following the collapse of the Soviet Union and the chaotic disintegration of the Socialist Federal Republic of Yugoslavia.[41] More recently, it has emerged in relation to Kosovo's decision in 2008 to declare its independence from Serbia. While the ICJ had the opportunity to state its position on whether Kosovo was entitled to secede in *Accordance with International Law of the Unilateral Declaration of Independence in Respect of Kosovo*, the Court unfortunately refrained from doing so. It limited itself to stating that there are 'radically different views' on whether the right to self-determination offers a right to secession for other peoples than those in 'non-self-governing territories and peoples subject to alien subjugation, domination and exploitation'[42] but that international law does not preclude Kosovo from issuing a declaration of independence.[43]

The most authoritative statement on the link between the right to self-determination and statehood remains an advisory opinion from 1998 issued by the Canadian Supreme Court on whether the Canadian province of Quebec was entitled to secede from Canada. In *Reference re Secession of Quebec*, the Court distinguished between an 'internal' and an 'external' right to self-determination. It found that the right to self-determination of a people is normally fulfilled by *internal* self-determination—autonomy—according to which a people pursue their political, economic, social and cultural development *within* the framework of an existing state. A right to *external* self-determination—with the option of seceding—on the other hand arises 'only in the most extreme of cases'.[44] According to the Court, it is undisputed that colonial people under imperial rule and other people who find themselves subject to alien subjugation, domination or exploitation have a right to external self-determination that may entitle them to create their own independent state.[45] With regard to the claim that a right to secede also exists, as a last resort, for other peoples who are blocked

---

[39] *Aaland Islands* (n 12) 5.

[40] See, inter alia, GA Res. 1514 (XV) Declaration on the Granting of Independence to Colonial Countries and Peoples (14 December 1960), UN Doc. A/RES/1514(XV).

[41] See, inter alia, Alain Pellet, 'The Opinions of the Badinter Arbitration Committee: A Second Breath for the Self-Determination of Peoples' (1992) 3 *European Journal of International Law* 178.

[42] *Kosovo* (n 4) para. 82   [43] Ibid, para. 83.

[44] *Reference re Secession of Quebec* [1998] 2 SCR 217, para. 126. On the distinction between internal and external self-determination, see also Committee on the Elimination of Racial Discrimination, 'General Recommendation 21: The right to self-determination' (8 March 1996), UN Doc. A/51/18, para. 4.

[45] *Reference re Secession of Quebec* (n 44) paras 131–133.

from meaningful exercise of their right to self-determination internally within a state, the Court merely noted that international law is 'unclear' on this point and that this potential exception was nevertheless not relevant to the question of Quebec as it 'cannot plausibly be said to be denied access to government'.[46]

It is very doubtful whether a people who are neither colonized nor subject to alien subjugation, domination or exploitation can claim a right to external self-determination and thus be entitled to secede. While some argue for the existence of an additional right to secede for peoples in cases of extreme oppression and the almost total denial of meaningful internal self-determination—also referred to as 'remedial secession'[47]—accepting such a right requires truly exceptional circumstances. International stability speaks in favour of keeping the territorial integrity of a 'mother-state' intact and requiring people to pursue their right to self-determination within the existing state.[48] The need for stability and respect for existing territorial borders is reflected in the so-called 'safeguard clause' that was first introduced in the General Assembly's 1970 Declaration on Friendly Relations.[49] The clause stipulates that there can be no question of remedial secession in a state where the government represents the whole of the people or peoples within its territory on a basis of equality and without discrimination.[50]

In October 2017, the Parliament of Catalonia in Barcelona sought to arrange a local referendum on the region's potential independence from Spain. The referendum was deemed to be invalid by the Spanish Constitutional Court since it was unlawful under Spain's Constitution. On the basis of the discussion above, the right to self-determination does not support a Catalonian claim to secede from Spain, especially in the light of Catalonia's enjoyment of widespread internal self-determination within Spain.

Two final points must be made with regard to the right to self-determination and statehood. First, an affirmed right to external self-determination need not lead to a claim for secession. A people with a right to statehood may well decide that their interests as a people are presently best served by remaining within an existing state. An example of that is Greenland. In 1953, on the basis of an amendment to the Danish Constitution, Greenland became an integral part of the Kingdom of Denmark. The amendment was approved by the National Council of Greenland, and in a 1954 resolution the General Assembly noted that 'the people of Greenland have freely exercised their right to self-determination'.[51] Although Denmark recognizes that 'the people of Greenland is a people pursuant to international law with the right of self-determination'[52] and that it will not stand in the way of Greenlandic independence, the people of Greenland have so far preferred to remain part of the Kingdom of Denmark albeit with extensive self-rule.[53] The second point to note is that international law does

---

[46] Ibid, paras 134–138.   [47] See also Crawford (n 3) 119.
[48] See also *Aaland Islands* (n 12) 5.   [49] Declaration concerning Friendly Relations (n 36) para. 5(7).
[50] See also *Reference re Secession of Quebec* (n 44) para. 130.
[51] See also GA Res. 849 (IX) (22 November 1954), UN Doc. A/RES/849(IX).
[52] Preamble to Act of Greenland Self-Government (n 26).
[53] For the latest grant of devolution, see n 26.

not prevent a 'mother-state' from consenting to the secession of part of its territory. The 2014 referendum in Scotland on potential Scottish independence from the UK was arranged after the British government had accepted that Scotland could potentially leave the Union if they so wished.

4.2.6 The acquisition of new territory

An issue somewhat related to conditions for the creation of states concerns an existing state's acquisition of additional territory. A state can acquire title to new territory in a number of ways. First, it can purchase territory from another state through *cession*. There are many historical examples of 'land purchases'. Among the more well-known are the US purchase of Alaska from Russia in 1867 and the 1917 US acquisition of the Danish West Indies from Denmark. During the Cold War, the United States indicated an interest in purchasing Greenland from Denmark.[54] Cession of territory was also the primary method by which European states acquired territory in Africa and Asia during the period of colonialization.[55] Acquisition of territory by cession may also result from an agreement to resolve a border dispute between two or more states. The mutual transfer of territory—'land swap'—is, for example, likely to be an important element in a future final peace agreement between Israel and Palestine. Whatever its exact form, the transfer of territory is governed by certain basic principles. The state that acquires the territory cannot obtain more rights to the territory than those possessed by the ceding state. Additionally, the acquiring state must respect the potential rights of third states.[56]

The second way whereby a state can acquire title to new territory is through *accretion*. Here, new land is created gradually by nature. On rare occasions, new islands are formed by volcanic eruption. In 1963, for example, volcanic eruptions off the coast of Iceland created the—new—island of Surtsey. Importantly, man-made additions—'artificial accretion'—are not covered. Such additions require that the new territory does not infringe on the rights of other states or that such states give their consent. For years, China has constructed artificial 'islands' on already existing maritime features, such as reefs and low-tide elevations in the South China Sea. In *South China Sea Arbitration*, a court of arbitration in 2016 concluded that the artificial constructions and installation entities cannot form the basis of Chinese claims to title. According to the court, the status of a maritime feature should 'be ascertained on the basis of its earlier, natural condition, prior to the onset of significant human modification'.[57] *Erosion* is the opposite of accretion and refers to the gradual disappearance of territory caused by natural forces. Accretion does not cover sudden or violent changes to territory, for example as a result of storms or natural disasters. Such changes are instead referred to as *avulsion*. The distinction between

---

[54] Dansk Udenrigspolitisk Institut, 'Danmark under Den Kolde Krig' (1997).

[55] See Crawford (n 3) 266.   [56] *Island of Palmas* (n 23) 842.

[57] *The Republic of the Philippines and the People's Republic of China*, Award PCA Case No. 2013-19, 12 July 2016, para. 306. See also para. 511.

accretion and avulsion is relevant for alterations of rivers that form the territorial boundary between two states. It is only when a change to the course of the river is caused by accretion that it will move the boundary line between the two states.[58]

The third and fourth means of acquiring title to additional territory bear certain similarities. The principles of *occupation* stipulate that a state can obtain title to territory that has never been the subject of any state—also known as *terra nullius* or simply 'no-man's land'.[59] It bears noting that the concept of *terra nullius* is different from that of '*res communis*', which refers to an area that is not subject to the legal title of any state, most notably the high seas.[60] Title is acquired through occupation when a state demonstrates that it exercises effective control over a territory of 'no-man's land' and intends to obtain title. While occupation is of limited relevance today, it served as the basis for numerous historical claims to territory 'discovered' by European explorers, including Australia and the South Island of New Zealand.[61] Another historical example of occupation of *terra nullius* is that of Svalbard (formerly known as Spitsbergen), an archipelago to the north of continental Europe in the Arctic Ocean.[62] While occupation is the means whereby a state acquires territory that does not belong to anyone, it is through *prescription* that it obtains title to territory previously under the sovereignty of another state. Unlike occupation, the acquisition of territory by prescription is derived from some form of implied consent from the state whose rights are being displaced by the acquiring state. The element of consent means that the acts of the acquiring state must be peaceful and that sustained protests and objections by the 'old' state will prevent prescription.[63]

In practice, it can be difficult to determine if a state's attempt to acquire territory should rightfully be considered as a case of occupation or one of prescription. Most territorial disputes involve contesting claims by states that have performed a series of more or less 'sovereign' acts. Often, title over the disputed territory will not be awarded because one of the states has been able to prove beyond any doubt that it holds title over the territory but, rather, because it has a claim that is superior to that of a competing state. Regardless of whether a claim to title is based in occupation or prescription, it must rest on the *effective possession* of the territory. The leading case on the issue remains Judge Huber's 1928 arbitral award in the *Island of Palmas* case that originated in Spain's 1898 cession of the Philippines to the United States. The Netherlands and the United States disagreed about whether the cession included the Island of Palmas—an isolated island located around halfway between the outermost island in the Philippines and the closest island in a group of islands that belonged at that time to the Netherlands. Judge Huber ruled in favour of the Netherlands and articulated the principle that 'the continuous and peaceful display of territorial sovereignty is as good as title'.[64] While the initial discovery of an as yet unknown territory could establish

---

[58] *The Chamizal Case (Mexico v United States)* (1911) XI RIAA 309.

[59] *Western Sahara* (n 19) para. 79.   [60] See also Chapter 8.   [61] Crawford (n 3) 265–266.

[62] Geir Ulfstein, *The Svalbard Treaty: From Terra Nullius to Norwegian Sovereignty* (Aschehoug, 1995).

[63] *Land and Maritime Boundary between Cameroon and Nigeria (Cameroon v Nigeria: Equatorial Guinea intervening)*, Judgment [2002] ICJ Rep 303, paras 67, 70.

[64] *Island of Palmas* (n 23) 839.

'inchoate' title, the initial act of discovery must be followed up by effective occupation of the territory within a reasonable time.[65] If not, it will be displaced by 'a definite title founded on continuous and peaceful display of sovereignty'.[66]

The requirement that a state must 'display territorial sovereignty' means that it must *behave as a state* in the disputed territory. How much sovereignty is required varies and even limited exercises of sovereignty may suffice in isolated and sparsely populated territory, such as remote islands or in areas of inhospitable terrain.[67] In *Eastern Greenland*, Denmark's display of sovereignty mainly consisted of minimal acts of administration and the granting of concession rights in the area. Since what is decisive is the display of sovereignty, acts performed by private citizens or private companies without the assistance of state authorities do not qualify. It is also worth mentioning that the public acts must reflect an intention on the part of the state to acquire title.

A few more points must be made about acquiring title to contested territory. Geographical contiguity/proximity is not in itself decisive, and it may well be that a contested island is not awarded to the state whose mainland is in closest proximity.[68] Also, resolving a case about disputed territory often requires the determination of a so-called 'critical date'. This is the moment when the potential rights of the parties manifested themselves to such an extent that subsequent acts could not alter the legal positions of the parties. In the *Pulau Ligitan* case, the ICJ stated that it could not:

> take into consideration acts having taken place after the date on which the dispute between the Parties crystallized unless such acts are a normal continuation of prior acts and are not undertaken for the purpose of improving the legal position of the Party which relies on them.[69]

In the *Island of Palmas* case, the critical date was the date of Spain's cession of the Philippines to the United States. The identification of the critical date is important because the doctrine of 'intertemporal law' stipulates that the law to be applied in a concrete case is that which existed at the critical date. Thus, when Judge Huber decided who had title to the Island of Palmas in 1923, he relied on the law as it existed at the critical date in 1898.[70]

As for acquisition of territory by prescription, an apparent display of sovereignty will not prevail and secure a state's title to territory if another state can prove the existence of a pre-existing legal right to the territory, such as a treaty-based title; and the conduct of the latter cannot be interpreted as acquiescence in the establishment of a change in treaty title. Thus, as the ICJ has stated in a number of cases, while a display of sovereignty may confirm legal title, it cannot by *itself* alter it. In the *Frontier Dispute*

---

[65] Ibid, 845–846.   [66] Ibid, 869.

[67] Ibid, 840; *Legal Status of Eastern Greenland*, 1933, PCIJ, Series A/B, No. 53, pp. 50–51/32–33.

[68] *Island of Palmas* (n 23) 854–855. See also *Territorial and Maritime Dispute between Nicaragua and Honduras in the Caribbean Sea (Nicaragua v Honduras)*, Judgment [2007] ICJ Rep 659, para. 161.

[69] *Sovereignty over Pulau Ligitan and Pulau Sipadan (Indonesia v Malaysia)*, Judgment [2002] ICJ Rep 625, para. 135.

[70] *Island of Palmas* (n 23) 845–846.

case, the Court stated that if the disputed territory 'is effectively administered by a State other than the one possessing the legal title, preference should be given to the holder of the title'.[71]

A final point to note about acquisitions of territory concerns *conquest*. For most of history, using force to conquer foreign territory was a well-recognized means of acquiring new territory. Since 1945, however, a state can no longer obtain title through conquest. Instead, as we shall return to in Chapter 14, one state's military occupation of the territory of another state activates the international legal regime on belligerent occupation. Legally, the presence of the foreign state is temporary and it does not result in any transfer of sovereignty.[72] So while the displaced sovereign loses *de facto* possession of the territory, it does not lose *de jure* possession.[73] As Oppenheim famously stated, there 'is not an atom of sovereignty in the authority of the occupant'.[74] The prohibition against forceful territorial acquisitions is reflected in the 1945 Charter of the United Nations and the 1970 General Assembly Resolution on Friendly Relations.[75] It is also supported by state practice. Thus, Iraq's attempt to annex Kuwait following its invasion of that state in 1990 was unanimously rejected by states as having no legal validity.[76] The same has been the case for Russia's 2014 annexation of the Crimean Peninsula in Ukraine. The General Assembly responded to the annexation by reaffirming that state territory shall not be the object of acquisition by force and that attempts to disrupt the territorial integrity of a state are incompatible with the purposes and principles of the Charter.[77] The prohibition against forceful territorial acquisitions is also relevant to the conflict in the Middle East between Israel and Palestine. Without an agreement between the parties, under international law Israel cannot obtain title over those parts of Palestine that it occupies.[78] With the exception of East Jerusalem and the Golan Heights, the latter of which has been annexed by Israel, this is also acknowledged by the Israeli Supreme Court.[79]

4.2.7 **State succession**

It is vital for the maintenance of international stability and predictability that international society is able to manage the disappearance of old states or the emergence

---

[71] *Frontier Dispute (Burkina Faso v Mali)*, Judgment [1986] ICJ Rep 554, para. 63. See also *Land and Maritime Boundary* (n 63) paras 67–70.

[72] See also SC Res. 252 (21 May 1968), UN Doc. S/RES/252.

[73] See also Yoram Dinstein, *The International Law of Belligerent Occupation* (Cambridge University Press, 2009) 49–50.

[74] Lassa Oppenheim, 'The Legal Relations between an Occupying Power and Its Inhabitants' (1917) 33 *Law Quarterly Review* 363, 364. See also *Construction of a Wall* (n 38).

[75] Declaration concerning Friendly Relations (n 36).

[76] See, inter alia, SC Res. 662 (9 August 1990), UN Doc. S/RES/662.

[77] See the Preamble to GA Res. 68/262 (27 March 2014), UN Doc. A/68/L.39 and Add. 1.

[78] SC Res. 252 (21 May 1968), UN Doc. S/RES/252. See also SC Res. 478 (20 August 1980), UN Doc. S/RES/478; *Construction of a Wall* (n 38) para. 78.

[79] CA 1432/03, *Yinon Production and Marketing of Food Products Ltd v Qaraan et al.* [2004] 59(1) PD 345, 355–356.

of new states in a stable and predictable manner. As a concept under international law, 'state succession' concerns 'the replacement of one state by another in the responsibility for the international relations of territory'.[80] Issues of state succession can arise in many circumstances and the legal regime governing successions is among the most complicated and disputed in international law. Two conventions on state succession exist: the 1978 Vienna Convention on Succession of States in Respect of Treaties and the 1983 Vienna Convention on Succession of States in Respect of State Property, Archives and Debts. Although only the 1978 Convention is in force, many of the provisions of the 1983 Convention reflect customary international law.

Changes of statehood always raise important legal questions, including issues relating to the status of existing treaties, membership of international organizations and nationality. The practical manner in which succession is dealt with varies from case to case and in many instances the 'old' and the 'new' states will settle the most important issues in a bilateral treaty. But whenever a new territorial entity emerges it is necessary to initially determine if the entity should be considered as a continuation of a pre-existing state or as a new and separate entity. When the Soviet Union disintegrated, for example, the Russian Federation generally continued that state, albeit, of course, with a smaller territory. Russia therefore continued the membership of the Soviet Union in relevant international organizations, including the UN and the Security Council. The outcome was different when the Socialist Federal Republic of Yugoslavia collapsed. Here, disintegration of the Yugoslavian state was so profound that it ceased to exist as a 'state'.[81] Thus, Serbia and Montenegro was not considered as the continuation of the now dissolved Yugoslavian 'mother-state'.[82] Among other things, Serbia was denied the right to continue Yugoslavia's membership of the UN.[83] Issues of state succession also arise when two states merge and form a single state. In the case of the 1990 German unification, the German Democratic Republic (East Germany) was technically assimilated into the Federal Republic of Germany (West Germany).[84]

The rules on succession to treaties are complex and largely depend on the subject matter at hand. As a point of departure, however, international law seems to adopt a so-called 'clean slate' approach according to which the emerging state is not considered bound by the treaties and agreements concluded by its predecessor. Thus, the successor state is free to become or not to become a party to treaties entered into by the predecessor state. There are, however, a number of exceptions. The first concerns the principle of *uti possidetis juris* according to which geographical boundaries created by treaties remain in force regardless of whether or not the boundaries coincide with (new) ethnic, tribal, religious or political affiliations.[85]

---

[80] Vienna Convention on Succession of States in Respect to Treaties (adopted 23 August 1978, entered into force 6 November 1996), 1946 UNTS 3, art. 2(1)(b).

[81] See the Arbitration Commission of the Peace Conference on Yugoslavia, Opinion No. 8.

[82] Ibid, Opinion No. 10.

[83] See, inter alia, SC Res. 757 (30 May 1992), UN Doc. S/RES/757 and SC Res. 777 (19 September 1992), UN Doc. S/RES/777.

[84] Treaty on the Final Settlement with Respect to Germany (12 September 1990).

[85] Vienna Convention on Succession of States in Respect to Treaties (n 80) art. 11.

Predictability and stability would be greatly jeopardized if territorial boundaries were subject to negotiation whenever a state changed its legal status. In *Frontier Dispute*, the ICJ applied the *uti possidetis* principle to an old colonial border and noted its 'exceptional importance for the African continent'.[86] The principle has also been applied in non-colonial settings and to the drawing of internal boundaries. In *Territorial Dispute*, the ICJ noted that a boundary agreed upon in a treaty, 'achieves a permanence which the treaty itself does not necessarily enjoy. The treaty can cease to be in force without in any way affecting the continuance of the boundary.'[87]

A second—possible—exception to the clean-slate approach concerns obligations under human rights and humanitarian law conventions. If a state disintegrates and ceases to exist, as was the case with the former Yugoslavia, the clean-slate approach would mean that the population of the seceding territory ceases to be protected by such conventions until the emerging state (maybe) decides to become a party. According to the UN Human Rights Committee, protection under the UN Covenant on Civil and Political Rights continues 'notwithstanding change in government of the State party, including dismemberment in more than one State or State succession'.[88] In *Genocide*, two of the ICJ judges concluded that the Genocide Convention 'does not come to an end with the dismemberment of the original State, as it transcends the concept of State sovereignty'.[89] And in *Delalić et al.*, the Appeals Chamber for the International Criminal Tribunal for the former Yugoslavia (ICTY) concluded that there is 'automatic State succession to multilateral humanitarian treaties in the broad sense, i.e., treaties of universal character which express fundamental human rights'[90] and that state succession did not impact obligations arising from 'fundamental humanitarian conventions'.[91]

4.2.8 **Extinction**

Once a state has been established, it is almost impossible for it to lose its statehood involuntarily. As we have already seen, the absence of an effective government, as is presently the case in both Somalia and Yemen, will not cause a state to cease being a state, and a state will similarly not be extinguished through the unlawful use of force and subsequent efforts of annexation by another state, as was the case with Iraq's invasion of Kuwait in 1990.[92] As the disintegration of Yugoslavia illustrates, however,

---

[86] *Frontier Dispute* (n 71) 20.

[87] *Territorial Dispute (Libyan Arab Jamahiriya v Chad)*, Judgment [1994] 1CJ Rep 6, para. 73.

[88] Human Rights Committee, 'CCPR General Comment No. 26: Continuity of Obligations' (8 December 1997), UN Doc. CCPR/C/21/Rev.1/Add.8/Rev.1, para. 4.

[89] *Application of the Convention on the Prevention and Punishment of the Crime of Genocide*, Preliminary Objections, Separate Opinion of Judge Weeramantry [1996] ICJ Rep 595, 646. See also Separate Opinion of Judge Shahabuddeen, 636.

[90] *Prosecutor v Zejnil Delalić et al.*, Judgment, ICTY-96-21-A (20 February 2001), para. 111.

[91] Ibid, para. 113. As we saw in Section 2.4.1, if a human rights obligation is customary international law, it is also binding on newly emerging states.

[92] On the rare cases of so-called *debellation*, see Michael N. Schmitt, 'Debellation' in Rüdiger Wolfrum (ed.), *Max Planck Encyclopedia of Public International Law* (Oxford University Press, 2009).

a state may cease to exist if it disintegrates and subsequently splinters into a range of new states. A state may, of course, decide to alter its legal status and voluntarily dissolve itself.

Two or more states may decide to merge into a single state as occurred in 1990 with the unification of the German Democratic Republic (GDR, East Germany) and the Federal Republic of Germany (FRG, West Germany). Another example was the merger in the same year of North Yemen and South Yemen into a unified Republic of Yemen. A state may also cease to exist on a voluntary basis if it decides to split into two or more independent states. This took place in 1993 when the Czech Republic and Slovakia were created from the former state of Czechoslovakia.

4.3 International organizations

The international organization is an actor that plays an increasing role in international law. International organizations come in many forms and the most authoritative definition is found in the International Law Commission's (ILC's) 2011 Draft Articles on the Responsibility of International Organizations. Here, an international organization is defined as:

> an organization established by a treaty or other instrument governed by international law and possessing its own international legal personality. International organizations may include as members, in addition to States, other entities.[93]

International organizations are created by treaty and must not be confused with so-called 'non-governmental organizations' (NGOs) that are private entities which, as we return to in Section 4.5.4, do not generally have international legal personality.[94] Organizations such as the UN, the North Atlantic Treaty Organization (NATO) and the institutions of the EU are international organizations whereas entities like Amnesty International, Human Rights Watch and the World Wildlife Federation (WWF) are NGOs.

As the historical overview in Chapter 1 illustrated, the first international organizations were created in the 19th century when organizations such as the International Telegraphic Union and the Universal Postal Union were established in order to further technical cooperation and facilitate international communications. However, it was not until after the turn of century that states began to set up organizations to deal with more contentious political matters, including issues relating to peace and security. The first such organization was the League of Nations, which was created after the end of the First World War to maintain world peace. After the end of the Second World War, the League was replaced with the UN, which quickly established itself as an umbrella organization for a myriad of

---

[93] ILC, Draft Articles on the Responsibility of International Organizations (2011), UN Doc. A/66/10, art. 2(a).

[94] See also Section 4.5 and the special case of the International Committee of the Red Cross.

international organizations. That period also saw the birth of a variety of regional organizations of great importance, including NATO, and the European Coal and Steel Community that would eventually develop into the EU and the Council of Europe.[95] The UN remains by the far most important global international organization. Its membership is practically universal and, as we shall see throughout this book, it covers a wide range of activities of vital importance to the effective functioning of international society. In addition, as noted in Chapter 2, it is generally presumed that obligations undertaken under the UN Charter must prevail over potentially competing international obligations.[96]

Since most of the important features of the UN are dealt with elsewhere in this book, only a few of its characteristics will be noted here. It is composed of six principal organs. The *General Assembly* has the competence to discuss and make recommendations on all matters that fall within the scope of the organization's constituent treaty—the UN Charter.[97] All 193 members of the UN have a seat in the Assembly. As discussed in more detail in Chapter 13, the *Security Council* is endowed with primary responsibility for maintaining international peace and security and is composed of 15 members, including five permanent members who retain a veto power. The *Secretariat*, headed by the Secretary-General who is usually selected for a term of five years, services the different UN organs. The *Economic and Social Council* (ECOSOC) holds the primary responsibility for economic and social matters within the UN and is composed of 54 members. Over the years, it has established a wide range of subsidiary organs. The *International Court of Justice* is the principal judicial organ of the UN. Its competences are dealt with in Chapter 12. The final principal organ of the UN is the now suspended *Trustee Council*, which was set up to administer the trustee system.

International organizations have the rights and obligations accorded to them by states.[98] This generally includes a power to conclude necessary agreements governed by international law[99] and immunity from the exercise of jurisdiction by national courts.[100] In *Reparations*, the ICJ clarified that the UN is a legal subject under international law capable of possessing international rights and duties and with a capacity to protect its rights by bringing international claims for injury to its personnel.[101] The extent of an organization's rights and obligations will depend on 'its purposes and functions as specified or implied in its constituent documents and developed in practice'.[102] In Chapter 7 we shall briefly see that international organizations may also incur international responsibility.

[95] See also Chapter 1. For a treatment of the Council of Europe, see Chapter 9.

[96] UN Charter art. 103.

[97] Ibid, art. 10. On the legal status of the resolutions by the General Assembly, see Chapter 2.

[98] *Legality of the Use of Nuclear Weapons in Times of Armed Conflict*, Advisory Opinion [1996] ICJ Rep 226, para. 25.

[99] See Vienna Convention on the Law of Treaties between States and International Organizations or between International Organizations (1986).

[100] *Difference Relating to Immunity from Legal Process of a Special Rapporteur of the Commission on Human Rights*, Advisory Opinion [1999] ICJ Rep 62.

[101] *Reparations* (n 2) 179.

[102] Ibid, 180, 182. See also *Jurisdiction of the European Commission of the Danube between Galatz and Braila*, Advisory Opinion, 1927, PCIJ, Series B, No. 14, 64.

4.4 Individuals

Like international organizations, individuals possess those rights and obligations that states bestow on them.[103] In the *LaGrand* case, the ICJ concluded that the United States had violated its obligations not only to Germany but also to two German nationals when it brought criminal proceedings against the German nationals without informing them of their rights under the Vienna Convention on Consular Relations. The Court noted that the clarity of the relevant provisions of the Vienna Convention, viewed in their context, 'admits of no doubt'. They created individual rights which 'may be invoked in this Court by the national State of the detained person'.[104] It is primarily in human rights law that international law grants *rights* to individuals. As we shall discuss in more detail in Chapter 9, up until the middle of the 20th century the manner in which states dealt with their own citizens was generally of no concern to international law. Things began to change after the end of the Second World War when states adopted conventions bestowing rights on individuals under international law. As we shall see in more detail in Chapter 15, states have also imposed *obligations* under international law on individuals. In 1946, the International Military Tribunal (IMT) at Nuremberg rejected the argument that international law cannot serve as the basis for the criminal prosecution of individuals: 'Crimes against International Law are committed by men, not by abstract entities, and only by punishing individuals who commit such crimes can the provisions of International Law be enforced.'[105]

4.5 Other actors in international law

4.5.1 Territorial entities other than states

States are not the only territorial entities with international legal personality. In fact, there are numerous historical examples of *territorial entities other than states* that have been created and managed by treaty, as was the case with Berlin from the end of the Second World War to the unification of Germany in 1990. Another example of international administration of territory was the post-First World War mandate system created by the League of Nations for the administration of territories that had belonged to the defeated states in the war.[106] The mandate system was replaced by a trustee system after the dissolution of the League of Nations and the creation of the UN.[107] More recent examples of international administration of territories

---

[103] See the thorough overview in Kjeldgaard-Pedersen (n 1). For early jurisprudence, see *Jurisdiction of the Courts of Danzig*, Advisory Opinion, 1928, PCIJ, Series B, No. 15, 17–18.

[104] *LaGrand (Germany v United States)*, Judgment [2001] ICJ Rep 466, para. 77.

[105] *Judgment of the Nuremberg International Military Tribunal 1946* (1947) 41 *American Journal of International Law* 172, 221.

[106] Covenant of the League of Nations (adopted 28 June 1919, entered into force 10 January 1920) art. 22.

[107] See Chapters XII and XIII of the UN Charter.

include the different UN regimes established with regard to the preparation of East Timor for independence after decades of Indonesian occupation[108] and the administration of Kosovo after the civil war in the former Yugoslavia.[109] *Taiwan* is a special case in international law. While it appears to fulfil the formal requirements for statehood in the Montevideo Convention, it finds itself in a delicate relationship with mainland China and adopts a policy of deliberate ambiguity about its status. It fact, it has never formally proclaimed its independence.[110] It does, however, possess separate legal personality on certain issues, including in the area of the law of the sea. It also has relations with several international organizations.[111] *Hong Kong* is another territorial entity with a degree of international legal personality. Since China took over the territory in 1997 from the UK, its status has been one of a 'Special Administrative Region' of China with the competence to enter into international agreements and participate in some international organizations.[112] Reference should also be made to the *Holy See*, which functions as the central government of the Roman Catholic Church. Italy has recognized the Holy See as the holder of exclusive sovereignty and jurisdiction over the Vatican City in Rome, Italy.[113] As a legal person, the Holy See is a *sui generis* entity. It is, for example, a party to many treaties and has diplomatic relations with a substantial number of states. It also has status as a permanent observer to the UN.

4.5.2 **Groups of individuals**

As collective entities, groups of individuals may also have legal personality. As we saw in Section 4.2.5, the right to self-determination is based on the notion that *peoples* possess certain rights under international law. As we shall see in Chapter 9, *indigenous groups* are another example. In 2007, the General Assembly adopted a Declaration on the Rights of Indigenous Peoples. Among other things, the Declaration stipulates that indigenous people have a right to the full enjoyment as a collective or as individuals of all human rights and fundamental freedoms and have the right to be free from any kind of discrimination.[114] *Insurgent groups* and *national liberation movements* are also endowed with rights and obligations in international law, most notably within the laws of armed conflict.[115] For example, the 1977 Additional Protocol I to the 1949 Geneva Conventions specifies that national liberation movements may under certain circumstances have rights and obligations under the Protocol.

---

[108] See SC Res. 1272 (25 October 1999), UN Doc. S/RES/1272.

[109] SC Res. 1244 (10 June 1999), UN Doc. S/RES/1244.

[110] See the overview in Crawford (n 3) 198–221.   [111] Crawford (n 3) 198–221.

[112] Sun Zhichao, 'International Legal Personality of the Hong Kong Special Administrative Region' (2008) 7 *Chinese Journal of International Law* 339.

[113] Lateran Treaty (adopted 11 February 1929) art. 3.

[114] GA Res. 61/295 Declaration on the Rights of Indigenous Peoples (13 September 2007), UN Doc. A/RES/295, arts 1–2.

[115] See Liesbeth Zegveld, *Accountability of Armed Opposition Groups in International Law* (Cambridge University Press, 2008).

4.5.3 **Private corporations**

A focus of increasing attention has been whether *private corporations* have rights and—in particular—obligations under international law. In practice, rights may under certain circumstances be bestowed on private corporations under international human rights law and particularly in international economic law. As for obligations, there is a booming literature in the area of so-called 'Corporate Social Responsibility' (CSR) and in 2011 the UN Human Rights Council adopted a number of Guiding Principles on Business and Human Rights that stress the obligations of states to respect, protect and fulfil human rights and fundamental freedoms.[116] The Guiding Principles are not legally binding, however, and at present the obligations that corporations undertake in that area remain voluntary. International law does not, for example, recognize 'international corporate crimes'. Nevertheless, in some circumstances a contractual relationship between a state and a corporation will be governed by international law. For example, concession agreements for the extraction of oil are often 'internationalized'.[117]

4.5.4 **Non-governmental organizations**

Non-governmental organizations, including such organizations as Amnesty International, Human Rights Watch and environmental organizations, have a growing influence on the processes that lead to the creation of international law. In many cases, they enhance enforcement of international law by providing vital information to monitoring bodies. They also contribute to better transparency in international decision-making. Their increasing role is reflected in the 1991 European Convention on the Recognition of the Legal Personality of International NGOs and in the 1998 UN Declaration on the Rights of Human Rights Defenders. Currently, however, NGOs do not as such possess rights or obligations under international law. A notable exception, however, is the *International Committee of the Red Cross* (ICRC), which, although it is a private organization, has a mandate (the provision of protection and assistance to victims in times of armed conflict) grounded in international conventions.

Summary

The answer to the question of who international law actually applies to is traditionally found in the concepts of 'legal subjectivity' or 'legal personality'. Since being a subject or having 'personality' in a legal system means having the capacity to hold rights, powers and obligations that can be enforced in that system, the subjects of international law are those to whom the international legal system gives exercisable rights, powers and obligations. Importantly, though, not all participants in the international legal system hold the same rights and obligations and legal personality is a relative concept.

---

[116] See UNHRC Res. 17/4 (16 June 2011), UN Doc. A/HRC/17/L.17/Rev.1.

[117] See, inter alia, *Texaco Overseas Petroleum Co. v The Government of the Libyan Arab Republic* (1979) *Yearbook of Commercial Arbitration* 177ff.

International society is first and foremost a society of individual states and states remain the most central actor possessing those capacities in international law. States are not the only actors in international law, however, and other actors with rights and obligations under international law have been created. Such actors will possess the powers they are given by states. Apart from states, the primary actors are international organizations and individuals.

Recommended reading

On the issue of legal personality, see Roland Portmann, *Legal Personality in International Law* (Cambridge University Press, 2010); Rosalyn Higgins, *Problems & Process* (Oxford University Press, 1994) ch. 3; Jean d'Aspremont (ed.), *Participants in the International Legal System* (Routledge, 2011).

On statehood, see the seminal work by James Crawford, *The Creation of States in International Law* (2nd edn, Oxford University Press, 2006). See also Matthew Craven, 'Statehood, Self-Determination, and Recognition' in Malcolm D. Evans (ed.), *International Law* (4th edn, Oxford University Press, 2014).

A classic work on the role of recognition is Sir Hersch Lauterpacht, *Recognition in International Law* (Cambridge University Press, 1947). See also Stefan Talmon, *Recognition of Government in International Law: With Particular Reference to Governments in Exile* (Oxford University Press, 2001); John Dugard, *Recognition and the United Nations* (Grotius, 1987).

For a presentation and discussion of the right to self-determination, see Antonio Cassese, *Self-Determination of Peoples* (Cambridge University Press, 1995).

On international organizations under international law, see C. F. Amerasinghe, *Principles of the International Law of International Organizations* (2nd edn, Cambridge University Press, 2005); Jan Klabbers, *An Introduction to International Institutional Law* (Cambridge University Press, 2009); Dapo Akande, 'International Organizations' in Malcolm D. Evans (ed.), *International Law* (4th edn, Oxford University Press, 2014).

A convincing discussion of the individual as a legal person is Astrid Kjeldgaard-Pedersen, *The International Legal Personality of the Individual* (Oxford University Press, 2018). See also Robert McCorquodale, 'The Individual and the International Legal System' in Malcolm D. Evans (ed.), *International Law* (4th edn, Oxford University Press, 2014).

Questions for discussion

1. Why is legal personality a relative concept?
2. What is the problem with the two approaches to the role of recognition (the declaratory and the constitutive)?
3. What is the difference between an internal and an external right to self-determination? Why is the distinction important?
4. Does Kosovo have a right to secede from Serbia?

5. What did Judge Huber mean when he stated that 'the continuous and peaceful display of territorial sovereignty is as good as title'?

6. Does Palestine fulfil the four Montevideo criteria for being considered a state under international law?

7. From where do international organizations derive their legal personality? How do you determine the extent of an international organization's rights and obligations under international law?

8. When it comes to the issue of statehood, can you provide some examples of where there might be a tension between, on the one hand, notions of justice and, on the other, international stability?

5

Jurisdiction

CENTRAL ISSUES

1. This chapter discusses the international legal concept of jurisdiction as well as the content of the relevant legal principles.

2. It presents the difference between, respectively, the jurisdiction to prescribe and the jurisdiction to enforce and the main elements thereof.

3. The chapter analyses the different principles of prescriptive jurisdiction (the principle of territoriality, nationality, universality, protection and so-called passive 'personality') and discusses the issue of concurring jurisdictions as well as jurisdiction on ships and aircraft.

4. The chapter also discusses the prohibition on enforcing jurisdiction on the territory of another state as well as the legal consequences of violating that prohibition.

5.1 Introduction

International law primarily seeks to maintain international order by compartmentalizing territory and individuals into sovereign states. One of the defining aspects of sovereignty, then, is the exclusive right of each state to govern its internal affairs. As the Permanent Court of Arbitration stated in the *Island of Palmas* case: 'Sovereignty in the relations between States signifies independence. Independence in regard to a portion of the globe is the right to exercise therein, to the exclusion of any other State, the functions of a State.'[1] In the *Lotus* case, the Permanent Court of International Justice (PCIJ) also stressed how the 'first and foremost restriction imposed by international law upon a State is that—failing the existence of a permissive rule to the contrary—it may not exercise its power in any form in the territory of another State'.[2] This principle against physically exercising sovereignty in another state is supplemented by another principle that flows from state sovereignty. In the *Lotus* case, the PCIJ stated that the prohibition against physically exercising jurisdiction in other states did not mean that a state was prohibited from exercising jurisdiction in its own territory 'in respect of

---

[1] *Island of Palmas (Netherlands v United States)* (1928) II RIAA 829, 838.
[2] *The Case of the SS Lotus (France v Turkey)*, Judgment, 1927, PCIJ, Series A, No. 10, 18–19.

any case which relates to acts which have taken place abroad, and in which it cannot rely on some permissive rule of international law'.[3]

In international law, these dual aspects of sovereignty are reflected in the principles of the lawful exercise of jurisdiction. The term jurisdiction relates to the authority of a state to exert its influence and power—in practice make, apply and enforce its rules—and create an impact or consequence on individuals or property.[4] In practice, the principles of jurisdiction translate into important distinctions between various forms of jurisdiction, the primary being jurisdiction to *prescribe* (make law) and jurisdiction to *enforce* (physically ensuring compliance with the law). In general, as the *Island of Palmas* and the *Lotus* cases illustrate, a state is entitled to *regulate* (prescribe) conduct that occurs abroad but it may not *enforce* its laws outside its territory. The two forms of jurisdiction are independent of each other. International law also operates with a jurisdiction to *adjudicate* that concerns the right of domestic courts to receive, treat and determine cases referred to them. The three forms of jurisdiction can be illustrated with a case of robbery. The domestic *criminalization* of robbery is an act of prescriptive jurisdiction while the physical *apprehension* of a suspected robber is a case of enforcing jurisdiction. Jurisdiction to adjudicate relates to the *subsequent* criminal prosecution of the individual. In practice, there is rarely reason to distinguish between prescriptive and adjudicatory jurisdiction, and in this chapter adjudicative jurisdiction is only touched upon in the discussion in Section 5.3 of the prosecution of individuals brought before a court in violation of the prohibition against enforcing jurisdiction in other states. The concept of 'extraterritorial' jurisdiction relates to those rare cases where a state may be authorized to enforce its jurisdiction on the territory of another state. It must not, then, be confused with the different forms of prescriptive jurisdiction that are not based on the principle of territoriality (see Sections 5.2.3–5.2.6).

The principles of jurisdiction seek to balance the rights of a sovereign state to legislate and thereby exert its influence over matters of its concern with the interests of other sovereign states not to be subjected to undue encroachment on their right to conduct their affairs. The attempt by a state to exercise jurisdiction over individuals or events on the territory of another state will be perceived as an infringement of the sovereignty of the latter because it interferes with how it exercises its own jurisdiction. By seeking to ensure that states do not assert jurisdiction over affairs that are properly the domain of other states, the principles of jurisdiction seek to prevent undue friction between states and they are therefore part of the international law of coexistence.

The source of jurisdiction is state sovereignty and the role of international law is merely to limit the exercise of jurisdictional powers. As we shall see in Chapter 6, at times state immunity requires a state to refrain from exercising jurisdiction. In practice, respect for sovereignty may lead to conflicting interpretations of the limits of jurisdiction. Respect for the sovereignty of a state that wants to influence a matter speaks in favour of adopting an expansive view of jurisdiction, while respect for the sovereignty of a state that is subjected to the first state's exercise of jurisdiction

---

[3] Ibid, 19.

[4] For an extensive overview, see Cedric Ryngaert, *Jurisdiction in International Law* (Oxford University Press, 2008).

dictates otherwise. Most states assert less jurisdiction than international law allows them to. There is no comprehensive convention regulating jurisdiction, and the law is primarily derived from state practice. An influential Draft Convention on Jurisdiction with Respect to Crime was, however, published by a group of researchers at Harvard University in 1935.[5]

Importantly, the different forms of jurisdiction we discuss in this chapter must not be confused with the interpretation of various jurisdictional provisions in individual human rights conventions, such as the European Convention on Human Rights (ECHR), which we discuss in Chapter 6.[6]

The overview is divided into two sections. We start in Section 5.2 with jurisdiction to prescribe before we examine jurisdiction to enforce in Section 5.3.

5.2 Jurisdiction to prescribe

5.2.1 **Introduction**

The jurisdiction to prescribe relates to the authority under international law of a state to apply its national laws to any individual, property or event no matter where they may be located or occur. It is now well established that states are only entitled to exercise their legislative jurisdiction when it is supported by a permissive principle in international law.[7] Thus, the debate about the jurisdictional authorities of states revolves around identifying the limits of the existing—but not always uncontroversial—categories of (potentially) permissible prescriptive jurisdiction. In general, a state may only extend its laws and exercise its prescriptive jurisdiction over an individual or a particular matter if the state is somehow affected or deemed to have a reasonable interest in doing so.[8] Thus, there must be some sort of real link—a 'connecting factor'—between the acts or the behaviour that the state wants to prescribe and the legitimate interests of the state. Furthermore, this nexus must exist at the time the particular conduct was performed. In most cases, of course, it is unlikely that a state will take steps to prescribe acts it does not have any interest in. It must be noted that the existence of an entitlement under international law for a state to exercise prescriptive jurisdiction over an individual or a matter does not mean that the national authorities of that state are necessarily competent under domestic law to exercise such jurisdiction. For that to be the case, the state must have adopted the required national measures and as already noted, states generally assert less jurisdiction than international law permits.

---

[5] The draft convention is available in (1935) 29 *American Journal of International Law* 439.

[6] See also Marko Milanovic, *Extraterritorial Application of Human Rights Treaties* (Oxford University Press, 2011) 26.

[7] In *Lotus*, the PCIJ implied that there is a presumption against limiting a state's jurisdiction to apply its national law to matters abroad when it stated that international law leaves states 'a wide measure of discretion which is only limited in certain cases by prohibitive rules; as regards other cases, every State remains free to adopt the principles which it regards as best and most suitable'. See *Lotus* (n 2) 19. On this point, the Court went too far. See also *Arrest Warrant of 11 April 2000 (Congo v Belgium)*, Judgment, Separate Opinion of President Guillaume [2002] ICJ Rep 3, 43.

[8] Ryngaert (n 4) 31.

The power to prescribe is asserted according to five principles. They have primarily been developed in relation to jurisdiction over criminal offences,[9] but as the exercise of civil jurisdiction is less intrusive than criminal jurisdiction they are generally considered equally valid for claims in civil law. In the following, we discuss each of the five principles. We start with the principle of territoriality (Section 5.2.2) before we examine nationality (Section 5.2.3), passive personality (Section 5.2.4), protective jurisdiction (Section 5.2.5) and universal jurisdiction (Section 5.2.6). Following that, Section 5.2.7 briefly discusses the question of concurring/overlapping jurisdictions and Section 5.2.8 will provide an overview of jurisdiction over aircraft and on board ships.

5.2.2 Territorial jurisdiction

The most basic and uncontroversial basis of jurisdiction is the principle of territoriality derived from state sovereignty. In a sense, all other principles of jurisdiction can be considered 'extraterritorial'.[10] The territoriality principle holds that a state has jurisdiction over all acts, whether criminal or not, committed on its territory and over everyone located on the territory of that state.[11] The principle cannot, however, be used by a state to assert jurisdiction over an offence that has taken place abroad merely because the alleged offender subsequently enters the territory of the state. Subject to limitations imposed under international law, most notably human rights law, a state can legislate as it pleases on whatever matter it desires on its own territory. 'Territory' includes not only territory on land but also the territorial sea and the airspace above the land and sea territory.[12]

The *2017 Tallinn Manual 2.0 on the International Law Applicable to Cyber Operations* specifies that the principles of territorial jurisdiction also apply to persons, natural and legal, involved in cyber activities that are present within the territory of a state as well as to cyber infrastructure and data located on the territory.[13] As a point of departure, therefore, a state may also restrict access to the internet, or parts thereof, for anyone who is physically present on its territory.[14]

The practical application of the principle of territorial jurisdiction may occasionally cause problems. What does it mean that an act is committed or occurs on the territory of a state? Often, a sequence of events that cause an effect does not occur wholly within one state. A criminal offence, for example, may often be initiated or planned in one state but committed in another. International law has developed two approaches to deal with such 'cross-border' activities. 'Objective territoriality' focuses on the effects of an offence and holds that a state will have jurisdiction over an offence that is *completed*

---

[9] See, *inter alia*, Draft Convention on Jurisdiction with Respect to Crime (n 5).

[10] See also Rosalyn Higgins, *Problems and Process: International Law and How We Use It* (Oxford University Press, 1994) 73.

[11] See also Draft Convention on Jurisdiction with Respect to Crime (n 5) art. 3.

[12] As we will see in Section 5.2.8, special rules apply with regard to jurisdiction on board aircraft and vessels registered in the state.

[13] Michael N. Schmitt (ed.), *The Tallinn Manual 2.0 on the International Law Applicable to Cyber Operations* (Cambridge University Press, 2017) Rule 9, see para. 1.

[14] Ibid, Rule 2, para. 8.

on its territory even though some of the elements of the offence took place abroad. 'Subjective territoriality', on the other hand, stipulates that a state has jurisdiction over all acts that are completed abroad as long as they are initiated or planned on the territory of the state in question. The subjective approach is of great practical importance in fighting transnational crime, such as international cybercrime. The distinction between objective and subjective territoriality can be illustrated by the 11 September 2001 terrorist attacks in the United States. As the attacks were completed on US territory, the United States could assert jurisdiction over the attacks on the basis of objective territoriality. But since a substantial part of the planning and preparation of the attacks occurred elsewhere, most notably in Afghanistan and Germany, such states could claim jurisdiction on the basis of subjective territoriality.

It is disputed whether the principle of territoriality permits a state to prescribe and thus extend its legislation to acts committed abroad that only have an economic effect on the state. The issue is primarily relevant with regard to antitrust legislation. The United States has adopted a so-called 'effects doctrine', and in *Alcoa* a US Court of Appeals in 1945 found that 'any state may impose liabilities, even upon persons not within its allegiance, for conduct outside its borders that has consequences within its borders which the state reprehends; and these liabilities other states will ordinarily recognize'.[15] The US has even prescribed acts that are lawful in the states in which they are committed.[16] European states responded by adopting 'blocking laws' that prohibited their national companies from cooperating and complying with the US authorities in antitrust cases. The blocking laws were based on the principle that a state cannot require an individual to comply with an order if doing so would result in a violation of the laws in the territory where the potentially complying act must be done.[17] US courts backed down from their most aggressive assertions of jurisdiction[18] with the result that jurisdictional relations have improved.[19] The United States is not the only state that has adopted an expansive interpretation of the reach of its competition laws. In the 1993 *Wood Pulp* case, the (then) European Court of Justice accepted legislative jurisdiction on the basis of what were essentially local effects/consequences of foreign conduct.[20]

According to the *2017 Tallinn Manual*, the effects doctrine has become increasingly accepted and may now be considered customary international law although its conditions are yet to be 'fully settled in international law'.[21] The Manual also notes how effects-based jurisdiction should be reserved for cyber operations that have a

---

[15] *United States v Aluminium Co. of America et al.*, 148 F.2d 416, 443 (2d Cir. 1945).

[16] See, inter alia, *Rio Tinto Zinc Corp. v Westinghouse Electric Corp.* (1978) 1 All ER 434 (HL).

[17] For an overview, see Vaughan Lowe, 'Blocking Extraterritorial Jurisdiction: The British Protection of Trading Interests Act, 1980' (1980) 75 *American Journal of International Law* 257.

[18] See *Timberlane Lumber Co. v Bank of America*, 549 F.2d 597, § 67 (9th Cir. 1976). See also *Hartford Fire Insurance v California*, 529 US 764, 797–799 (1993) and *F. Hoffmann-La Roche Ltd v Empagran SA*, 542 US 155, 164–165 (2004).

[19] See, inter alia, Agreement on the Application of Positive Comity Principles in the Enforcement of their Competition Laws (European Community–United States) (adopted 4 June 1998), OJ L173/28.

[20] See Joined Cases 89, 104, 114, 116, 117 and 125–129/85 *Ahlström and Others v Commission* [1988] ECR 5193. The Court did not rely on an 'effects doctrine' but on an expansive interpretation of the territoriality principle and the fact that the relevant agreement was 'implemented' in the EU.

[21] Schmitt (n 13), Rule 9, paras 10–13.

'substantial effect' upon a state[22] and that it should be exercised in a 'reasonable fashion and with due regard for the interest of other States'.[23]

5.2.3 Jurisdiction on the basis of nationality

States may extend their laws to their own nationals regardless of where they are located. Indeed, as a basis for jurisdiction, the so-called 'active personality' principle has a longer history than any other principle of jurisdiction.[24] The state of nationality has traditionally enjoyed basically unlimited control over its nationals, and until the advent of international human rights law the manner in which a state treated its own citizens was of no interest to international law. States have a legitimate interest in the behaviour of their own citizens abroad, and since they are reluctant to extradite their nationals to criminal prosecution in other states (see Section 5.3), preventing impunity for serious offences occasionally requires the state of nationality to prosecute its own nationals for crimes they have committed abroad. At present, the active personality principle has become relevant where a state of nationality may wish to criminally prosecute a national for acts committed abroad, such as in areas of conflict in places like Iraq and Syria—a 'foreign fighter'.

If an individual has dual nationality, both states of nationality may assert jurisdiction on the basis of nationality. States are generally free to decide who they consider to be their 'nationals' and under what circumstances an individual qualifies for citizenship.[25] In the *Nottebohm* case, however, the International Court of Justice (ICJ) stated that the exercise of rights associated with nationality may sometimes be challenged by other states and that nationality requires a 'genuine connection' with the state that seeks to protect the rights of its citizens.[26]

5.2.4 The passive personality principle

Jurisdiction on the basis of territory and nationality usually provide a state with sufficient jurisdictional means to protect its interests from potential harm. After all, most offences are committed by individuals physically located on the territory of the state or by the nationals of the state abroad. However, under the so-called 'passive personality' principle, a state can also assert its jurisdiction over an offence committed abroad on the sole ground that the *victim* of the offence was a national of the state. As a principle of prescriptive jurisdiction, this has historically been controversial, and Harvard Research in International Law did not include it in its 1935 Draft Convention on Jurisdiction with Respect to Crime because it found that it would only 'invite controversy without serving any useful objective'.[27] In *Lotus*, a number of the dissenting

---

[22] Ibid, para. 15.   [23] Ibid, para. 13.   [24] Ryngaert (n 4) 42–47.

[25] See also *Constitution of the Maritime Safety Committee of the Inter-Governmental Maritime Consultative Organization*, Advisory Opinion [1960] ICJ Rep 150. See also *Nationality Decrees Issued in Tunis and Morocco*, Advisory Opinion, 1923, PCIJ, Series B, No. 4, 24.

[26] *Nottebohm (Second Phase) (Liechtenstein v Guatemala)*, Judgment [1955] ICJ Rep 4, 23.

[27] Commentary to art. 10 in the Draft Convention on Jurisdiction with Respect to Crime (n 5) 579.

judges were also critical of Turkey's claim that it could assert jurisdiction over an incident at sea on the basis of the Turkish nationality of the drowned seaman.[28] The passive personality principle makes it practically impossible for a potential offender to anticipate which state's laws he or she may be subjected to and it creates uncertainty about acceptable behaviour within a state.

Passive personality has nevertheless become increasingly accepted in recent years, in particular in the context of international terrorism.[29] In *Yunis*, the United States prosecuted a Lebanese citizen for hijacking a Jordanian civilian airliner in Beirut even though the only connection to the United States was the presence among the passengers of American citizens.[30] Aside from basing its claim of jurisdiction on the principle of universality (see later) and the 1970 Convention for the Suppression of Unlawful Seizure of Aircraft, the US court relied on the passive personality principle, which it found was supported by international law 'at least where the state has a particularly strong interest in the crime'. The United States also relied on the passive personality principle in relation to the 1985 *Achille Lauro* incident in which terrorists took control of an Italian cruise ship in the Mediterranean and caused the death of an American passenger.[31]

Assertions of jurisdiction on the basis of passive personality should only be made in relation to serious offences (e.g. crimes of terrorism) that are prescribed in all states. This ensures that a state does not prosecute an individual for a crime that was lawful in the territory where it was committed and that potential offenders will know that their conduct constitutes a serious crime.[32] Passive personality should also serve as a mere subsidiary means of jurisdiction and preferably only relied upon when the state in which the offence occurred does not intend to prosecute the offender.

5.2.5 **Protective jurisdiction**

The 'protective principle' holds that a state may extend its jurisdiction over any matter that has a deleterious effect on it regardless of where the act occurs or who has committed it. It is derived from the sovereign right of all states to conduct their affairs without outside interference.[33] Importantly, the exercise of protective jurisdiction requires the existence of a genuine threat to a *vital* state interest. It must, therefore,

---

[28] See *Lotus* (n 2) Dissenting Opinion by M. Loder 36, Dissenting Opinion by Lord Finlay 57–58, Dissenting Opinion by M. Nyholm 62, Dissenting Opinion by Mr Moore 91–93. Interestingly, the principle is not included as a jurisdictional basis in the International Convention on Certain Rules Concerning Civil Jurisdiction in Matters of Collision (adopted 10 May 1952, entered into force 14 September 1955), 439 UNTS 217 or the United Nations Convention on the Law of the Sea (UNCLOS, also known as LOSC) (adopted 10 December 1982, entered into force 16 November 1994) 1833 UNTS 2.

[29] Higgins (n 10) 66–69. See also Ryngaert (n 4) 94–96. See also the US Omnibus Diplomatic Security and Antiterrorism Act of 1986 and see Geoffrey R. Watson, 'The Passive Personality Principle' (1993) 28 *Texas International Law Journal* 1; See too *Arrest Warrant* (n 7) Joint Separate Opinion of Judges Higgins, Kooijmans and Buergenthal, para. 47.

[30] *United States v Fawaz Yunis, A/k/a Nazeeh, Appellant*, 924 F.2d 1086 (DC Cir. 1991).

[31] For a brief overview, see Watson (n 29) 10–11.   [32] Ibid, 25.

[33] Ryngaert (n 4) 96–97. See also commentary to art. 7 of the Draft Convention on Jurisdiction with Respect to Crime (n 5) 543–561.

be distinguished from the (controversial) effects doctrine discussed in Section 5.2.2 whereby a state extends its laws to acts that merely have a negative economic effect in the state. The classic example of assertions of protective jurisdiction is the criminalization of falsification or counterfeiting of 'seals, currency, instruments of credit, stamps, passports, or public documents', issued by a state.[34] In the 1960s, some states also prescribed so-called 'pirate radio broadcasting' to stop unauthorized radio stations on ships on the high seas or from installations fixed to the seabed in areas outside the territorial sea of the coastal state.[35]

The 1935 Harvard Research in International Law Draft Convention argues for limitations to protective jurisdiction.[36] In general, however, this form of prescriptive jurisdiction has not been a cause of great contention and states in most cases limit their reliance on this form of jurisdiction to serious offences that are not condoned by anyone.[37] In recent decades, the principle has been relied on to combat drug smuggling and international terrorism. There are examples, though, where the principle seems to have been used in order to prescribe activity that cannot reasonably be said to have a serious negative impact on the legislating state's vital interests. The best examples are so-called 'secondary boycott'/'secondary sanctions' laws that are imposed by a state to deter non-nationals or foreign companies from doing business with a state or other entity that is the direct target of a sanction. The sanctions are 'secondary' because they supplement the (primary) sanctions. The seminal example is the 'secondary boycott' laws adopted in the 1996 US Helms–Burton Act and the D'Amato Act. While the former sought to extend a long-existing US embargo on Cuba by penalizing foreign companies for trading in Cuban property confiscated from American citizens, the latter imposed penalties on persons who made certain investments in Iranian and Libyan oil and natural gas resources.[38] Since the legislation primarily seemed to serve as a tool for US foreign policy, it was met with protests from other states and both Canada and the EU enacted 'blocking legislation'.[39] Recently, the United States has threatened to resort to secondary boycotts to supplement the (primary) sanctions regime imposed on North Korea. The potential new US laws would target third-country businesses and individuals, primarily Chinese, who do business with North Korea.[40]

---

[34] Draft Convention on Jurisdiction with Respect to Crime (n 5) art. 8. See also the commentary to art. 8 at 561–563.

[35] See, inter alia, Horace B. Robertson Jr, 'The Suppression of Pirate Radio Broadcasting: A Test Case of the International System for Control of Activities outside National Territory' (1982) 45 *Law and Contemporary Problems* 71.

[36] Commentary to art. 7 of the Draft Convention on Jurisdiction with Respect to Crime (n 5) 557–561. See also Manuel R. García-Mora, 'Criminal Jurisdiction over Foreigners for Treason and Offenses Against the Safety of the State Committed upon Foreign Territory' (1957–1958) 19 *University of Pittsburgh Law Review* 567, 588–589.

[37] Ryngaert (n 4) 98–99.

[38] For more, see Stefaan Smis and Kim Van der Borght, 'The EU–US Compromise on the Helms Burton and D'Amato Acts' (1999) 93 *American Journal of International Law* 227.

[39] Ibid. In May 1998, the EU and the US reached an agreement according to which the latter would limit the application of the Acts on European companies and citizens.

[40] Jung Suk-Yee, 'N. Korea Highly Likely to Trigger Economic Conflict between US and China', *Business Korea* (5 September 2017): http://www.businesskorea.co.kr/news/articleView.html?idxno=19202.

5.2.6 **Universal jurisdiction**

International law recognizes that certain offences are so serious and/or disruptive to international society that any state may claim jurisdiction over them no matter where they have been committed, who they have been committed against or the nationality of the perpetrator. The lack of a direct link between the state and the offence makes so-called 'universal jurisdiction' stand out from the other principles of jurisdiction. Originally, it was the crime of piracy that gave rise to the notion of universal jurisdiction.[41] Since pirates roamed the high seas outside the territorial jurisdiction of any state it made good practical sense to allow all states to prosecute any pirate they could get their hands on and customary international law thus established a right for all states to assert their prescriptive jurisdiction over the crime.[42] Universal jurisdiction was thereby created to fulfil a potential jurisdictional vacuum. Nowadays, universal jurisdiction is mostly applied in order to prevent impunity for perpetrators of particularly serious offences. The underlying rationale and justification behind universal jurisdiction was forcefully articulated by the District Court in Jerusalem in the 1961 *Eichmann* trial in Israel where the court had to justify prosecuting the former high-ranking German Nazi Adolph Eichmann under an Israeli law that gave Israeli courts national jurisdiction to prosecute crimes committed outside Israel at a time when the State of Israel had not yet been established. The court stated that the 'abhorrent' crimes in question were not just crimes under Israeli law alone. According to the court:

> These crimes which offended the whole of mankind and shocked the conscience of nations are grave offences against the law of nations itself ('*delicta juris gentium*'). Therefore, so far from international law negating or limiting the jurisdiction of countries with respect to such crimes, in the absence of an International Court, the international law is in need of the judicial and legislative authorities of every country, to give effect to its penal injunctions and to bring criminals to trial. The jurisdiction to try crimes under international law is universal.[43]

The legal basis for asserting universal jurisdiction over the most serious offences in international law is found in customary international law. For the time being, the offences appear to be limited to the crime of genocide, crimes against humanity, serious war crimes and torture—all violations of norms of a peremptory character/*jus cogens*.[44]

In its most 'pure' form, a state will assert universal jurisdiction over an offence even though the alleged offender is not present on the territory of the state—also referred to as universal jurisdiction *in absentia*. In 1993, for example, Belgium adopted legislation that granted its courts national jurisdiction over a range of offences regardless of where they were committed, who the perpetrators or victims were or whether the alleged offender was present in Belgium. In *Arrest Warrant*, the Democratic Republic of Congo (DRC) brought a case against Belgium after Belgian authorities had relied on the new legislation and issued an arrest warrant for the acting minister of foreign

---

[41] See Commentary to art. 9 in the Draft Convention on Jurisdiction with Respect to Crime (n 5) 563–572.
[42] See also the discussion in Chapter 15.
[43] *Adolph Eichmann*, District Court of Jerusalem, Criminal Case No. 40/61, para. 12.
[44] Roger O'Keefe, *International Criminal Law* (Oxford University Press, 2015) 23–24 and 371.

affairs in the DRC.[45] As we shall see in Chapter 6, the ICJ concluded that a sitting minister of foreign affairs is immune from criminal prosecution and the court did not therefore determine if the Belgian legislation was compatible with the international law of jurisdiction. In their separate opinions, however, some of the judges offered quite varying positions on the issue.[46]

Since prescriptive jurisdiction concerns the authority of a state to apply its laws to an act *at the time it occurs*, the legality of an assertion of universal jurisdiction cannot be contingent on the subsequent presence of the alleged offender on the territory of the asserting state.[47] A state may, however, decide that it is not desirable to be as aggressive as the Belgians and thus only make assertions of universal jurisdiction in cases where the alleged offender is physically present on its territory. In fact, that is what most states opt to do. While the fight to end impunity for serious violations of international law speaks in favour of an aggressive use of universal jurisdiction, upholding peaceful and amicable interstate relations speaks against doing so. In 2003, Belgium gave in to international pressure and repealed its (controversial) legislation.

A more limited form of universal jurisdiction is derived from the obligation of a state in a number of treaties to either prosecute or extradite—*aut dedere aut judicare*—an alleged offender suspected of specific offences who is located on the territory of that state. As we shall see in Chapter 15, in practice the obligation requires a state to extend its prescriptive jurisdiction to certain individuals present on the territory of the state suspected of having committed certain specified crimes regardless of where the offence is committed, the nationality of the offender or the nationality of the victim. Since the legal basis for the obligation to prosecute or extradite is a treaty, non-state parties are not obliged to assert their (universal) jurisdiction over the offence in question.

The obligation to prosecute or extradite certain individuals found its way into treaty law in the early 1970s in relation to international terrorism. The 1970 Hague Convention for the Suppression of Unlawful Seizure of Aircraft, for example, specifies that a state must take the required measures to ensure that it can establish its jurisdiction over an offence covered by the Convention in relation to an individual who takes refuge on its territory. Similar provisions were introduced into the 1971 Montreal Convention for the Suppression of Unlawful Acts against the Safety of Civil Aviation, the 1979 Convention against the Taking of Hostages, the 1997 Convention for the Suppression of Terrorist Bombings and the 1999 Convention for the Suppression of the Financing of Terrorism. The obligation is also found in the 1984 UN Convention against Torture and Other Cruel, Inhuman or Degrading Treatment or Punishment.

5.2.7 **Concurring/overlapping jurisdictions**

Since states can rely on a number of principles in order to assert jurisdiction to prescribe in respect of a given person or matter, it is not uncommon for more than one

---

[45] *Arrest Warrant* (n 7).

[46] See, inter alia, *Arrest Warrant* (n 7) Separate Opinion of President Guillaume, para. 16.

[47] See the discussion in Roger O'Keefe, 'Universal Jurisdiction: Clarifying the Basic Concept' (2004) 2 *Journal of International Criminal Justice* 750–755.

state to claim jurisdiction in a given case. If, say, a citizen of state A kills citizens of state B on the territory of state C, international law may potentially entitle all three states to assert jurisdiction over the offence. State A may assert jurisdiction on the basis of the offender's nationality while state C may rely on the principle of territoriality and the fact that the offence was committed on its territory. Depending on the circumstances, as described earlier, state B could also be entitled to assert jurisdiction on the basis of the nationality of the victims. In addition, the principle of universality may also entitle all states to exercise jurisdiction over an offence irrespective of a link between those states and the crime.

The issue of *concurrent jurisdiction* and the simultaneous exercise of jurisdiction by more than one state over the same matter may give rise to considerable international friction and it is therefore somewhat unfortunate that states are not under a legal obligation to exercise their jurisdiction in a particularly reasonable manner. The aggressive jurisdictional assertions by US courts in antitrust cases and the Helms–Burton and D'Amato Acts illustrate the need for principles that resolve jurisdictional conflicts in a mutually satisfactory manner. In a Separate Opinion in *Barcelona Traction*, Judge Fitzmaurice noted that states are obliged 'to exercise moderation and restraint as to the extent of the jurisdiction assumed by its courts in cases having a foreign element, and to avoid undue encroachment on a jurisdiction more properly exercised by another state'.[48] The 2001 Convention on Cybercrime stipulates that, when more than one state claims jurisdiction over an alleged offence under the Convention, the states involved shall 'consult with a view to determining the most appropriate jurisdiction for prosecution'.[49]

In most cases, the territorial state will claim that it has the closest link to a particular offence and therefore has a more privileged position compared to states with 'competing' claims of jurisdiction. In practical terms, it will be the state with physical custody of the offender that determines which state will exercise jurisdiction over the individual. The principle *aut dedere aut judicare* discussed earlier can be perceived as a principle of resolving a potential jurisdictional dispute.

Although there is no formal hierarchy of jurisdictional claims, attempts have been made to establish second-order discretionary principles for identifying the state with the strongest claim or interest in a given matter.[50] A principle of comity familiar to US lawyers suggests that a state should limit the reach of its laws and defer to other states if those states have a stronger link to a situation.[51] An example is the so-called jurisdictional 'rule of reason' in the 1987 *Restatement (Third) of the Foreign Relations Law of the United States* introduced in response to the contentious issue of jurisdiction in antitrust cases. The purpose of the rule is to oblige the United States not to exercise its jurisdiction when it is deemed 'unreasonable'. It also lists a range of relevant factors, including 'the link of the activity to the territory

---

[48] *Barcelona Traction, Light and Power Co., Ltd (Belgium v Spain)*, Judgment, Separate Opinion of Judge Sir Gerald Fitzmaurice [1970] ICJ Rep 3, para. 70.

[49] Budapest, 23 November 2001, European Treaty Series 185, see art. 22(5).

[50] Ryngaert (n 4), 136–153.

[51] Ibid, 136–142. See also the Harold G. Maier, 'Extraterritorial Jurisdiction at a Crossroads: An Intersection between Public and Private International Law' (1982) 76 *American Journal of International Law* 280. On the concept of comity in international law in general, see Joel R. Paul, 'Comity in International Law' (1991) 32 *Harvard International Law Journal* 1.

of the regulating state', 'the character of the activity to be regulated', 'the extent to which another state may have an interest in regulating the activity' and 'the likelihood of conflict with regulation by another state'.[52] As noted earlier, US courts have become more sensitive to the jurisdictional concerns voiced by other states, in particular in the area of antitrust jurisdiction. European states are generally more reluctant to overtly balance interests in jurisdiction disputes and instead reach similar results by other means.

5.2.8 **Jurisdiction over aircraft and ships**

Jurisdiction over a state's airspace and aircraft is regulated in a number of conventions. The 1944 Chicago Convention on International Civil Aviation stipulates that all states have complete and exclusive sovereignty over the airspace above their territory, including the airspace over their territorial waters.[53] The 1963 Tokyo Convention on Offences and Certain Other Acts Committed on Board Aircraft specifies that the state of registration of an aircraft has authority to apply its laws to matters that occur on board its aircraft while in flight regardless of where it is located.[54] It also establishes the general rule that a contracting state which is not the state of registration may not interfere with an aircraft in flight in order to exercise its criminal jurisdiction over an offence committed on board.[55] The Tokyo Convention also provides the aircraft commander (the captain) with the authority to use reasonable force to deal with individuals who have committed or are about to commit a crime or acts that may jeopardize safety on board the aircraft.[56] In cases of hijacking of an aircraft, contracting states are obliged to 'take all appropriate measures to restore control of the aircraft to its lawful commander or to preserve his control of the aircraft'. The Tokyo Convention's regulation on the prevention of hijacking has since been supplemented by numerous other conventions including the 1970 Hague Convention for the Suppression of Unlawful Seizure of Aircraft according to which, as we saw earlier, contracting states are obliged to extradite or prosecute hijackers.

In Chapter 8 we will explore the issue of jurisdiction over ships on the high seas and the principles of innocent passage through a coastal state's territorial sea or exclusive economic zone (EEZ). As a point of departure, the flag state has sole jurisdiction over a ship.

5.3 **Jurisdiction to enforce**

International law is clear when it comes to a state's *physical* enforcement of its laws. As the PCIJ stated in the *Lotus* case, the 'first and foremost restriction imposed by international law upon a state is that—failing the existence of a permissive rule to

---

[52] The American Law Institute, *Restatement (Third) of the Foreign Relations Law of the United States* (1988) para. 403.

[53] Convention on International Civil Aviation (Chicago Convention) (adopted 7 December 1944, entered into force 14 April 1947), 15 UNTS 295, arts 1–2.

[54] Convention on Offences and Certain Other Acts Committed on Board Aircraft (Tokyo Convention) (adopted 14 September 1963, entered into force 4 December 1969), 704 UNTS 219, art. 3(1).

[55] Ibid, art. 4.   [56] Ibid, arts 6–7.

the contrary—it may not exercise its power in any form in the territory of another State'.[57] Thus, unless the territorial state gives its consent, a state cannot enter another state in order to secure the arrest of an alleged offender or confiscate stolen property unless it can point to some specific legal justification, such as an authorization from the UN Security Council (see Chapter 13). If a state nevertheless does so, it will have committed a breach of sovereignty. According to the *2017 Tallinn Manual 2.0 on the International Law Applicable to Cyber Operations*, the principles of enforcement jurisdiction also apply in cyberspace, and a state is therefore barred from enforcing its laws via cyberspace if it would thereby violate the sovereignty of another state.[58]

In criminal law, the practical problems associated with the prohibition against physical enforcement in other states are solved by *extradition* where a state hands over an individual located on its territory who is wanted for criminal prosecution in another state. In practice, states are very reluctant to extradite their own citizens to criminal prosecution abroad. Extraditions are generally governed by a number of principles. First, the principle of 'double criminality' stipulates that the offence involved must be a criminal offence in both the extraditing and the receiving state. Secondly, the principle of 'double jeopardy' (*ne bis in idem*) specifies that an individual should not be punished twice for the same offence. In addition, extraditing states are bound by obligations in human rights conventions. The most important of these is the obligation not to extradite an individual to another state if there is a risk that the individual may be subjected to inhuman or degrading treatment in the receiving country or in a third state to which the individual may subsequently be transferred.[59] The obligation is found in article 3 of the ECHR,[60] article 7 of the UN Covenant on Civil and Political Rights[61] and article 3 of the UN Convention against Torture and Other Cruel, Inhuman or Degrading Treatment or Punishment.[62] In the *Niels Holck* case in June 2011, a Danish court of second instance concluded that article 3 of the ECHR prevented the extradition of a Danish national to India where he would face criminal prosecution in connection with his alleged role in providing weapons to local insurgents in the Indian state of West Bengal.[63] Human rights law may also bar extradition to a state where there is a risk of the death penalty being imposed[64] or of a trial that constitutes a 'flagrant denial of justice'.[65] In 1990, the UN General Assembly adopted

---

[57] *Lotus* (n 2) 18–19.   [58] Schmitt (n 13) 2.0, Rule 11. See also the debate in Section 13.2.3.

[59] See also the overview in Chapter 9.

[60] See also ECtHR, *Soering v UK*, App. no. 14038/88, 7 July 1989, para. 91.

[61] For case law from the Human Rights Committee on the prohibition on transfer to a risk of ill-treatment, see *Kindler v Canada* (Communication No. 470/1991, CCPR/C/48/D/470/1991, 11 November 1993); *Chitat Ng v Canada* (Communication No. 469/1991, CCPR/C/49/D/469/1991, 7 January 1994).

[62] For relevant case law from the Committee Against Torture, see *Mutombo v Switzerland* (Communication No. 13/1193, CAT/C/12/D/13/1993, 27 April 1994) and *Haydin v Sweden* (Communication No. 101/1997, CAT/C/21/D/101/1997, 20 November 1998).

[63] U.2011.2904Ø.

[64] In the ECHR, the death penalty is proscribed under the 1983 Protocol No. 6 to the ECHR concerning the abolition of the death penalty and the 2002 Protocol No. 13 to the ECHR concerning the abolition of the death penalty in all circumstances.

[65] For case law from the ECtHR, see *Othman (Abu Qatada) v UK*, App. no. 8139/09, 17 January 2012, para. 282.

a 'model treaty for extradition' to serve as a guide for the establishment of bilateral extradition treaties.[66]

A state can consent to another state's enforcement of jurisdiction on its territory. Under a so-called 'Status of Forces Agreement' (SOFA), for example, a host state consents to the presence of foreign troops on its territory.[67] Parties to the Schengen Treaty have accepted that law enforcement officers from other state parties may in certain circumstances continue the active pursuit of a suspected criminal into their territories without prior authorization.[68]

History is full of examples where state officials have enforced jurisdiction in another state without permission from the host state. A well-known case was Israeli agents' apprehension and subsequent transfer in 1960 from Argentina to Israel of the former high-ranking Nazi officer Adolph Eichmann.[69] In Israel, Eichmann was subsequently convicted and executed for atrocities committed during the Second World War. The UN Security Council responded to the unlawful Israeli incursion into Argentina by requesting Israel to offer compensation.[70] A more recent example of a potentially unlawful exercise of enforcement jurisdiction was the extraordinary rendition programme initiated by the United States after the terrorist attacks on 9/11.[71]

In its 1935 Draft Convention on Jurisdiction with Respect to Crime, Harvard Research in International Law stated that a state should refrain from prosecuting an individual brought into the state through measures that violated international law.[72] In practice, however, international law does not seem to impede subsequent prosecution. Most states follow the maxim of *mala captus, bene detentus* whereby a state can try an individual even if the state believes that the defendant was brought there by irregular means. In *Eichmann* mentioned earlier, for example, the District Court of Jerusalem stated that a state must only abstain from prosecution if the defendant is tried for an offence different from that for which he or she was extradited.[73] In *Stocke*, the German Federal Constitutional Court similarly concluded that national courts should generally only refuse jurisdiction if another state has protested about the abduction of an individual and requested that the person be returned.[74] US courts are notorious for their refusal

---

[66] GA Res. 45/116 (14 December 1990), UN Doc. A/RES/45/116.

[67] Paul J. Conderman, 'Status of Armed Forces on Foreign Territory Agreements (SOFA)' in Rüdiger Wolfrum (ed.), *Max Planck Encyclopedia of Public International Law* (Oxford University Press, 2013).

[68] Convention Implementing the Schengen Agreement of 14 June 1985 between the Governments of the States of the Benelux Economic Union, the Federal Republic of Germany and the French Republic, on the Gradual Abolition of Checks at their Common Borders, OJ L239/19, 19 June 1990, art. 41.

[69] See, *inter alia*, J. E. S. Fawcett, 'The *Eichmann* Case' (1963) 38 *British Yearbook of International Law* 181.

[70] SC Res. 138 (23 June 1960), UN Doc. S/RES7138.

[71] It must be noted that at least some states have actively cooperated with the United States: see, inter alia, ECtHR, *Husayn (Abu Zubaydah) v Poland*, App. no. 7511/13, 24 July 2914; *Al Nashiri v Poland*, App. no. 28761/11, 24 July 2014.

[72] Draft Convention on Jurisdiction with Respect to Crime (n 5) art. 16. See also the commentaries to the article at 623–632. See also the debate in, inter alia, Higgins (n 10) 71–73.

[73] *Eichmann* (n 43) paras 41–52.

[74] Decision of 17 July 1985, AZ: 2 BvR 1190/84. Bundesverfassungsgericht (Federal Constitutional Court), see § 1 c. For similar French practice, see the Klaus Barbie case, *Fédération Nationale des Désportés et Internes Resistants et Patriotes and Others v Barbie*, Court of Cassation, 6 October 1983.

to be influenced by the potentially unlawful manner in which a defendant is brought before court.[75] In *Alvarez-Machain*, the US Supreme Court did not find that the kidnapping and subsequent transport to the United States of a Mexican citizen in Mexico was a bar to prosecuting the individual for participating in the murder of a US official and a local pilot in Mexico.[76] Courts in other common law countries have been more reluctant. In *R v Horseferry Road Magistrates' Court*, the UK House of Lords refused to allow the criminal trial of an individual who was abducted from South Africa to England in disregard of the established extradition procedures in place between the two states.[77]

Summary

In international law, jurisdiction is concerned with the authority of a state to exert its influence and power over individuals or property. The rules can be divided into three forms of jurisdiction: jurisdiction to prescribe, jurisdiction to enforce and jurisdiction to adjudicate. The purpose of the rules is to strike a balance between the rights of a sovereign state to exert its influence on matters of interest to it and the interests of other sovereign states that may be at risk of undue encroachments on their own right to conduct their affairs as they please. International law generally operates with five bases for the exercise of prescriptive jurisdiction. These are jurisdiction on the basis of territoriality, nationality, universality, protective principles and so-called passive personality. While the first three are well accepted, the latter basis of jurisdiction—passive personality—is particularly controversial. International law prohibits a state from physically enforcing its jurisdiction on the territory of another state unless the latter gives its consent. In practice, however, this has not generally precluded national courts from bringing criminal proceedings against an individual who has been brought before the court in violation of that principle.

Recommended reading

For a broad overview of jurisdiction in international law, see Cedric Ryngaert, *Jurisdiction in International Law* (Oxford University Press, 2008). See also Rosalyn Higgins, *Problems and Process: International Law and How We Use It* (Oxford University Press, 1994) 56–77 and Frederick A. Mann, 'The Doctrine of Jurisdiction in International Law' (A. W. Sijthoff, 1964).

For an overview of the concept of 'blocking legislation', see Vaughan Lowe, 'Blocking Extraterritorial Jurisdiction: The British Protection of Trading Interests Act, 1980' (1980) 75 *American Journal of International Law* 257.

On the protective principle, Manuel R. García-Mora, 'Criminal Jurisdiction over Foreigners for Treason and Offenses Against the Safety of the State Committed upon Foreign Territory' (1957) 19 *University of Pittsburgh Law Review* 567.

---

[75] The classic case is *Ker v Illinois*, 119 US 436, 438 (1866).

[76] *United States v Alvarez-Machain*, 504 US 655 (1992) (US Supreme Court). Remarkably, the Court did not find the abduction of the defendant from Mexican territory incompatible with an existing extradition treaty between the United States and Mexico because that treaty did not expressly prohibit such abductions: see at 664.

[77] *R v Horseferry Road Magistrates' Court, ex p. Bennett* [1994] 1 AC 42, 62. See also *R v Hartley* [1978] 2 NZLR 199, 216 (New Zealand Court of Appeal).

On passive personality, see Geoffrey R. Watson, 'The Passive Personality Principle' (1993) 28 *Texas International Law Journal* 1.

On universal jurisdiction, Luc Reydams, *Universal Jurisdiction: International and Municipal Legal Perspectives* (Oxford University Press, 2003).

Other works include Harold G. Maier, 'Extraterritorial Jurisdiction at a Crossroads: An Intersection between Public and Private International Law' (1982) 76 *American Journal of International Law* 280, and the same author in 'Resolving Extraterritorial Conflicts, or "There and Back Again"' (1984) 7 *Virginia Journal of International Law* 7.

As for the different approaches to jurisdictional conflicts in various states, see Hannah L. Buxbaum, 'Territory, Territoriality, and the Resolution of Jurisdictional Conflict' (2009) 57 *American Journal of International Law* 631.

Questions for discussion

1. What does it mean that jurisdiction flows from sovereignty and not from international law?
2. State sovereignty may speak in favour of both a wide and a narrow authority to assert jurisdiction. Why?
3. Why is the 'effects doctrine' in the area of prescriptive jurisdiction controversial?
4. Can you think of some examples where a state's assertion of prescriptive jurisdiction on the basis of the protective principle would be problematic?
5. What do you think is the best way to handle cases of concurring jurisdiction?
6. Why is the maxim of *mala captus, bene detentus* problematic from the point of view of international law?

6

Immunity from national jurisdiction and diplomatic protection

CENTRAL ISSUES

1. The chapter discusses the different forms of immunity from national jurisdiction enjoyed by a state and its representatives.

2. It presents state immunity and the distinction between sovereign (*jure imperii*) and commercial (*jure gestionis*) acts. It discusses the exception to state immunity for commercial acts as well as some of the additional exceptions.

3. The chapter also discusses the immunities of state representatives and the distinction

between immunity *ratione personae* and immunity *ratione materiae* and shows how the distinction is applied to different state representatives.

4. It briefly discusses the immunities and protection of diplomatic representatives and diplomatic missions as well as the issue of consular protection and the immunities enjoyed by so-called special missions.

6.1 Introduction

We saw in Chapter 5 that a state has full and absolute jurisdiction within its own territory. So, not only can the territorial state legislate as it pleases, it can also generally enforce its laws and regulations over all matters and individuals. In some circumstances, however, the territorial state will be obliged to refrain from exercising its jurisdiction. Most importantly, under the principles of sovereign immunity a foreign state and its representatives are entitled to certain immunities from the exercise of jurisdiction by other states and a violation of these immunities will give rise to international responsibility. The principles of immunity from national jurisdiction are applied by national courts pursuant to national law.

Respect for sovereign immunity is mandated by international law and not simply a matter of expediency or comity.[1] In *Jurisdictional Immunities of the State*, the International

---

[1] *Jurisdictional Immunities of the State (Germany v Italy: Greece intervening)*, Judgment [2012] ICJ Rep 99, paras 53–57. But see practice from US courts: a classic example is *The Schooner Exchange v McFaddon*, 11 US (7 Cranch) 116, 136–137 (1812).

Court of Justice (ICJ) stated that the obligation of a host state—the 'forum' state—to refrain from exercising its jurisdiction over another state derives from the sovereign equality of states.[2] A state cannot require another sovereign state to submit to its national courts. State representatives enjoy immunity in part because they—and in particular high-ranking officials—'personify' the state on whose behalf they act. Alongside this 'representational' justification are functional considerations. As the ICJ noted in *Arrest Warrant*, a foreign minister can only perform his or her official functions if the individual can travel freely and remain in constant communication with not only the home government but also with diplomatic missions and representatives of other states.[3] This also helps explain the rights and privileges of diplomatic missions and representatives.

The chapter is divided into three sections. Section 6.2 concerns the immunity of *the state and its property*. Since a state cannot be found criminally liable, the discussion concerns immunity from *civil* claims. Section 6.3 discusses the immunities of *state representatives*, which may involve questions of immunity from *both* civil and criminal jurisdiction. Section 6.4 examines the immunities and protections accorded to envoys of a foreign state in a 'host state'—generally known as *diplomatic and consular immunity*.

Although the present chapter focuses on the immunities of states, it is worth noting that international organizations and their representatives also enjoy certain immunities from national jurisdiction. An international organization generally enjoys the immunities that are required for it to fulfil its functions without interference from local authorities.[4] In relation to the UN, this is reflected in article 105 of the UN Charter and in the 1946 Convention on the Privileges and Immunities of the United Nations, which governs the immunity and inviolability of UN property, funds and assets, communications and representatives and officials. The relations between an international organization and the state on whose territory the organization is located are often governed by a headquarters agreement.

6.2 State immunity

6.2.1 Introduction

State immunity is a principle of customary international law whose modalities have primarily been developed through national legislation and the jurisprudence of national courts.[5] Two conventions regulate state immunity. The European

---

[2] *Jurisdictional Immunities* (n 1) para. 57. See also ECtHR, *Al-Adsani v UK*, App. no. 35763/97, 21 November 2001, para. 54. See also *Arrest Warrant of 11 April 2000 (Congo v Belgium)*, Joint Separate Opinion of Judges Higgins, Kooijmans and Buergenthal [2002] ICJ Rep 3, para. 72. For a—critical—analysis of the basis of state immunity, see Xiaodong Yang, *State Immunity in International Law* (Cambridge University Press, 2012) 44–58.

[3] *Arrest Warrant of 11 April 2000 (Congo v Belgium)*, Judgment [2002] ICJ Rep 3, para. 53.

[4] *Difference Relating to Immunity from Legal Process of a Special Rapporteur of the Commission on Human Rights*, Advisory Opinion [1999] ICJ Rep 62, para. 66. On the immunity of international organizations, see August Reinisch (ed.), *The Privileges and Immunities of International Organizations in Domestic Courts* (Oxford University Press, 2013).

[5] See the discussion in Hazel Fox, *The Law of State Immunity* (2nd edn, Oxford University Press, 2008) 20–25.

Convention on State Immunity was adopted by the Council of Europe in 1972 and entered into force in 1976. By October 2018, however, only eight states had ratified it.[6] The UN Convention on Jurisdictional Immunities of States and Their Property—in this chapter referred to as the '2004 UN Convention'—was prepared by the International Law Commission (ILC) and adopted by the General Assembly in 2004. While it is not yet in force, many of its provisions reflect customary international law.

It is important to distinguish between pleas of immunity for *adjudicative* jurisdiction on the one hand, and *enforcement* jurisdiction on the other. While the former relates to the jurisdiction of a court to render a judgment in a matter, the latter concerns the exercise of administrative and executive powers by whatever measures or procedures and by whatever authorities of the forum state. The question of immunity from enforcement only arises *after* the issue of jurisdictional immunity has been dealt with and has decided against granting the foreign state immunity. Since the imposition of coercive measures is more intrusive than court proceedings, states are almost completely protected from enforcement.

In practice, state immunity from adjudication means that a state cannot be sued before a foreign court unless it gives its consent. Immunity is a procedural matter and it must therefore be dealt with *prior* to an inquiry into the merits of the case. Since it is unrelated to the substantive legal issues of the case, a finding by a national court that it must refrain from exercising its jurisdiction says nothing about the extent to which the foreign state has breached its legal obligations.[7] In reality, of course, a decision by a national court not to exercise jurisdiction will often mean that the substantive legal issues of the case are not dealt with. If the foreign state waives its immunity and consents to the national court's exercise of jurisdiction, however, the court can move forward with the case and deal with its merits.[8] As we shall see later, immunity from execution requires an additional and separate waiver.

According to the 2004 UN Convention, a state 'shall ensure that its courts determine on their own initiative' whether the immunity of a foreign state is respected.[9] It is therefore not necessary for the foreign state to appear before the court and invoke immunity.

In practice, immunity is just one of the ways a national court decides it lacks competence to deal with a dispute involving the interests of a foreign state.[10] In common law jurisdictions, a national court may also find that an issue should be dealt with by another branch of government, usually the executive,[11] or it may rely on the doctrine of 'acts of state' and decide that it lacks competence to rule on acts by foreign

---

[6] Council of Europe, 'Chart of signatures and ratifications of Treaty 074: European Convention on State Immunity', http://www.coe.int/en/web/conventions/full-list/-/conventions/treaty/074/signatures?p_auth=n6lNcTH9 (accessed 30 September 2018).

[7] *Jurisdictional Immunities* (n 1) para. 58.

[8] United Nations Convention on Jurisdictional Immunities of States and Their Property (adopted 2 December 2004), UN Doc. A/RES/59/38 (UN Convention on Jurisdictional Immunities), art. 7.

[9] Art. 6(1). See also art. 23(1)(c).   [10] For an overview, see Fox (n 5) 100–138.

[11] From US practice, see *Baker v Carr*, 639 US 186, 217 (1962) and more recently *Sarei v Rio Tinto plc*, 456 F.3d 1069 (2006).

governments and reject the case as *non-justiciable*.[12] In civil law jurisdictions, sensitive issues relating to the effects of laws in foreign states will usually be dealt with pursuant to principles of private international law and the doctrine of '*ordre public*'. This section deals only with immunity.

It is only independent and sovereign states that can assert state immunity. If there is doubt about an entity's statehood, national courts will usually follow instructions from the executive branch, often a ministry of foreign affairs. For the purposes of state immunity, the term 'state' includes the state and its various organs of government—ministries, diplomatic missions, armed forces etc.—as well as any other instrumentality that perform acts in the exercise of sovereign authority.[13] So, if an entity that would otherwise qualify as being 'private', for whatever reason, performs official sovereign acts, it may be entitled to assert state immunity.

We begin the discussion of state immunity with the principles of adjudicative jurisdiction and the distinction between official acts—*jure imperii*—and commercial acts—*jure gestionis* (Section 6.2.2). Attention then turns to the exceptions to state immunity (Section 6.2.3) and state immunity from adjudicative jurisdiction for violations of international law (Section 6.2.4). The chapter ends with a discussion of state immunity from enforcement jurisdiction (Section 6.2.5).

6.2.2 The distinction between sovereign and commercial acts in adjudicative jurisdiction

6.2.2.1 Background

Historically, the international law of state immunity from adjudication has progressed from absolute to restrictive immunity whereby immunity is only granted for *certain acts* of a state. Until the middle of the 20th century, a foreign state was generally entitled to immunity before national courts in relation to *any* subject matter, and it could therefore not be sued unless it consented. The only general exception related to immovable/'real' property, such as land or houses, which has always been found to form an integral part of the territorial state and not subject to any other laws.[14] The practical effect of absolute immunity was that a national court did not exercise jurisdiction over a dispute if one of the parties was a state. But as states became increasingly involved in commercial activities, states began to adopt a more nuanced view[15] and after the end of the Second World War, national courts started applying a *restrictive* approach to immunity from adjudicative jurisdiction.[16] In 1950 in *Hoffmann Dralle*

---

[12] See, inter alia, *Banco National de Cuba v Sabbatino*, 376 US 398, 428 (1964). For UK practice, see *Buttes Gas and Oil Co. v Hammer* [1982] AC 888, 938 (HL). For a more narrow conception of 'acts of state', see *Kuwait Airways Corp. v Iraqi Airways Co.* [2002] UKHL 19, [2002] 2 AC 883, [29], [114], [140], [149].

[13] UN Convention on Jurisdictional Immunities (n 8) art. 2(b). See also ILC, Draft Articles on Jurisdictional Immunities of States and Their Property, with commentaries, *Yearbook of the International Law Commission*, 1991, vol. II, Part Two, pp. 14–18, paras 5–19.

[14] Yang (n 2) 10–11.

[15] For a historical overview, see Draft Articles on Jurisdictional Immunities (n 13) pp. 36–40, paras 14–25.

[16] For developments in the US, see 'The Tate Letter' (1952) 26 *Department of State Bulletin* 984. For subsequent case law, see, inter alia, *Alfred Dunhill of London, Inc. v Republic of Cuba*, 425 US 682 (1976).

v *Czechoslovakia*, the Austrian Supreme Court found that a foreign state was only exempted from Austrian jurisdiction for sovereign acts, and in *Empire of Iran* in 1963, the German Federal Constitutional Court concluded that absolute immunity was no longer customary international law. It introduced a distinction between acts of a sovereign—*jure imperii*—and non-sovereign—*jure gestionis*—character.[17] In treaty law, restrictive immunity was introduced in both the 1972 European Convention on State Immunity[18] and the 2004 UN Convention.[19] Thus, according to article 10(1) of the latter, a state cannot invoke immunity from jurisdiction of a court of another state in proceedings arising out of 'commercial transactions' with a foreign national or juridical person. In 2013, the European Court of Human Rights (ECtHR) found that Russia—a signatory state to the 2004 UN Convention—had violated its obligations under the European Convention on Human Rights by relying on absolute immunity (immunity *ratione personae*).[20] Today, a foreign state only enjoys immunity from a territorial state's exercise of adjudicative jurisdiction for sovereign acts (acts *jure imperii*) and not for commercial acts (acts *jure gestionis*).

6.2.2.2 *Jure imperii* v *jure gestionis* acts

The reason for refusing state immunity from adjudicative jurisdiction for commercial activities is clear: when a state engages in commercial activities and competes with private actors it must be treated like its competitors and not be immune from scrutiny by the courts of the state in which it competes. In practice, however, it has been difficult to develop a workable definition of what a commercial act is.[21] Traditionally, the determination is made by applying a 'private individual test' and asking if the activity in question could be performed by a private individual. If yes, it is a commercial act.[22]

To further assist with the determination, certain approaches have been put forward. One such approach focuses on the *purpose* of the activity. Here, an activity is 'sovereign' (and thus immune) if performed for public/governmental purposes. The problem is, however, that states generally act for public purposes and the purpose test therefore ends up excluding a very wide range of acts from adjudication. In *Empire of Iran*, the German Federal Constitutional Court therefore rejected the purpose test[23] and instead focused on the *nature* of the activity.[24] Thus, if the *type* of act cannot be performed by a private individual, it is sovereign. Since private individuals can purchase most goods and commodities, the vast majority of contracts for purchases and acquisitions entered into by states would then be commercial—and thus not immune—acts. In 1999, the

---

[17] *Empire of Iran* (1963) 45 ILR 57, 79–81. Only later did courts in the UK begin to abandon absolute immunity, see *Owners of the Philippine Admiral v Wallem Shipping (Hong Kong) Ltd (The Philippine Admiral)* [1977] AC 373 (Privy Council).

[18] Art. 7(1).   [19] See Part III of the Convention.

[20] ECtHR, *Oleynikov v Russia*, App. no. 36703/04, 14 March 2013, paras 60–61.

[21] For an overview, see Fox (n 5) 502–532; Yang (n 2) 75–132.

[22] From the UK, see *I Congreso del Partido* [1983] AC 244, 262, from the US, *Argentina v Weltover*, 504 US 607, 614–617 (1992) and, from Austria, *Holubek v The Government of the United States*, Austrian Supreme Court, 10 February 1961.

[23] *Empire of Iran* (n 17) 27. See also *Argentina v Weltover* (n 22) 614.

[24] *Empire of Iran* (n 17) 80. US Foreign Sovereign Immunities Act 1976, § 1603(d).

Danish Supreme Court found that an embassy's purchase of airline tickets as a private law transaction was a non-immune activity.[25] But while the purpose test may be over-inclusive, a nature test may be the opposite because it effectively ignores the fact that states sometimes exercise their sovereignty through seemingly commercial activities.

In practice, therefore, distinguishing between commercial and non-commercial acts often requires a *contextual* approach taking account of *both* the purpose and the nature of the activity. According to the 2004 UN Convention, the determination of what is a commercial transaction should be made with regard 'primarily to the nature of the contract or transaction'. However, 'its purpose should also be taken into account if the parties to the contract or transaction have so agreed, or if, in the practice of the State of the forum, that purpose is relevant to determining the non-commercial character of the contract or transaction'.[26] In *Holland v Lampen-Wolfe*, the UK House of Lords adopted a contextual approach in a case concerning proceedings for defamatory damages in the UK against a US official for statements made in the individual's official capacity as an educational officer at a US base in the UK. Although the act in question—the writing of a memorandum by a civilian educational services officer in connection with an educational programme provided by civilian staff employed by a university—did not appear at first sight to be a sovereign act (*jure imperii*), the court found otherwise. The court referred to the broader context of the statement, including where and to whom the educational programme was provided and whom it was designed to benefit. Among other things, the court noted that the 'whole activity was designed as part of the process of maintaining forces and associated civilians on the base by U.S. personnel to serve the needs of the U.S. military authorities'.[27]

Some states try to overcome the difficulties of distinguishing between sovereign and commercial activities by enacting legislation that lists acts deemed to be of a non-sovereign and thus non-immune character.[28] According to article 2(1)(c) of the 2004 UN Convention, commercial transactions are: (i) any commercial contract or transaction for the sale of goods or supply of services; (ii) any contract for a loan or other transaction of a financial nature, including any obligation of guarantee or of indemnity in respect of any such loan or transaction; (iii) any other contract or transaction of a commercial, industrial, trading or professional nature, but not including a contract of employment of persons.

6.2.3 **Other exceptions to state immunity**

Commercial activities are not the only exception to state immunity in the 2004 UN Convention. Articles 11–17 supplement the general exception for commercial activities by listing the most important examples of activities that may (also) be deemed to be of a non-immune character. One such example is *employment contracts*.[29] Such

---

[25] U.1999.939H. See also *Argentina v Weltover* (n 22) 615.

[26] Art. 2(2). See also Draft Articles on Jurisdictional Immunities (n 13) para. 27.

[27] *Holland v Lampen-Wolfe* [2000] 1 WLR 1573, 1576ff, 1581ff (HL).

[28] See UK State Immunity Act 1978, ss 2–11. See also US Foreign Sovereign Immunities Act 1976, §§ 1604, 1605 and 1607.

[29] For an overview of the rules, see Fox (n 5) 547–563 and Yang (n 2) 132–198.

contracts merit specialized treatment because the traditional way of distinguishing between *jure imperii* and *jure gestionis* activities is of little assistance. Since private individuals and companies hire people all the time and there is nothing inherently 'governmental' about employing someone, a nature test would make all employment contracts *jure gestionis* acts and thus non-immune. This, however, is not acceptable to states, and courts often grant extensive immunity to states in proceedings concerning employment contracts. Thus, article 11 lists a number of instances where a foreign state can invoke immunity from adjudicative jurisdiction in relation to an employment contract for work performed on the territory of the forum state. A foreign state remains immune, for example, if the employee has 'been recruited to perform functions in the *exercise of governmental authority*'.[30] State immunity is generally also maintained in relation to *diplomatic missions*.[31]

Another exception to state immunity is found in article 12 of the 2004 UN Convention, which excludes immunity:

> in a proceeding which relates to pecuniary compensation for death or injury to the person, or damage to or loss of tangible property, caused by an act or omission which is alleged to be attributable to the State, if the act or omission occurred in whole or in part in the territory of that other State and if the author of the act or omission was present in that territory at the time of the act or omission.

The 1972 European Convention on State Immunity contains a similar provision.[32] This exception is primarily meant to apply to insurable risks from injuries and damage caused by traffic accidents and it does not cover non-physical damage, such as proceedings related to allegedly false or defamatory statements.[33] Since the exception only covers wrongful conduct that has occurred or been committed in the territory of the forum state where the author of the act or omission is also present in the forum state, it similarly does not justify refusing immunity when injury or damage is inflicted abroad, such as in the territory of the foreign state itself.[34] The application of article 12 to acts committed by a state on the territory of the forum state *in times of armed conflict* has been debated. In Greece and Italy, national courts have found that Germany could *not* invoke state immunity for civil claims arising from German atrocities committed during the Second World War.[35] In *Jurisdictional Immunities of the State*, however, the ICJ found that customary international law affords a state immunity for claims arising from *jure imperii* acts committed on the territory of another state by its armed forces

---

[30] Art. 11(2)(a).

[31] Art. 11(2)(b). Relevant rules are also found in the Vienna Convention on Diplomatic Relations (VCDR) (adopted 18 April 1961, entered into force 24 April 1964), 500 UNTS 95 and the Vienna Convention on Consular Relations (VCCR) (adopted 24 April 1963, entered into force 19 March 1967), 596 UNTS 261. See also ECtHR, *Fogarty v UK*, App. no. 37112/97, 21 November 2001, paras 37–38.

[32] See art. 11.   [33] Draft Articles on Jurisdictional Immunities (n 13) para. 5.

[34] The practical application of the exception in art. 12 is not uniform and a number of issues remain unresolved. For ECtHR practice, see *McElhinney v Ireland*, App. no. 31253/96, 21 November 2001.

[35] For practice in Greece, see *Prefecture of Voiotia v Federal Republic of Germany*, Supreme Court (Areios Pagos) case No. 11/2000, 4 May 2000. But see also *Margellos v Federal Republic of Germany*, case No. 6/2002, Supreme Court of Greece, 17 September 2002. For Italian practice, see *Ferrini v Federal Republic of Germany*, Corte di Cassazione (Sezioni Unite), judgment No. 5044 of 6 November 2003, registered 11 March 2004 (2004) 87 *Rivista diritto internazionale* 539.

and other organs of the state during the course of armed conflict.[36] It bears mentioning, however, that a number of the ICJ judges dissented.[37]

The third exception to state immunity worth noting concerns the issue of immovable property located on the territory of the forum state. As we saw earlier, even in the age of absolute immunity it was well established that an exception from immunity was made in relation to immovable/'real' property situated in the forum state. Immovable property forms an integral part of the forum state and is therefore not subject to other laws—in Latin this is known as the *lex situs* rule. This is reflected in article 13(a) of the 2004 UN Convention.[38] The lack of immunity for immovable property does not, however, alter the privileges and immunities a foreign state enjoys under other parts of international law with regard to its diplomatic missions and other representative offices.[39] However, premises used as a private residence by a member of a diplomatic mission are covered by the exception from immunity, and there is also practice to support the conclusion that a national court may exercise jurisdiction over the premises of the diplomatic mission itself when it is purely the ownership or title that is in issue if there is no interference with the performance of diplomatic duties.[40]

6.2.4 **State immunity and violations of international law**

Since state immunity serves as a procedural bar to the exercise of jurisdiction by a national court, the court must dismiss a case against a state entitled to state immunity, regardless of the nature of the allegations against the state. In recent decades, some national courts have nevertheless found that a foreign state cannot assert state immunity in relation to civil claims arising from alleged violations of *international* law, including breaches of fundamental human rights.[41] In the previous subsection, reference was made to some of the cases that also concerned state immunity for acts committed in times of armed conflict. In 2000, in *Distomo*, the Supreme Court of Greece found that Germany was not protected by state immunity in relation to claims for compensation for atrocities committed by German armed forces during the German occupation of Greece in the Second World War.[42] The 2004 UN Convention does not include any exceptions to state immunity for civil claims arising from international crimes, but the question was treated extensively by the ICJ in *Jurisdictional Immunities of the State*, where Italy argued that Germany was not entitled to immunity because its acts involved the most serious violations of rules of international law of a peremptory character (*jus cogens*).[43] The ICJ did not agree with Italy, however.[44] The Court could not find any practice that supported the Italian argument, and it noted how a state's entitlement to immunity does not depend upon the 'gravity of the act ... or the peremptory nature of the rule which it is alleged to

---

[36] *Jurisdictional Immunities* (n 1) paras 72–78.

[37] See, inter alia, the Dissenting Opinions of Judge ad hoc Gaja and Judge Yusuf. See also the discussion in the Separate Opinion of Judge Bennouna. See also Separate Opinion of Judge Koroma, para. 7.

[38] See also European Convention on State Immunity (n 6) art. 9.

[39] See UN Convention on Jurisdictional Immunities (n 8) art. 3.   [40] Fox (n 5) 594–595.

[41] For an overview, see ibid, 139–166. Immunity from individual criminal responsibility for international crimes for state representatives is discussed in Section 6.3.

[42] *Prefecture of Voiotia v Federal Republic of Germany* (n 35).

[43] *Jurisdictional Immunities* (n 1) para. 61.   [44] Ibid, para. 81.

have violated'.[45] The Court referred to case law from the ECtHR according to which a state is not 'deprived of immunity by reason of the fact that it is accused of serious violations of international human rights law or the international law of armed conflict'.[46] It also rejected the notion that upholding state immunity would conflict with the existence of *jus cogens* rules from which no derogation is permitted.[47] In 2006, the UK House of Lords found that Saudi Arabia was entitled to state immunity in relation to alleged violations of the prohibition against torture in the UN Convention against Torture.[48]

6.2.5 **Immunity from enforcement**

As already noted, a distinction exists between state immunity from *adjudicative* jurisdiction and immunity from subsequent *enforcement* measures of the orders of a court by the host state. Since the issue of immunity from enforcement only arises after jurisdictional immunity has been dealt with and a national court has decided the case against the foreign state, immunity from enforcement constitutes 'the last bastion of State immunity'.[49] The different treatment of the two kinds of jurisdiction means that the principles of state immunity for each are distinct and must be so applied. One of the consequences is that, as already noted, a waiver of immunity from execution must be expressed separately. This is also reflected in article 20 of the 2004 UN Convention.

Unlike immunity from adjudication, immunity from enforcement is by and large absolute. It is therefore possible that a national court does not find that a foreign state is immune from proceedings but that it is immune from enforcement measures. In *Jurisdictional Immunities of the State*, the ICJ found that it could rule on whether a measure of constraint on property owned by the German state in Italy violated Germany's immunity from enforcement without determining if the underlying decision by a Greek court against Germany that formed the basis for the constraint was in itself a breach of the rules on jurisdictional immunity.[50]

Historically, states have been very reluctant to accept limitations on immunity from enforcement,[51] but in response to the introduction of restrictive adjudicative jurisdiction as discussed earlier, a number of continental European states slowly began to permit enforcement measures against property used for commercial purposes located in the forum state.[52] Now, international law distinguishes between property located in the forum state used for public purposes and property used for commercial purposes. Only the former category is protected from enforcement.[53]

---

[45] Ibid, para. 84.

[46] Ibid, para. 90. For ECtHR case law, see *Al-Adsani v UK* (n 2) para. 66 (regarding alleged torture). See also *Kalogeropoulou v Greece and Germany*, App. no. 59021/00, 12 December 2002, 9.

[47] *Jurisdictional Immunities* (n 1) para. 95.

[48] *Jones v Ministry of Interior of Kingdom of Saudi Arabia et al.* [2006] UKHL 26, [33].

[49] Draft Articles on Jurisdictional Immunities (n 13) para. 2.

[50] *Jurisdictional Immunities* (n 1) para. 114.   [51] For an overview, see Fox (n 5) 600–609.

[52] See the overview in August Reinisch, 'European Court Practice Concerning State Immunity from Enforcement Measures' (2006) 17 *European Journal of International Law* 803.

[53] See also *The 'Ara Libertad' (Argentina v Ghana)*, Provisional Measures, Order of 15 December 2012, ITLOS Rep 21.

The 2004 UN Convention covers immunity from enforcement in Part IV—articles 18–21. Article 18 concerns immunity for pre-judgment measures and article 19 deals with immunity for post-judgment measures. In both instances, enforcement measures require that the foreign state has either expressly consented to such measures or has allocated or earmarked property for the satisfaction of the particular claim. In addition, post-judgment measures of enforcement can only be taken if the property in question is based in the forum state and is specifically used or intended to be used by the foreign state for commercial purposes, and the enforcement measure is taken against property that 'has a connection with the entity against which the proceeding was directed'.[54] With regard to the use of the property, then, it is purpose and not nature that is decisive. Article 21 then lists a number of types of property which due to their purpose or use are considered to be non-commercial and thus immune. These include bank accounts for use in the performance of functions of a diplomatic mission or consular post, military property, property of a central bank or other monetary authority, property that is part of the cultural heritage of the state or part of its archives and property that forms part of an exhibition of objects of scientific, cultural or historical interest.

The issue of enforcement of a local judgment against real property used *in part* for commercial purposes was discussed by the Swedish Supreme Court in *Sedelmayer v Russian Federation*. Here, the court concluded that state immunity did not preclude execution against a multi-unit building owned by the Russian state whose units were for the most part rented out to either individuals employed at the Russian embassy or trade mission or otherwise used in connection with Swedish–Russian scientific exchanges or other governmental activities.[55] Since the building was only used for official purposes to a limited extent, the property was not immune. In *Jurisdictional Immunities of the State*, the ICJ concluded that the measures of constraint taken by the Italian authorities against property owned by the German state in the absence of express German consent violated international law. The Court noted that the property in question—a cultural centre intended to promote cultural exchanges between Germany and Italy—was used for governmental non-commercial purposes and thus for sovereign purposes.[56]

6.3 The immunities of state representatives

6.3.1 Introduction

State representatives enjoy certain immunities from national jurisdiction because they 'personify' the state on whose behalf they act and because they need protection from national jurisdiction in order to fulfil their functions as state representatives.[57] As the

---

[54] Art. 19(c).

[55] *Sedelmayer v Russian Federation*, No. O 170–10. 2011. See the discussion in Pål Wrange, '*Sedelmayer v Russian Federation*' (2012) 106 *American Journal of International Law* 347.

[56] *Jurisdictional Immunities* (n 1) paras 119–120.

[57] For an overview of the different rationales for immunity for state representatives, see Roman Anatolevich Kolodkin, 'Preliminary Report on immunity of State officials from foreign criminal jurisdiction' (ILC, 2008), UN Doc. A/CN.4/601, paras 84–97. See also Hazel Fox, *The Law of State Immunity* (Oxford University Press, 2015) 547.

ICJ noted in *Arrest Warrant*, a foreign minister can only perform his or her official functions if the individual can travel freely and remain in constant communication with not only the home government but also with diplomatic missions and representatives of other states.[58] The immunities are therefore not granted for the personal benefit of the representative but so that the individual can fulfil his or her official functions.[59]

At the outset, a few important points must be noted. First, the extent of immunity offered to various representatives differs substantially. While some representatives enjoy almost absolute immunity, others enjoy more limited protection. Thus, when determining what immunity a particular state representative is entitled to it is important to identify the category of state representatives to which the representative belongs. The second important point to note is that the extent of immunity offered to state representatives revolves around an important distinction between immunity *ratione personae*—or 'personal immunity'—and immunity *ratione materiae*—'functional immunity'. Immunity *ratione personae* flows from the *position* a representative holds in a state, and as we shall see in Section 6.3.2, it is enjoyed only by a small group of individuals with high-level governmental positions as well as by diplomatic agents and by representatives on 'special missions'. As a form of immunity, it applies to both *official* and *private* acts as well as to acts committed both *before* and *while* the representative occupied his or her public position. Immunity *ratione materiae*, on the other hand, relates to the functions the representative performs and is enjoyed by all state representatives. It does not apply to private acts but applies after the representative leaves his or her position in respect of public acts committed while in public service.

The overview begins with the immunities of high-ranking state representatives (Section 6.3.2) before we examine the immunity of other state representatives (Section 6.3.3).

6.3.2 **The immunity of certain high-ranking representatives**

6.3.2.1 Introduction

A limited number of state representatives are so closely tied to the sovereignty of the state that they enjoy particularly extensive legal protection.[60] They hold a special position and enjoy immunity *ratione personae*/personal immunity. *Heads of state* have always had a privileged status in international law and in earlier periods of international law there was a tendency to consider the ruler of a state as the embodiment of the state.[61] In *Questions of Mutual Assistance in Criminal Matters*, the ICJ stated that the immunity of heads of state is derived from customary international law.[62] In *Arrest*

---

[58] *Arrest Warrant* (n 3) para. 53.   [59] Ibid.

[60] This appears to be accepted everywhere apart from in the United States where immunity for heads of state seemingly remains 'a matter of grace and comity, rather than a matter of right'. See, inter alia, *Lafontant v Aristide*, 844 F.Supp. 128, 132 (1994) and *Flatow v Islamic Republic of Iran et al.*, 999 F.Supp. 1, 24 (DDC 1998).

[61] See also Lord Millett in *R v Bow Street Metropolitan Stipendiary Magistrate, ex p. Pinochet Ugarte (No. 3)* [2000] 1 AC 147, 269 (HL).

[62] *Certain Questions of Mutual Assistance in Criminal Matters (Djibouti v France)*, Judgment [2008] ICJ Rep 177, para. 174.

Warrant, the Court found that not just a head of state but also a head of government and a minister for foreign affairs enjoy personal immunity from jurisdiction in other states.[63] In the light of the representative powers these representatives possess, this is not surprising. For example, as we saw in Chapter 3, these representatives may enter into legally binding commitments on behalf of their states without having to produce full powers.[64] In 2001, a French court adopted a *de facto* assessment and concluded that Muammar Gaddafi was to be considered the 'head of state' of Libya even though he did not formally appear to qualify under the Libyan constitution.[65] While immunity *ratione personae* would appear to be limited to the head of state, head of government and the minister for foreign affairs,[66] UK courts have found that an Israeli minister of defence and a Chinese minister for commerce and international trade also benefitted from personal immunity.[67] In *Khurts Bat*, however, personal immunity was denied to a head of an office of national security.[68]

6.3.2.2 The protection offered

Personal immunity offers widespread protection from both civil and criminal prosecutions and in relation to official as well as private acts. Protection from *civil jurisdiction* is less extensive, however, and certain acts performed in a private capacity do not seem to be immune from adjudicative jurisdiction. For practical purposes, the protection offered may be parallel to that enjoyed by diplomatic agents (see Section 6.4).[69] It follows that protection is unavailable for certain acts relating to private immovable property, succession in which the official is involved as an executor, administrator, heir or legatee as a private person or professional or commercial activities exercised outside their official functions.[70]

Immunity *ratione personae* from *criminal jurisdiction* applies to both acts done in both an official as well as in a private capacity and to conduct performed both before and during the period in office.[71] And unlike the situation that applies to civil claims, there is no need to distinguish between immunity from jurisdiction and immunity from execution with regard to criminal jurisdiction. Criminal jurisdiction refers to *all* criminal

---

[63] *Arrest Warrant* (n 3) para. 51.

[64] Vienna Convention on the Law of Treaties (adopted 23 May 1969, entered into force 27 January 1980), 1155 UNTS 331, art. 7(2).

[65] *Arrêt* of the Cour de Cassation, 13 March 2001, No. 1414.

[66] See also Concepción Escobar Hernández, 'Second Report on the immunity of State officials from foreign criminal jurisdiction' (ILC, 2013), UN Doc. A/CN.4/661, paras 56–68.

[67] See, respectively, the ruling of 12 February 2004 in the case regarding General Shaul Mofaz, and the ruling of 8 November 2005 in the case regarding Re Bo Xilai, quoted in Kolodkin, 'Preliminary Report on immunity of State officials from foreign criminal jurisdiction' (n 57) para. 118. See also the debate in paras 118–121.

[68] *Khurts Bat v Investigating Judge of the German Federal Court* [2011] EWHC 2029 (Admin). For an extensive overview and debate, see Andrew Sanger, 'Immunity of State Officials from the Criminal Jurisdiction of a Foreign State' (2013) 62 *International and Comparative Law Quarterly* 193.

[69] See generally *Certain Questions of Mutual Assistance* (n 62) para. 174.   [70] VCDR art. 31(1).

[71] *Arrest Warrant* (n 3) para. 55. See also *Prosecutor v Omar Hassan Ahmad al-Bashir*, Decision on the Cooperation of the Democratic Republic of the Congo Regarding Omar al-Bashir's Arrest and Surrender to the Court, ICC-02/05-01/09 (9 April 2014), para. 25. In *Certain Questions of Mutual Assistance* (n 62) the ICJ also concluded that the rules on the inviolability of diplomatic agents in art. 29 of the VCDR are equally applicable to heads of state: see para. 174.

procedural measures in respect of a foreign representative. In *Arrest Warrant*, the ICJ stated that the protection extends to 'any act of authority of another State which would hinder' the representative in performing his or her duties.[72] The state that considers exercising criminal jurisdiction against a foreign head of state, head of government or a minister for foreign affairs must consider the issue of immunity and make its own determination as to whether or not immunity bars the proceedings.[73]

Importantly, personal immunity does not offer absolute protection from criminal jurisdiction. In *Arrest Warrant*, the Court stated that criminal prosecution of a minister for foreign affairs is possible in four circumstances.[74] First, the minister can be criminally prosecuted by courts in his or her *own* state. Secondly, prosecution in the forum state is possible if the home state agrees to the prosecution by waiving immunity. A waiver of immunity must, however, be express.[75] Thirdly, as we shall return to in Chapter 15, criminal prosecution may occur before international courts. As a fourth and final avenue for possible criminal prosecution, the Court stated that a foreign minister can be prosecuted *after* his or her term expires for acts committed either *prior* or *subsequent* to the period of office or for *private acts* committed during the period in office. By implication, the Court thereby seemed to conclude that immunity remains intact in relation to *all* official acts performed during the period in office. As we shall see in Section 6.3.3.2, however, this is a statement that may no longer be correct.

6.3.3 The immunity of other state representatives who perform official acts

6.3.3.1 Introduction

As we have just seen, only a limited number of very high-ranking state representatives enjoy immunity for both official and private acts—immunity *ratione personae*. All other state representatives are merely protected by immunity in relation to the acts they perform on behalf of the state they represent—immunity *ratione materiae* (functional immunity). Functional immunity is derived from the understanding that it is not the representative but the state that he or she represents that is the real object of the proceedings. The grant of immunity therefore prevents an applicant from circumventing state immunity by bringing a case against the representative of the state rather than the state. Like immunity *ratione personae*, functional immunity can be waived by the state on whose behalf the state official has acted.

The determination of whether conduct is 'official' or 'personal' is made according to the principles on state responsibility and attribution of conduct that will be discussed in Chapter 7.[76] Here, a few points are worth noting. First, as long as an act is performed

---

[72] *Arrest Warrant* (n 3) para. 54. See also *Certain Questions of Mutual Assistance* (n 62) para. 170.

[73] Roman Anatolevich Kolodkin, 'Third Report on immunity of State officials from foreign criminal jurisdiction' (ILC, 2011), UN Doc. A/CN.4/646, para. 19.

[74] *Arrest Warrant* (n 3) para. 61.   [75] Ibid, para. 41.

[76] See also Eileen Denza, *Diplomatic Law: A Commentary on the Vienna Convention on Diplomatic Relations* (2nd edn, Oxford University Press, 1998) 363.

by an individual with official authority ('under the colour of authority') it is an 'official' act. Secondly, acts that fall outside the official functions of a state representative—conduct *ultra vires*—are also official acts if performed in a public capacity.[77] The same conclusion applies to illegal acts carried out by a state representative. Indeed, since it is precisely in cases of suspicion of unlawful conduct that the question of jurisdiction arises, it would run counter to the whole idea of immunity to exclude illegal acts from immunity *ratione materiae*. As we shall return to below, however, it is hotly debated whether there are exceptions to criminal immunity, in particular for international crimes. It is also worth noting that the distinction between acts *jure imperii* and *jure gestionis* is irrelevant for the purposes of attribution and that nothing precludes classifying a commercial act as an official act. In practice, then, a representative who performs a commercial act on behalf of a state enjoys immunity whereas the state does not (due to the commercial character of the act).

6.3.3.2 The protection offered

Immunity *ratione materiae* protects all state officials from *civil proceedings* in respect of their official acts. If it were otherwise, an applicant would be able to circumvent state immunity by bringing a case against the representative who represents the state. This is also reflected in the 2004 UN Convention, according to which the concept of a 'state' for the purposes of immunity includes 'representatives of the State acting in that capacity'.[78] Similar conclusions were reached by the UK House of Lords in *Jones v Ministry of Interior of Kingdom of Saudi Arabia et al.*[79] and by a Canadian appeals court in *Bouzari v Islamic Republic of Iran*.[80] In both cases, the courts rejected the argument that an exception to immunity from civil proceedings could be made in relation to allegations of breach of the (*jus cogens*) prohibition against torture.

Functional immunity from *criminal proceedings* for non-high-ranking state representatives differs from that applied to *civil proceedings* and *criminal proceedings against high-ranking state officials*. In contrast to what applies in relation to the criminal immunity of high-ranking state officials, the forum state does not appear to be obliged to consider the immunity of other state representatives unless the foreign state invokes it.[81] So if the state of a non-high-ranking representative wants to protect its own official from foreign criminal prosecution it must notify the forum state and assert that the representative acted in an official capacity and should thus enjoy immunity. If not, the forum state may proceed with the case. In *Certain Questions of Mutual Assistance in Criminal Matters*, the ICJ concluded that the head of national security in Mongolia was not entitled to immunity *ratione materiae* and that this was partly because his home state had never invoked it.[82]

---

[77] See also Draft Articles on Jurisdictional Immunities (n 13) art. 7.   [78] Art. 2(1)(b)(iv).

[79] *Jones v Ministry of Interior of Kingdom of Saudi Arabia et al.* (n 48).

[80] *Bouzari v Islamic Republic of Iran*, 71 OR (3d) 675, para. 91.

[81] Kolodkin, 'Third Report on immunity of State officials from foreign criminal jurisdiction' (n 73) para. 18. See also Ingrid Wuerth, 'Pinochet's Legacy Reassessed' (2012) 106 *American Journal of International Law* 731, 745–747.

[82] *Certain Questions of Mutual Assistance* (n 62) para. 196.

Unlike the circumstances with regard to the functional immunity of non-high-ranking officials in civil proceedings, it is not clear if state representatives are always immune in relation to criminal prosecution before national courts. As we saw earlier, in *Arrest Warrant* the ICJ indicated that a high-ranking state representative (in the absence of a waiver of immunity) remains immune after the end of his or her term for *official* acts committed during their period in office. National case law is not, however, exactly in line with that statement. Two potential exceptions to immunity *ratione materiae* are currently under debate.

First, a number of national cases indicate that functional immunity from criminal jurisdiction may not always apply in relation to official acts committed *on the territory of the forum state*. The existence of a territorial exception to criminal immunity seems to be supported by the ILC's first Special Rapporteur.[83] The rationale for refusing criminal immunity in such circumstances would be the jurisdictional priority of the forum state on its own territory. It would also correlate with article 12 of the UN Convention discussed in Section 6.2.3 whereby a state cannot invoke immunity from civil jurisdiction in relation to pecuniary compensation for death or injury to the person, or damage to or loss of tangible property, caused by an act or omission that occurred in whole or in part on the territory of that other state.

The second possible exception to immunity *ratione materiae* from criminal jurisdiction relates to international crimes.[84] In 1999, the House of Lords in the UK concluded that immunity did not protect the former head of state of Chile—August Pinochet—from extradition to criminal prosecution in Spain for acts of torture.[85] A majority of the law lords found that Pinochet was not immune after his official term had ended in relation to an established international crime where both the forum and the home states had accepted that they were under an obligation to prosecute. The House of Lords limited the conclusion to torture. After *Pinochet*, a number of arguments have been advanced in support of the general conclusion that functional immunity from criminal jurisdiction cannot be asserted in relation to international crimes.[86] Some argue, for example, that international crimes cannot be considered official acts that are protected by immunity. It is, however, difficult to see why the gravity of a criminal offence alters the attribution of the act, especially since it is often precisely the presence of a complete state apparatus that enables the perpetration of the worst atrocities. After all, most international crimes are perpetrated in furtherance of some sort of public policy, however reprehensible. Another argument holds that the prohibition against the commission of certain core international crimes, including torture, is of a

---

[83] Roman Anatolevich Kolodkin, 'Second Report on immunity of State officials from foreign criminal jurisdiction' (ILC, 2000), UN Doc. A/CN.4/631, paras 82 and 94. But see also *Pinochet* (n 61) and the discussion of that judgment in Sanger (n 68) 207–209.

[84] See also the overview in Lee M. Caplan, 'State Immunity, Human Rights, and *Jus Cogens*: A Critique of the Normative Hierarchy Theory' (2003) 97 *American Journal of International Law* 741.

[85] *Pinochet* (n 61). See also Hazel Fox, Colin Warbrick and Dominic McGoldrick, 'The Pinochet Case No. 3' (1999) 48 *International and Comparative Law Quarterly* 687.

[86] See, inter alia, Antonio Cassese and others, *Cassese's International Criminal Law* (3rd edn, Oxford University Press, 2013) 242–246 and 320. See also Andrea Bianchi, 'Immunity versus Human Rights: The Pinochet Case' (1999) 10 *European Journal of International Law* 237.

peremptory/*jus cogens* nature and therefore overrides any claim of immunity *ratione materiae*.[87] As discussed previously, however, in *Jurisdictional Immunities of the State* the ICJ did not find that immunity depended upon the 'gravity of the act',[88] and while the case concerned immunity from civil and not criminal jurisdiction, it is hard to see why the outcome would revolve around the type of jurisdiction. In addition, the peremptory nature of some international crimes relates to the *commission* of the crime and not to the obligation to *prosecute*. Thus, it is the state that perpetrates the crime of, say, genocide or torture, that violates an obligation of a *jus cogens* nature, and not the state that fails to prosecute.[89] A further argument bases the non-availability of immunity *ratione materiae* on case law from national courts and the emergence of an alleged customary law-based exception to immunity. National cases are not, however, as clear-cut as their proponents would like to portray them. In many cases, immunity is not even discussed by the courts, and while this could be due to an understanding that a plea of immunity would be unsuccessful, it could also be explained by the absence of an assertion of immunity on behalf of the foreign state or by the existence of a waiver of immunity—either explicit or implicit—by that state.[90]

The law appears to be unclear.[91] While the present author is not persuaded by the current practice, a majority of the members of the International Law Commission seems to hold the view (as does the current Special Rapporteur) that functional immunity is (now) unavailable in relation to the following international crimes: genocide, crimes against humanity, war crimes, torture and enforced disappearances.[92] As we shall return to in Chapter 15, some international crimes are no longer only attributed to the state on whose behalf they are committed but also to the individual officials who perpetrate them.

6.4 Diplomatic immunities and protection

6.4.1 Introduction

In day-to-day relations, the majority of interstate communication is conducted through the many diplomatic missions that states have established around the world. Due to their physical location on the territory of another state, diplomatic representatives, their staff and their premises find themselves in a particularly vulnerable situation and in need of extensive international protection. The rules that govern the rights

---

[87] *Arrest Warrant* (n 3) Dissenting Opinion of Judge Al-Khasawneh, para. 7.

[88] Ibid, para. 84. See also *Al-Adsani v UK* (n 2) para. 66 and *Jones v Ministry of Interior of Kingdom of Saudi Arabia et al.* (n 48) para. 33.

[89] See also Dapo Akande and Sangeeta Shah, 'Immunities of State Officials, International Crimes, and Foreign Domestic Courts' (2011) 21 *European Journal of International Law* 815, 835–836.

[90] For a critical discussion, see Kolodkin, 'Second Report on immunity of State officials from foreign criminal jurisdiction' (n 83) paras 68–71. See also Wüerth (n 81).

[91] For discussions, see Fox (n 57) 560–561 and Akande and Shah (n 89) 842–846.

[92] See draft art. 7(1), as proposed by the Special Rapporteur in her fifth report, and the discussion in Report of the International Law Commission, 69th Session (1 May–2 June and 3 July–4 August 2017), A/72/10.

and privileges of diplomatic representatives and missions are primarily derived from functional needs and the understanding that state representatives must enjoy certain privileges in order to perform their official functions. Accordingly, the purpose of diplomatic law is to benefit not the state representative in his or her personal capacity but the state he or she represents. The relevant rules are found in the 1961 Vienna Convention on Diplomatic Relations (VCDR), which has been ratified by the majority of states and the provisions of which generally reflect customary international law.[93] In *Tehran Hostages*, the ICJ noted the 'extreme importance' of the law of diplomatic protection, 'carefully constructed by mankind over a period of centuries, the maintenance of which is vital for the security and well-being of the complex international community of the present day'.

The purpose of diplomatic law is to strike a balance between the legitimate concerns of the sending state and those of the state in which the representatives and the diplomatic mission are based. Diplomatic relations are always based on mutual consent, and states are not obligated to enter into diplomatic relations with each other. A host state is always free to revoke its consent to the presence of a diplomatic mission of another state without having to offer any justification.[94] In addition, the host state must give its consent and thus accept the appointment of the head of the mission (and the military attaché) by 'accreditation'.[95] The host state may at any time and without justification declare that the head of the mission or any other member of the diplomatic mission is not welcome on its territory—'*persona non grata*'—in which event the sending state must recall the person or terminate his or her functions with the mission.[96] If the sending state does not do so 'within a reasonable time', the host state may refuse to recognize the individual concerned as a member of the mission.

In this section we examine not only the immunity from national jurisdiction offered by international law to diplomatic representatives but also other forms of protection afforded to diplomats, diplomatic premises and their communications. The relevant rules are found in articles 29–39 of the VCDR. The overview begins with the immunities offered to diplomatic agents (Section 6.4.2) and then turns to the other forms of protection offered by international law (Section 6.4.3). Brief attention is then aimed at the obligations of the sending state (Section 6.4.4). To supplement the treatment of diplomatic protection, we will also briefly discuss consular relations (Section 6.4.5) and the immunities afforded to so-called 'special missions' or 'ad hoc diplomacy' (Section 6.4.6).

6.4.2 **Immunity of diplomatic agents**

Article 31 of the VCDR stipulates that a diplomatic agent enjoys immunity *ratione personae* and has (full) immunity from the criminal jurisdiction of the host state.

---

[93] *United States Diplomatic and Consular Staff in Tehran (United States v Iran)*, Judgment [1980] ICJ Rep 3, para. 62.
[94] See also VCDR art. 2.   [95] Ibid, art. 4.   [96] Ibid, art. 9(1).

Diplomatic agents also benefit from civil and administrative immunity, except in proceedings that relate to one of the following:

(a) A real action relating to private immovable property situated in the territory of the receiving State, unless he holds it on behalf of the sending State for the purposes of the mission;

(b) An action relating to succession in which the diplomatic agent is involved as executor, administrator, heir or legatee as a private person and not on behalf of the sending State;

(c) An action relating to any professional or commercial activity exercised by the diplomatic agent in the receiving State outside his official functions.

Article 31 also specifies that a diplomatic agent is not obliged to give evidence as a witness.

With regard to immunity from enforcement jurisdiction, no such measures can be taken unless they relate to the three exceptions mentioned above and provided the measures taken do not infringe upon the inviolability of the diplomatic agent or his or her residence.[97] In general, and with few exceptions, diplomatic agents are also exempt from all dues and taxes[98] and military obligations.[99] The diplomat's family—unless they are nationals of the host state—enjoy the same immunities.[100] Provided they are not nationals or permanently residing in the host state, members of the administrative and technical staff of a mission, as well as their families, are afforded similar immunities to those of diplomatic agents, except that they enjoy immunity from civil and administrative jurisdiction only in relation to official—and not private—acts (immunity *ratione materiae*).[101] Other members of the staff are offered progressively fewer rights.[102]

Since the immunity from jurisdiction enjoyed by diplomatic staff is not granted for the personal benefit of the representatives but to enable them to perform their functions, it can be waived by the sending state.[103] A waiver must, however, be explicit.[104] In addition, a waiver from jurisdiction in relation to civil and administrative proceedings does not imply a waiver from execution. Here, a separate waiver is required.[105]

6.4.3 Other forms of protection of diplomats, diplomatic premises and property

Diplomatic representatives are not just afforded extensive immunity but also benefit from other forms of protection.[106] The extent of protection differs, however, depending on the status and functions of the diplomatic staff. Most importantly, according to article 29, a *diplomatic agent* is inviolable and shall not be liable to any form of arrest or detention and all attacks on his person, freedom and liberty must be prevented by the host state. With regard to *diplomatic premises* of the mission, article 22 of the VCDR stipulates

---

[97] Ibid, art. 31(3).   [98] Art. 34.   [99] Art. 35.   [100] Art. 37.   [101] Art. 37(2).

[102] Art. 37(3) and (4).   [103] Art. 32(1).   [104] Art. 32(2).   [105] Art. 32(4).

[106] *United States Diplomatic and Consular Staff in Tehran (United States v Iran)*, Judgment [1980] ICJ Rep 3, para. 92.

that these 'shall be inviolable' and that 'agents of the receiving state may not enter them, except with the consent of the head of the mission'. Under article 30, the private residence of the diplomat benefits from the same extensive protection. In addition, the host state is under 'a special duty to take all appropriate steps to protect the premises of the mission, including its means of transport, against any intrusion or damage and to prevent any disturbance of the peace of the mission or impairment of its dignity'. Also inviolable are the *archives and documents* of the mission no matter where they are located.[107] While violations of the obligation to protect foreign diplomatic missions are rare, they are not unheard of. In *Tehran Hostages*, for example, the ICJ concluded that Iran had violated its obligations under the VCDR by failing to protect, inter alia, the US embassy in Tehran from local protesters who stormed the diplomatic premises in 1979 and took the staff hostage.[108] A more recent example of disregard for the obligations under article 22 of the VCDR includes the passivity of local authorities in relation to the attacks and torching by local crowds of the Danish embassies in Lebanon and Syria following the publication in a Danish newspaper in 2005 of cartoons depicting the Prophet Muhammad.

Article 26 of the VCDR specifies that the host state shall ensure that members of a diplomatic mission can move and travel freely in its territory and that exceptions can only be made for reasons of national security in relation to certain zones. According to article 27, the host state shall permit and protect *free communication* 'on the part of the mission for all official purposes', and the diplomatic mission is generally free to employ all appropriate means of communicating including 'diplomatic couriers and messages in code or cipher'. The article also stipulates that all correspondence relating to the mission and its functions 'shall be inviolable'.[109] Extensive protection is additionally offered to the so-called 'diplomatic bag' that may be neither opened nor detained. The courier of the bag also enjoys inviolability and will not be liable to any form of arrest or detention.[110] The 'bag' can vary in size but must bear visible external marks. In 1989, the ILC issued a set of Draft Articles on the Status of the Diplomatic Courier and the Diplomatic Bag not accompanied by Diplomatic Courier.

6.4.4 **Obligations of the sending state and abuse of privilege**

Despite the widespread immunity and protection offered to diplomatic agents by international law, diplomats of the sending states are not above the laws of the host state. Article 41 of the VCDR explicitly states that all persons protected by the Convention must respect local laws and regulations. The representatives are also obliged not to 'interfere in the internal affairs' of the host state.[111] The premises of the diplomatic mission must not be used in any manner incompatible with the functions of the mission.[112] If a sending state abuses its rights and privileges, the VCDR offers the host state a number of remedies. Most notably, as mentioned in Section 6.4.1, under article 9 of the Convention it can withdraw its consent in respect of a member of the mission by declaring the representative *persona non grata*, in which cases the sending state must

---

[107] Art. 24.   [108] *Tehran Hostages* (n 106) para. 63.   [109] Art. 27(2).   [110] Art. 27(3)–(7).
[111] Art. 41(1).   [112] Art. 41(3).

recall the individual or terminate his or her functions. The host state can also decide to respond to a serious case of abuse by completely breaking off diplomatic relations.

But, even in cases of abuse, diplomatic protection and the inviolability of the diplomatic premises remain intact. In *Tehran Hostages*, the Iranian government claimed that its occupation of the US embassy should be considered in the light of more than '25 years of continual interference by the United States in the internal affairs of Iran, the shameless exploitation of our country, and numerous crimes perpetrated against the Iranian people, contrary to and in conflict with all international and humanitarian norms'. The ICJ responded, however, by noting that the rules of diplomatic law are a 'self-contained régime which specifies the means at the disposal of the receiving State to counter any such abuse'. The inviolability of diplomatic premises was confirmed in the so-called 1984 'St James's Square Incident', during which shots fired from inside the Libyan embassy in London killed a British policewoman. Despite a public outcry, the UK authorities refrained from entering the embassy. More recently, the British authorities have respected the inviolability of the premises of the Ecuadorian embassy in London even though the premises are being (ab)used to shield the founder of WikiLeaks, Julian Assange, from arrest and subsequent extradition to Sweden in relation to charges of sexual assault.

6.4.5 Consular immunity and protection

Unlike diplomatic agents, the functions of consular agents are generally limited to offering assistance in relation to more technical, commercial and/or private matters to the nationals of the sending state, including when nationals somehow find themselves in difficulty.[113] In *LaGrand*, the ICJ concluded that the United States had violated its obligations under consular law when the authorities of the State of Arizona tried and sentenced to death two German nationals without informing them of their rights to consular assistance.[114] The main body of consular rules are found in the 1963 Vienna Convention on Consular Relations, the structure of which in many ways resembles that of the Vienna Convention on Diplomatic Relations. The less 'political' role traditionally played by consuls is reflected in the less extensive degree of protection from the jurisdiction of the host state than international law offers to consular agents. In contrast to diplomats, consular officers only enjoy immunity *ratione materiae* in relation to functions performed in the exercise of their official functions.[115] Like diplomatic premises, consular premises are inviolable, and the authorities of the host state are not allowed to enter the premises without consent.[116]

6.4.6 Immunity for representatives on 'special missions'

As an alternative—or a supplement—to permanent diplomatic and consular relations, a state can conduct so-called 'ad hoc diplomacy' and send state representatives on

---

[113] For an overview of normal functions, see art. 5 of the Vienna Convention on Consular Relations.
[114] *LaGrand (Germany v United States)*, Judgment [2001] ICJ Rep 466. See the rights under art. 36 of the Vienna Convention on Consular Relations.
[115] Art. 43.   [116] Art. 31.

'special missions' to other states. In essence, a special mission is a temporary diplomatic mission. A 1969 Convention on Special Missions has entered into force but has yet to be widely ratified. Its status under customary international law is unclear. It is, however, well established that members of a special mission enjoy immunity *ratione personae* and are immune from the jurisdiction of the national courts of the host state.[117] But since the immunities of a representative on a special mission derive from the consent of the forum state to the presence of the mission on its territory, the foreign state must obtain the prior consent of the host state. In October 2011, the UK declined to issue an arrest warrant for an Israeli politician in relation to alleged war crimes because the British government had consented to her presence on a special mission. In *Khurts Bat*, a Mongolian state official could not claim the protections of a special mission because the local authorities had not consented to his presence prior to his arrival in the UK.[118]

Summary

Respect for the sovereign equality of states generally requires that a territorial state refrains from exercising its jurisdiction—whether adjudicative or in relation to enforcement—over another state and its representatives. Immunity is a procedural matter and must therefore be dealt with *prior* to an inquiry into the merits of the case. It is now well established that foreign states only enjoy immunity from a territorial state's exercise of adjudicative jurisdiction in relation to sovereign or governmental acts (acts *jure imperii*) and not with regard to commercial or private acts (acts *jure gestionis*). Thus, immunity is denied when a state engages in commercial activities and competes with private individuals or corporations. State immunity also applies in cases of serious violations of international law. The immunity offered to state representatives revolves around the distinction between immunity *ratione personae*—or 'personal immunity'—and immunity *ratione materiae*—'functional immunity'. The former is derived from the *position* a representative holds and the latter relates to the functions the representative performs. Personal immunity is more extensive than functional immunity. It is at present unclear if functional immunity can be limited in cases of international crimes. Foreign diplomats and diplomatic premises enjoy widespread immunities and protection under international law.

Recommended reading

A seminal work on state immunity is Hazel Fox, *The Law of State Immunity* (Oxford University Press, 2008). See also Xiaodong Yang, *State Immunity in International Law* (Cambridge University Press, 2012) and the elaborate work in Roger O'Keefe and Christian J. Tams (eds), *The UN Convention on Jurisdictional Immunities of States and Their Property: A Commentary* (Oxford University Press, 2013).

---

[117] For discussion, see Sanger (n 68).
[118] *Khurts Bat v Investigating Judge of the German Federal Court* (n 68).

A good—and shorter—overview is contained in Hazel Fox, 'International Law and Restraints on the Exercise of Jurisdiction by National Courts of States' in Malcolm D. Evans (ed.), *International Law* (4th edn, Oxford University Press, 2014). See also James Crawford (ed.), 'Privileges and Immunities of Foreign States' in *Brownlie's Principles of Public International Law* (8th edn, Oxford University Press, 2012).

For the distinction between sovereign and commercial acts, see James Crawford, 'Foreign Sovereigns: Distinguishing Immune Transactions' (1983) 54 *British Yearbook of International Law* 75.

On practice in relation to immunity from enforcement, see August Reinisch, 'European Court Practice Concerning State Immunity from Enforcement Measures' (2006) 17 *European Journal of International Law* 803.

A good introduction and discussion of immunity for state representatives is Chanaka Wickremasinghe, 'Immunities Enjoyed by Officials of States and International Organizations' in Malcolm D. Evans (ed.), *International Law* (4th edn, Oxford University Press, 2014). See also the latest edition of Hazel Fox, *The Law of State Immunity* (Oxford University Press, 2015).

There is a vast literature on the immunities from criminal jurisdiction of state representatives: see, inter alia, Dapo Akande and Sangeeta Shah, 'Immunities of State Officials, International Crimes, and Foreign Domestic Courts' (2011) 21 *European Journal of International Law* 815. See also Andrew Sanger, 'Immunity of State Officials from the Criminal Jurisdiction of a Foreign State' (2013) 62 *International and Comparative Law Quarterly* 193.

On diplomatic law, see the seminal work of Eileen Denza, *Diplomatic Law: A Commentary on the Vienna Convention on Diplomatic Relations* (2nd edn, Oxford University Press, 1998).

Questions for discussion

1. How would you justify state immunity?

2. Can you identify some of the tensions that respect for state immunity creates in relation to other considerations in international law?

3. Why has it proven to be difficult to introduce a workable definition of a sovereign (*jure imperii*) act on the one hand and a commercial (*jure gestionis*) act on the other?

4. In the *Arrest Warrant* case, the ICJ stated that immunity from criminal jurisdiction for a foreign minister is not the same as impunity. What did the Court mean by that?

5. How would you justify limiting immunity *ratione materiae* in relation to international crimes?

6. Why are there generally more exceptions to immunity in relation to civil proceedings than with regard to criminal jurisdiction?

7. Where is the consensual character of diplomatic relations reflected in diplomatic law?

8. What options does a forum state have in relation to criminal activities emanating from a foreign diplomatic mission located on its territory?

7

State responsibility

CENTRAL ISSUES

1. This chapter discusses the international law of state responsibility as primarily reflected in the 2001 International Law Commission's Articles on the Responsibility of States for Internationally Wrongful Acts.

2. It discusses the core principles of state responsibility, including the dual requirements of wrongful conduct and state attribution.

3. The chapter provides an overview of the different means whereby a state will be held internationally responsible for wrongful conduct (attribution) and the different circumstances that preclude the wrongfulness of conduct that is otherwise a violation of an international obligation.

4. It also analyses the primary consequences that flow from international responsibility for wrongful conduct and when a state may invoke the international responsibility of another state, including the principles of so-called 'diplomatic protection'.

7.1 Introduction

All systems of law must deal with the issue of responsibility for breaches of the obligations contained in the system. To supplement the rules that identify the concrete rights and obligations, a legal system must have rules specifying what happens when a subject violates its obligations and how an aggrieved party can vindicate its rights. In international law, these rules are primarily found within the field of state responsibility, supplemented by the rules on the responsibility of international organizations. State responsibility is an area of international law that is indispensable for the well functioning of international law and the international society that the law regulates. The international rules relating to the responsibility of individuals are found in international criminal law and they are discussed in Chapter 15. As noted in Chapter 4, international corporations do not hold responsibility under international law.

Theoretically, the laws on responsibility are rules of a *secondary* nature.[1] While *primary* rules are those that define the substantial obligations that a state must follow

---

[1] The distinction was introduced by Roberto Ago in his capacity as the second Special Rapporteur; see also the discussion in James Crawford, *State Responsibility* (Cambridge University Press, 2013) 64–66.

to comply with international law, secondary rules determine the consequences of violating the primary rules. The rules on immunity from national jurisdiction discussed in Chapter 6, for example, are primary rules because they specify when a territorial state must refrain from exercising its jurisdiction in a case that involves a foreign state and the representatives of a foreign state. The secondary rules on state responsibility identify the legal consequences that are associated with a breach of the law on state immunity. It is important to note that the question of responsibility is distinct from the treaty law question of whether a treaty obligation is binding upon a state or not. Thus, whereas the law of treaties determines if a treaty is in force, it is the law on responsibility that determines if a breach of an (existing) treaty obligation involves the responsibility of the breaching actor and what the consequences of a breach may be.[2]

This chapter primarily focuses on the responsibility of states. The most relevant rules and principles are found in a series of Articles on Responsibility of States for Internationally Wrongful Acts prepared by the International Law Commission (ILC) on the basis of the work of successive Special Rapporteurs. Although state responsibility was one of the first issues taken up by the ILC, the final set of articles was not adopted until May 2001.[3] In December 2001, the UN General Assembly recommended the articles.[4] The ILC articles are unlikely to be developed into a treaty, but they are generally considered to reflect customary international law.[5]

The discussion in the chapter is based on the structure of the ILC articles. It therefore opens in Section 7.2 with the basic principles of state responsibility. Section 7.3 covers the issue of state attribution before Section 7.4 discusses joint and collective state responsibility. Section 7.5 examines the various circumstances that may preclude the wrongfulness of conduct otherwise in violation of a (primary) legal obligation, and Section 7.6 examines the consequences of state responsibility. Section 7.7 discusses who is entitled to invoke state responsibility, and Section 7.8 focuses on the right of a state to invoke the responsibility of another state for injury caused to a national of the former state—also known as 'diplomatic protection'. Section 7.9 provides a brief overview of the responsibility of international organizations.

7.2 The basic principles of state responsibility

The starting point for any discussion of state responsibility is one that is often overlooked in the treatment of the topic: the existence of an international obligation. Obviously, if a state is free to act within a given area, its acts cannot give rise to state responsibility. Aside from this, the fundamental principle of state responsibility is

---

[2] See also *Gabčíkovo-Nagymaros Project (Hungary v Slovakia)*, Judgment [1997] ICJ Rep 7, para. 47.
[3] For an overview of the process, see Crawford (n 1) 35–44.
[4] GA Res. 56/83 (12 December 2001).
[5] See, inter alia, *Application of the Convention on the Prevention and Punishment of the Crime of Genocide (Bosnia and Herzegovina v Serbia and Montenegro)*, Judgment [2007] ICJ Rep 43, para. 401.

reflected in article 1 of the ILC articles, which stipulates that 'Every internationally wrongful act of a State entails the international responsibility of that State'. Article 2 of the ILC articles illustrates that state responsibility consists of two elements: (1) conduct must be a breach of an international obligation and (2) that conduct must be attributable to a state. The International Court of Justice (ICJ) referred to the two core elements in reverse order in the *Tehran Hostages* case, where Iranian citizens overran US diplomatic installations in Iran including the US embassy in Tehran, in a prelude to a lengthy state-sanctioned occupation of the premises. The Court had to determine, first, 'how far, legally, the acts in question may be regarded as imputable to the Iranian State' and, secondly, 'their compatibility or incompatibility with the obligations of Iran'.[6] *Tehran Hostages* illustrates that both acts and omissions can constitute wrongful conduct. In the case, the ICJ found that Iran had breached its international obligations under the Vienna Convention on Diplomatic Relations (the primary rules) by failing to offer protection from Iranian citizens to the US premises.[7]

A few basic points about *liability* in international law are worth making. National legal systems generally operate with different forms of liability depending on the primary obligation. Thus, there is usually one standard of liability for contracts, another for torts and yet another standard in criminal law. Such distinctions do not exist in international law, and article 12 of the ILC articles simply states that an international obligation is breached by a state 'when an act of that State is not in conformity with what is required of it by that obligation, regardless of its origin or character'.[8] Thus, the standard of liability depends on the primary legal source. It is also worth noting the absence of a distinction between 'civil' and 'criminal' illegality. The attempt to introduce the concept of an 'international crime' into the ILC articles on state responsibility was not supported by states. State representatives may, however, be held criminally accountable as individuals for certain violations of international law.[9]

State responsibility does not always require that damage in the form of material or other actual losses has been caused by an act or omission. It depends on the primary rules. For example, while rules relating to marine pollution require that actual damage has occurred, this is not the case for rules that set out standards of behaviour that must be followed regardless of whether breaches result in tangible effects on other states. In such instances, responsibility arises as soon as a state's conduct is at variance with the legal obligation. As we shall see in Section 7.5, the existence of actual damage, such as financial losses, may, however, be relevant for determining the right level of reparations for wrongful conduct. In addition, as Section 7.6 will illustrate, actual damage may also be relevant to determining who is entitled to invoke the responsibility of the state that is in breach of its obligations.

---

[6] *United States Diplomatic and Consular Staff in Tehran (United States v Iran)*, Judgment [1980] ICJ Rep 3, para. 56.

[7] Ibid, para. 67. See also *Corfu Channel (UK v Albania)*, Judgment of 9 April 1949 [1949] ICJ Rep 4, 22–23.

[8] See also *Rainbow Warrior (New Zealand v France)* (1990) XX RIAA 217, para. 75.

[9] International criminal law is discussed in Chapter 15.

The last principle worth mentioning here is reflected in article 3 of the ILC articles. It is the well-known principle that the characterization of an act of a state as internationally wrongful is governed solely by international law. Thus, a state cannot justify a breach of its international legal obligations by invoking its national laws and a state must also comply with international obligations even if it requires breaching its national laws.[10]

7.3 Attribution of conduct

7.3.1 Introduction

One of the core elements of state responsibility is that wrongful conduct must be attributable to a state. The issue of attribution is dealt with in articles 4–11 in Chapter III of the ILC articles. The provisions illustrate the fundamental principle that states are only responsible for their own acts and generally not for those of private individuals. As *Tehran Hostages* illustrates, however, a state can still be found to be in breach of its international obligations in relation to acts of private individuals if a state is under a (primary) legal obligation to offer effective protection from such private acts. The existence of a more general due diligence obligation was implied in *Corfu Channel* where the ICJ stated that a state may not 'allow knowingly its territory to be used for acts contrary to the rights of other States'.[11] As we shall see in Chapter 10, the due diligence obligation plays a prominent role in international environmental law where it is translated into a state's obligation to use all means 'to avoid activities which take place in its territory, or in any area under its jurisdiction, causing significant damage to the environment of another State'.[12] More recently, due diligence has been brought up in relation to the activities of private individuals in cyberspace.[13]

In this section, we examine the principles governing when the conduct of state organs, as well as private groups and individuals, is attributable to a state. We begin with the general principle of attribution (Section 7.3.2) before we turn to attribution for acts performed by (other) organs that perform governmental authority (Section 7.3.3). We then examine attribution for acts by organs on 'loan' from other states (Section 7.3.4), attribution for acts *ultra vires* (Section 7.3.5) and attribution for acts by private individuals (Section 7.3.6). Then, acts by insurrectional movements are discussed (Section 7.3.7) and in the final section, the issue of attribution for acts subsequently acknowledged and adopted (Section 7.3.8).

---

[10] See, inter alia, *SS 'Wimbledon'*, 1923, PCIJ Series A, No. 1, 15, see 29–30, and *Reparations for Injuries Suffered in the Service of the United Nations*, Advisory Opinion of 11 April 1949 [1949] ICJ Rep 174, 180. See also art. 26 of the Vienna Convention on the Law of Treaties discussed in Chapter 3.

[11] *Corfu Channel* (n 7) 20. On the concept of due diligence more generally, see also the International Law Association's Study Group on Due Diligence in International Law, First Report, Duncan French and Tim Stephens, 7 March 2014.

[12] *Pulp Mills on the River Uruguay (Argentina v Uruguay)*, Judgment [2010] ICJ Rep 14, para. 101. See also *Trail Smelter (United States v Canada)* (1938 and 1941) III RIAA 1905.

[13] See, inter alia, Michael N. Schmitt (ed.), *The Tallinn Manual 2.0 on the International Law Applicable to Cyber Operations* (Cambridge University Press, 2017) Rule 6.

7.3.2 **Attribution for acts performed by the state and its organs**

The first principle of state attribution is straightforward and uncontroversial. According to article 4 of the ILC articles, all conduct of state organs is considered an act of the state regardless of whether the organ in question 'exercises legislative, executive, judicial or any other functions'. Thus, all three branches of government may implicate the international responsibility of the state. It is immaterial what position the organ holds within the state and if it is an organ of the central government or of a regional/territorial entity of the state. The term 'organ' is interpreted broadly and it includes any person or entity with an official status in the internal law of the state. Attribution is also triggered by conduct by low-level state officials as long as they act in an official capacity. Furthermore, a state cannot avoid responsibility for acts or omissions of an entity that in practice functions as a state organ by denying it an official status in its internal laws. This was also noted by the ICJ in *Genocide*, where the Court had to determine if the Federal Yugoslavian government in Belgrade was internationally responsible for the 1995 Srebrenica massacres in Bosnia perpetrated by local Bosnian Serb forces who were not officially state organs in Yugoslavia. According to the Court, the Bosnian forces would only be considered organs of the Federal Yugoslavian state if they acted in 'complete dependence on the State, of which they are ultimately merely the instrument'. And that could not be established in the case.[14] The Court also stated that 'to equate persons or entities with State organs when they do not have that status under internal law must be exceptional'.[15] As a main rule, conduct by the authorities of subunits in a federal state is attributable to the state. In *LaGrand*, the United States was responsible for the conduct of federal authorities in the state of Arizona and acts that fell within the jurisdiction of the governor of that US state.[16] Limited exceptions may apply, however, in relation to the acts of certain constituent units of a federation.[17]

7.3.3 **Attribution for acts performed by organs exercising governmental authority**

Article 5 of the ILC articles concerns a state's responsibility for acts of individuals and entities that exercise authority normally exercised by a state even though they do not have an official status. The article specifies that conduct of individuals and entities empowered to exercise governmental authority is attributable to the state whenever they act in that capacity. Thus, a state cannot avoid responsibility by privatizing/outsourcing functions that are properly governmental. Article 5 is of relevance, therefore, to the privatization of certain military and police functions, matters relating to the running of detention and prison facilities and the delegation of powers relating to immigration and

---

[14] *Genocide* (n 5) paras 388–392. See also *Military and Paramilitary Activities in and against Nicaragua (Nicaragua v United States)*, Merits [1986] ICJ Rep 14, para. 109.

[15] Ibid, para. 393.

[16] *LaGrand (Germany v United States)*, Order, Request for the Indication of Provisional Measures [1999] ICJ Rep 9, para. 28.

[17] See the Draft Articles on the Responsibility of States for Internationally Wrongful Acts, with commentaries, *Yearbook of the International Law Commission*, 2001, vol. II, Part Two, p. 42, para. 10.

border control to private airlines or ships. It may be difficult to determine if an activity should be considered as an exercise of 'governmental authority' and the assessment may differ from state to state. The commentary to article 5 notes that the content of the powers granted as well as 'the way they are conferred on an entity, the purposes for which they are to be exercised and the extent to which the entity is accountable to government for their exercise' may offer some assistance.[18] Attribution under article 5 is limited to cases where the entity is empowered by the internal laws of the state to conduct the governmental authority in question. It should therefore not be conflated with attribution for the conduct of private individuals who (merely) act under the direction or control of a state. That falls under article 8 (see Section 7.3.6).

7.3.4 Attribution for acts by organs 'on loan' from another state

Article 6 of the ILC articles covers the rather exceptional situation where a state places one of its organs at the disposal of another state. Examples include health service units in crisis situations and the occasional appointment of judges. The article stipulates that the acts of the 'loaned' organ are attributed to the receiving and not the sending state. This, however, requires that the organ in question is actually placed under the authority or structure of the receiving state and does not retain its autonomy and that the organ exercises governmental authority.[19] In *Jaloud v Netherlands*, the European Court of Human Rights did not find that Dutch troops stationed in an area in south-eastern Iraq in 2004, where all relevant forces were under the command of an officer from the UK, were placed 'at the disposal' of, inter alia, the UK.[20] The Netherlands was responsible for providing security in the area, to the exclusion of other troop-participating states, and retained full command over its contingent.[21]

7.3.5 Responsibility for acts *ultra vires*

A state remains responsible for conduct performed by its organs and officials in cases where the organ or official acted contrary to orders and instructions or in excess of authority—conduct *ultra vires*. This is reflected in article 7 of the ILC articles. As the Inter-American Court of Human Rights stated in *Velásquez Rodriguez*, which concerned the disappearance of a student at the hands of the armed forces of Honduras, the determination of whether a state has breached its obligations under international law is 'independent of whether the organ or official has contravened provisions of internal law or overstepped the limits of his authority'. A state is 'responsible for the acts of its agents undertaken in their official capacity and for their omissions, even when those agents act outside the sphere of their authority or violate internal law'.[22] Responsibility is a fact as long as an organ or official has acted with 'apparent authority'.[23]

---

[18] Ibid, p. 43, para. 6.   [19] See also *Genocide* (n 5) para. 389.
[20] *Jaloud v the Netherlands*, App. no. 47708/08, 20 November 2014, para. 151.
[21] Ibid, para. 149.
[22] *Velasquez Rodriguez*, Judgment of 29 July 1988, Inter-AmCtHR, Series C, No. 4 (1988), see paras 169–170.
[23] Draft Articles (n 17) p. 46, para. 8.

7.3.6 **Attribution for acts performed by private individuals**

We have already seen that states are generally not responsible for the acts of private individuals. Exceptions do exist, however, and one of the more contentious issues within the field of state responsibility concerns the responsibility of a state for the acts committed by private persons or private organizations that are somehow linked to or supported by the state. The issue was brought to the fore in connection with the 11 September 2001 terrorist attacks on the United States that were perpetrated by the al Qaida network, at the time based in Afghanistan, where it was provided sanctuary by the Taleban regime. The relationship between al Qaida and the Taleban led to a debate about how closely related a state must be to a private terrorist organization before the acts of the terrorists can be attributed to the state.

Article 8 of the ILC articles specifies that a state is only responsible for the conduct of a person or a group of persons if they are 'in fact acting on the instructions of, or under the direction or control of, that state in carrying out the conduct'. State responsibility therefore only exists in two situations. Either the private individuals must be *acting on the instructions or orders* of the state or they must *act under the direction or control* of the state. While it is fairly obvious that a state should be responsible for acts that it instructs someone to do on its behalf, it has proven more difficult to reach agreement on what is contained in the concept of 'direction and control'. The seminal case is *Nicaragua* in which the ICJ, among other things, had to determine if the United States was internationally responsible for violations of the laws of armed conflict committed by a paramilitary force—the *contras*—in Nicaragua, who were heavily subsidized and supported by the US government. The Court did not find that the acts of the *contras* could be attributed to the United States because it would require that the US 'had effective control of the military or paramilitary operations in the course of which the alleged violations were committed'.[24] The key, in other words, was the concept of 'effective control'. In *Tadić*, the Appeals Chamber of the International Criminal Tribunal for the former Yugoslavia (ICTY) in 1999 criticized the threshold for attribution in *Nicaragua* for being too high and concluded that the required degree of control over the private actors 'var[ies] according to the factual circumstances of each case'.[25] Thus, according to the Chamber, the exercise of 'overall control' may in some circumstances suffice in relation to the acts of militarily organized groups.[26] The ICTY was not, however, concerned with attribution under the principles of state responsibility, but rather for the purpose of classifying an armed conflict as either of an international or of a non-international character. As noted earlier, in the 2007 *Genocide* case, the ICJ had to determine if the Federal Yugoslavian government could be held internationally responsible for, among other things, the 1995 Srebrenica massacres perpetrated by Bosnian Serb forces supported by the Yugoslavian government. The Court rejected the ICTY's arguments for lowering the threshold for control and stated that the standard in *Nicaragua* still reflected customary international law.[27] Thus, attribution (still)

---

[24] *Nicaragua* (n 14) para. 115.

[25] ICTY, *Tadić*, Appeals Chamber, Judgment, para. 117. See also para. 137.　　　[26] Ibid, para. 145.

[27] *Genocide* (n 5) paras 404–406. It did leave open, however, the possibility that an 'overall control' test could be applied in relation to determining whether or not an armed conflict is international: see para. 404.

requires that effective control can be established 'in respect of each operation in which the alleged violations occurred, not generally in respect of the overall actions taken by the persons or groups of persons having committed the violations'.[28] The Court did not find that to be the case with regard to the Srebrenica massacre because the decision to kill the adult male population of the Muslim community in Srebrenica was seemingly taken by the Bosnian Serbs without instructions from or effective control by the Yugoslavian government in Belgrade.[29] The Court did not find that the particular (reprehensible) nature of the conduct—in this case, the crime of genocide— justified lowering the threshold for attribution in the absence of a clearly expressed *lex specialis*.[30] This, of course, would also seem to rule out the standard for attribution being lower for acts of international terrorism. As we shall return to in Chapter 13, the 9/11 attacks may have paved the way for an 'unable or unwilling' doctrine whereby a state can resort to self-defence against a private actor, such as a terrorist organization, located in another state if the host state does not have the ability or willingness to stop the private actor's activities. That doctrine does not hold, however, that the host state is internationally responsible for the acts of the private actor, and it does not therefore constitute a lowering of the standard for attribution under article 8.

An additional point must be noted at this stage. We saw earlier that a state is responsible for conduct of its own organs that is contrary to or in excess of directions of the state— *ultra vires*—. The same does not hold in relation to *ultra vires* acts performed by persons or groups of persons who merely operate under the direction or effective control of the state.[31]

7.3.7 **Acts of an insurrectional movement**

It is a well-established principle that the acts of insurrectional movements are not attributable to the state. If, however, the movement succeeds in assuming power and establishes itself as the new government of the state, or manages to form a new state in part of the territory of the pre-existing state, article 10 of the ILC articles stipulates that the state will be responsible for the acts of the movement. Theoretically, attribution can be justified in such cases by arguing that the movement should be considered as a continuation of the former government.

7.3.8 **Responsibility for acts subsequently acknowledged and adopted**

Article 11 of the ILC articles illustrates that a state may become responsible for conduct that was not attributable to it when it was committed if the state *subsequently* acknowledges the conduct and adopts it as its own. The best example is *Tehran Hostages*, where the ICJ concluded that the acts of the Iranian government subsequent to the storming and occupation of the US embassy by private Iranian citizens meant that the conduct became acts of the Iranian state. Not only did the Iranian government give its approval to the occupation of the embassy and the taking of its staff as

---

[28] Ibid, para. 400.   [29] Ibid, para. 413.   [30] Ibid, para. 401.
[31] Draft Articles (n 17) p. 48, para. 8.

hostages, it decided to perpetuate it and use it as a means of exerting pressure on the US government. From then on, the 'militants, authors of the invasion and jailers of the hostages, had now become agents of the Iranian State for whose acts the State itself was internationally responsible'.[32] Conduct will only be attributed to a state under article 11 if it somehow acknowledges and adopts the conduct as *that of its own*. It must show a willingness to assume responsibility for the acts in question. Mere statements of support or sympathy or general acknowledgements of factual circumstances are not sufficient. For example, the fact that the Taleban regime refused to cooperate with the United States and surrender those deemed responsible for the 9/11 attacks was not enough to make Afghanistan internationally responsible for the attacks.

7.4 State responsibility in relation to acts of other states

As noted earlier, it is a fundamental principle of state responsibility that a state is only responsible for its own conduct. This, however, does not mean that a state cannot be found internationally responsible in situations where it cooperates with another state. The relevant principles are found in Chapter IV of the ILC articles.[33] Joint or collective responsibility is relatively underdeveloped and relevant case law is still limited.[34] The most relevant principle is found in article 16 whereby a state will be internationally responsible for aiding or assisting another state in the commission of an international wrongful act if (1) the aid or assistance is given with knowledge of the circumstances of the international wrongful act and (2) the act would be internationally wrongful if it was committed by the aiding or assisting state. In *Genocide*, the ICJ stated that article 16 reflects customary international law.[35] Article 16 may be applicable, for example, if a state assists another state with using force in violation of the prohibition on the use of force in article 2(4) of the UN Charter or if it assists another state with secretly detaining and torturing suspected terrorists in violation of human rights law.[36] But the threshold in article 16 is high. For one thing, the aid or assistance must be given with *knowledge* of the circumstances of the wrongful act and a state will not normally assume that its aid or assistance to another state is to be used to perpetrate internationally wrongful acts. If the state is unaware of the circumstances it will not be responsible. In addition, an assisting state is only responsible for aid or assistance if it *intended* to facilitate the occurrence of the wrongful conduct and that conduct was actually committed by the aided or assisted state.[37] In *Genocide*, the ICJ found that the Bosnian Serbs committed the Srebrenica massacre, at least in part, with resources they had acquired as a result

---

[32] *Tehran Hostages* (n 6) para. 74.

[33] On shared responsibility with international organizations, see Draft Articles on Responsibility of International Organizations, arts 14–18.

[34] See also Crawford (n 1) 325–328. For a recent presentation, see André Nollkaemper and Ilias Plakokefalos (eds), *Principles of Shared Responsibility in International Law: An Appraisal of the State of the Art* (Cambridge University Press, 2017).

[35] *Genocide* (n 5) para. 420.

[36] See, inter alia, *El Masri v the Former Republic of Macedonia*, App. no. 39630/09, 13 December 2012.

[37] Draft Articles (n 17) p. 66, paras 4–5.

of a general policy of aid and assistance by the Federal Yugoslavian government in Belgrade. But since it had not been established that the latter was fully aware that the aid would be used to commit genocide, its responsibility was not engaged.[38]

7.5 Circumstances precluding wrongfulness

7.5.1 Introduction

Chapter V of the ILC articles lists a number of circumstances the existence of any one of which will preclude the international wrongfulness of an act otherwise in breach of international law. In practice, then, the circumstances listed serve as justifications for not complying with an international obligation. They are general in the sense that, unless specifically regulated in the primary rules, they will apply to any wrongful act regardless of whether it constitutes a breach of a treaty or any other source of international law. The existence of a circumstance precluding wrongfulness does not, however, terminate the underlying legal obligation. As the ICJ stated in *Gabčíkovo-Nagymaros Project*, in relation to a claim of a state of necessity, even if 'found justified, it does not terminate a Treaty … As soon as the state of necessity ceases to exist, the duty to comply with treaty obligations revives.'[39]

7.5.2 Consent

The first of the circumstances precluding wrongfulness mentioned in the ILC articles is *consent*. According to article 20, valid consent by a state to the commission of an act precludes the wrongfulness of that act as long as the act does not exceed the limits of that consent. As the article illustrates, consent must be 'valid', and in some cases this may require a determination of whether the individual who gave the consent was actually authorized to do so by his or her state.[40] Different officials may be authorized to give consent to different conduct. In cases of doubt, the relevant question will be whether the state that acts on the contested consent is in good faith. Consent must be given freely without coercion and it must be clearly expressed. It must, furthermore, be given either beforehand or at the time the otherwise wrongful conduct occurs. Consent plays an important practical role in everyday international relations (overflight of aircraft, disaster assistance, rescue operations etc.) and is usually not a cause of great controversy. However, there are also instances where it is controversial to rely on consent as a justification for using force.[41]

7.5.3 Self-defence

Article 21 of the ILC articles specifies that the wrongfulness of an otherwise unlawful act is precluded if it is *in conformity with the inherent right to self-defence* in article 51

---

[38] *Genocide* (n 5) paras 422–424.   [39] *Gabčíkovo-Nagymaros Project* (n 2) para. 101.

[40] On this issue, see inter alia the Vienna Convention on the Law of Treaties, arts 27 and 46, discussed in Chapter 3.

[41] See Chapter 13.

of the UN Charter. The two articles must therefore be interpreted together and conduct that does not comport with article 51 of the Charter cannot be justified under article 21.[42] Article 21 does not preclude the wrongfulness of conduct that is in breach of the international obligations that are meant to apply in times of armed conflict.[43]

7.5.4 **Lawful countermeasures**

The third circumstance that may preclude the wrongfulness of an otherwise unlawful act is derived from the understanding that the absence of centralized mandatory enforcement in international law means that states are often left with no choice but to enforce their own rights. In a system of self-help, a state must be allowed to respond to another state's international wrongful acts by taking certain *countermeasures* in order to bring the wrongful acts to an end.[44] Thus, according to article 22 of the ILC articles, a state is entitled to breach its international obligations towards another state 'if and to the extent that the act constitutes a countermeasure taken against the latter State'.[45] The modalities that govern countermeasures are contained in articles 49–54 of the ILC articles. It follows that countermeasures are subject to certain conditions. First of all, article 49 stipulates that a countermeasure can only be directed against a state that has breached its international obligations and that the *purpose* of the measure must be to induce the other state to comply with its international obligations. It must therefore be of a temporary nature and applied in a way that permits the resumption of performance of the obligations in question.[46] The second condition is found in article 50(1) and (2), according to which *some obligations cannot be the object of countermeasures*.[47] These include the obligation to refrain from the threat or use of force contained in the UN Charter. A state is therefore barred from responding to a wrongful act by resorting to force.[48] Also, countermeasures may not infringe 'obligations for the protection of fundamental human rights'. It is not clear which human rights are considered 'fundamental', but they would seem to include at least those that cannot be derogated from even in times of war or other public emergency.[49] Article 50(1) also prohibits countermeasures that affect obligations of a 'humanitarian character prohibiting reprisals'. It seems, therefore, that a state cannot respond to another state's breach of international law by suspending the basic rules in the laws of armed conflict/international humanitarian law.[50] Also prohibited under article 50(1) are countermeasures offending against peremptory/*jus cogens* norms. Article 50 stipulates that the right to resort to countermeasures does not relieve a state

---

[42] The right to self-defence is discussed in Chapter 13.

[43] In general, see also *Legality of the Threat or Use of Nuclear Weapons*, Advisory Opinion [1996] ICJ Rep 226.

[44] *Gabčíkovo-Nagymaros Project* (n 2) para. 83. For an overview, see also Nigel White and Ademola Abass, 'Countermeasures and Sanctions' in Malcolm D. Evans (ed.), *International Law* (Oxford University Press, 2010) 531–545.

[45] See also *Air Services Agreement (US v France)*, Arbitral Award, 9 December 1978, XVIII RIAA 417–493.

[46] Art. 49. *Gabčíkovo-Nagymaros Project* (n 2) para. 87.   [47] Art. 50(1).

[48] See also GA Res. 2625 (XXV) (24 October 1970), UN Doc. A/25/2625

[49] For derogation and non-derogable rights, see Chapter 9.

[50] Crawford (n 1) 694. For more on such principles, see Section 14.5.

from fulfilling its obligations under a relevant 'dispute settlement' or respecting the inviolability of diplomatic or consular agents, premises, archives and documents.[51]

The third condition is found in article 51 and it concerns *proportionality* and a state's obligation to strike a fair balance between the initial breach of international law and the measures taken. If a measure is not proportionate it may be interpreted as a reaction aimed at exerting revenge or punishment on the targeted state and therefore fall outside the boundaries of lawful countermeasures. There is, however, no requirement that a countermeasure must be reciprocal in nature, and a state may be justified in responding to another state's breach of international law by adopting measures that are different in kind. In practice, assessments of proportionality are usually difficult.[52] In the *Gabčíkovo-Nagymaros Project* case, the ICJ concluded that a Czechoslovakian project aimed at diverting part of the Danube in response to Hungary's failure to comply with a treaty on the construction of a dam was not proportionate.[53] Before initiating countermeasures, a state must take every possible measure to avoid affecting a third party.[54]

The fourth condition for resorting to countermeasures is a set of *procedural requirements*. Thus, under article 52(1), before initiating countermeasures, the state must call upon the responsible state to fulfil its international obligations and notify it of the initiation of countermeasures and offer it a chance to negotiate. However, in urgent circumstances the state may 'take such urgent countermeasures as are necessary to preserve its rights'.[55] Article 52(3) specifies that countermeasures cannot be taken if the wrongful act has ceased and the dispute is pending before a court or tribunal with the authority to make a binding decision.

The fifth and final condition is that a countermeasure must be *terminated* as soon as the internationally wrongful acts on the part of the other state have ceased. This is required by article 53.[56]

The overview of countermeasures has so far focused on the right of an injured state to resort to such measures in order to bring a halt to another state's breach of international law. As we shall return to in Section 7.7, however, a *non-injured state* may sometimes be entitled to invoke the responsibility of another state if the obligation breached is 'owed to the international community as a whole'—also known as obligations *erga omnes*. This raises the question whether a non-injured state is entitled to initiate individual countermeasures against a state that has breached *erga omnes* obligations. In article 54, the ILC leaves the question open and the commentary to the articles merely notes that state practice is sparse and that there does not 'at present' appear to be a 'clearly recognized entitlement of third states to take countermeasures in the collective interest'.[57] Others are more positive.[58] The US missile strikes against Syria in 2017 and 2018 in response to the Assad regime's use of (prohibited) chemical weapons could be interpreted as a

---

[51] See art. 50(2).

[52] Thomas Franck, 'On Proportionality of Countermeasures in International Law' (2008) 102(4) *American Journal of International Law* 763.

[53] *Gabčíkovo-Nagymaros Project* (n 2) para. 87.   [54] See also Draft Articles (n 17) p.130, para. 4.

[55] Art. 52(2).   [56] See also art. 52(3).   [57] Draft Articles (n 17) p. 139, para. 6.

[58] Christian J. Tams, *Enforcing Obligations Erga Omnes in International Law* (Cambridge University Press, 2005) 250.

countermeasure by a non-injured state. But since countermeasures may not constitute a use of force, the strikes cannot be justified as lawful countermeasures.[59]

7.5.5 *Force majeure*

The fourth circumstance that may preclude the wrongfulness of otherwise unlawful conduct is *force majeure*. According to article 23 of the ILC articles, a state may justify non-performance of an obligation in the case of the 'occurrence of an irresistible force or of an unforeseen event, beyond the control of the State' that makes it 'materially impossible in the circumstances' to perform the obligation. A plea of *force majeure* is not available, however, if the state that invokes it has contributed to the situation or if it has 'assumed the risk' of the situation occurring.[60] In the *Rainbow Warrior* case, the Permanent Court of Arbitration (PCA) stated that *force majeure* requires 'absolute or material impossibility' and that circumstances that merely render performance of the obligation more difficult or burdensome do not suffice.[61] The Court also noted that *force majeure* is generally relied upon in relation to involuntary or at least unintentional conduct and that it is based on the premise that no one can be required to do the impossible.[62]

7.5.6 **Distress**

The fifth circumstance precluding wrongfulness is *distress*, according to which an agent of a state may be justified in not performing an international obligation if it has no other reasonable way of saving the agent's life or that of other persons in the agent's care. It is covered by article 24 of the ILC articles. As the PCA noted in *Rainbow Warrior*, distress differs from *force majeure* in the sense that it can be relied upon in a situation where the state could in theory fulfil its international obligation but where it would require a sacrifice that it was unreasonable to demand.[63] According to article 24(2), distress cannot be invoked if the situation of distress is due to the state's own conduct or if the act that constitutes a breach of the international obligation 'is likely to create a comparable or greater peril'.

7.5.7 **Necessity**

The final circumstance precluding wrongfulness mentioned in the ILC articles is *necessity*, contained in article 25. It relates to those rare cases where the only way for a state to safeguard an 'essential interest' that is threatened by 'a grave and imminent peril' is, for the time being, to refrain from performing another international obligation that is considered to be of a lesser weight or urgency. In *Gabčíkovo-Nagymaros Project*,

---

[59] Anders Henriksen, 'Trump's Missile Strike on Syria and the Legality of Using Force to Deter Chemical Warfare' (2018) 23 *Journal of Conflict and Security Law* 45. For a discussion of the legality of the strikes, see also Section 13.6.4.
[60] Art. 23(2). [61] *Rainbow Warrior* (n 8) para. 77.
[62] Ibid. See also Draft Articles (n 17) p. 76, para. 2. [63] *Rainbow Warrior* (n 8) para. 78.

the ICJ stated that a plea of necessity can only be accepted 'on an exceptional basis'[64] and in his capacity as ILC Special Rapporteur, James Crawford described necessity as being 'at the outer edge of the tolerance of international law for otherwise wrongful acts'.[65] As already noted, an 'essential interest' must be at stake and the international obligation that is not performed must be of a lesser value. In addition, the wrongful act must be 'the only way' for the state to safeguard its vital interest. In *The Wall*, the ICJ concluded that Israel's construction of a security barrier on Palestinian territory violated its obligations under international law and that a plea of necessity could not preclude the wrongfulness of Israel's conduct. While the Court noted the existence of 'indiscriminate and deadly acts of violence against its civilian population' and that Israel had both the right and duty to protect the life of its citizens, it was not convinced that the construction of the wall along the route chosen was the only means to safeguard the interests of Israel against that peril.[66]

According to article 25, when invoking necessity a state may not 'seriously impair an essential interest of the State or States towards which the obligation exists, or of the international community as a whole'.[67] It also follows from the article that necessity is unavailable if the 'international obligation in question excludes the possibility of invoking necessity', or if the state has contributed to the situation of necessity. Importantly, even if a state of necessity exists, it will only justify a state not performing a treaty-based obligation for as long as that state of necessity lasts. The underlying obligation and the treaty are not terminated and as soon as the state of necessity ceases to exist, the state is under a duty to resume compliance with its treaty obligations.[68] A plea of necessity does not cover conduct regulated by a primary rule. It follows, therefore, that it does not cover an assertion of military necessity that is subject to regulation in the substantive provisions in the laws of armed conflict.[69] Whether a plea of necessity can justify a use of force not in accordance with the UN Charter is discussed in Section 13.5.

7.5.8 Circumstances precluding wrongfulness and *jus cogens*

Articles 20–25 of the ILC articles must all be read in conjunction with article 26, according to which a state cannot preclude the wrongfulness of any act that violates a peremptory norm/*jus cogens*. As we saw in Chapter 2, it is not clear what norms can be said to be of a peremptory character, but it appears to include, at a minimum, the crime of genocide, the prohibition on torture, the ban on slavery, piracy, aggression, crimes against humanity, the right to self-determination and the prohibition of apartheid and other forms of gross racial discrimination.

---

[64] *Gabčíkovo-Nagymaros Project* (n 2) para. 51. See also the general scepticism displayed in *Rainbow Warrior* (n 8) para. 78 and in the Draft Articles (n 17) p. 80, para. 2 and p. 83, para. 14.

[65] Report of the International Law Commission on its work of its 51st Session (1999), UN Doc. A/54/10, para. 378.

[66] *Legal Consequences of the Construction of a Wall in the Occupied Palestinian Territory*, Advisory Opinion [2004] ICJ Rep 136, paras 140–141.

[67] Art. 25(1).   [68] *Gabčíkovo-Nagymaros Project* (n 2) para. 101.

[69] Draft Articles (n 17) p. 84, para. 21.

7.6 Consequences of wrongful conduct

7.6.1 Introduction

In this section we examine the *consequences* that flow from a conclusion that a state is found to be internationally responsible. The two most important consequences are the obligations of the state to cease the wrongful conduct and the obligation to make reparations. These dual obligations are listed in articles 30 and 31 of the ILC articles respectively. At the outset it is important to note, however, that the obligations to cease wrongful conduct and make reparations do not affect the duty of the responsible state to perform the obligation that it has breached. The pre-existing legal obligation remains.[70] Thus, in *Gabčíkovo-Nagymaros Project*, the ICJ noted that the treaty for the construction of a dam on the Danube entered into by Czechoslovakia and Hungary was still in force even though both states had materially breached its provisions.[71] Thus, regardless of their wrongful conduct, both parties remained under an obligation to consider how the 'multiple objectives of the Treaty could best be served, keeping in mind that all of them should be fulfilled'.[72]

7.6.2 The cessation of wrongful conduct

The first and primary obligation incumbent on a state that is responsible for an internationally wrongful act is to cease the act in question. Thus, in *The Wall*, after having concluded that Israel had violated its international obligations by constructing a security barrier on occupied Palestinian territory, the ICJ concluded that Israel must put an end to the violations that flowed from the construction of the barrier.[73] The duty of cessation is listed in article 30(1) of the ILC articles. Paragraph (2) of the article stipulates that the responsible state may be obliged to 'offer appropriate assurances and guarantees of non-repetition' if that is required by the circumstances. In *LaGrand*, where the United States was found to be in violation of its obligations under the Vienna Convention on Consular Relations for not notifying foreign nationals in their custody of their rights to consular assistance, Germany requested an assurance from the United States that it would in future comply with the Convention. The Court found, however, that a commitment expressed by the United States to ensure future compliance was sufficient.[74]

7.6.3 The duty to make reparation

Article 31 of the ILC articles reflects the fundamental principle that a responsible state is under an obligation to 'make full reparation for the injury caused by the

---

[70] See also art. 29.

[71] *Gabčíkovo-Nagymaros Project* (n 2) paras 114 and 132. See also the Vienna Convention on the Law of Treaties, art. 60.

[72] *Gabčíkovo-Nagymaros Project* (n 2) para. 139.   [73] *The Wall* (n 66) paras 149–150.

[74] *LaGrand* (n 16) para. 124.

internationally wrongful act'.[75] Thus, since both parties in the *Gabčíkovo-Nagymaros Project* case had committed an international wrong, both were in theory entitled to compensation.[76] The seminal case is *Factory at Chorzów* where the Permanent Court of International Justice (PCIJ) stated that the 'breach of an engagement involves an obligation to make reparation in an adequate form' and that reparation is the indispensable complement to a failure to apply a convention.[77] It also found that the purpose of reparation is to 'as far as possible, wipe out all the consequences of the illegal act and re-establish the situation which would, in all probability, have existed if that act had not been committed'.[78] As we shall see in Chapter 11, the issue of the proper standard of reparation and compensation has been debated in relation to the expropriation of foreign property in the case of Communist states and developing states during the Cold War seeking to lower the standard of compensation from that of 'full' to 'appropriate' compensation.

The concept of 'injury' includes not just material but also moral damage. While material damage relates to losses etc. that are measurable in financial terms, moral damage includes more intangible losses, including pain and suffering.

As noted in the introduction to this chapter, it is not a general requirement in international law that a state must have suffered material harm or damage before it can seek reparation. In *Rainbow Warrior*, the Permanent Court of Arbitration (PCA) concluded that the French breach of its obligations towards New Zealand had been an 'affront to the dignity and prestige of New Zealand' and led to damage 'of a moral, political and legal nature'.[79] Articles 34–38 list the different forms that reparation may take. The list includes restitution, compensation, satisfaction and interest. Of these, compensation is the most relevant means of reparation and a court or tribunal with jurisdiction over a case usually awards compensation for the damage suffered.[80]

7.6.4 **Obligations of third states following breaches of *jus cogens***

As discussed in Chapter 2, *jus cogens* norms (peremptory norms) have a special status in international law.[81] This is also reflected in the law on state responsibility, where articles 40 and 41 of the ILC articles specify that all states must cooperate to bring to an end through lawful means any serious breach of a *jus cogens* norm, must refrain from recognizing 'as lawful a situation created by a serious breach' of a peremptory norm and must not 'render aid or assistance in maintaining that situation'.[82] The breach of *jus cogens* must, however, be serious.[83] The obligations in articles 40 and 41 are reflected in the ICJ's Advisory Opinion on *Namibia*,[84] the General

---

[75] See also *Factory at Chorzów*, 1928, PCIJ, Series A, No. 17, 21.

[76] *Gabčíkovo-Nagymaros Project* (n 2) para. 152.   [77] *Factory at Chorzów* (n 75) 21.

[78] Ibid, 47. See also *Gabčíkovo-Nagymaros Project* (n 2) para. 150.

[79] *Rainbow Warrior* (n 8) para. 110.   [80] See also Draft Articles (n 17) p. 99, para. 2.

[81] See art. 53 of the Vienna Convention on the Law of Treaties.   [82] Art. 41(1) and (2).

[83] See also the overview in Draft Articles (n 17) pp. 112–116.

[84] *Legal Consequences for States of the Continued Presence of South Africa in Namibia (South West Africa) notwithstanding Security Council Resolution 276 (1970)*, Advisory Opinion [1971] ICJ Rep 16, para. 126.

Assembly's Declaration on Friendly Relations[85] and in the international reaction to the Iraqi invasion and attempt at annexation of Kuwait in 1990.[86] In *The Wall*, the ICJ found that all states are obliged not to 'recognize the illegal situation resulting from the construction of the wall in the Occupied Palestinian Territory, including in and around East Jerusalem' just as all states are 'under an obligation not to render aid or assistance in maintaining the situation created by such construction'.[87] In March 2014, the General Assembly responded to Russia's annexation of Crimea by calling upon states, international organizations and specialized agencies not to recognize any alteration of the status of Crimea and to 'refrain from any action or dealing that might be interpreted as recognizing any such altered status'.[88]

7.7 Who may invoke a breach of international law?

7.7.1 Introduction—the injured state

In this section, we identify the state that is entitled to invoke the international responsibility of another state. Who can, in other words, demand that another state cease its wrongful conduct and claim a right to reparation? The main rule in international law is that it is only the state whose individual rights have been violated or denied—the 'injured state'—that is entitled to invoke the international responsibility of the responsible state and demand cessation and reparation.[89] If the rights of more than one state have been violated, there may be more than one injured state.[90] In practice, however, it may be difficult to determine when a state can reasonably be considered to be 'injured' by the wrongful act of another state. To that end, article 42 of the ILC articles specifies that a state is injured if the obligation breached was owed to it individually. That, of course, will be the case in relation to breaches of bilateral treaties and other obligations that directly concern the state.[91] A state will also be injured if the obligation is not owed to it individually but instead to a group of states and the breach 'specially affects' the state or if the obligation breached radically changes the position of all other states to which the obligation is owed.[92]

7.7.2 Obligations *erga omnes*

Sometimes a state that is not 'injured' may invoke the responsibility of another state. We saw in Chapter 2 that some legal obligations are 'communitarian' in the sense that they are owed not just to the state that has been injured by a breach of the obligation but to the international community as a whole.[93] The norms in question are referred to as *erga omnes* and when such norms are breached all states will be found to have the

---

[85] GA Res. 2656 (XXV) (24 October 1970), UN Doc. A/25/2625.
[86] SC Res. 662 (9 August 1990), UN Doc. S/RES/662.   [87] *The Wall* (n 66) para. 159.
[88] GA Res. 68/262 (27 March 2014), UN Doc. A/68/L.39 and Add.1, para. 6.
[89] Art. 42.   [90] See also art. 46.   [91] Art. 42(a).   [92] Art. 42(b).
[93] See Section 2.9.

required legal interest to invoke them. In practice, as article 48(1) of the ILC articles illustrates, there are two types of *erga omnes*/'communitarian' obligations. The first type is found in article 48(1)(a) and it refers to *erga omnes partes* obligations. These are owed 'to a group of States' and they are 'established for the protection of a collective interest of the group'. Here, a non-injured state among the group of states can invoke the responsibility of another state.[94] Examples of such obligations *erga omnes partes* include obligations under multilateral human rights treaties. For example, any state that is party to the European Convention on Human Rights may invoke another state's breach of the Convention, regardless of whether the invoking state is injured by the breach. In *Certain Questions Relating to the Obligation to Prosecute or Extradite*, the ICJ stated that obligations under the UN Torture Convention 'are owed by any State party to all the other States parties to the Convention' and that 'each State party has an interest in compliance with them in any given case'.[95]

The second type of *erga omnes* obligations is found in article 48(1)(b) and it concerns the broader category of (pure) *erga omnes* obligations that are owed to *all* states. Breaches can therefore also be invoked by all states. In *Barcelona Traction*, the Court had to determine if Belgium had the required legal standing to bring a case against Spain on behalf of Belgian shareholders in a Canadian company. According to the Court:

> … an essential distinction should be drawn between the obligations of a State towards the international community as a whole, and those arising vis-à-vis another State in the field of diplomatic protection. By their very nature the former are the concern of all States. In view of the importance of the rights involved, all States can be held to have a legal interest in their protection; they are obligations *erga omnes*.[96]

As we saw in Chapter 2, there is a close link between *erga omnes* obligations and norms of a peremptory/*jus cogens* nature. We also saw that the obligations in question include the prohibition of aggression and genocide, the principles and rules concerning the basic rights of the human person, including protection from slavery, the prohibition of apartheid and racial discrimination, the ban on crimes against humanity and grave breaches of the laws of armed conflict, the prohibition of piracy and the right to self-determination. As we shall see in Chapter 10, *erga omnes* obligations have also been brought up in relation to breaches of international environmental law.

A final point is worth noting about *erga omnes* obligations. While all states can invoke breaches of these communitarian norms, a state that is not injured by a breach of an *erga omnes* norm will have fewer rights than an injured state. Thus, according to article 48(2), the rights of non-injured states are limited to claiming cessation of the wrongful act, seeking assurances and guarantees of non-repetition[97] and claiming compensation in the interest of an injured state.[98] Since the invoking state is not injured, it cannot claim compensation in its own right.

---

[94] Art. 48(1)(a).

[95] *Questions relating to the Obligation to Prosecute or Extradite (Belgium v Senegal)*, Judgment [2012] ICJ Rep 422, para. 68.

[96] *Barcelona Traction, Light and Power Co., Ltd*, Judgment [1970] ICJ Rep 3, para. 33.

[97] Art. 48(2)(a).   [98] Art. 48(2)(b).

7.8 **Diplomatic protection**

'Diplomatic protection' refers to the right of a state to invoke the international responsibility of another state for an international wrongful act to a natural or legal person who is a national of the invoking state in order to implement the responsibility. Thus, since the rules on diplomatic protection are linked to the rules of state responsibility, it is natural to discuss them in that connection.

Historically, diplomatic protection was derived from the understanding that the state is exercising such protection because the injury to one of its nationals is considered as an injury to the state itself. In practice, however, the state also asserts the rights of the injured national.[99] The basic principles of diplomatic protection are listed in 19 draft articles adopted by the ILC in 2006. As article 1 of these articles illustrates, diplomatic protection is essentially a procedure whereby the state of nationality of an injured person seeks to secure protection from and potential reparation for the international wrongful act inflicted on that person by another state. Once a state exercises diplomatic protection, the claim becomes one of the state in the sense that the state is now asserting its own right.[100] In article 19, the ILC recommends a practice that states should follow when they exercise diplomatic protection. According to the article, the state that is entitled to exercise diplomatic protection should (a) 'give due consideration' to the option of exercising such protection in particular in instances where 'a significant injury has occurred'; (b) 'take into account, wherever feasible, the views of injured persons with regard to resort to diplomatic protection and the reparation to be sought' and (c) 'transfer to the injured person any compensation obtained for the injury from the responsible State subject to any reasonable deductions'. As the term 'recommend' illustrates, however, the practice is not legally binding on the state.

The rules on diplomatic protection deal with both natural and legal persons. Importantly, they primarily protect nationals who are not officially representing the state. As we saw in Chapter 6, state representatives are protected by the 1961 Vienna Convention on Diplomatic Relations and the 1963 Vienna Convention on Consular Relations. According to article 2 of the ILC articles on diplomatic protection, the exercise of diplomatic protection is a right for a state and not a duty. While the national laws of a state may oblige state authorities to offer diplomatic protection to nationals of the state who have been the victim of an international wrongful act by another state, international law contains no such obligation. This is also reflected in *Barcelona Traction*[101] and in a 2002 decision by a UK court of appeal.[102]

Article 4 of the ILC articles on diplomatic protection concerns protection of *natural persons*. The article reflects how it is generally for the state of nationality to set the conditions by which individuals qualify as nationals of the state. This is in line with early practice from the PCIJ, the 1930 Hague Convention on Certain Questions

---

[99] See also the discussion in Draft Articles on Diplomatic Protection with commentaries, *Yearbook of the International Law Commission*, 2006, vol. II, Part Two, p. 25.

[100] See also *Mavrommatis Palestine Concessions*, 1924, PCIJ, Series A, No. 2, p. 12.

[101] *Barcelona Traction* (n 96) para. 78.

[102] *Abbasi v Secretary of State* [2002] EWCA Civ 1598, [69].

Relating to the Conflict of Nationality Laws and the 1997 European Convention on Nationality.[103] While the ICJ in *Nottebohm* indicated that a state is only obliged to respect a grant of nationality by another state if the latter can point to an effective and genuine link between itself and the individual granted nationality,[104] the ILC does not find that the state offering diplomatic protection must prove the existence of such a link.[105]

Diplomatic protection of *corporations* is covered in article 9. It follows therefrom that the nationality of a corporation is the state where it is incorporated. As with natural persons, it is generally the state of nationality that decides who it chooses to incorporate and thus grant its nationality to.[106] However, article 9 makes an exception in those cases where there is no significant link between the state of incorporation and the corporation *and* where significant connections exist with another state. In such instances, the latter state will be regarded as the state of nationality for the purposes of diplomatic protection. According to article 11 of the ILC articles on diplomatic protection, as a general point of departure, the state of nationality of shareholders in a corporation is not entitled to exercise diplomatic protection in respect of the shareholders.[107] This also follows from the ICJ's decision in *Barcelona Traction*.[108]

It is a well-established principle that a state cannot present an international claim before the injured person has *exhausted local remedies*.[109] This is also reflected in article 14 of the articles on diplomatic protection. Thus, a state that has violated the rights of a national of another state must be afforded the opportunity to correct the wrong through its own means. In *Diallo*, however, the ICJ found that a number of exceptions exist.[110] Among other things, the injured person is not required to exhaust local remedies if these are manifestly not available.[111]

A few points are worth noting regarding the relationship between the rules on diplomatic protection and other areas of international law. First, according to article 16 of the ILC articles on diplomatic protection, the principles of diplomatic protection do not affect the rights of states, persons or other entities to secure redress for international wrongful acts under other procedures in international law. In practice, therefore, diplomatic protection is complementary to the specialized rules for the protection of human rights.[112] Secondly, under article 17, the rules on diplomatic protection do not apply if they are inconsistent with special rules of international law, including treaties for the protection of investments. As we shall return to in Chapter 11, treaties on foreign investments usually have special rules on dispute settlement. A final rule to note is article 18, which concerns the protection of a ship's crew. According to that

---

[103] See the Convention's art. 3.

[104] *Nottebohm (Second Phase) (Liechtenstein v Guatemala)*, Judgment [1955] ICJ Rep 4, 23.

[105] ILC Draft Articles on Diplomatic Protection (n 99) p. 32.

[106] See also *Ahmadou Sadio Diallo (Republic of Guinea v Democratic Republic of the Congo)*, Preliminary Objections, Judgment [2007] ICJ Rep 582, para. 61.

[107] But see art. 11(a) and (b) and art. 12.

[108] *Barcelona Traction* (n 96), see inter alia para. 46.

[109] See *Diallo* (n 106) para. 44. See also *Interhandel (Switzerland v United States)*, Preliminary Objections [1959] ICJ Rep 6, see p. 27.

[110] See also art. 15.   [111] See art. 15(d).   [112] See the discussion in Chapter 9.

article, both the state of nationality of the ship as well as the state of nationality of the members of the crew can exercise diplomatic protection on behalf of the crew.[113]

7.9 The international responsibility of international organizations

The 2002 ILC Articles on the Responsibility of States explicitly state that they do not apply to the responsibility of international organizations.[114] Instead, that falls within a series of Draft Articles on Responsibility of International Organizations adopted by the ILC in 2011. These articles are largely based on the articles on state responsibility, and in the following only a limited number of issues will be dealt with.

Article 2(a) defines an international organization as 'an organization established by a treaty or other instrument governed by international law and possessing its own international legal personality'. Article 3 stipulates the basic principle whereby 'Every internationally wrongful act of an international organization entails the international responsibility of that organization.'[115] In addition, under article 4, an international wrongful act of an international organization exists when conduct attributable to that organization 'constitutes a breach of an international obligation of that organization'. Conduct may cover both acts and omissions.

One of the most interesting issues is attribution of conduct. An international organization is, after all, unlike a state in the sense that it does not have any territory and merely exists in order to fulfil certain functions assigned to it by the creating states.[116] According to article 6, conduct is attributable to an international organization when performed by an organ or an agent of the organization, regardless of the position held by that organ or agent. Importantly, the term 'agent' is given a wide application and it includes an individual who does not hold any official position in the organization as long as the conduct performed by the individual is done on the instruction or under the direction or control of the organization.[117]

Article 7 concerns the important question of responsibility for conduct performed by an actor (or agent) that has been 'loaned' to an international organization by a state or another international organization. The issue is particularly relevant to UN peacekeeping operations. The UN does not have its own 'UN forces' and instead relies on forces put forward by the member states, which generally retain certain powers, such as the power to discipline and criminally prosecute individual soldiers. According to article 7, the UN

---

[113] See also *SS I'm Alone Case (Canada v United States)* (1935) III RIAA 1609 and *The M/V 'Saiga' (No. 2) (Saint Vincent and the Grenadines v Guinea)*, Case No. 2, Judgment, 1 July 1999, para. 106.

[114] See ILC Articles on State Responsibility, art. 57.

[115] See also *Difference Relating to Immunity from Legal Process of a Special Rapporteur of the Commission on Human Rights*, Advisory Opinion [1999] ICJ Rep 62, para. 66.

[116] See also ILC, Draft Articles on the Responsibility of International Organizations, with commentaries, *Yearbook of the International Law Commission*, 2011, vol. II, Part Two, p. 3.

[117] See also *Reparations* (n 10) 177. See also ILC, Draft Articles on the Responsibility of International Organizations (n 116) commentary to art. 6, paras 10–11.

is responsible for the conduct of the forces it lends when it exercises 'effective control' over their conduct. It is, however, not entirely clear what 'effective control' means.

In 2007 in *Behrami and Behrami v France*, the Grand Chamber of the European Court of Human Rights held that acts committed by the UN Kosovo Force (KFOR) troops in Kosovo were attributed to the UN and not the troop-contributing NATO states because the UN Security Council had retained 'ultimate authority and control' and only delegated operational control to the states.[118] The decision was, however, widely (and justifiably) criticized for allowing states to escape their international responsibilities,[119] and in *Al-Jedda* the Court seemed to backtrack somewhat from its controversial conclusions in *Behrami*.[120] In its 2011 commentary to article 7, the ILC noted that the decisive issue is the element of 'factual control' and that 'operational' control would seem more significant than 'ultimate' control, since the latter hardly implies a role in the act in question.[121] Thus, what is decisive is who actually directs the forces when the relevant conduct occurs. The Supreme Court of the Netherlands has also concluded that 'all factual circumstances and the special context of the case must be taken into account'[122] and it has upheld a decision from a lower court that had found that conduct by a Dutch battalion deployed in Bosnia under the UN Protection Force (UNPROFOR) could be attributed to the Netherlands.[123] The Court limited its decisions to the responsibility of the Netherlands and left open the possibility that the conduct by the Dutch forces could *also* have been attributed to the UN.[124] The case therefore illustrates the important point that article 7 does not rule out that conduct can be attributed to both the international organization and the lending state or organization.[125]

Summary

The international law on state responsibility specifies what happens when a state violates its obligations under international law. The most relevant rules are found in a set of 2001 articles on state responsibility adopted by the ILC. State responsibility generally arises when conduct is in breach of an international obligation and the conduct can be attributed to a state. As a main rule, a state is only internationally responsible for its own acts and not for the acts of private actors. International law recognizes that the existence of one of a number of circumstances precludes the international wrongfulness of an act otherwise in breach of international law. The circumstances in question may justify not

---

[118] *Behrami and Behrami v France*, App. no. 71412/01 and *Saramati v France, Germany and Norway*, App. no. 78166/01 (Grand Chamber), Admissibility, 2 May 2007, paras 57–61.

[119] See, inter alia, Marko Milanovic and Tatjana Papic, 'As Bad as it Gets: The European Court of Human Rights's *Behrami and Saramati* Decision and General International Law' (2009) 58 *International and Comparative Law Quarterly* 267.

[120] *Al-Jedda v UK*, App. no. 27021/08 (Grand Chamber), Judgment, 7 July 2011, paras 83–84.

[121] Commentary to art. 7, p. 23, para. 103. See also the 2007 decision by the UK House of Lords in *R (on the application of Al-Jedda) (FC) v Secretary of State for Defence* [2007] UKHL 58, see e.g. the judgment of Lord Bingham of Cornhill, [22]–[24].

[122] Supreme Court of the Netherlands, *The State of the Netherlands v Hasan Nuhanović*, Case 12/03324, 6 September 2013. For the particular circumstances, see para. 3.12.2.

[123] Ibid, paras 3.11.3 and 3.12.3.   [124] Ibid, para. 3.9.4.

[125] See also Draft Articles on the Responsibility of International Organizations (n 116) p. 16, para. 4. See also Supreme Court of the Netherlands, *Hasan Nuhanović* (n 124) paras 3.11.2–3.11.3.

complying with an international obligation. The two most important consequences that follow from wrongful conduct are the obligations of the responsible state to cease the wrongful conduct and the obligation to make reparations. Some breaches of international law are so serious that they will trigger obligations for third parties. Although a state that is injured by another state's breach of international law may always invoke the responsibility of the latter, non-injured states may also be entitled to invoke breaches of international law. According to the rules on diplomatic protection, a state is entitled to invoke the international responsibility of another state for an international wrongful act to a natural or legal person who is a national of the invoking state in order to implement the responsibility.

Recommended reading

On the topic of state responsibility in general, see the seminal work by James Crawford, *State Responsibility* (Cambridge University Press, 2013). Another helpful source is the commentaries to the 2001 Articles on the Responsibility of States for Internationally Wrongful Acts, see *Yearbook of the International Law Commission*, 2001, vol. II, Part Two. For a more concise overview and discussion of state responsibility, see James Crawford and Simon Olleson, 'The Character and Forms of International Responsibility' in Malcolm D. Evans (ed.), *International Law* (4th edn, Oxford University Press, 2014) 443–476.

A good presentation of the issue of consent as a circumstance precluding wrongfulness and its role in relation to the use of force, is Ashley S. Deeks, 'Consent to the Use of Force and International Law Supremacy' (2013) 54 *Harvard International Law Journal* 1.

For the topic of countermeasures, see Nigel White and Ademola Abass, 'Countermeasures and Sanctions' in Malcolm D. Evans (ed.), *International Law* (Oxford University Press, 2010) 531–545 and Thomas Franck, 'On Proportionality of Countermeasures in International Law' (2008) 102(4) *American Journal of International Law* 715.

The issue of necessity is covered in Ole Spiermann, 'Humanitarian Intervention as a Necessity and the Threat or Use of *Jus Cogens*' (2002) 71 *Nordic Journal of International Law* 543.

The concept of *erga omnes* is discussed in M. Cherif Bassiouni, 'International Crimes: "*Jus Cogens*" and "*Obligatio Erga Omnes*"' (1996) 59(1) *Law and Contemporary Problems* 63.

A good overview of the rules on diplomatic protection is found in the commentary to the ILC's Draft Articles on Diplomatic Protection, see *Yearbook of the International Law Commission*, 2006, vol. II, Part Two.

Questions for discussion

1. Why are the rules on state responsibility classified as secondary rules of international law?
2. Can a state be in breach of its international obligations due to acts of private individuals?
3. What is the relationship between treaty law and state responsibility?
4. What are the conceptual differences between peremptory norms/*jus cogens* and *erga omnes* obligations?
5. Why was the 2007 *Behrami* decision from the European Court of Human Rights criticized?
6. When can a state invoke the responsibility of another state?

8

The international law of the sea

CENTRAL ISSUES

1. This chapter discusses the main principles and rules that make up the international legal regulation of the seas.

2. It presents the rationale behind the division of the sea into a set of different jurisdictional zones in which states hold various rights and obligations.

3. The chapter discusses the regulation of the different maritime zones and the question of how overlapping zones are delimited.

4. The chapter also discusses a number of issues related to the conservation of marine life and the different means by which disputes about the proper interpretation of the law of the sea can be adjudicated peacefully.

8.1 Introduction

The international law of the sea is one of the oldest disciplines of public international law. In fact, the identification and application of principles for governing the roughly 70 per cent of the earth's surface that consists of water has been a topic of interest for centuries. A substantial part of the modern interest in the regulation stems from the age of the explorers, when the extent to which the oceans could be traversed without obstacles was of crucial importance to powerful maritime powers, such as the British and the Dutch, and their 'colonial companies'. It is therefore within the international law of the sea that some of the most noteworthy contributions to international law were published. A notable example is that of Hugo Grotius's *Mare Liberum* (1609), which offered a strong defence of the principle of the freedom of the seas.[1]

The identification of the balance between the needs and sovereign concerns of coastal states and the interests of other states that wish to enjoy the benefits of the seas is vital to the maintenance of peaceful international relations, and the law of the sea is part of the international law of coexistence. In contemporary international law, the competing interests between coastal states and other states is primarily reflected

---

[1] Hugo Grotius, *Mare Liberum* (1609).

in a spatial partitioning of the sea into jurisdictional zones. In this 'zonal system', the rights of coastal states decrease the further away one moves from the shore. More recently, by classifying the deep seabed and the resources of its subsoil as the 'common heritage of mankind', the law of the sea recognizes collective rights alongside the rights of individual states. Not all concerns and interests can be accommodated through a spatial division of the sea, however, and international law seeks to facilitate international cooperation on matters of concern to all states, such as the preservation of marine life and the limitation of marine pollution.[2]

We begin in Section 8.2 with an overview of the legal sources, including the 1982 United Nations Convention on the Law of the Sea (UNCLOS). Section 8.3—which constitutes the bulk of the chapter—discusses the spatial partitioning of the sea and the different maritime zones. Section 8.4 analyses the regulation of piracy before Section 8.5 discusses some selected issues in relation to conservation of marine life. Section 8.6 introduces dispute settlement in the law of the sea.

8.2 The sources of the international law of the sea

The most important legal source in the international law of the sea is the 1982 United Nations Convention on the Law of the Sea (UNCLOS), which entered into force in November 1994. It is a massive document and its 320 articles cover the majority of issues in the law of the sea. It is built on a holistic understanding of the challenges associated with regulating the oceans.[3] In fact, the mandate of the 1973–1982 Third UN Conference on the Law of the Sea (UNCLOS III), which adopted the Convention, was to reach agreement on 'all matters relating to the law of the sea'.[4] Thus, UNCLOS is a 'package deal' that disallows reservations unless expressly permitted.[5] By October 2018, 168 states had become parties to the Convention. Some important maritime states, including the United States and Turkey, remain outside.

UNCLOS is the result of years of complicated negotiations[6] and it builds upon existing treaty-based regulation, most notably four conventions adopted at the First UN Conference on the Law of the Sea in 1958 in Geneva. Unlike the 1958 Conventions, however, the Third UN Conference managed to reach agreement on a host of contentious issues, most notably the maximum breadth of the territorial sea and coastal states' rights to the natural resources of the sea adjacent to their shores. The Conference also took account of recent technological advances that enable mining of the deep seabed. After tough negotiations and a noticeable delay, it established a system that balances the interests of states willing to exploit the deep seabed with a fair distribution of the wealth therefrom. Other notable accomplishments in UNCLOS include the creation of the International Tribunal for the Law of the Sea (ITLOS) (see Section 8.6).

---

[2] Protection of the marine environment is covered in Chapter 10.   [3] UNCLOS Preamble.
[4] See GA Res. 3067 (XXVIII) (16 November 1973).   [5] See art. 309.
[6] For an overview of the process, see James Harrison, *Making the Law of the Sea: A Study in the Development of International Law* (Cambridge University Press, 2013) 27–61.

Customary international law is also an important legal source in the international law of the sea. In fact, some of the most important statements by the International Court of Justice (ICJ) on customary international law are found in decisions that deal with the law of the sea.[7]

8.3 The spatial partitioning of the sea

8.3.1 Introduction

As noted already, it is a prime concern of international law to find a reasonable balance between the legitimate interests of coastal states that wish to extend their sovereignty to the waters that run adjacent to their shores and the often equally legitimate interests of other states that want to utilize the sea for a myriad of purposes. The result is a finely marked legal system that divides the sea into different maritime zones in which coastal and other states hold a variety of rights and obligations. Since the aim is to balance the rights of a coastal state with the freedom of other states, it is not surprising that the rights of the former decrease with the distance from the shore.

Conceptually, one can distinguish between marine spaces *within the national jurisdiction of a coastal state* (internal waters, territorial sea, archipelagic waters, international straits, the contiguous zone, the exclusive economic zone (EEZ) and the continental shelf) and spaces *beyond the jurisdiction of a coastal state* (the high seas and the seabed and subsoil thereof, also known as the Area). The first category—the zones of national jurisdiction—can be subdivided into two additional 'spaces'. The first type of space consists of areas that fall *within the territorial sovereignty of a coastal state* where the state has the exclusive right to enforce its laws and regulations. These areas include the internal waters, the territorial sea, the archipelagic waters and international straits. The second type of space is made up of those areas situated *beyond the territorial sovereignty of a coastal state* where the state may only assert certain jurisdictional powers. These areas include the contiguous zone, the EEZ and the continental shelf. Under international law, the 'sea' consists of three elements: the atmosphere above the sea, the water in the sea and the seabed and subsoil.

Our overview of the zonal system starts with the concept of the baseline (Section 8.3.2). We then discuss the regulation of internal waters and the territorial sea (Section 8.3.3), the contiguous zone (Section 8.3.4), and the EEZ (Section 8.3.5). Attention is then turned to the exploitation of the continental shelf (Section 8.3.6) and the deep seabed (Section 8.3.7), before we examine the regulation of the high seas (Section 8.3.8). The final section is devoted to delimitation of overlapping maritime zones (Section 8.3.9).

---

[7] See, inter alia, *North Sea Continental Shelf Cases*, Judgment [1969] ICJ Rep 53, para. 63 and *Norwegian Fisheries (UK v Norway)*, Judgment [1951] ICJ Rep 116, 131.

8.3.2 **The concept of baselines**

To measure the breadth of the various maritime zones one must first identify the physical point from where the breadth of the zone is measured—the *baseline*.[8] In practical terms, the baseline serves two purposes. First, as already mentioned, it is the point from which the breadth of the various maritime zones is measured. Secondly, it also delimits the internal waters of a state from those of its territorial sea. Thus, a coastal state has an interest in pushing its baseline as far as possible out into the sea. The practical drawing of baselines is governed by certain principles that take account of the different physical configurations of coastlines.

The main rule is found in article 5 of UNCLOS whereby the 'normal baseline ... is the low-water line along the coast as marked on large-scale charts officially recognized by the coastal State'.[9] In *Anglo-Norwegian Fisheries*, however, the ICJ accepted that Norway could draw *straight baselines* between fixed points on the mainland and on islands or rocks where the coast 'is deeply indented and cut into' or where there is a fringe of islands along the coast in its immediate vicinity.[10] Article 7(1) of UNCLOS accepts straight baselines as an exception to a normal baseline.[11] Straight baselines are drawn across the water with the practical effect that water on the landward side of the line becomes internal waters. Article 8(2) specifies that other states enjoy a right of innocent passage (see more in Section 8.3.3) in such territorial waters.

Article 7(3) contains a number of conditions for drawing straight baselines.[12] First, the baseline may not depart 'to any appreciable extent from the general direction of the coast'. Secondly, the 'sea areas lying within the lines must be sufficiently closely linked to the land domain to be subject to the regime of internal waters'. In *Anglo-Norwegian Fisheries*, the ICJ also noted that 'certain economic interests peculiar to the region, the reality and importance of which are clearly evidenced by a long usage' may be a relevant factor when determining if a straight baseline is called for.[13] In either case, a coastal state has a fairly wide discretion in drawing its baseline.[14]

Article 10 of UNCLOS concerns *bays* on coastal lines belonging to a single state. A 'bay' is defined as a 'well-marked indentation whose penetration is in such proportion to the width of its mouth as to contain land-locked waters and constitute more than a mere curvature of the coast'. An indentation is not a bay, however, if its area is smaller than that of a 'semi-circle whose diameter is a line drawn across the mouth of that indentation'.[15] If an indention fulfils the conditions for constituting a 'bay', a coastal state may draw the baseline across the mouth of the bay and turn the water inside

---

[8] For an overview, see Yoshifumi Tanaka, *The International Law of the Sea* (2nd edn, Cambridge University Press, 2015) 44–74.

[9] See also the 1958 Geneva Convention on the Territorial Sea and the Contiguous Zone (TSC), art. 3 and *Fisheries* (n 7) 128.

[10] *Fisheries* (n 7) 128–129. See also *Maritime Delimitation and Territorial Questions between Qatar and Bahrain*, Merits, Judgment [2001] ICJ Rep 40, 103, para. 212.

[11] See also TSC art. 4. All of the Scandinavian states have drawn straight baselines.

[12] See also *Fisheries* (n 7) 133.   [13] *Fisheries* (n 7) 131. See also UNCLOS art. 7(5).

[14] See also *Fisheries* (n 7) 131. But see *Maritime Delimitation and Territorial Questions between Qatar and Bahrain* (n 10) 103, para. 212.

[15] Art. 10(2).

the bay into internal waters. But a bay cannot be closed by a baseline if the distance between the two sides of the mouth exceeds 24 nautical miles.[16] The ICJ has indicated that the provisions on bays in UNCLOS reflect customary international law.[17] Special rules apply to large *historic bays* over which a coastal state has continuously exercised jurisdiction with the general acceptance of other states.[18]

Mention should also be made of the issue of *port and harbour installations* that extend into the water. Article 11 of UNCLOS stipulates that harbour installations can be regarded as forming part of the coastline. The works must, however, be attached to the coast.

Article 121(2) of UNCLOS specifies that *islands* generate the same jurisdictional rights (territorial sea, contiguous zone etc.) as other territory. An 'island' is a 'naturally formed area of land, surrounded by water, which is above water at high tide'.[19] ICJ case law illustrates that there is no rule on the minimum size of an island.[20] The requirements of attachment to the seabed and natural formation mean that artificial installations, such as lighthouses or oil platforms, do not constitute 'islands' and do not therefore possess territorial seas or other maritime zones. An island is different from *a low-tide elevation* that is a naturally formed area of land 'surrounded by and above water at low tide but submerged at high tide'.[21] A low-tide elevation may be used as the baseline for measuring the territorial sea if it is situated at a distance not exceeding the breadth of the territorial sea from the mainland or an island, but it does not have a territorial sea if located outside.[22] According to article 121(3), a maritime feature is only an 'island' if it can 'sustain human habitation or economic life' of its own. If not, it is a *rock* that does not have an EEZ or a continental shelf. The definition of an island in UNCLOS reflects customary international law.[23] What is decisive is the *ability* of the feature to sustain human habitation or economic life—not whether humans actually have a presence on it.[24] The size of feature does not seem to be relevant.[25]

Article 121(3) was discussed in *South China Sea Arbitration*, which concerned Chinese claims in the South China Sea. One of the issues concerned the legal status of some of the maritime features in the area. According to the tribunal, the term 'human habitation'

---

[16] Art. 10(4).

[17] *Land, Island and Maritime Frontier Dispute* [1992] ICJ Rep 588, para. 383.

[18] See also *Continental Shelf (Tunisia v Libyan Arab Jamahiriya)*, Judgment [1982] ICJ Rep 18, 74, para. 100.

[19] Art. 121(1).

[20] *Maritime Delimitation and Territorial Questions between Qatar and Bahrain* (n 10) 97, para. 185.

[21] UNCLOS art. 13(1).

[22] Art. 13(2). On low-tide elevations, see also *Fisheries* (n 7) 128; *Maritime Delimitation and Territorial Questions between Qatar and Bahrain* (n 10) 99, para. 193.

[23] *Territorial and Maritime Dispute (Nicaragua v Colombia)* [2012] ICJ Rep 624, para. 139. For a sceptical view, see Tanaka (n 8) 69.

[24] *The Republic of the Philippines and the People's Republic of China*, Award, PCA Case No. 2013-19, 12 July 2016, paras 482 and 545.

[25] Ibid, para. 482. See also *Territorial and Maritime Dispute (Nicaragua v Colombia)* (n 23) paras 139 and 37. The Norwegian Supreme Court has held, however, that a feature may simply be too large to be considered a mere 'rock': see *Public Prosecutor v Haraldson et al.*, Rt. 1996 p. 624. For an overview in English, see Robin Churchill, 'Norway: Supreme Court Judgment on Law of the Sea Issues' (1996) 11 *International Journal of Marine and Coastal Law* 576–580.

refers to the 'non-transient character of the inhabitation, such that the inhabitants can fairly be said to constitute the natural population of the feature'. It refers to 'a stable community of people for whom the feature constitutes a home and on which they can remain'. So while an indigenous population would suffice, a non-indigenous inhabitation may also suffice if the population truly intends 'to reside in and make their lives on the islands in question'.[26] The term 'economic life of their own' refers to a notion of 'economic life' and not 'economic value'. The economic life 'must be oriented around the feature itself and not focused solely on the waters or seabed of the surrounding territorial sea'. Importantly, the extraction of natural resources 'for the benefit of a population elsewhere' falls outside the definition.[27] The Court also noted that in practice, a maritime feature will ordinarily only possess an economic life of its own if it is also inhabited by a stable human community.[28] With regard to China's construction on the maritime features in the area, as we saw in Chapter 4, the Court found that the status of a feature takes its departure point as the *natural condition* and not man-made/artificial alterations/installations. Thus, a low-tide elevation remains a low-tide elevation 'regardless of the scale of the island or installation built atop it',[29] just as 'a rock cannot be transformed into a fully entitled island through land reclamation'.[30] The Court concluded that none of the maritime features could be considered islands for the purposes of international law.[31]

8.3.3 **Internal waters and the territorial sea**

Internal waters primarily consist of water on the landward side of a straight baseline from which the territorial sea is measured and water on the landward side of an enclosed bay.[32] In general, a state enjoys full sovereignty over its internal waters and transit in such waters is not governed by the rules on innocent passage (see later in this section).[33] In its internal waters, a coastal state is entitled to regulate all access to its ports and it is only in the event of distress that it is obliged to allow entry to a foreign vessel. A coastal state enjoys full sovereignty over all vessels located in its internal waters, including over ships in its ports. In practice, however, a coastal state tends to exercise its jurisdiction with restraint and with due consideration to the fact that the flag state will often be in a more natural position to exercise jurisdiction.

The *territorial sea* is a belt of the sea that runs adjacent to the coast. The maximum breadth of the territorial sea has been a long-standing issue in international law and it was not until the adoption of the 1982 UNCLOS that agreement was reached. UNCLOS sets the maximum breadth to 12 nautical miles when measured from the baseline.[34] The majority of states now claim a territorial sea of 12 miles and the limit appears to be reflected in customary international law. The territorial sea is not

---

[26] *The Republic of the Philippines and the People's Republic of China* (n 24) para. 542.

[27] Ibid, para. 543.   [28] Ibid, para. 544. See also the debate in Tanaka (n 8) 67.

[29] *The Republic of the Philippines and the People's Republic of China* (n 24) para. 305.

[30] Ibid, para. 508.

[31] See the Court's conclusions in ibid, paras 554, 557, 560, 563, 566, 569, 625–626 and 643–648.

[32] UNCLOS art. 8(1). On internal waters, see also V. D. Degan, 'Internal Waters' (1986) 17 *Netherlands Yearbook of International Law* 3–44.

[33] See Art. 8(1).   [34] Art. 3

limited to the water in the sea but also includes the air space above the sea as well as the seabed and its subsoil. Unlike the contiguous zone and the EEZ (see Sections 8.3.4 and 8.3.5), the territorial sea is an inseparable appurtenance of the land territory and thus an inherent feature of sovereignty over the land.

In general, a coastal state enjoys exclusive territorial sovereignty in its territorial sea and may lawfully exert the same jurisdictional powers in the area as it does on land.[35] According to the right of *innocent passage*, however, foreign vessels may traverse the territorial sea of another state without entering the internal waters or a port facility within the territorial sea.[36] For navigation to be considered 'passage', it must be 'continuous and expedited' and stopping and anchoring must be either an incidental element to ordinary navigation or justified under principles of *force majeure*, distress or in order to render assistance to others in danger or distress. Passage is considered 'innocent' when it is not 'prejudicial to the peace, good order or security of the coastal State'.[37] UNCLOS lists a number of acts that are deemed to be at variance with innocent passage. These include exercises with weapons, spying, acts of propaganda, the loading or unloading of commodities, currency or persons contrary to the regulations of the coastal state, serious pollution, fishing activities, research activities or interferences with coastal communications.[38] Submarines and other underwater vehicles must navigate on the surface and show their flag.[39] *Foreign warships* can also rely on a right of innocent passage.[40] So can ships that are either *nuclear-powered or which carry dangerous or noxious materials.*[41] A coastal state may, however, designate certain sea lanes for the passage of such vessels.[42] If a coastal state suspects that passage in its territorial waters is not innocent, it may take the steps necessary to prevent the passage from occurring.[43]

Article 27 of UNCLOS governs the important issue of the coastal state's exercise of criminal jurisdiction on foreign ships in passage in its territorial sea. Article 27(1) stipulates that a state should refrain from exercising such jurisdiction to arrest any person or to conduct any investigation in connection with any crime committed on board the ship during its passage unless it concerns the following circumstances:

(a) the consequences of the crime extend to the coastal state;

(b) the crime is of a kind to disturb the peace of the country or the good order of the territorial sea;

(c) the assistance of the local authorities has been requested by the master of the ship or by a diplomatic agent or consular officer of the flag state; or

(d) such measures are necessary for the suppression of illicit traffic in narcotic drugs or psychotropic substances.

A coastal state is also entitled to exercise measures of criminal jurisdiction on board foreign ships that pass through the territorial sea after leaving the internal waters.[44] When considering if, and in what manner, an arrest should be made, the local authorities must always have 'due regard to the interests of navigation'.[45] UNCLOS is even stricter in relation

---

[35] Art. 17.   [36] Art. 18(1).   [37] Art. 19(1).   [38] Art. 19(2).   [39] Art. 20.
[40] See the discussion in Tanaka (n 8) 89–92.   [41] Art. 23.   [42] Art. 22(2).
[43] Art. 25(1).   [44] Art. 27(2).   [45] Art. 27(4).

to a coastal state's exercise of *civil jurisdiction*. Thus, according to article 28(1), a coastal state 'should not stop or divert a foreign ship passing through the territorial sea for the purpose of exercising civil jurisdiction in relation to a person on board the ship'.

Special rules apply for *archipelagic waters* within an archipelagic state—generally speaking, a group of islands situated in the middle of an ocean that form a geographical, economic and political unit.[46] Examples of archipelagic states include Indonesia, the Philippines and Fiji. Although the water within the baselines of an archipelagic state would prima facie appear to be 'internal' in nature, navigation in archipelagic waters is generally governed by the right of innocent passage.[47] The archipelagic state may designate sea lanes and air routes that it deems suitable for continuous and expeditious passage through its waters.[48]

The vital importance of *international straits* also calls for a special legal regime.[49] UNCLOS defines an 'international strait' as a strait used for international navigation between one part of the high seas or an EEZ and another part of the high seas or an EEZ.[50] Well-known international straits include the Malacca Strait (connecting the Pacific with the Indian Ocean), the Strait of Hormuz (linking the Persian Gulf with the Gulf of Oman and Arabian Sea) and the Strait of Gibraltar (connecting the Atlantic Ocean and the Mediterranean). In international straits, the sovereignty and jurisdiction of coastal states must be exercised with respect to the importance of straits for the well functioning of international communication and trade. Importantly, navigation through an international strait is governed by the right of *transit passage*.[51] Unlike the right of innocent passage through the territorial seas, transit passage cannot be suspended by a coastal state.[52] In addition, it is not only ships that enjoy a right to transit passage; aircraft that overfly the international strait also possess the right. Ships and aircraft must 'proceed without delay' as well as 'refrain from any threat or use of force'. There is also a requirement to comply with generally accepted international regulations regarding safety procedures.[53] A coastal state may designate sea lanes and prescribe similar schemes if necessary to enhance the safe passage of ships.[54]

The dramatic decrease of ice in the Arctic region has led to speculation that navigation through the so-called 'Northwest Passage' may soon be possible for commercial shipping. The passage consists of a number of alternative maritime transit routes that link Europe and the Atlantic Ocean with Asia and the Pacific Ocean above the North American continent. Canada claims that the route would lie within Canadian territorial or even internal waters. The United States and the EU, on the other hand, argue that the Passage must be conceived of and governed as an international strait.[55] Issues about status under international law also arise in relation to the so-called 'Northeast Passage' and passage from the Atlantic Ocean to the Pacific Ocean along the Norwegian and Russian Arctic coasts.[56]

---

[46] For a definition, see art. 46(a).   [47] Art. 52(1).   [48] Art. 53.
[49] For an overview, see Tanaka (n 8) 97–110.   [50] Art. 37.   [51] Art. 38.
[52] Art. 38(1).   [53] Art. 39.   [54] Art. 41(1).
[55] For a discussion, see James Kraska, 'The Law of the Sea Convention and the Northwest Passage' (2007) 22(2) *International Journal of Marine and Coastal Law* 257–282.
[56] See Erik Franckx, 'The Legal Regime of Navigation in the Russian Arctic' (2008–2009) 18 *Journal of Transnational Law and Policy* 327–342.

Historic straits are exempt from the regulation of international straits in UNCLOS. A historic strait is one 'in which passage is regulated in whole or in part by long-standing international conventions in force specifically relating to such straits'.[57] Examples include the Great Belt (Storebælt) and Øresund in Denmark, which are governed by the 1857 Copenhagen Convention.[58] *Great Belt* concerned the construction of a bridge in an international strait. Finland initiated proceedings against Denmark when the latter decided to build a bridge across 'Storebælt' (Great Belt) that would affect access to the North Sea for a certain type of very high Finnish vessel.[59] Denmark and Finland reached a settlement before the Court could hear oral arguments (Denmark paid Finland 90 million Danish kroner) and the Court did not therefore offer its views on the legality under international law of constructing bridges in international straits.

8.3.4 **The contiguous zone**

The contiguous zone is a stretch of the sea contiguous to the territorial sea where the coastal state may exercise necessary control to prevent and punish 'infringements of its customs, fiscal, immigration or sanitary laws and regulations within its territory or territorial sea'.[60] The maximum breadth of the zone is 24 nautical miles when measured from the baseline.[61] The purpose of the contiguous zone is to allow a coastal state to extend the reach of its enforcement jurisdiction for a range of specified purposes only. The term 'punish' suggests that a coastal state has the authority to arrest a ship that has committed an offence in the territorial sea but has since left and is now located in the contiguous zone. The term 'prevent', on the other hand, indicates that a coastal state is authorized to impede/stop a ship that is suspected of committing such an offence before it enters its territorial waters.

8.3.5 **The exclusive economic zone (EEZ)**

One of the primary concerns of a coastal state is to claim a privileged position with regard to harvesting the economic resources, primarily fish, in the waters off its shores. Disagreements about fishing rights and legitimate concerns about overfishing have been a recurrent source of animosity between states and vastly different positions have been adopted by states. In the 1970s, for example, some Latin American states claimed a right to exploit the natural resources of the sea for up to 200 nautical miles from their

---

[57] Art. 35(c).

[58] See Copenhagen Convention, 14 March 1857. See also Denmark's declaration on ratification, Declaration of Denmark dated 16 November 2004 ('It is the position of the Government of the Kingdom of Denmark that the exception from the transit passage regime provided for in article 35 (c) of the Convention applies to the specific regime in the Danish straits (the Great Belt, the Little Belt and the Danish part of the Sound), which has developed on the basis of the Copenhagen Treaty of 1857. The present legal regime of the Danish straits will therefore remain unchanged').

[59] See ICJ, *Passage Through the Great Belt (Finland v Denmark)*, Application Instituting Proceedings, 17 May 1991 and the subsequent Order of 12 September 1992.

[60] UNCLOS art. 33(1).   [61] Art. 33(2).

coasts.[62] In *Fisheries Jurisdiction*, the UK brought a case against Iceland in relation to the latter's proclamation of a 50-mile exclusive fishing zone.[63] In UNCLOS, the issue is dealt with by the establishment of an EEZ—a *sui generis* area of the sea adjacent to the coast. According to article 57, the EEZ may reach a maximum breadth of 200 nautical miles from the baseline. In the zone, a coastal state may claim and hold the exclusive right to the economic resources of the sea. Since the adoption of UNCLOS, most states have replaced their demands for exclusive fishing zones (EFZ) with EEZs. The ICJ has found that the existence of an EEZ is part of customary international law.[64]

Two initial things must be noted about the EEZ. First, it consists of not only the water within the area but also the seabed and subsoil as well as the airspace above the water.[65] Secondly, it is an 'economic' zone in the broad sense and therefore covers more than just fishing. Article 56(1) stipulates that the rights of a coastal state relate to 'exploring and exploiting, conserving and managing the natural resources, whether living or non-living' as well as 'other activities for the economic exploitation and exploration of the zone, such as the production of energy from the water, currents and winds'.[66] Thus, a coastal state has the exclusive right to construct and operate offshore wind farms in its EEZ, as Denmark has done. The rights that a coastal state possesses in the EEZ are exclusive in the sense that other states are barred from undertaking economic activities in the zone unless the coastal state has given its consent.

In general, under article 73 a coastal state may take the necessary measures to ensure compliance with its laws and regulations in conformance with UNCLOS. In practice, therefore, a coastal state may exercise both legislative and enforcement jurisdiction over foreign vessels in the EEZ. According to article 73(1), for example, a coastal state may board and inspect foreign vessels suspected of unlawful fishing activities and, if necessary, arrest the ship and initiate judicial proceedings. A coastal state's jurisdiction is limited, however, to that required to protect its economic rights. In *M/V 'Saiga' (No. 2)*, ITLOS did not find that Guinea could generally extend its customs laws to its EEZ.[67] In *M/V 'Virginia G'*, however, the Tribunal found that the regulation by a coastal state of so-called 'bunkering' (refuelling) of foreign vessels fishing in the EEZ was included in the measures which a coastal state could take to conserve and manage its living resources.[68]

The exclusive right to exploit and explore the resources of the EEZ includes the right to construct and operate necessary artificial islands or other structures as long as they do not interfere with the use of recognized sea lanes essential to international navigation.[69] A coastal state may also regulate, authorize and conduct marine scientific research in its EEZ,[70] as well as protect and preserve the marine environment.[71]

---

[62] See 1952 Declaration of Santiago and the 1974 Montevideo Declaration on the Law of the Sea. See also the overview in *Maritime Dispute (Peru v Chile)*, Judgment [2014] ICJ Rep 3, para. 19.

[63] *Fisheries Jurisdiction (UK v Iceland)*, Merits, Judgment [1974] ICJ Rep 3.

[64] *Continental Shelf (Libyan Arab Jamahiriya v Malta)* [1985] ICJ Rep 13, para. 34.

[65] See UNCLOS art. 56(1).   [66] Art. 56(1)(a).

[67] *The M/V 'Saiga' (No. 2) (Saint Vincent and the Grenadines v Guinea)*, Case No. 2, Judgment, 1 July 1999, para. 127.

[68] The *M/V 'Virginia G' (Panama v Guinea-Bissau)*, Judgment, Case No. 19, 14 April 2014, paras 215, 217 and 223.

[69] Arts 56(1)(b) and 60(1) and (7).   [70] Arts 56(1)(b)(ii) and 246(2).   [71] Art. 56(1)(iii).

As a main rule, article 58(1) specifies that other states are entitled to enjoy the free-doms of navigation and overflight as well as other related freedoms of the high seas (see Section 8.3.8) as long as they do not interfere with the coastal state's exclusive right to exploit and explore its EEZ. Navigation, however, may be subject to coastal state regulation to protect the marine environment. As long as *military exercises* are conducted with due regard to a coastal state's rights to exploit and explore the marine resources in its EEZ, they are not incompatible with the rights of the coastal state.[72]

8.3.6 The continental shelf

In September 1945, US President Truman proclaimed that the natural resources of the subsoil and seabed of the continental shelf beneath the high seas but contiguous to the coasts of the US appertained to the United States. At the time, recent technological developments had made it possible to exploit the resources (primarily oil and subsequently natural gas) contained in the seabed and subsoil below the surface of the sea. Many states soon followed the US policy and the 1958 Geneva Convention on the Continental Shelf states that a coastal state exercises sovereign rights over the continental shelf for the 'purposes of exploring it and exploiting its natural resources'.[73] In *North Sea Continental Shelf*, the ICJ referred to the latter as a reflection of the 'emergent rules of customary international law'.[74] Today, the sovereign rights of a coastal state over the continental shelf can be regarded as part of customary law. Unlike the EEZ, the continental shelf is an inherent feature of sovereignty and does not need to be proclaimed by a coastal state.[75]

In practice, the continental shelf is primarily relevant to the extraction of oil and gas. In UNCLOS, the shelf is regulated in Part IV. According to article 76(1), the shelf is composed of the seabed and subsoil of the submarine areas that extend beyond the territorial sea throughout the natural prolongation of the land territory to the outer edge of the continental margin, or to a distance of 200 nautical miles from the baselines from which the breadth of the territorial sea is measured where the outer edge of the continental margin does not extend up to that distance. There are, in other words, two alternative modes of determining the outer limits of the shelf: one based on geological factors (the edge of the continental margin) and one based on distance (200 nautical miles). The 200-miles limit—which ties the legal regime for governing the shelf to that governing the EEZ—is reflected in customary international law.[76]

If the outer edge of the continental margin goes beyond 200 miles, the limit of the shelf may under certain circumstances be set on the basis of a number of fairly com-plicated geological criteria. Thus, under article 76(4)(a), two modes of setting the limit of the shelf beyond 200 miles may be relevant. While the first takes its departure point in the thickness of sedimentary rocks, the second relies on a distance criterion of fixed points not more than 60 miles from the foot of the continental shelf. Regardless of the method, however, article 76(5) specifies that the extension of the continental shelf

---

[72] See the discussion in Tanaka (n 8) 394–397.   [73] See art. 2(1).
[74] *North Sea Continental Shelf* (n 7) para. 63.   [75] Art. 77(3).
[76] *Continental Shelf (Libyan Arab Jamahiriya v Malta)* (n 64) para. 34.

cannot exceed 350 miles from the baseline or more than 100 miles from a point at which the depth of the water is 2,500 metres. In practice, it may be difficult to locate the points of the 2,500-metre isobaths. In this case, it is less easy to apply the rule that involves measuring 100 nautical miles from the 2,500-metre isobaths.

Claims to a continental shelf exceeding 200 miles must be forwarded to a Commission on the Limits of the Continental Shelf, which assesses the claim and issues a recommendation to the state.[77] The Commission does not offer its view on delimitation of overlapping claims to the shelf. The first state to submit a claim to the Commission was Russia, which in December 2001 made extensive claims to the continental shelf in the Arctic and Pacific Oceans.[78] A number of states have since made overlapping claims to certain areas of the continental shelf in the Arctic Ocean. In November 2006, for example, Norway claimed parts of the shelf north of Svalbard and in December 2014, on behalf of the Kingdom of Denmark, the Danish government forwarded its claim to a large part of the continental shelf situated to the north of Greenland.[79]

Article 77(2) specifies that a coastal state's sovereign rights to explore and exploit the natural resources of the continental shelf are exclusive in the sense that if the coastal state does not explore the continental shelf or exploit its natural resources, no one may undertake those activities without the express consent of the coastal state. According to article 77(4), the natural resources in the continental shelf consist of the 'mineral and other non-living resources of the seabed and subsoil together with living organisms belonging to sedentary species'. The latter refers to 'organisms which, at the harvestable stage, either are immobile on or under the seabed or are unable to move except in constant physical contact with the seabed or the subsoil'. While the organisms in question certainly include clams and oysters, there is less agreement about whether crabs and lobsters are also included. With regard to its EEZ, a coastal state also possesses the right to construct artificial islands or other structures that do not obstruct the use of recognized sea lanes essential to international navigation.[80]

A coastal state may exercise both legislative and enforcement jurisdiction over foreign individuals and vessels in its EEZ to ensure respect for its rights on the continental shelf. It also has jurisdiction in relation to marine scientific research. In practice, of course, there are only limited means by which other states can interfere with a coastal state's exploitation of its continental shelf. As a point of departure, other states are entitled to lay submarine cables and pipelines on the surface of the continental shelf.[81]

8.3.7 **The Area—exploitation of the deep seabed**

The deep seabed beyond the outer limit of where states claim a right to the continental shelf is called the 'Area'.[82] Reaching agreement on the regulation of the Area was one of the most difficult aspects of the negotiations of UNCLOS and dissatisfaction about the legal regime created was so profound that it threatened to undermine the almost

---

[77] Art. 76(8). See Annex II to the Convention.
[78] See http://www.un.org/depts/los/clcs_new/submissions_files/submission_rus.htm.
[79] Ibid. See submission nos 7 and 76 respectively.   [80] Art. 80.   [81] Art. 79.
[82] Art. 1(1).

universal support for the Convention.[83] An Implementation Agreement was therefore adopted in 1994 to modify the original regime.

The regulation of the Area is based on the premise—articulated in article 136—that the deep seabed and its resources form part of the 'common heritage of mankind'.[84] Thus, no state can claim or exercise sovereignty or sovereign rights over the Area and exploitation must be carried out for the benefit of all.[85] In addition, the Area may only be used for peaceful purposes.[86] 'Resources' are defined as 'all solid, liquid or gaseous mineral resources in situ in the Area at or beneath the seabed, including polymetallic nodules'.[87] Importantly, marine genetic resources are not covered. When recovered from the Area, the resources are referred to as 'minerals'.[88] To ensure that exploitation of the Area benefits all of mankind, activities are organized, carried out and controlled by an International Seabed Authority (ISA) based in Jamaica.[89] No activity can be undertaken without the approval of the ISA. All parties to UNCLOS are automatically members of the ISA.

Activities in the Area can be undertaken either by the ISA itself, acting through its own operational entity—the Enterprise (not yet established)—or by state parties or other entities, in association with the ISA.[90] In the latter instances, an application for exploitation must include two areas, one for the activities of the applicant and one reserved for activities by the ISA, acting through the Enterprise.[91] The obligations and responsibilities of activities in the Area are governed by a number of general principles, including core principles of international environmental law, listed in a 2011 advisory opinion by ITLOS.[92]

8.3.8 The high seas

Under article 86 of UNCLOS, the high seas are 'all parts of the sea which are not included in the EEZ, in the territorial sea or in the internal waters of a State, or in the archipelagic waters of an archipelagic State'. The high seas are *res communis* and thus beyond the sovereignty and jurisdiction of any state and they are governed by the principle of the freedom of the high seas. All states have an equal right, among other things, to navigation and overflight and, subject to certain stipulations, to lay submarine cables and pipelines as well as to construct artificial islands and other installations and to fish and conduct scientific research.[93] It is reserved for peaceful purposes[94] but military exercises that comply with article 2(4) of the UN Charter are allowed.[95]

---

[83] For an overview, see Bernard H. Oxman, 'The 1994 Agreement and the Convention' (1994) 88 *American Journal of International Law* 687–696. See also James Harrison, *Making the Law of the Sea: A Study in the Development of International Law* (Cambridge University Press, 2013) 85–99.

[84] See also art. 137(1) and UN Res. 2749 (XXV) Declaration of Principles Governing the Sea-Bed and the Ocean Floor, and the Subsoil Thereof, Beyond the Limits of National Jurisdiction (1970).

[85] UNCLOS art. 140(1).   [86] Art. 141.   [87] Art. 133(a).   [88] Art. 133(b).

[89] Art. 153(1).   [90] Art. 153(2).   [91] Art. 153(3). See also art. 3 of Annex III.

[92] *Responsibilities and Obligations of States Sponsoring Persons and Entities with Respect to Activities in the Area*, Case No. 17, Advisory Opinion, 1 February 2011.

[93] Art. 87(1).   [94] Art. 88.   [95] Art. 301.

Article 92(1) contains the well-established principle of both customary and treaty law that the flag state has exclusive jurisdiction over a vessel on the high seas.[96] The jurisdiction of the flag state includes both prescriptive and enforcement jurisdiction. It is up to each state to set the conditions for granting a vessel its nationality/flag and it is a well-known fact that some states profit from a policy of 'flags of convenience' whereby they permit shipowners with very limited connection to the state to register their ships and their national flags. Article 91(1) requires 'a genuine link' between the state and the ship.[97] In M/V 'Virginia G', ITLOS stressed that, once a ship is registered, the flag state must 'exercise effective jurisdiction and control over that ship in order to ensure that it operates in accordance with generally accepted international regulations, procedures and practices'.[98]

Although vessels enjoy widespread freedom from the jurisdiction of foreign states on the high seas, a number of exceptions do exist. Article 110(1) contains *a right to visit* whereby a foreign warship may board a ship on the high seas if there are reasonable grounds for suspecting that:

(a) the ship is engaged in piracy;

(b) the ship is engaged in the slave trade;

(c) the ship is engaged in unauthorized broadcasting and the flag state of the warship has jurisdiction under article 109;

(d) the ship is without nationality; or

(e) though flying a foreign flag or refusing to show its flag, the ship is, in reality, of the same nationality as the warship.

Some conventions contain provisions whereby contracting parties accept that a ship of another contracting party may request authorization from the flag state to board a vessel suspected of engaging in certain prescribed activities, such as illicit trafficking of narcotics or illegal transportation of migrants.[99] If individuals found on 'visited' vessels are forced to return to their home states it may raise issues in relation to the human rights prohibition against the return of individuals to states where there is a risk of ill-treatment.[100]

According to article 111 of UNCLOS, a warship or military aircraft or other governmental ship or aircraft may pursue a vessel out on to the high seas—also known as a right of *hot pursuit*—if it has breached the laws of the state in one of the maritime zones.[101] The pursuit must be 'hot' and continuous. In the M/V 'Saiga' (No. 2) case, ITLOS found that the recall of a small patrol boat engaged in the alleged pursuit of a ship constituted a 'clear interruption' with the effect that Guinea could not rely on article 111.[102] A hot pursuit must cease if

---

[96] See also art. 92(2).   [97] See also *The M/V 'Saiga' (No. 2)* (n 67) para. 63.

[98] *The M/V 'Virginia G'* (n 68) para. 113.

[99] See, inter alia, the 1988 Vienna Convention Against Illicit Traffic in Narcotic Drugs and Psychotropic Substances and the 2000 Protocol Against the Smuggling of Migrants by Land, Sea and Air, supplementing the 2000 UN Convention against Transnational Organized Crime.

[100] ECtHR, *Hirsi Jamaa and Others v Italy*, App. no. 27765/09 (Grand Chamber), 23 February 2012. See also Chapter 9.

[101] A violation committed in the contiguous zone must relate to violations of customs, fiscal, immigration or sanitary laws.

[102] *The M/V 'Saiga' (No. 2)* (n 67) para. 148.

the vessel pursued enters the territorial sea of another state. The *M/V 'Saiga' (No. 2)* case also stipulated the principle that the use of force 'must be avoided as far as possible, and where force is unavoidable, it must not go beyond what is reasonable and necessary in the circumstances'.[103]

8.3.9 Delimitation of maritime zones

The various maritime zones discussed so far will often overlap with the zones of other states and it is therefore of vital importance that international law stipulates how overlapping maritime zones must be delimited.[104] In practice, a delimitation issue may arise in relation to the delimitation of the territorial sea, the contiguous zone, the EEZ and the continental shelf. In most cases, states tend to draw a single boundary for both the EEZ and the continental shelf.

UNCLOS's approach to delimitation differs according to the zones in question. Overlapping claims to the territorial sea and contiguous zone are governed by the so-called 'equidistance—special circumstance rule'.[105] According to this, the territorial sea between two coastal states that are opposite or adjacent to each other is divided by a median line every point of which is the same distance from the nearest points on the baselines from which the breadth of the territorial seas of the two states are measured. The exception is where reasons of historic title or other special circumstance require a different delimitation. What warrants classification as a 'special circumstance' is not mentioned in UNCLOS and must therefore be clarified by state practice and case law.

Overlapping claims to the EEZ and the continental shelf are dealt with on the basis of an 'equitable solution'.[106] But what this means in practice is not clear and international case law has not been uniform. Initially, the ICJ adopted the position that there was no generally applicable method of delimiting maritime zones and it repeatedly stated that it was focused on the goal—the identification of an equitable delimitation—and not the method used to reach that goal.[107] While the advantage of this 'goal-oriented approach' was that it gave a high degree of flexibility to the judges, it suffered from a lack of predictability. The goal-oriented approach was subsequently replaced with a more fixed method of delimiting maritime zones. In *Jan Mayen*, the ICJ stated that it is 'in accord with precedents' to initiate delimitation with 'the median line' and then enquire whether 'special circumstances' exist that 'require any adjustment or shifting of that

---

[103] Ibid, para. 155. See also *SS 'I'm Alone' (Canada v United States)* (1935) III RIAA 1609–1618 and the *Red Crusader* incident: see *Investigation of certain incidents affecting the British trawler Red Crusader* (1962) XXIX RIAA 521–539.

[104] For a thorough discussion, see Yoshifumi Tanaka, *Predictability and Flexibility in the Law of Maritime Delimitation* (Hart Publishing, 2006).

[105] Art. 15 (territorial sea), TSC art. 24 (contiguous zone). UNCLOS is silent with regard to delimitations of the contiguous zone.

[106] Arts 74(1) and 83(1).

[107] *Continental Shelf (Tunisia v Libyan Arab Jamahiriya)* (n 18) para. 70. See also *North Sea Continental Shelf* (n 7) paras 101B and 92; *Delimitation of the Maritime Boundary in the Gulf of Maine Area*, Judgment [1984] ICJ Rep 246, para. 112 and *Continental Shelf (Libyan Arab Jamahiriya v Malta)* (n 64) paras 28 and 45.

line'.[108] A similar approach has been adopted in subsequent cases.[109] Thus, while this test allows for the consideration of circumstances that may be peculiar to the delimitation in question, it also requires that the delimitation must take its point of departure as the median line and thus it introduces more predictability in delimitation cases. Then, in *Maritime Delimitation in the Black Sea*, the ICJ developed the latter approach by introducing a three-stage process to the delimitation of a maritime boundary. According to the Court, the first step is to identify the provisional line of equidistance. The second phase consists of an examination of whether relevant circumstances exist that call for an adjustment of the equidistance line with a view to reaching an equitable result. The third and final stage is a proportionality test carried out on a case-by-case basis to verify whether the delimitation line leads to an inequitable result.[110] The latest test—which is referred to as the 'equidistance/relevant circumstances method'—has since been applied in a number of decisions, including by the International Tribunal for the Law of the Sea (ITLOS) in *Delimitation in the Bay of Bengal*[111] and the 2017 *Delimitation Between Ghana and the Côte d'Ivoire*.[112] It was also relied upon by the ICJ in *Maritime Dispute (Peru v Chile)*[113] and a 2018 dispute between Costa Rica and Nicaragua.[114] The three-stage approach ensures that cases can be resolved in an equitable manner while at the same time ensuring clarity about the principles and methods applied.

The question is, of course, what circumstances may require a variance from the line of equidistance? Case law illustrates that the ICJ attributes particular weight to certain *geographical* conditions, including the direction of the coastline and the configuration of the coasts of the two states, a proportionality assessment of the amount of marine space allotted to each state compared to the length of their coastlines and the presence of islands. In *North Sea Continental Shelf*, for example, the ICJ found that it was unacceptable for Germany to be allotted a continental shelf considerably different from those of its neighbours merely as a result of its concave coastline.[115] In *Libya v Malta*, the Court disregarded the existence of an uninhabited Maltese island when it drew a provisional median line.[116] It also rejected, however, a claim by Libya that it should be allotted a greater

---

[108] *Maritime Delimitation in the Area between Greenland and Jan Mayen*, Judgment [1993] ICJ Rep 38, para. 51.

[109] See *Maritime Delimitation and Territorial Questions between Qatar and Bahrain* (n 10) 40, paras 167 and 230; *Land and Maritime Boundary between Cameroon and Nigeria (Cameroon v Nigeria: Equatorial Guinea intervening)*, Judgment [2002] ICJ Rep 303, paras 288–290.

[110] *Maritime Delimitation in the Black Sea (Romania v Ukraine)*, Judgment [2009] ICJ Rep 61, paras 115–122.

[111] *Dispute Concerning Delimitation of the Maritime Boundary Between Bangladesh and Myanmar in the Bay of Bengal*, Case No. 16, Judgment, 14 March 2012, para. 240.

[112] *Dispute Concerning Delimitation of the Maritime Boundary Between Ghana and Côte d'Ivoire in the Atlantic Ocean*, Case No. 23, Judgment, 23 September 2017, para. 284.

[113] *Maritime Dispute (Peru v Chile)* (n 62) paras 180–195. See also *Territorial and Maritime Dispute (Nicaragua v Colombia)* (n 23) paras 190–199.

[114] *Maritime Delimitation in the Caribbean Sea and the Pacific Ocean (Costa Rica v Nicaragua) and Land Boundary in the Northern Part of Isla Portillo (Costa Rica v Nicaragua)*, General List Nos 157 and 165, Judgment, 2 February 2018, para. 135.

[115] *North Sea Continental Shelf* (n 7) para. 91. On the direction of the coastline, see also *Continental Shelf (Tunisia v Libyan Arab Jamahiriya)* (n 18) para. 120 and *Delimitation of the Maritime Boundary in the Gulf of Maine Area* (n 107) para. 225.

[116] *Continental Shelf (Libyan Arab Jamahiriya v Malta)* (n 64) paras 64 and 71.

proportion of the continental shelf because it had a greater landmass than Malta.[117] In its 2018 judgment in the maritime dispute between Costa Rica and Nicaragua, the ICJ (only) assigned half weight to, respectively, a string of islands that was of limited size and located fairly far from the mainland coast and a sparsely populated peninsula.[118] *Economic considerations* are unlikely to be given any weight in the delimitation of maritime zones. As the ICJ noted in *Libya v Malta*, it did not find that it should be 'influenced by the relative economic position of the two States in question'.[119] Marine delimitation is concerned with limiting geography and physical space and not economic fairness or redistribution.

8.4 Piracy

Piracy has a long history in international law, and states frequently resorted to using pirates as proxies in times of war during the 17th and 18th centuries. In recent decades, however, it re-emerged as a topic of substantial international attention and concern, primarily due to the explosion of incidents from the 2000s and onwards in the waters of Somalia and the Horn of Africa. As noted in Chapter 5, customary international law grants all states a right to assert universal jurisdiction over the crime of piracy. In UNCLOS, piracy is governed by articles 100–107 and article 110. According to article 101, piracy consists of any of the following acts:

(a) any illegal acts of violence or detention, or any act of depredation, committed for private ends by the crew or the passengers of a private ship or a private aircraft, and directed:

  (i)   on the high seas, against another ship or aircraft, or against persons or property on board such ship or aircraft;

  (ii) against a ship, aircraft, persons or property in a place outside the jurisdiction of any State;

(b) any act of voluntary participation in the operation of a ship or of an aircraft with knowledge of facts making it a pirate ship or aircraft;

(c) any act of inciting or of intentionally facilitating an act described in subparagraph (a) or (b).

As the wording illustrates, the definition of piracy in article 101—regarded as customary international law—is limited in a number of important ways. First, the illegal acts of violence must be committed for 'private ends'. It is, however, not entirely clear what 'private ends' means. Does it cover, for example, politically motivated acts of violence, such as acts of terrorism? Courts in Belgium and the United States have found that it included acts of violence perpetrated by environmental groups, such as Greenpeace and the Sea Shepherd Conservation Society.[120]

---

[117] Ibid, para. 49.

[118] *Maritime Delimitation in the Caribbean Sea and the Pacific Ocean (Costa Rica v Nicaragua) and Land Boundary in the Northern Part of Isla Portillo (Costa Rica v Nicaragua)* (n 114) paras 154 and 194.

[119] *Continental Shelf (Libyan Arab Jamahiriya v Malta)* (n 64) para. 50. See also *Land and Maritime Boundary between Cameroon and Nigeria (Cameroon v Nigeria: Equatorial Guinea intervening)* (n 109) para. 304.

[120] See *Castle John v NV Mabeco*, Cour de Cassation, 19 December 1986, 77 ILR 537 (Belgium) and *Institute of Cetacean Research v Sea Shepherd Conservation Society*, 725 F.3d 940 (9th Cir. 2013).

The second limitation is that piracy must involve two ships, a pirate ship and a victim ship. So-called 'internal hijacking', where the seizure of a ship is perpetrated by members of its own crew or its passengers, is therefore not covered by UNCLOS but instead by the 1988 Rome Convention on the Suppression of Unlawful Acts Against the Safety of Maritime Navigation.[121] The Rome Convention was adopted in the wake of the *Achille Lauro* incident in October 1985 when four members of the Palestinian Liberation Front (PLF) disguised as tourists hijacked an Italian-flagged cruise ship in the Mediterranean.[122]

The third important limitation is that piracy must be committed either on the high seas or in an EEZ[123] or in a place outside the jurisdiction of any state. Acts of violence committed in the territorial sea or internal waters of a state fall outside the definition in article 101. Instead, such acts are often classified as 'armed robbery' and they may be covered by the 2009 International Maritime Organization (IMO) Code of Practice for the Investigation of the Crimes of Piracy and Armed Robbery against Ships.[124]

Article 105 states that 'every State may seize a pirate ship or aircraft, or a ship or aircraft taken by piracy and under the control of pirates, and arrest the persons and seize the property on board'. In addition, the courts of the state which 'carried out the seizure may decide upon the penalties to be imposed, and may also determine the action to be taken with regard to the ships, aircraft or property, subject to the rights of third parties acting in good faith'.

In response to widespread piracy in the Gulf of Aden that began in 2008, the UN Security Council greatly expanded the existing authorities under UNCLOS to fight piracy.[125] In December 2008, for example, the Council authorized states to use necessary means to fight piracy in the territorial waters of Somalia.[126] Two weeks later, it authorized states to use a force on land in Somalia.[127] The counter-piracy operations in the Gulf of Aden have raised a host of challenges. Participating states have, for example, struggled to find local states willing to prosecute suspected pirates. Agreements have, however, been concluded with states such as Kenya, Mauritius and the Seychelles.[128] Human rights law has also complicated counter-piracy efforts. In *Medvedyev v France*, the European Court of Human Rights (ECtHR) concluded that the transfer of suspected pirates is governed by the prohibition against transfer when there is a risk of ill-treatment in the receiving state.[129]

---

[121] The Rome Convention entered into force in 1992 and it has 156 parties.

[122] Malvina Halberstam, 'Terrorism on the High Seas: The *Achille Lauro*, Piracy and the IMO Convention on Maritime Safety' (1988) 82(2) *American Journal of International Law* 269–310.

[123] See also Anna Petrig and Robin Geiss, *Piracy and Armed Robbery at Sea: The Legal Framework for Counter-Piracy Operations in Somalia and the Gulf of Aden* (Oxford University Press, 2011) 64.

[124] See the Convention's art. 2(2).

[125] See also the overview in Tullio Treves, 'Piracy, Law of the Sea, and Use of Force: Developments off the Coast of Somalia' (2009) 20 *European Journal of International Law* 399–414. As at July 2018, two international naval task forces are conducting counter-piracy operations in the Gulf of Aden. The EU operates 'Operation Atalanta', see http://eunavfor.eu/ (accessed 30 July 2018) and a number of states are engaged in the activities of 'Combined Task Force 151', see https://combinedmaritimeforces.com/ctf-151-counter-piracy/ (accessed 30 July 2018).

[126] SC Res. 1846 (2 December 2008), para. 10.   [127] SC Res. 1851 (16 December 2008), para. 6.

[128] For an overview, see Håkan Friman and Jens Lindborg, 'Initiating Criminal Proceedings with Military Force: Some Legal Aspects of Policing Somali Pirates by Navies' in Douglas Guilfoyle (ed), *Modern Piracy, Legal Challenges and Responses* (Edward Elgar Publishing, 2013) 172–200.

[129] ECtHR, *Medvedyev and Others v France*, App. no. 3394/03 (Grand Chamber), Judgment, 29 March 2010.

8.5 Conservation of marine life

It is a prime concern of the international law of the sea to conserve the living resources of the sea and oceans.[130] Many communities depend for their livelihood on the exploitation of marine life, primarily fishing, and the risk of depletion of certain forms of marine life is an ongoing concern in many parts of the world. International awareness of the need for conservation rose in the decades after the end of the Second World War and some of the early treaties that contain explicit obligations to conserve marine life were adopted in the 1950s. An example is the 1958 Convention on Fishing and Conservation of the Living Resources of the High Seas.

The zonal system discussed in Section 8.3 imposes only limited obligations on coastal states when it comes to conserving marine life. In its territorial waters, a coastal state exercises sovereignty and is generally free to catch all the fish it wants. A general freedom to fish in the high seas also exists for all states. In the EEZ—where the vast majority of fish are caught—UNCLOS introduced a special regime that seeks to balance conservation and the proper utilization of the living resources of the zone. Thus, in order to prevent over-fishing, article 61 requires coastal states to determine the allowable catch of the living resources in their EEZ and ensure that 'the maintenance of the living resources in the exclusive economic zone is not endangered by over-exploitation'. The conservation aims in article 61 must, however, be considered in the light of article 62, which stipulates that coastal states shall also 'promote the objective of optimum utilization of the living resources' in the EEZ. According to that article, a coastal state that does not have the capacity to harvest all of the allowable catch itself, must allow other states access to the surplus. In its practical implementation and the determination of the allowable catch, articles 61 and 62 leave a substantial amount of discretion to the coastal state.

The highly migratory nature of many species of marine life makes the maritime zone system in UNCLOS a less than optimal tool for conservation purposes. Thus, when it comes to protecting marine life, the primary approach is to tailor regulation around the needs of the individual species. Article 63(1) of UNCLOS, for example, obliges states to cooperate in ensuring the conservation and development of *shared and straddling fish stocks*, such as herring and mackerel, that occur within the EEZs of two or more coastal states. Similar obligations exist in relation to *highly migratory species*, such as tuna, marlin, dolphin and shark.[131] In 1995, the UN Agreement on Straddling Stocks and Highly Migratory Species was adopted to enhance the conservation and management of such fish stocks, and it sets up minimum standards of conservation and introduces a system for compliance and enforcement on the high seas. UNCLOS also regulates *anadromous stocks*, such as salmon and sturgeon, which spawn in fresh water but otherwise spend the majority of their lives in the sea.[132] Conservation of anadromous stocks is also subject to fairly detailed regional and bilateral regulation, including in the 1992 Convention for the Conservation of Anadromous Stocks in the North Pacific Ocean.

---

[130] See also the Preamble to UNCLOS.   [131] Art. 64(1).   [132] Art. 66.

The exploitation of *marine mammals*, such as whales, dolphins, polar bears and seals, had been a topic of major attention for decades. Article 65 of UNCLOS specifies that the Convention does not prejudice the right of a coastal state or an international organization to regulate the exploitation of marine mammals more strictly than provided for in the Convention. In some cases, conservation of marine mammals is covered by the 1973 Convention on International Trade in Endangered Species of Wild Fauna and Flora (CITES), which we shall return to in more detail in Chapter 10. CITES seeks to ensure that international trade in specimens of plants and wild animals, such as some marine mammals, does not threaten their survival. Regionally, numerous relevant conventions exist for the conservation and protection of marine mammals.[133]

The regulation of *whaling* has been a particularly sensitive topic since the advent in the first decades of the 20th century of large factory ships that enabled whaling far from land. Thus, conventions on whaling had already began to be adopted in the 1930s.[134] The key international legal instrument is the 1946 International Convention for the Regulation of Whaling (ICRW), which was adopted in Washington DC and entered into force in November 1948. The ICRW is a framework convention, which established the International Whaling Commission, tasked with adopting the relevant rules and regulations for whaling in the form of amendments to a schedule that is an integral part of the ICRW.[135] The ICRW applies to whaling in all waters and, in 1982, the Commission adopted a moratorium to suspend all commercial whaling commencing in the 1985–1986 season.[136] The moratorium remains in force but certain exemptions have been made for *aboriginal communities*, such as those in Greenland.[137] Unlike commercial whaling, whaling by indigenous peoples does not seek to maximize catches or profit. It is up to states to provide the Commission with the required information on the needs of their indigenous people in the form of 'Needs Statements'. Despite the moratorium, Norway resumed commercial whaling of minke whales in 1993.[138] Iceland objects to the moratorium and also hunts whales. Both states set their own catch limits but provide relevant information about their catches to the ICRW. The Commission has established two 'whale sanctuaries', one in the Indian Ocean and the other in the Southern Ocean in the Pacific. Despite the moratorium, states are allowed to grant permits that authorize whaling for the purposes of scientific research. In *Whaling in the Antarctic*, the ICJ concluded that a special whaling programme instituted by Japan in the Southern Ocean breached the 1982 moratorium because the permits granted did not have an entirely scientific purpose.[139]

---

[133] See, inter alia, the 1971 Agreement on Sealing and the Conservation of the Seal Stocks in the Northwest Atlantic, the 1972 Convention for the Conservation of Antarctic Seals, the 1973 Agreement on the Preservation of Polar Bears and the 1992 Agreement on the Conservation of Small Cetaceans of the Baltic and North Seas.

[134] See the 1931 Convention for the Regulation of Whaling and the 1937 International Agreement for the Regulating of Whaling.

[135] ICRW art. 5.   [136] See rule 10(c) of the schedule.   [137] See rule 13.

[138] See Martha Howron, 'International Regulation of Commercial Whaling: The Consequences of Norway's Decision to Hunt the Minke Whale' (1994) 18 *Hastings International and Comparative Law Review* 175–193.

[139] *Whaling in the Antarctic (Australia v Japan: New Zealand intervening)*, Judgment [2014] ICJ Rep 226, paras 227–233.

8.6 Dispute settlement in the law of the sea

In Part XV, UNCLOS establishes an elaborate system for the settlement of disputes that combines voluntary and mandatory measures.[140] The voluntary component is reflected in article 280 whereby states agree to settle a dispute between them concerning the interpretation of the Convention by any peaceful means of their own choice. The mandatory element only enters the picture if the disputing states cannot settle their disagreement by themselves. Article 286 stipulates that any party to the dispute may bring it before the court or tribunal that has been given jurisdiction under Part XV. Under article 287, a contracting state is free to choose one or more of four possible options for the settlement of disputes:

- the International Tribunal for the Law of the Sea;
- the International Court of Justice;
- an arbitral tribunal constituted in accordance with Annex VII of UNCLOS;
- a special arbitral tribunal constituted in accordance with Annex VIII of UNCLOS.

When ratifying UNCLOS, Denmark, Sweden, Norway and the Netherlands all declared that they chose the ICJ for the settlement of disputes.[141] If the parties to a dispute have accepted the same settlement procedure for a dispute, it can only be submitted according to that procedure, unless the parties agree otherwise.[142] If, however, the parties have not accepted the same settlement procedure, it may only be submitted to arbitration pursuant to Annex VII, unless the parties agree otherwise.[143] Thus, Annex VII arbitration is the fall-back dispute settlement mechanism, and it has been resorted to with increasing frequency. A well-known example was the 2016 award in the *South China Sea* case.[144]

Importantly, certain of the discretionary powers enjoyed by coastal states are not covered by compulsory dispute settlement, such as setting an allowable catch in an EEZ.[145] In addition, article 298 allows a state to exempt itself from submitting certain categories of dispute to the settlement mechanisms, such as disputes concerning the application of the rules on sea boundary delimitations, historic bays or titles[146] or military activities.[147]

One of the notable features of UNCLOS was the creation of the *International Tribunal for the Law of the Sea* (ITLOS) as a permanent judicial organ that is open to state parties to UNCLOS as well as other entities when specifically provided for in the Convention. ITLOS consists of 21 members, who serve in their individual capacity. It has jurisdiction over any dispute that concerns the interpretation and application of UNCLOS, as well as any other related international law of the sea agreement that confers jurisdiction on it.[148] The Tribunal has multiple Chambers, including a Seabed Disputes Chamber established in 1997 to deal with disputes related to activities in the Area. The decisions

---

[140] For an overview, see Natalie Klein, *Dispute Settlement in the UN Convention on the Law of the Sea* (Cambridge University Press, 2006).

[141] For an overview of statements and declarations, see http://www.un.org/depts/los/convention_agreements/convention_declarations.htm.

[142] Art. 287(4).   [143] Art. 287(5).   [144] See n 24.   [145] See art. 297(3)(a).

[146] Art. 298(1)(a).   [147] Art. 298(1)(b).   [148] See the ITLOS Statute, arts 21–22.

of the Tribunal in contentious cases are final and must be complied with by the parties to the dispute.[149] The Tribunal may prescribe provisional measures if deemed 'appropriate under the circumstances to preserve the respective rights of the parties to the dispute or to prevent serious harm to the marine environment'.[150] Decisions on provisional measures are binding.[151] The Statute of the Tribunal includes a provision that grants the Tribunal jurisdiction to render advisory opinions.[152] The first contentious case submitted to the Tribunal was the *M/V Saiga* case. By October 2018, a total of 25 contentious cases had been referred to the Tribunal and, in addition, it has issued two advisory opinions.[153]

Summary

The international law of the sea is one of the oldest disciplines of public international law. The most important rules are found in the 1982 UNCLOS. The primary purpose of the law is to balance the legitimate interests of coastal states with the interests of other states. The practical result is the division of the sea into maritime zones in which coastal and other states hold a variety of rights and obligations. As a main rule, the rights of a coastal state decrease relative to the distance from the shore. Maritime zones can be divided into those spaces that are located *in the national jurisdiction of a coastal state* and those that lie *beyond*. It is a primary concern of the international law of the sea to conserve the living resources of the seas and oceans. To that end, the law relies less on the zonal system and focuses more on individual species of marine life and the particular needs of those species. UNCLOS has an elaborate system for dispute settlement that combines voluntary and mandatory measures.

Recommended reading

A solid presentation of the law of the sea is Yoshifumi Tanaka, *The International Law of the Sea* (2nd edn, Cambridge University Press, 2015).

See also Donal Rothwell and Tim Stephens, *The International Law of the Sea* (2nd edn, Hart Publishing, 2016); James Harrison, *Making the Law of the Sea: A Study in the Development of International Law* (Cambridge University Press, 2013).

For some of the legal challenges in the Arctic, see Michael Byers, *International Law and the Arctic* (Cambridge University Press, 2013); James Kraska, 'The Law of the Sea Convention and the Northwest Passage' (2007) 22(2) *International Journal of Marine and Coastal Law* 257.

On piracy, see Anna Petrig and Robin Geiss, *Piracy and Armed Robbery at Sea: The Legal Framework for Counter-Piracy Operations in Somalia and the Gulf of Aden* (Oxford University Press, 2011).

Maritime delimitation is dealt with in Yoshifumi Tanaka, *Predictability and Flexibility in the Law of Maritime Delimitation* (Hart Publishing, 2006).

---

[149] UNCLOS art. 296. See also ITLOS Statute, art. 33.   [150] UNCLOS art 290(1).
[151] Art. 290(6).   [152] See ITLOS Statute, art. 138.
[153] An overview of contentious cases and advisory proceedings is available at https://www.itlos.org/cases/list-of-cases.

On dispute settlement, see Natalie Klein, *Dispute Settlement in the UN Convention on the Law of the Sea* (Cambridge University Press, 2006). See also chapter 8 in Yoshifumi Tanaka, *The Peaceful Settlement of International Disputes* (Cambridge University Press, 2018).

Questions for discussion

1. Can you come up with some examples of where the interests of a coastal state collide with the interests of other states?
2. Which actors are deemed to have a legitimate interest in the regulation of the seas?
3. What is the difference between internal waters and territorial waters? And to what extent does the regulation of the two zones differ?
4. What is the difference between the right of innocent passage and the right of transit passage?
5. What is the difference between an 'island' and a 'rock'? Does it matter?
6. Which principles govern the delimitation of overlapping continental shelves?
7. Why is the zonal system a less than ideal system for conserving marine life? What approach does international law adopt towards the system?

9

International human rights law

CENTRAL ISSUES

1. This chapter examines the system of human rights protection that has emerged since the end of the Second World War.

2. It also discusses the mechanisms for the enforcement of human rights within the realm of the United Nations and on a regional level, including the robust European system for the protection of human rights.

3. The chapter analyses the territorial scope of the most important human rights conventions and the applicability of human rights conventions in times of emergency, including in times of armed conflict.

4. It also provides an overview of the international legal protection of refugees.

9.1 Introduction

As we have seen throughout this book, international law is at its core a horizontal legal system, the primary purpose of which is to avoid undue friction between sovereign states. In fact, up until the middle of the 20th century, the manner in which sovereign authority was exercised within a state was by and large considered a matter in which other states had no business meddling. With a few exceptions, it was not until after the end of the Second World War that international law began to afford individuals protection from their own state. Human rights law is not a field of public international law because its substance is inherently international (in fact, it is not). Rather, it is part of international law because states have decided to turn the manner in which they treat individuals under their jurisdiction into a matter of international concern through the adoption of treaties. Human rights law belongs, in other words, within the international law of cooperation.

The idea that a person possesses certain rights as an individual vis-à-vis his or her own state, has its origins in the era of the Enlightenment in the 18th century and in early Western constitutional thought.[1] In the 19th century, many states adopted national

---

[1] See the English Bill of Rights (1689), the US Declaration of Independence (1776), the French Declaration of the Rights of Man and of the Citizen (1789).

constitutions containing fundamental rights protection. In general, though, the rights granted were tied to citizenship or a similar nexus to the state, and often based on theories of 'social contract', and could therefore not be relied on by all individuals. In contrast, the modern conception of human rights is based on the premise—derived from natural law thinking—that some human rights are inherent in *all* individuals regardless of citizenship. Thus, human rights are universal.[2] The modern human rights law system started with the establishment of the United Nations in 1945 and the ambition to prevent any reoccurrence of the kinds of persecutions perpetrated by the Axis Powers in the latter part of the 1930s and first half of the 1940s. Article 1(3) of the UN Charter stipulates that promoting respect for human rights and fundamental freedoms is one of the primary purposes of the organization.[3] An early achievement was the adoption in 1948 of the General Assembly's Universal Declaration of Human Rights (UDHR). In its first article, the UDHR declares that all 'human beings are born free and equal in dignity and rights' and 'endowed with reason and conscience and should act towards one another in a spirit of brotherhood'.[4]

The understanding that certain human rights are universal has been criticized by 'cultural relativists' for unjustifiably imposing one particular conception of justice on all others.[5] During the Cold War, the communist states in the East defended their dismal human rights record by arguing that the implementation of civil and political rights (see Section 9.3.2) depended on the political ideology of a state, and they in turn criticized the capitalist states in the West for not sufficiently respecting economic and social rights (see Section 9.3.3). While the disagreements between the East and the West disappeared with the collapse of Communism after the end of the Cold War, a debate began to emerge between the developed states in the North and the less developed states in the South, with the latter arguing that the priority afforded to certain civil and political rights by the North comes at the expense of the' right of all states to self-determination and development. Human rights' claim to universalism is also challenged by arguments that greater account should be taken of religious dogma, most notably those derived from Islam. In Europe and North America, for the large influx of immigrants and refugees has led to complicated exchanges about the extent to which secular societies based on fundamental rights protection must make room for what are often perceived as 'foreign' cultural practices and religious beliefs.[6] The debate about how much an immigrant must give up and how much the receiving state must compromise is often cast in terms of human rights relativism.

---

[2] See also preamble to the 1966 ICCPR and ICESCR.   [3] See also art. 53 of the Charter.

[4] GA Res. 217 (III) (10 December 1948). Also of major importance was the 1975 Final Act of the Conference on Security and Co-operation in Europe—also known as the Helsinki Act—that helped pave the way for the spread of democracy and human rights protection to Eastern Europe after the end of the Cold War: see Conference on Security and Co-operation in Europe Final Act, 1 August 1975.

[5] Jack Donnelly, 'Cultural Relativism and Universal Human Rights' (1984) 6(4) *Human Rights Quarterly* 400–419. For a critique of cultural relativism, see John J. Tilley, 'Cultural Relativism' (2000) 22(2) *Human Rights Quarterly* 501–547.

[6] For a good overview, see the selection of articles and perspectives in Henry J. Steiner, Philip Alston and Ryan Goodman, *International Human Rights in Context* (Oxford University Press, 2007) 616–639.

International human rights law is a huge area of international law and it is impossible to cover all aspects in the present chapter. Here, the primary focus is on the human rights law *system*. We begin in Section 9.2 with the primary sources of human rights law, before Section 9.3 discusses the different categories of human rights. Section 9.4 analyses the obligation to offer protection from acts of private individuals. Section 9.5 provides an overview of the enforcement mechanisms in the UN and Section 9.6 focuses on the regional protection of human rights. Section 9.7 examines the territorial scope of human rights treaties and Section 9.8 concerns the application of human rights in times of emergency. Section 9.9 provides an overview of the international legal protection of refugees.

9.2 Sources of human rights law

As noted in the introduction, the modern history of international human rights law can be said to begin with the 1948 UDHR. Since then, the United Nations has been instrumental in the drafting of a host of human rights conventions,[7] including nine core universal human rights treaties open to all states. Among those are the 1966 International Covenant on Civil and Political Rights (ICCPR) and the 1966 International Covenant on Economic, Social and Cultural Rights (ICESCR). The ICCPR and the ICESCR are *general conventions* in the sense that they contain a wide range of different human rights. The UN has, however, also adopted universal conventions that focus on *a particular human rights issue*, such as the 1965 International Convention on the Elimination of All Forms of Racial Discrimination (CERD), the 1984 Convention Against Torture and Other Cruel, Inhuman or Degrading Treatment or Punishment (CAT) and the 2006 International Convention for the Protection of All Persons from Enforced Disappearance (ICPPED). Other UN human rights conventions focus on the *protection of certain categories of vulnerable individuals*. Such conventions include the 1979 Convention on the Elimination of All Forms of Discrimination Against Women (CEDAW) and the 1989 Convention on the Rights of the Child (CRC). A particularly important universal convention is the 1951 Convention Relating to the Status of Refugees, which we shall return to in Section 9.8.

To supplement the universal human rights conventions, there are a range of *regional* human rights conventions. The earliest was the 1950 European Convention on Human Rights (ECHR) adopted by the Council of Europe. In fact, as we shall return to in Section 9.6.2, the protection of human rights is particularly strong in Europe. Other notable regional human rights conventions include the 1969 American Convention on Human Rights and the 1981 African Charter on Human and Peoples' Rights. In 2004, the Arab League adopted an Arab Charter on Human Rights that replaced an earlier charter that never entered into force.

---

[7] For an overview, see http://www.ohchr.org/EN/ProfessionalInterest/Pages/UniversalHumanRights Instruments.aspx.

Fundamental human rights are also protected under *customary international law* and thus binding on all states regardless of their treaty obligations. This is particularly the case for most civil and political rights. Certain rights are also protected as norms of a peremptory/*jus cogens* nature. As discussed in Chapter 2, these rights include (at least) the prohibition against torture, slavery, genocide, violations of rights that rise to the level of crimes against humanity and various forms of gross racial discrimination. As we shall see in Section 9.8, some of the rights are 'non-derogable' and must therefore be respected even in times of public emergency.

9.3 The categories of human rights

9.3.1 Introduction

Conceptually, individual human rights can be divided into different categories, or classes, that reflect the evolution of the law and the nature of the rights. The categories are civil and political rights (Section 9.3.2), economic and social rights (Section 9.3.3) and collective rights (Section 9.3.4). Since civil and political rights play a more dominant role in international law, the following overview affords priority to these rights. It must be noted, however, that it is now generally considered that the rights are interrelated as well as interdependent.[8]

9.3.2 Civil and political rights

The 'oldest' category is rights of a *civil and political nature*. These rights—at times referred to as 'first generation' human rights—constitute the backbone of the general human rights treaties, including the ICCPR and the ECHR. They include the prohibition against torture and slavery, the right to life, liberty, fair trial, equality before the law, freedom of speech, religious freedoms as well as certain political participatory rights. Most of these rights are 'negative' in the sense that they primarily seek to offer protection from the excesses of the state. They are concerned, in other words, with freedom *from* government. In practice, though, effective enjoyment of civil and political rights often requires at least a minimum degree of positive action on the part of the state, such as the creation of an effective police force and a well-functioning judicial system.

Civil and political rights are derived from a set of core principles and values that inform their articulation and practical application. One such principle or value is *human dignity*. The preamble to the ICCPR states, for example, that the Convention is derived from the inherent dignity of the human person. Some civil and political rights are directly linked to respect for human dignity, the clearest example being the right to life and the prohibition against torture and cruel, inhuman or degrading treatment or punishment. Other examples include the abolition of the death penalty

---

[8] See also the 1993 Vienna Declaration and Programme of Action, 25 June 1993.

and the prohibition against enforced disappearances. Rights derived from human dignity are generally formulated in absolute terms in the sense that they do not allow for limitations or balancing. Another core value is *freedom* which can be translated into both intellectual and physical freedom. Notions of *intellectual* freedom are visible in those rights that protect freedom of expression, freedom of thought, freedom of conscience, freedom of religion, freedom of association and freedom of peaceful assembly. Since the practical exercise of intellectual freedoms may collide with the interests of other individuals and/or with wider societal goals, they can usually be limited if required to fulfil a legitimate purpose and the limiting measure is deemed proportionate. In practice, this limitation often takes the form of a balancing act where the right is held up against a competing value or consideration. Respect for *physical freedom* is reflected in the right to liberty and the accompanying prohibition against arbitrary detention as well as the freedom of movement. Equality and *non-discrimination* are yet other powerful values in international human rights law. Differential treatment based solely on the basis of traits and attributes that cannot be altered or should not be required to be altered is hard to reconcile with basic notions of justice and the equal status of all individuals. Non-discrimination is reflected in the overall obligation on all states to respect and ensure the enjoyment of rights without distinction on the basis of race, sex, language, religion, political opinion or national or social origin. Importantly, the principle of non-discrimination does not prohibit a state from taking account of a particular ground (race, sex, language etc.) when it is a legitimate consideration to the issue at hand. Principles of *justice and fairness* are core human rights values in their own right. They are most clearly reflected in the legal principles of proper administration of justice in the legal system. Most notably, the principle of justice is translated into a requirement of a legal basis for interfering with a right and the right to a fair trial—also known as 'due process'—and in the prohibition against retroactive criminality (*nullum crimen sine lege*). The last set of principles or values worth noting are those concerning *political participation*. The right of citizens to participate in the political processes of their societies has become a fundamental principle in international human rights protection, in particular in Europe. In practice, political participation is reflected in the intellectual freedoms noted earlier as well as in more direct rights of access to public service, to participate in general elections and to run for political office.

9.3.3 Economic and social rights

The second category of rights concerns *economic and social issues* and, on the universal level, these rights—at times referred to as 'second generation' human rights—are primarily found in the ICESCR. In Europe, they are listed in the European Social Charter. The rights include a right to work, adequate working conditions including fair wages, a right to social security, an adequate living standard, physical and mental health and a right to education. As the examples illustrate, the rights differ from civil and political rights not only due to their character and the values they seek to promote[9] but also because of the role the state must play in order to fulfil those rights. In practice, enjoyment of economic and social rights, such as work, social security and education, requires a substantial element of state action and initiative. For this reason, the rights are also referred to as 'positive' rights, in the sense that their fulfilment requires not freedom from government but rather action *by* it. Economic and social rights are generally formulated in fairly abstract terms, thus leaving a wide discretion to the states. This also helps explain why judicial enforcement of social and economic rights is much weaker than enforcement of civil and political rights.

9.3.4 **Collective rights**

Some human rights instruments focus on the protection of various *groups of individuals*, most often those groups deemed to be particularly vulnerable and thus in need of special protection. The *1948 Genocide Convention*, for example, obliges states to prevent and punish acts intended to destroy, in whole or in part, 'a national, ethnical, racial or religious group as such'.[10] The notion of 'group rights' is also central to *the right to self-determination* discussed in Chapter 4, whereby all 'peoples' have a right to freely determine their political status and pursue their economic, social and cultural development. The right is listed in article 1 in the two 1966 UN Covenants. International human rights law also grants protection to various *minorities*, such as ethnic or religious minorities. According to article 27 of the ICCPR, for example, individuals belonging to ethnic, religious or linguistic minorities 'shall not be denied the right, in community with the other members of their group, to enjoy their own culture, to profess and practise their own religion, or to use their own language'.[11] In Europe, minority protection was enhanced with the adoption of the 1994 European Framework Convention for the Protection of National Minorities. *Indigenous peoples* enjoy a particular form of human rights protection.[12] In 1989, the International Labour Organization (ILO) updated an existing 1957 Convention on Indigenous and Tribal Peoples in Independent Countries.[13] Indigenous rights have also been brought up in a number of cases before the Inter-American Court of Human Rights.[14]

Claims have additionally been made for the existence of other more intangible 'third generation' rights, such as a right to development, a right to peace and a right to the environment.[15] In 1986, the UN General Assembly adopted a Declaration on the Right to Development according to which such a right 'is an inalienable human right by virtue of which every human person and all peoples are entitled to participate in, contribute

---

[9] The value of human dignity is also reflected in some of the economic and social rights.

[10] See art. 2. See also the definition in Chapter 15.

[11] See also GA Res. 47/135 Declaration on the Rights of Persons Belonging to National or Ethnic, Religious or Linguistic Minorities (8 December 1992).

[12] See generally, S. James Anaya, *Indigenous Peoples in International Law* (2nd edn, Oxford University Press, 2004).

[13] See also the 2007 Declaration on the Rights of Indigenous Peoples.

[14] See, inter alia, *The Mayagna (Sumo) Awas Tingni Community v Nicaragua*, Judgment of 31 August 2001, Inter-AmCtHR, Series C, No. 79 (2001).

[15] See the overview in Steiner and others (n 6) 1433–1462.

to, and enjoy economic, social, cultural and political development in which all human rights and fundamental freedoms can be fully realized'.[16] It remains unclear, however, how the content of a (vague) right to development differs from that already subsumed under the well-established right to self-determination, let alone how it can be applied in practice. In fact, the existence of these 'alternative' third generation rights probably remain mere political aspirations. The vagueness of these alleged rights makes any practical application, let alone enforcement, almost impossible.

9.4 Human rights and responsibility for private acts

As a main rule, international human rights law is only binding on states.[17] This, however, does not mean that a state's responsibility cannot be triggered by the acts of private actors, most notably private individuals. Especially in relation to the enjoyment of civil and political rights, a state may be obliged to offer positive protection from private acts. The European Court of Human Rights (ECtHR) has concluded, for example, that the prohibition against torture or inhuman or degrading treatment or punishment requires positive measures on the part of a state to ensure that individuals are not subjected to prohibited treatment at the hands of private individuals. In practice, the obligation—at times also referred to as a 'horizontal' obligation—must 'at least, provide effective protection in particular of children and other vulnerable persons and should include reasonable steps to prevent ill-treatment of which the authorities had or ought to have had knowledge'.[18] In *Begheluri and Others v Georgia*, the ECtHR stressed the existence of a positive obligation to offer protection in relation to religiously motivated violence perpetrated by private individuals.[19]

9.5 Enforcement of human rights in the United Nations

9.5.1 Introduction

Over the years, the UN has developed an elaborate system for monitoring and enforcing compliance with human rights law. In practice, there are two parallel systems: one based on the UN Charter and one based on the universal human rights treaties. We begin with the Charter-based system in Section 9.5.2 and then turn to the treaty-based system in Section 9.5.3.

---

[16] GA Res. 41/28 (1986), art. 1

[17] But see General Recommendation No. 30 on women in conflict prevention, conflict and post-conflict situations (18 October 2013), UN Doc. CEDAW/C/GC/30, paras 13–18. When determining if an act is a 'state act', reference must be made to the general principles of state responsibility and attribution in international law that we visited in Chapter 7.

[18] *O'Keeffe v Ireland*, App. no. 35810/09, 28 January 2014, para. 144. See also *X and Y v The Netherlands*, App. no. 8978/80, 26 March 1985, paras 23–27.

[19] *Begheluri and Others v Georgia*, App. no. 28490/02, 7 January 2015, paras 160, 164.

9.5.2 **Charter-based human rights mechanisms**

In 1946, the Economic and Social Council (ECOSOC) created the *Human Rights Commission* to enhance respect and set standards for the human rights conduct of the members of the UN. Beginning in the 1960s, the Commission developed a number of Special Procedures to facilitate the study and discussion of human rights issues and country-specific compliance. Among other things, the Commission created ad hoc working groups of experts and a series of Special Rapporteurs on thematic topics. The first thematic procedure created was the Working Group on Enforced or Involuntary Disappearances created in 1980. It was followed by the creation of a Special Rapporteur on extra-judicial, summary and arbitrary executions (1982) and one on torture and ill-treatment (1985). The Human Rights Commission was, however, criticized for being too politicized and intentionally ignoring obvious situations of gross human rights violations.[20] In 2006 it was therefore replaced by the *Human Rights Council* (HRC), which is established as a subsidiary organ under the General Assembly. The Council has 47 members divided regionally and elected by a majority of the Assembly. With the Council also came a new mechanism—the Universal Periodic Review—whereby the human rights compliance of *all* states is examined by the Council. The Council retained the system of Special Procedures and by October 2018, 44 thematic and 12 country-specific mandates had been created.[21]

Unfortunately, the creation of the Council did not bring an end to excessive politicization and, as early as its first year, the departing Secretary-General noted how the Council had 'clearly not justified all the hopes' placed in it.[22] In June 2018 the United States resigned its membership of the Council, citing frustration with what it perceived to be a bias against Israel and a lack of appetite for criticizing states like North Korea, Iran and Syria.

In 1993, the General Assembly created the position of *High Commissioner for Human Rights* to promote the enjoyment and protection of all human rights and to coordinate and facilitate, among other things, advisory services and technical assistance in the field of human rights.[23]

9.5.3 **Treaty-based enforcement mechanisms**

The second system in the UN for the protection and promotion of human rights is the collection of committees that have been created to monitor implementation and compliance with the nine 'core' universal human rights treaties mentioned earlier.

---

[20] For an overview, see also Paul Gordon Lauran, 'To Preserve and Build on Its Achievements and to Redress Its Shortcomings: The Journey from the Commission on Human Rights to the Human Rights Council' (2007) 29(2) *Human Rights Quarterly* 307–345.

[21] https://www.ohchr.org/en/hrbodies/sp/pages/welcomepage.aspx (accessed 20 October 2018).

[22] 'Secretary-General urges human rights activists to "fill leadership vacuum", hold world leaders to account' (8 December 2006), UN Doc. SG/SM/10788-HR/4909-OBV/601.

[23] GA Res. 48/141 (20 December 1993).

The committees are composed of between 10 and 25 experts who serve in their independent capacity for terms of, typically, four years. Importantly, the experts are chosen due to their expertise in the given subject matter and they need not be trained lawyers. With a few exceptions, the functions and competences of the committees are broadly similar.[24]

Arguably, the most notable of the committees is the *Human Rights Committee* (CCPR), which monitors the implementation of the ICCPR. The CCPR comments on *periodic reports* submitted by states on the national measures of relevance to their obligations under the ICCPR.[25] In practice, the reports are to be submitted every three to six years depending on the human rights situation in the state in question. At a hearing before the Committee, a state may be asked to respond to a previously notified 'list of issues' of particular interest. The treatment of the periodic reports concludes with the Committee's adoption of 'concluding observations' primarily containing a list of concerns about compliance with the Convention and recommendations for improvement. Since the early 1980s, the CCPR has also adopted non-binding *General Comments* on the interpretation and application of the ICCPR. The CCPR may also hear complaints brought by one state party against another regarding the latter's non-fulfilment of its obligations under the ICCPR.[26] So far, however, this procedure has not yet been used. Of greater practical importance is the procedure for *individual complaints* under which parties to an optional protocol to the Convention accept that the CCPR may consider complaints ('communications') from individuals who claim to be victims of a violation of the ICCPR.[27] In cases of irreparable harm, the Committee may request a state to adopt interim measures.[28] Like its General Comments, the Committee's conclusions in individual cases are not binding on the states. The *Committee Against Torture* (CAT) is also worth highlighting. It monitors implementation and compliance with the 1984 Convention Against Torture and, like the CCPR, it receives periodic reports from the state parties[29] and has a procedure for both interstate and individual complaints if the relevant state has accepted the competence of the Committee.[30] The Committee's conclusions are not binding. A 2002 optional protocol to the Convention established a Subcommittee on Prevention (SPT) and a system of regular visits by independent international and national bodies to detention facilities in order to prevent treatment contrary to the Convention.[31]

It is worth noting that while the various recommendations and findings by the different UN committees are not legally binding in their own right, they may carry substantial interpretative value for determining the content of international law.

---

[24] For a complete overview of the committees, see http://www.ohchr.org/EN/HRBodies/Pages/TreatyBodies.aspx.

[25] See ICCPR art. 40.   [26] ICCPR arts 41–42.   [27] See Optional Protocol 1 to the ICCPR.

[28] HRC, 'General Comment No 33' (2008), UN Doc. CCPR/C/GC/33, para. 19.

[29] Art. 19.

[30] Arts 21 and 22.

[31] Subcommittee on Prevention of Torture and other Cruel, Inhuman or Degrading Treatment or Punishment.

9.6 Regional systems for the protection of human rights

9.6.1 Introduction

The human rights system in the UN is supplemented by regional human rights protection. The protection differs substantially from region to region, stretching from the robust system of human rights protection in Europe to the fairly toothless systems in the Middle East and Asia. The following overview is limited to the human rights system in Europe (Section 9.6.2) and—to a lesser extent—the system created in the Americas (Section 9.6.3) and Africa (Section 9.6.4).

9.6.2 Human rights protection in Europe

9.6.2.1 Introduction—the ECHR

The Council of Europe was founded in 1949 to strengthen intergovernmental and inter-parliamentary cooperation in a ravaged post-Second World War Europe. The Council is composed of, among other things, a Committee of Ministers with a seat for the foreign ministers of the member states and a Parliamentary Assembly consisting of delegations from the national parliaments of the state parties. The Council's greatest achievement was its adoption in 1950 of the *European Convention on Human Rights* (ECHR), which remains the cornerstone of human rights protection in Europe. Accession to the ECHR is now a precondition for membership of the Council of Europe. The ECHR entered into force in 1953 and today has 47 parties.

9.6.2.2 The European Court of Human Rights

The key to the success of the ECHR is the *European Court of Human Rights* (ECtHR), which is competent to make binding decisions. The Court deals with both interstate and individual complaints, but since states are generally reluctant to bring legal cases against each other, *interstate* complaints are relatively rare. Recently, however, a number of such complaints have been brought against Russia. In a case brought by Georgia, for example, the Court in 2014 found that Russia had violated its obligations under the ECHR in a policy of arresting, detaining and expelling Georgian nationals.[32] Ukraine has also lodged a series of interstate complaints against Russia in relation to the latter's intervention in Crimea and activities in Eastern Ukraine.[33]

The most important element of the ECHR's protection of human rights is the procedure for *individual complaints*, whereby the ECtHR receives applications from any person, non-governmental organization or group of individuals claiming to be victims of a violation of the Convention.[34] In fact, the individual complaints mechanism has been so successful that the Court has been forced to adopt a range of initiatives to deal effectively with its caseload. With the adoption of Protocol No. 14,

---

[32] *Georgia v Russia (I)*, App. no. 13255/07, 3 July 2014. See also *Georgia v Russia (II)*, App. no. 38263/08.

[33] *Ukraine v Russia*, App. no. 20958/14, *Ukraine v Russia (IV)*, App. no. 42410/15, *Ukraine v Russia (V)*, App. no. 8019/16 and *Ukraine v Russia (VI)*, App. no. 70856/16.

[34] ECHR art. 34.

the Court succeeded in streamlining the process substantially and it has since brought the number of pending cases down from a staggering 161,000 in September 2011 to a 'mere' 59,250 by October 2018.[35]

A couple of initial points are worth noting about the individual complaints system. First, the Court will only deal with an application if the applicant has *exhausted all domestic remedies*. Also, a complaint must be launched *within six months* after the adoption of the final decision or act that is the subject of the complaint.[36] When Protocol No. 15 to the ECHR enters into force, the complaint must be launched within four months. In the great majority of cases, the Court will declare an application to be inadmissible because it is considered *manifestly ill-founded*. But when the Court finds that the Convention has been violated, it will conclude accordingly and consider *satisfaction*.[37] Often, satisfaction consists of monetary compensation but other measures may also be decided upon. The Court's judgments and decisions are final and binding on the respondent states.[38] The states are free to determine how they will comply with a judgment but the Committee of Ministers in the Council of Europe monitors the proper implementation of the Court's judgments.[39]

On 1 August 2018, Protocol No. 16 to the ECHR entered into force. According thereto, the Court can now also give advisory opinions on questions of principle concerning the interpretation and application of the Convention and its protocols.[40]

9.6.2.3 The substantive rights

The ECHR primarily protects civil and political rights. The substantive rights are contained in section 1 of the Convention as well as in the additional protocols. The first substantive right is the protection of life in article 2 of the ECHR. Although the article allows for the imposition of a death sentence, a general ban on the death penalty was introduced in Protocol No. 13 from 2002.[41] Article 3 of the ECHR protects individuals from torture or inhuman or degrading treatment and punishment and it also protects an individual from being expelled or otherwise transferred to another state where there may be a real risk that the individual will be subjected to treatment contrary to article 3. As we shall return to in Section 9.9, this form of protection is referred to as protection from '*non-refoulement*'. Article 4 contains a prohibition on slavery and forced labour. The rights in articles 3 and 4 are absolute or unqualified rights in the sense that they allow for no limitations or balancing against other interests. Article 5 protects the right to liberty and security, while article 6 concerns the right to a fair trial. Article 7 prohibits retroactive criminal legislation—also an unqualified right. Article 8 protects private and family life; article 9 protects freedom of thought, conscience and religion; article 10 protects freedom of expression, and article 11 protects the freedom of assembly and association. Articles 8–11 are qualified rights that can be balanced against a set of specific interests and the four rights share common features. Thus, whereas the first paragraph of the articles stipulates the specific right, the second

---

[35] https://www.echr.coe.int/Documents/Stats_pending_month_2018_BIL.pdf (accessed 20 October 2018).

[36] Art. 35.   [37] ECHR art. 41.   [38] See, respectively, arts 44 and 46(1).

[39] Art. 46(2).   [40] See the Protocol's art. 1.   [41] See also Protocol No. 6 from 1983.

paragraph lays out the conditions under which interferences with the right may be justifiable. Article 12 contains a right to marry and article 13 protects the right to an effective remedy for anyone whose rights and freedoms under the Convention are violated. Article 14 prohibits discrimination in the enjoyment of the rights and freedoms of the Convention. Additional substantive rights and freedoms are contained in some of the 16 additional protocols to the ECHR. For example, Protocol No. 1 contains a right to property, a right to education and a right to free elections. Protocol No. 4 protects against imprisonment for debt, expulsion of nationals and collective expulsion of aliens and protects freedom of movement. As already noted, Protocol No. 13 bans the death penalty in all circumstances.

9.6.2.4 The ECtHR's interpretation

As discussed in Chapter 3, human rights conventions are generally interpreted less to accord with the original intention of the parties and more in order to ensure the effective, real and concrete protection of the individuals who find themselves under the jurisdiction of the states in question. This is also reflected in the practice of the ECtHR. The Court adopts an interpretation that is 'dynamic', and the Court has frequently stated that the Convention is a 'living instrument' whose provisions must be interpreted in the light of the current social and political climate rather than in accordance with the sentiments at the time the Convention was adopted.[42] According to the Court, a failure to maintain a dynamic approach to interpretation would risk rendering the Convention a bar to reform or improvement.[43] In particularly sensitive matters where there is no common European position, the Court will, however, often grant a state a certain *margin of appreciation* and thus a substantial degree of deference.[44] In *Handyside v UK*, for example, the Court found that national authorities, due to their 'direct and continuous contact with the vital forces of their countries', may in principle be in a 'better position than the international judge to give an opinion' on the exact content of the requirements of morals.[45] The case concerned the banning of a school book with sexual content. The margin of appreciation has also been relied on in relation to sensitive issues concerning religion[46] and blasphemy.[47] In recent years, the Court has been criticized for not affording states a sufficient degree of margin of appreciation in certain types of cases, including those where a state's decision to expel an alien convicted of criminal offences may interfere with the alien's family life under article 8 of the Convention.[48] In Protocol No. 15, the states therefore decided to insert a

---

[42] See, among others, *Tyrer v UK*, App. no. 5856/72, 25 April 1978, para. 31 and *Loizidou v Turkey*, App. no. 15318/89, 23 March 1995, para. 71.

[43] *Stafford v UK*, App. no. 46295/99, 28 May 2002, paras 68–69.

[44] For a thorough examination, see, inter alia, Jonas Christoffersen, *Fair Balance, Proportionality, Subsidiarity and Primarity in the European Convention on Human Rights* (Brill Nijhoff, 2009).

[45] *Handyside v UK*, App. no. 5493/72, 7 December 1976, para. 48.

[46] *Christine Goodwin v UK*, App. no. 28957/95, 11 July 2002, para. 58.

[47] *Leyla Şahin v Turkey*, App. no. 44774/98, 10 November 2005, para. 109.

[48] See, inter alia, the criticism voiced in the declarations adopted at the conferences held in, respectively, Brighton in 2012, Izmir in 2011 and Interlaken in 2010. See also the recent 2018 Copenhagen Declaration: https://www.coe.int/en/web/human-rights-rule-of-law/-/copenhagen-declaration-on-the-reform-of-the-european-convention-on-human-rights-system (accessed 20 October 2018).

new recital in the preamble to the Convention that explicitly affirms that states 'enjoy a margin of appreciation, subject to the supervisory jurisdiction of the European Court of Human Rights established by this Convention'.

9.6.2.5 Other Council of Europe human rights conventions

The ECHR is not the only human rights convention adopted by the Council of Europe. Other notable conventions include the 1994 European Framework Convention for the Protection of National Minorities mentioned earlier. Reference must also be made to the 1961 European Social Charter, later replaced by a revised Charter in 1996, which includes economic and social rights, such as entitlements associated with adequate and affordable housing, accessible health care, free education and employment and working conditions. Its implementation is monitored by a European Committee of Social Rights. In 1995, a mechanism for collective complaints was established in an additional protocol to the Charter.[49] Also worth noting is the 1987 European Convention for the Prevention of Torture and Inhuman and Degrading Treatment or Punishment, which created a Committee for the Prevention of Torture (CPT) with a fact-finding and reporting mandate.

9.6.2.6 Human rights protection in the EU

The treaties of the EU also offer protection of human rights and fundamental freedoms. In December 2000, the EU adopted a Charter of Fundamental Rights of the European Union addressed both to the EU institutions and to the individual member states.[50] When compared to the ECHR, the EU Charter contains more rights, including numerous rights of an economic and social nature. While it was initially without binding effect, that changed following the entry into force of the Treaty of Lisbon in December 2009.[51] Although the Lisbon Treaty also opened the way for the accession of the EU to the ECHR that was later blocked by the Court of Justice for the European Union (CJEU).[52]

The two-tier system of protection provided by the EU and the ECHR raises a number of questions about the relationship between the two systems and it requires a certain level of coordination to prevent inconsistency in the protection of fundamental rights developing in the case law of the CJEU and the ECtHR.[53] Importantly, the ECtHR maintains a prioritized position when it comes to the protection of human rights in Europe. The Court balances respect for the autonomy of the EU with its role as the guardian of the ECHR through a general doctrine of 'equivalent protection' whereby it presumes that a state has not departed from the requirements of the Convention when it implements legal obligations that flow from its membership of another organization

---

[49] Additional Protocol to the European Social Charter Providing for a System of Collective Complaints, 9 November 1995.

[50] Charter of Fundamental Rights of the European Union (18 December 2000), 2000/C 364/01.

[51] See Treaty of the European Union, art. 6(1).   [52] See Opinion 2/13 of 18 December 2014.

[53] Frederic van den Berghe, 'The EU and Issues of Human Rights Protection: Same Solutions to More Acute Problems' (2010) 16(2) *European Law Review* 112–157.

which provides for equivalent protection of fundamental rights.[54] 'Equivalent' means 'comparable' and not 'identical'.[55] In *Bosphorus*, the Grand Chamber of the ECtHR found that the protection of fundamental rights by EU law in general, and at the time of the case, could be considered 'equivalent' to that of the Convention system and that there was therefore a presumption that the state (Ireland) had not departed from the Convention when it implemented its EU obligations.[56] The Court also stated, however, that the presumption can be rebutted if the protection of Convention rights is 'manifestly deficient'.[57] The Court thereby placed itself on a higher footing than the CJEU in the hierarchy of fundamental rights issues.[58] The CJEU has on numerous occasions held that 'fundamental rights form an integral part of the general principles of law' it protects and that it draws particular inspiration from the ECHR.[59] It has stated that respect for fundamental human rights is a 'condition of the legality' of EU acts and it has also begun to refer directly to ECHR standards in its decisions.[60]

9.6.3 Human rights protection in the Americas

The primary human rights instrument in the Americas is the American Convention on Human Rights adopted by the Organization of American States (OAS) in 1969 and which entered into force in 1978. The Convention, which has 25 member states, builds on the 1948 American Declaration of the Rights and Duties of Man and lists both civil and political rights as well as economic, social and cultural rights. It also created the Inter-American Commission of Human Rights and the Inter-American Court of Human Rights.[61] The *Commission* promotes respect for human rights and deals with both interstate and individual complaints.[62] The Inter-American *Court* of Human Rights hears cases referred to it by the Commission.[63] Up until now, however, the Court has not received many contentious cases for consideration. The Court may also issue advisory opinions.[64] The OAS has additionally adopted a 1985 Convention to Prevent and Punish Torture, a 1998 Additional Protocol on Economic, Social and Cultural Rights, a 1990 Protocol on the Abolition of the Death Penalty, a 1994 Convention on Forced Disappearances and, more recently, a 2013 Convention Against Racism, Racial Discrimination and related forms of Intolerance.

---

[54] *Bosphorus Hava Yollari Turizm v Ireland*, App. no. 45036/98 (Grand Chamber), Judgment, 30 June 2005, para. 155.

[55] Ibid.   [56] Ibid, para. 165.   [57] Ibid, para. 156.

[58] See also the discussion in Cathryn Costello, 'The *Bosphorus* Ruling of the European Court of Human Rights: Fundamental Rights and Blurred Boundaries in Europe' (2006) 6(1) *Human Rights Law Review* 103–104.

[59] See, among others, Case 11/70 *Internationale Handelsgesellschaft* [1970] ECR 1125, para. 4 and Case C-36/02 *Omega Spielhallen- und Automatenaufstellungs-GmbH v Oberbürgermeisterin der Bundesstadt Bonn* [2004] ECR I-9609, para. 33.

[60] See, inter alia, Case C-117/01 *KB v National Health Service and the Secretary of State for Health* [2004] ECR I-541 and C-112/00 *Schmidberger Transporte und Planzüge v Austria* [2003] ECR I-5659.

[61] For an assessment of the Inter-American experience, see James L. Cavallaro and Stephanie Erin Brewer, 'Reevaluating Regional Human Rights Litigation in the Twenty-First Century: The Case of the Inter-American Court' (2008) 102(4) *American Journal of International Law* 768–827.

[62] Arts 44–45.   [63] Art. 61.   [64] Art. 64.

9.6.4 **Human rights protection in Africa**

Regional human rights protection in *Africa* is centred around the 1981 Banjul Charter on Human and Peoples' Rights adopted by the Organisation of African Unity (OAU). All 55 members of the African Union (AU) are parties to the Charter, which contains both civil and political rights, economic, social and cultural rights as well as 'collective' rights, including the right of all peoples to self-determination and to freely dispose of their wealth and natural resources, the right to national and international peace and security and the right to a generally satisfactory environment.[65] The Charter established an African Commission on Human and Peoples' Rights, which promotes and ensures the protection of the rights in the Charter and receives complaints from both states[66] and 'other parties', including individuals.[67] If the Commission finds that one of the communications relates to 'a series of serious or massive' violations of the rights contained in the Charter, it will notify the Assembly of Heads of State and Government, which may then ask the Commission to further study the issue and submit a factual report that includes both findings and recommendations.[68]

9.7 The territorial scope of human rights treaties

As a point of departure, a state is only obliged by its human rights obligations on its own territory. In practice, however, it is rarely as simple as that and the territorial reach of human rights conventions is a hotly debated topic.[69] At the outset it is important to note that a treaty can be said to have an 'extraterritorial' effect when a protected individual is not physically present on the territory of the state when the violation of the individual's rights occurs. This concept of 'extraterritoriality' must not, however, be conflated with the principle of '*non-refoulement*', noted earlier in relation to article 3 of the ECHR, according to which a human rights convention may prohibit the transfer of an individual *located on the territory of the state* to another state where the individual risks being treated in a manner that violates that convention. As noted in Chapter 5, the concept of 'jurisdiction' in human rights law is a *sui generis* concept that is unrelated to the different forms of jurisdiction found elsewhere in international law.[70]

Some treaties contain jurisdictional provisions that govern the geographical scope of the treaty. According to article 2(1) of the *ICCPR*, for example, a state party must respect and ensure the rights of the Convention to 'all individuals within its territory and subject to its jurisdiction'. In *The Wall*, the ICJ found that this means

---

[65] Banjul Charter on Human and Peoples' Rights, arts 20–24.   [66] Art. 47.
[67] Arts 55–56.   [68] Art. 58(1) and (2).
[69] Marko Milanovic, *Extraterritorial Application of Human Rights Treaties* (Oxford University Press, 2011).
[70] See, however, the erroneous remarks on this aspect in *Banković and Others v Belgium and Others*, App. no. 52207/99, 12 December 2001, paras 59–61 and *Issa v Turkey*, App. no. 31821/96, 16 November 2004, para. 67.

that jurisdiction under the ICCPR 'may sometimes be exercised outside the national territory'.[71] Among other things, the Court noted that the drafters of the ICCPR 'surely' did not intend to 'allow States to escape from their obligations when they exercise jurisdiction outside their national territory'.[72] According to the Human Rights Committee, the ICCPR applies as soon as a state has an individual in its physical custody abroad 'regardless of the circumstances in which such power or effective control was obtained'.[73] Following the revelations by Edward Snowden of extensive surveillance practices by, inter alia, the US National Security Agency, the Committee has expressed concern at the 'surveillance of communications in the interests of protecting national security, conducted by the National Security Agency (NSA) both within and outside the United States ... and their adverse impact on the right to privacy'.[74]

Article 1 of the ECHR specifies that state parties shall secure the rights and freedoms of the Convention to 'everyone within their jurisdiction'. Unfortunately, however, it has been somewhat difficult to ascertain when 'jurisdiction' exists.[75] The leading case is the Grand Chamber's judgment in 2011 in *Al-Skeini v UK*, which arose from the killing of a number of Iraqi nationals by British forces during the US/UK occupation of Iraq in 2003–20004. The Court listed a number of instances where extraterritorial acts fall within the concept of 'jurisdiction' in article 1.[76] The first relates to acts by diplomatic consular agents who exert authority and control over others.[77] The second is where a state 'through the consent, invitation or acquiescence of the Government of that territory' 'exercises all or some of the public powers normally to be exercised by that Government ... as long as the acts in question are attributable to it rather than to the territorial State'.[78] Thirdly, a state will exercise 'jurisdiction' in relation to an individual who is taken into the custody of state agents abroad. What is decisive in such cases is 'the exercise of physical power and control over the person in question'.[79] The fourth instance is when a state exercises 'effective control of an area' outside its own national territory as a consequence of military action.[80] In the case, the Court found that a number of Iraqis killed by British soldiers on patrol were within British 'jurisdiction' and the decisive factor seems to be that the UK (together with the United States) exercised 'some of the public powers normally to be exercised by a sovereign government' after the removal of the Baath regime and before the accession of the interim Iraqi

---

[71] *Legal Consequences of the Construction of a Wall in the Occupied Palestinian Territory*, Advisory Opinion [2004] ICJ Rep 136, paras 109–111.

[72] Ibid, para. 119. *Armed Activities on the Territory of the Congo (New Application: 2002) (Democratic Republic of the Congo v Rwanda)*, Jurisdiction and Admissibility [2006] ICJ Rep 6, paras 178–180, 216 and 345.

[73] Human Rights Committee, 'General Comment 31' (2004), UN Doc. CCPR/C/21/Rev.1/Add.13, para. 10. See also *Lopez Burgos v Uruguay*, Communication No. 52/1979, 29 July 1981, para. 12.3.

[74] Human Rights Committee, 'Concluding Observations on the Fourth Periodic Report of the United States of America' (23 April 2014), UN Doc. CCPR/C/USA/CO/4, para. 22.

[75] See also the discussion in Milanovic (n 69).

[76] *Al-Skeini and Others v UK*, App. no. 55721/07, 7 July 2011, paras 131–132.   [77] Ibid, para. 134.

[78] Ibid, para. 135.   [79] Ibid, para. 136.

[80] Ibid, paras 138–139. See also *Jaloud v the Netherlands*, App. no. 47708/08, 20 November 2014, para. 142.

government.[81] The judgment implies that a state is *not* bound by its obligations under the ECHR if it uses deadly force (e.g. through the use of a remotely piloted drone) against an individual who is neither within the physical control of the state nor located on a territory where the state has effective control or at least exercises 'public powers'. Some argue, however, that a state should be bound by the Convention in respect of *all* individuals whose lives it can affect no matter where the individuals are located.[82] Others claim that certain core human rights, such as the right to life, are protected in customary international law and that states are therefore always obliged to protect those rights no matter where their agents operate.[83] At the time of writing, however, there is little case law or actual state practice to support such views.

9.8 Human rights in times of public emergency

Human rights law does not cease to apply in times of emergency or even in times of armed conflict. This has been reiterated by the ICJ on numerous occasions.[84] This, however, does not mean that the application of specific human rights may not be affected by the emergency or armed conflict. First, as we shall return to in Chapter 14, the determination of what constitutes a violation of human rights law in times of armed conflict may be influenced by the content of the law of armed conflict that is the relevant *lex specialis*.[85] Secondly, a state may be entitled to 'derogate' from its human rights obligations and thus suspend the application of parts of a human rights convention in times of emergency, including in the event of war.[86] A valid 'derogation' is, however, subject to a number of conditions. First of all, there must be a public emergency of *a certain gravity*. Both the ICCPR and the ECHR require that 'the life of the nation' be under threat.[87] Practice from the ECtHR refers to a threat to 'the organized life of the community of which the State is composed'.[88] In addition, the emergency must be 'actual or imminent'.[89] The Court has found that the situation that previously existed in Northern Ireland,[90] the threat to Turkish society from Kurdish terrorism[91] and the fear of terrorist attacks from al

---

[81] *Al-Skeini* (n 76) para. 149. See also Marko Milanovic, '*Al-Skeini* and *Al-Jedda* in Strasbourg' (2012) 23(1) *European Journal of International Law* 121–139.

[82] See also *Al-Skeini*, Concurring Opinion of Judge Bonello, paras 11–16; Milanovic (n 69) 209.

[83] David Kretzmer, 'Targeted Killing of Suspected Terrorists: Extra-Judicial Executions or Legitimate Means of Defence?' (2005) 16 *European Journal of International Law* 184–185.

[84] *Legality of the Threat or Use of Nuclear Weapons*, Advisory Opinion [1996] ICJ Rep 226, para. 25. See also *The Wall* (n 71) para. 105 and *Armed Activities* (n 72) para. 216.

[85] See also ICJ, *Nuclear Weapons* (n 84) para. 25 and ECtHR, *Hassan v UK*, App. no. 29750/09, Judgment, 16 September 2014, paras 102–104.

[86] See ICCPR art. 4 (1) and ECHR art. 15(1). See also art. 27 of the American Convention on Human Rights.

[87] See also Siracusa Principles on the Limitation and Derogation of Provisions in the International Covenant on Civil and Political Rights (1985), UN Doc. E/CN.4/1985/4, para. 39.

[88] *Lawless v Ireland*, App. no. 332/57, 1 July 1961, para. 28.

[89] *Denmark, Norway, Sweden and the Netherlands v Greece*, App. nos 3321/67, 3322/67, 3323/67 and 3344/67, 5 November 1969, para. 113.

[90] *Ireland v UK*, App. no. 5310/71, 18 January 1978, para. 205.

[91] See, inter alia, *Aksoy v Turkey*, App. no. 21987/93, 18 December 1996, para. 68.

Qaida in the UK qualified for the suspension of certain provisions of the Convention.[92] In June 2015, Ukraine suspended a range of its obligations 'in respect of those areas in the Donetsk and Luhansk regions where Ukrainian authorities have been conducting an anti-terrorist operation in view of the actions of armed groups there'.[93] In November 2015, France derogated from the Convention after the declaration of a state of emergency in France after the 13 November terrorist attacks in Paris.[94] It is not clear if participation in military operations abroad warrants derogation.[95] Secondly, the measures that derogate from human rights obligations must be *strictly required* by the situation. The ECtHR has recognized, however, that 'a wide margin of appreciation should be left to the national authorities'.[96] In *A and Others*, the Court agreed with an earlier judgment by the UK House of Lords that had found that British legislation authorizing indefinite detention of a suspected terrorist of non-British nationality was disproportionate and therefore in violation of article 15 of the ECHR because the law did not allow for the detention of British nationals who posed a similar threat.[97] A third condition is that the measures do not infringe upon certain 'non-derogable' rights. In the ECHR, these rights include the right to life (except in respect of deaths resulting from lawful acts of war), the prohibition against torture and other forms of ill-treatment, the prohibition of slavery and the prohibition against retroactive criminal legislation.[98] It is also worth noting that a decision to derogate from a human rights convention does not alter a state's obligations under other parts of international law, such as under customary international law, and that a decision to derogate must be communicated and justified to the other state parties to that convention.[99]

9.9 International protection of refugees

9.9.1 Introduction–the Refugee Convention

It is a well-established principle of international law that sovereign states have the freedom to control the entry, residence and expulsion of aliens. States can, however, choose to limit this freedom by adopting treaty-based obligations. With regard to the legal protection of refugees, the most important such treaty is the 1951 Convention

---

[92] *A and Others v UK*, App. no. 3455/05, 19 February 2009, para. 177.

[93] See http://www.coe.int/en/web/conventions/full-list/-/conventions/treaty/005/declarations?p_auth= N5hF4XrW.

[94] Ibid.

[95] On this issue, see the House of Lords, *R (on the application of Al-Jedda) (FC) (Appellant) v Secretary of State for Defence (Respondent)* [2007] UKHL 58, [38].

[96] *Aksoy* (n 91) para. 68. See also *Ireland v UK* (n 90) para. 207 and *A and Others v UK* (n 92) para. 180.

[97] *A and Others v UK* (n 92) para. 190. For the House of Lords decision, see the individual judgments of the law lords in *A and others v Secretary of State for the Home Department* [2004] UKHL 56, see esp. [126] and [132].

[98] See ECHR art. 15 and art. 3 of Protocol No. 6 and art. 2 of Protocol No. 13. For the ICCPR, see art. 4(2) and HRC, 'General Comment No. 29: States of Emergency (article 4)' (2001), UN Doc. CCPR/C/21/Rev.1/ Add.11, paras 13–16.

[99] ICCPR art 4(3) and ECHR art. 15(3).

relating to the Status of Refugees—also known as the Refugee Convention—which has 145 state parties. The Convention is derived from the principle that all human beings shall enjoy fundamental rights and freedoms without discrimination.[100] While it was adopted with the primary purpose of dealing with people displaced by the Second World War and its definition of a refugee (see the following section) was originally limited to individuals who had acquired such a status as a result of events occurring before 1 January 1951, that temporal limitation was removed with a 1967 protocol.[101] The Convention does not create any courts or committees that decide how the Convention shall be interpreted and while the United Nations High Commissioner for Refugees (UNHCR) provides international protection to refugees it does not have any authority to make binding determinations of how the Convention should be interpreted. This falls upon the states themselves.[102] But since the Convention is 'law-making' and seeks to offer protection to individuals at risk of persecution, it should be interpreted in a manner that ensures an effective and modern level of protection. Its humanitarian purpose makes it natural to interpret its provisions with reference to contemporary standards and definitions in human rights conventions.

9.9.2 The protection of refugees in the Refugee Convention

The initial point to note about the protections found in the Refugee Convention is that the Convention does not oblige states to grant asylum to aliens seeking protection. Instead, it contains a (negative) obligation in article 33(1) whereby no contracting party 'shall expel or return ("refouler") a refugee' to a state where his or her life or freedom would be threatened. This obligation is also known as the *'non-refoulement'* principle. The Convention's aim is not limited to offering protection from *refoulement*, however. It seeks to provide surrogate national protection to individuals who cannot live in their country of citizenship and therefore also grants refugees a host of other rights that are traditionally associated with citizenship, such as protection from discrimination, religious freedoms, preservation of property rights, access to the courts, access to rationing systems and identity papers.[103]

As its name implies, the Convention (only) protects 'refugees'. The all-important definition of a refugee is found in article 1A(1). It follows that a refugee is an individual who:

> owing to well-founded fear of persecution for reasons of race, religion, nationality, membership of a particular social group or political opinion, is outside the country of his nationality and is unable or, owing to such fear, is unwilling to avail himself of the

---

[100] See the Convention's preamble

[101] Protocol relating to the Status of Refugees, 31 January 1967.

[102] The UNHCR publishes a handbook and a set of (non-binding) guidelines that may assist national decision-makers: see UNHCR, *Handbook and Guidelines on Procedures and Criteria for Determining Refugee Status under the 1951 Convention and the 1967 Protocol relating to the Status of Refugees*, Reissued Geneva, December 2011. A range of guidelines are available at http://www.unhcr.org/search?page=search& skip=0&docid=&cid=49aea93ae2&comid=4a27bad46&tags=RSDguidelines.

[103] James C. Hathaway and Michelle Foster, *The Law of Refugee Status* (2nd edn, Cambridge University Press, 2014) 51.

protection of that country; or who, not having a nationality and being outside the country of his former habitual residence as a result of such events, is unable or, owing to such fear, is unwilling to return to it.

Two initial comments are worth making about the definition. First, the Convention does not allow reservations to the definition.[104] Secondly, an individual is a 'refugee' as soon as he or she fulfils the criteria in the Convention, and refugee status is therefore not something that is 'granted' by a state but rather a status that is *recognized*.

According to the definition, to qualify as a 'refugee', and thus for protection under the Convention, an individual must fulfil five conditions. First, an individual must be *outside the country of origin*. Thus, the Convention does not protect the millions of people who are dislocated within their own countries—also known as 'internally displaced persons' (IDPs). The Convention allows a state to require that a refugee who requests its protection seek protection in another country if the consignment to such a 'safe third country' does not compromise the refugee's rights under the Convention. The second requirement is that the individual is *unable or unwilling* to seek the protection of his or her state of nationality. This requirement is relevant, for example, in those instances where an individual who fears persecution can find the required degree of protection in some other part of the country than where he or she originates. In such cases, the individual can be denied protection and asked to rely upon an 'international flight alternative'. Thirdly, the inability or unwillingness to seek the protection required must be due to a fear of persecution that is *well-founded*. In practice, the state that is confronted with a request for protection from an alien is forced to make a prediction about what will happen to the alien if he or she is returned to their country of origin. For the fear to be well-founded, it is not a requirement that the individual can demonstrate that he or she is at a greater risk of harm than other individuals in the state of origin. It is enough that the expected harm is sufficiently serious to find that the individual faces real harm if returned. The fourth condition is that the individual fears *persecution*. In practice, there is a minimum threshold of harm that must be surpassed and there must be a risk of serious harm, in most cases taking the form of severe violations of basic human rights. The risk of harm need not, however, originate from state authorities, and a risk of serious harm from non-state actors suffices if the state authorities do not offer the required degree of protection (and no internal flight alternative is available). The fifth—and last—requirement is that the persecution must be *based on one of five specific reasons*, namely race, religion, nationality, membership of a particular social group, or political opinion. Thus, the Convention is not concerned with all cases of persecution but merely those based on specific forms of discrimination. In addition, the persecution must be linked to the particular purpose.

Even if a person qualifies as a refugee under the definition in article 1A(1), the individual may still be denied protection under the Convention if he or she does not 'deserve' to be protected. Thus, according to article 1F, the Convention shall not apply to an individual in respect of whom there are serious reasons for considering that he or she has committed:

---

[104] See the Convention's art. 42.

(a) a 'crime against peace, a war crime, or a crime against humanity', as those crimes are defined in relevant international legal conventions;[105] (b) a 'serious non-political crime outside the country of refuge prior to his admission to that country as a refugee'; or (c) if the individual is 'guilty of acts contrary to the purposes and principles of the United Nations'. Article 1F was introduced to ensure state support for the Convention.

9.9.3 The protection of individuals who fear ill-treatment in other human rights conventions

The principle of *non-refoulement* is also found in a number of human rights conventions, most explicitly in the 1984 UN Convention Against Torture (CAT), which in article 3 stipulates that no state party 'shall expel, return ("refouler") or extradite a person to another State where there are substantial grounds for believing that he would be in danger of being subjected to torture'.[106] In addition, as noted earlier, the ECHR's article 3 also protects individuals from being transferred to a state where they face a real risk of being subjected to torture or other forms of ill-treatment.[107] The ECHR also protects against transfer to a state where there is a risk of a flagrant denial of a fair trial under ECHR, article 6,[108] or a breach of the right to liberty under article 5.[109] Unlike the protection found in the Refugee Convention, the *non-refoulement* principle in the human rights conventions protects everyone, regardless of why they fear ill-treatment in their states of origin or another state to which they may risk being transferred, and not just individuals who fulfil the conditions for being considered refugees. The ECtHR has found, for example, that article 3 may also prevent the removal of seriously ill persons if an 'absence of appropriate treatment in the receiving country or the lack of access to such treatment' may lead to 'a serious, rapid and irreversible decline' in health 'resulting in intense suffering or to a significant reduction in life expectancy'.[110]

Non-refoulement will become an example of extraterritorial application of a human rights treaty where an individual transferred to another state is physically located outside the territory of the state party, as may be the case in situations where soldiers on military operations abroad hand over detainees to the authorities of another state.

---

[105] See e.g. the discussion in Chapter 15.

[106] For the ICCPR and *non-refoulement*, see Human Rights Committee, 'General Comment No. 20' (10 March 1992), UN Doc. HRI/GEN/1/Rev.7.

[107] See *Soering v UK*, App. no. 14038/88, 7 July 1989, para. 88. See also *Cruz Varas and Others v Sweden*, App. no. 15576/89, 20 March 1991, para. 70 and *Vilvarajah and Others v UK*, App. nos 13163/87 etc., 30 October 1991, para. 107.

[108] Soering (n 107), para. 113. See also *Othman (Abu Qatada) v UK*, App. no. 8139/09, 17 January 2012, paras 258–260.

[109] *El-Masri v The Former Yugoslav Republic of Macedonia*, App. no. 39630/09, 13 December 2012, para. 239.

[110] *Paposhvili v Belgium*, App. no. 41738/10, 13 December 2016, para. 183.

Summary

International human rights law derives from a basic notion that human rights are inherent to *all* human beings. The modern human rights law system was created after the end of the Second World War with the establishment of the UN. The most important human rights instruments are those adopted under the auspices of the UN and a number of regional conventions, most notably the ECHR. Individual human rights are traditionally divided into categories or classes that reflect the nature of the rights and the evolution of international human rights law. Arguably, the most important human rights are those of a civil and political character. There are two systems for monitoring and enforcing compliance with human rights law in the UN, one based on the UN Charter and the other on universal human rights treaties. At the regional level, human rights protection is particularly strong in Europe, where the ECHR is a cornerstone of human rights protection. The geographical scope of human rights conventions is not necessarily limited to the territory of the state. The application of human rights does not cease in times of public emergency or armed conflict, but the determination of what constitutes a violation of human rights may be influenced by standards from the law of armed conflict. A state may also be allowed to temporarily suspend the application of parts of a human rights convention in the case of a public emergency. Refugees are primarily protected in the 1951 Refugee Convention.

Recommended reading

The literature on human rights is immense. A solid, comprehensive work on the law and politics of human rights is Henry J. Steiner, Philip Alston and Ryan Goodman, *International Human Rights in Context* (Oxford University Press, 2007).

For a comprehensive examination of the UN Covenant on Civil and Political Rights, see Manfred Novak, *UN Covenant on Civil and Political Rights, CCPR Commentary* (N. P. Engel Publishers, 1993) and Sarah Joseph and Melissa Castan, *The International Covenant on Civil and Political Rights: Cases, Materials, and Commentary* (3rd edn, Oxford University Press, 2013).

For a solid discussion of the ECHR, see Bernadette Rainey, Elizabeth Wicks and Clare Ovey, *Jacobs, White & Ovey: The European Convention on Human Rights* (6th edn, Oxford University Press, 2014).

For a discussion of human rights protection in the UN, see Paul Gordon Lauran, 'To Preserve and Build on Its Achievements and to Redress Its Shortcomings: The Journey from the Commission on Human Rights to the Human Rights Council' (2007) 29(2) *Human Rights Quarterly* 307.

On more recent human rights protection in the EU, see Frederic van den Berghe, 'The EU and Issues of Human Rights Protection: Same Solutions to More Acute Problems' (2010) 16(2) *European Law Review* 112.

The seminal work on the extraterritorial effect of the ECHR is Marko Milanovic, *Extraterritorial Application of Human Rights Treaties* (Oxford University Press, 2011).

The margin of appreciation and proportionality in the ECHR is thoroughly discussed in Jonas Christoffersen, *Fair Balance, Proportionality, Subsidiarity and Primarity in the European Convention on Human Rights* (Brill Nijhoff, 2009).

The classic work on the protection of refugees is James C. Hathaway and Michelle Foster, *The Law of Refugee Status* (2nd edn, Cambridge University Press, 2014).

Questions for discussion

1. What is the basis of the cultural relativist critique of human rights law?

2. The chapter notes that the human rights debate before the Human Rights Council is (still) highly politicized. Can you think of some examples?

3. What are some of the common features of the various monitoring organs that have been established with a view to monitoring compliance with specific UN human rights conventions?

4. The interpretational style of the ECtHR has been criticized for, among other things, disregarding state consent/intention. Why do you think that has been the case?

5. Case law from the ECtHR illustrates that a state party to the ECHR is not always bound by its obligations under the Convention when it acts abroad. Why could that be problematic when considered from the perspective of the alleged universal nature of human rights law?

6. What are the conditions for lawful derogation from a human rights convention?

7. How is the protection from '*refoulement*' in the 1951 Refugee Convention different from the protection from '*refoulement*' in article 3 of the ECHR?

10

International environmental law

CENTRAL ISSUES

1. This chapter discusses the most important areas of international environmental law and its main legal sources.

2. It presents the fundamental principles of international environmental law, including those that seek to prevent damage to the environment and those that seek to ensure a balanced approach to environmental protection.

3. The chapter provides an overview of the most important aspects of the substantial regulation in international environmental law, including the legal regime for the protection of the atmosphere and the marine environment, the conservation of nature and species and the regulation of hazardous substances.

4. The chapter also discusses a number of features related to implementation and enforcement that are particular to international environmental law.

10.1 Introduction

International environmental law emerged as a separate field of international law in the late 1960s and early 1970s as awareness of the need for international regulation to address environmental problems gradually arose. While existing international law had already regulated certain environmental issues, that regulation was primarily focused on protecting the environment as an economic resource[1]—such as a shared watercourse[2] or in order to alleviate the immediate economic costs of pollution[3]— and not on the protection of the environment *as such*.[4] International environmental

---

[1] See, inter alia, *Award between the United States and the United Kingdom relating to the rights of jurisdiction of the United States in the Bering's sea and the preservation of fur seals* (1893) XXVIII RIAA 263–276. See also the 1946 International Convention for the Regulation of Whaling.

[2] See *Lake Lanoux Arbitration (Spain v France)* (1957) XII RIAA 281f.

[3] See *Trail Smelter Arbitration (United States v Canada)* (1938 and 1941) III RIAA 1905. See the 1954 International Convention for the Prevention of Pollution of the Sea by Oil.

[4] See Philippe Sands and Jacqueline Peel, *Principles of International Environmental Law* (3rd edn, Cambridge University Press, 2012) 22–49. See also Pierre-Marie Dupuy and Jorge E. Viñuales, *International Environmental Law* (Cambridge University Press, 2015) 8–12.

law is an area of international law where states have decided to cooperate with each other in order to fulfil certain goals of common interest, and for the most part its rules and principles belong in the category of the international law of cooperation. It covers those parts of international law—whether public or private law—that relate to the environment and there is therefore often an overlap with other fields of international law, such as the law of the sea, international economic law and human rights law. It is not a separate and independent legal discipline and regulation is generally very piecemeal and sectoral. In addition, there is no international institution with overall competence on all matters of concern to the environment.

There is no authoritative definition of 'the environment' but in *Nuclear Weapons*, the International Court of Justice (ICJ) referred to the environment as 'the living space, the quality of life and the very health of human beings, including generations unborn'.[5] For present purposes, it suffices to note that there is an operational dimension to the term 'environment' that springs from the legal instruments generally referred to as falling within 'international environmental law'. Here, then, the 'environment' primarily consists of a range of physical components (air, water and land), as well as biological (species, habitats, ecosystems and diversity) and various cultural components.[6]

We begin in Section 10.2 with a brief overview of some of the major conferences and events that have served as important catalysts for the development of the law. Section 10.3 discusses the most relevant legal sources in this field of law and Section 10.4 deals with the main principles of international environmental law. Section 10.5 introduces the most important elements of the substantive regulation. Section 10.6 discusses implementation and enforcement.

10.2 From Stockholm to Rio and back to Rio

The development of international environmental law has been catapulted by major conferences. The first was the *1972 Stockholm Conference on the Human Environment*, which adopted a 'Declaration on the Human Environment'[7] with 26 principles, including as the first principle a right to 'an environment of a quality that permits a life of dignity and well-being', and an 'Action plan for the Human Environment'. It also paved the way for the UN Environment Programme (UNEP), which promotes international cooperation on environmental matters and has been instrumental in the development of legal instruments.[8] The Stockholm Conference also helped to create momentum for the establishment of many national environmental agencies and ministries and the conclusion of a range of environmental law treaties.

---

[5] *Legality of the Threat or Use of Nuclear Weapons*, Opinion [1996] ICJ Rep 226, para. 29. See also *Award in the Arbitration regarding the Iron Rhine ('Ijzeren Rijn') Railway between the Kingdom of Belgium and the Kingdom of the Netherlands*, Decision of 24 May 2005 (2005) XXVII RIAA 35–125, para. 58.

[6] See Dupuy and Viñuales (n 4) 27.

[7] Declaration of the United Nations Conference on the Human Environment, Stockholm, 16 June 1972, UN Doc. A/CONF48/14/Rev.1.

[8] GA Res. 2997 (XXVII) (15 December 1972).

The second major event was the *1992 Rio Conference on Environment and Development*—also known as the 'Earth Summit'.[9] The organizing principle of the Summit—often heralded as a 'foundational moment' in international environmental law—was the emerging concept of 'sustainable development' that would later be defined as 'development that meets the needs of the present without compromising the ability of future generations to meet their own needs'.[10] Like its Stockholm predecessor, the Rio Summit adopted a seminal declaration—the Rio 'Declaration on Environment and Development'.[11] The declaration contains a range of principles that illustrate how environmental protection and economic development had become increasingly linked in the years since Stockholm. The extent to which developing states should be allowed to exploit their natural resources without limitations imposed by international society remains an ongoing tension in international environmental law.[12] A number of the principles in the Rio Declaration are the building blocks on which the more substantial regulation is built. Examples include the principle of prevention (Principle 2), inter-generational equity (Principle 3), the principle of cooperation (Principles 5, 7, 9, 27), respect for the special needs of the least developed states (Principle 6), precaution (Principle 15) and Environmental Impact Assessments (Principle 17). Of particular interest was the introduction of Principle 7, which formulated a principle of common but differentiated responsibilities. The Rio Summit also led to the adoption of a plan of action—'Agenda 21'—and to a number of important conventions, including a framework convention on climate change and a convention on biological diversity. These treaties are highly complex instruments that integrate a host of issues that had up until then been dealt with as separate issues.

The ten-year anniversary of the Rio Conference was marked in 2002 with a World Summit on Sustainable Development in Johannesburg, South Africa. Though the results of the Summit were fairly modest, it illustrated the increasing importance of a variety of partnerships, including with the private sector. In September 2000, the General Assembly had adopted a Millennium Declaration with eight measurable goals—the Millennium Development Goals (MDGs)—to be reached before 2015. While the goals focused on poverty, references were also made to environmental sustainability (Goal 7) and developing a global partnership for development (Goal 8).

The most recent major conference was the 2012 (second) Rio Summit, which sought to secure a renewed commitment for sustainable development and to address new and emerging challenges. The conference adopted the document 'The Future We Want',[13] which replaced the MDGs with 17 Sustainable Development Goals (SDGs) setting out the global development agenda from 2015 to 2030.[14] Among the goals are

[9] See Dupuy and Viñuales (n 4) 16.

[10] Report of the World Commission on Environment and Development, 'Our Common Future', 10 March 1987.

[11] The Rio Declaration on Environment and Development (13 June 1992), see UN Doc. A/CONF.151/26 (vol. I).

[12] See also Nico Schrijver, *Sovereignty over Natural Resources: Balancing Rights and Duties* (Cambridge University Press, 1997).

[13] 'The Future We Want' (11 September 2012), UN Doc. A/Res/66/288.

[14] GA Res. 70/1 Transforming Our World: the 2030 Agenda for Sustainable Development (25 September 2015).

ending poverty in all forms (Goal 1), taking urgent action to end climate change and its impacts (Goal 13), conserving and sustainably using the oceans, sea and marine resources for sustainable development (Goal 14), protecting, restoring and promoting sustainable use of terrestrial ecosystems, sustainable management of forests, combating desertification, halting and reversing land degradation and halting biodiversity loss (Goal 15) and strengthening global partnerships (Goal 17).

10.3 Sources of international environmental law

International environmental law is primarily made up of treaties. In part, this is due to the recent 'birth' of the law and the detailed character of much of the substantive regulation. In order to take account of changes to the environment, shifting scientific assessments as well as political prioritization of the environment, states make frequent use of framework conventions, the primary purpose of which is not to exhaustively regulate a topic but rather to set up an organizational entity with the mandate to negotiate and adopt the substantive regulation. A well-known example is the 1992 UN Framework Convention on Climate Change (UNFCCC), which that—as we shall see later—only contains a few substantive provisions but establishes a Conference of the Parties (COP) as the 'supreme body' of the Convention. Some environmental law treaties adopt a so-called 'list technique' whereby the treaty-based obligations are tied to periodically updated lists in protocols or annexes. Examples include the 1972 World Heritage Convention, and its regularly updated World Heritage List of cultural and natural sites of outstanding universal interest, and the 1973 Convention on International Trade in Endangered Species of Wild Fauna and Flora (CITES) with its different lists/annexes of (more or less) endangered species of wild animals and plants. We return to both conventions later. An additional feature is the common differentiation in the substantial obligations imposed on the parties. For example, the 1992 UNFCCC is explicitly based on the notion that developed countries 'should take the lead in combating climate change and the adverse effects thereof'.[15] Differentiation may also take the form of different deadlines for reaching certain goals or through the transfer of technology and/or assistance.[16]

Customary international law plays only a limited role in international environmental law but, as we will see later, a number of customary legal principles do exist. The most well-established are the so-called 'no harm' principle—also known as the principle of due diligence; the obligation to consult and notify in the event of possible transboundary harm and the obligation to conduct a prior transboundary environmental impact assessment (EIA).

International courts have made important contributions to the development of international environmental law. Noticeable examples include the seminal award in

---

[15] Art. 3(1). See also Annex B to the 1997 Kyoto Protocol.
[16] P. Cullet, 'Differential Treatment in Environmental Law: Addressing Critiques and Conceptualizing the Next Steps' (2016) 5(2) *Transnational Environmental Law* 305–328.

the *Trail Smelter* case[17] and, from the ICJ, the *Gabčíkovo-Nagymaros Project* case and the *Pulp Mills* case.[18] Since environmental law is increasingly being applied and interpreted by specialized international courts, such as the European Court of Human Rights (ECtHR), the International Tribunal for the Law of the Sea (ITLOS) and the World Trade Organizations' Dispute Settlement Body (DSB), decisions from these organs are becoming of greater relevance.[19]

There is an abundance of non-binding 'soft law' instruments in international environmental law and some of the most cited instruments, including the 1972 Stockholm Declaration and the 1992 Rio Declaration, are for the most part of a non-binding character. The 2009 Copenhagen Accord on climate change is a case in point.[20] As discussed in Chapter 2, these instruments may assist in the formation of customary law. A possible example includes the principle of prevention listed in both the Stockholm and Rio Declarations.[21]

10.4 Basic principles of international environmental law

10.4.1 Introduction

In this section we shall examine some of the core principles/approaches that govern and guide the application of international environmental law.[22] The principles are of general application and apply to all actors and in respect of all activities. They are derived from a combination of state practice, treaties, soft law instruments and decisions from international courts, and their legal status varies. Some are mere aspirations of a soft law character[23] whose primary role is to guide the operation and implementation of more concrete and substantive obligations.[24] The principles can be divided into two groups, each seeking to fulfil a more overarching goal.[25] The first group of principles seeks *to prevent damage to the environment* while the second seeks to *ensure that environmental protection is balanced and—when necessary—distributed*. We begin with the principles of prevention (Section 10.4.2) before we turn to the balancing principles (Section 10.4.3).

---

[17] *Trail Smelter* (n 3).

[18] *Gabčíkovo-Nagymaros Project (Hungary v Slovakia)*, Judgment [1997] ICJ Rep 7; *Pulp Mills on the River Uruguay (Argentina v Uruguay)*, Provisional Measures, Order of 13 July 2006 [2006] ICJ Rep 113.

[19] See, inter alia, ECtHR, *López Ostra v Spain*, App. no. 16798/90, Judgment, 9 December 1994. From ITLOS, see *Responsibilities and Obligations of States Sponsoring Persons and Entities with Respect to Activities in the Area*, Advisory Opinion, 1 February 2011, ITLOS Rep 2011, 10.

[20] Copenhagen Accord (18 December 2009) in UNFCCC, Report of the Conference of the Parties on Its Fifteenth Session (hereinafter COP Report and session number), Addendum (30 March 2010), UN Doc. FCCC/CP/2009/11/Add.1, 5. See also Daniel Bodansky, 'The Copenhagen Climate Change Conference: A Postmortem' (2010) 104(2) *American Journal of International Law* 230–240.

[21] See, respectively, Principle nos 21 and 2 and *Nuclear Weapons* (n 5) para. 29, *Gabčíkovo-Nagymaros Project* (n 18) para. 53, *Pulp Mills* (n 18) para. 72.

[22] An overview is available in Sands and Peel (n 4) 187–237.   [23] *Iron Rhine* (n 5) para. 58.

[24] See also Sands and Peel (n 4) 188–190.

[25] For this approach, see Dupuy and Viñuales (n 4) 51–87.

10.4.2 **Principles that seek to prevent environmental damage**

The first principle is linked to the sovereign right of all states to their natural resources. Principle 21 of the 1972 Stockholm Declaration stipulates that 'States have ... the sovereign right to exploit their own resources pursuant to their own environmental policies'[26] but also have 'the responsibility to ensure that activities within their jurisdiction or control do not cause damage to the environment of other States or of areas beyond the limits of national jurisdiction'. The obligation not to cause damage to other states is known as the *'no harm' principle*. In the *Trail Smelter* case, where smoke from a smelting company located in Canada caused damage to crops and forests in the United States, an arbitrational court stated that:

> no State has the right to use or permit the use of its territory in such a manner as to cause injury by fumes in or to the territory of another or the properties or persons therein, when the case is of serious consequence and the injury is established by clear and convincing evidence.[27]

The ICJ has since confirmed that the principle reflects customary international law.[28] Importantly, though, it only applies to a risk of significant or serious harm.[29] While the no harm principle was initially solely relied on in the context of transboundary harm, the ICJ has indicated the existence of a more overarching *principle of prevention* and a corresponding duty not to cause damage to areas *beyond the territorial confines of states*.[30] In *Nuclear Weapons*, the Court found that:

> the existence of the general obligation of States to ensure that activities within their jurisdiction and control respect the environment of other States or of areas beyond national control is now part of the corpus of international law relating to the environment.[31]

This points to the existence of a (vague and ill-defined) obligation under international law not to cause harm to the environment per se.

In the *Pulp Mills* case, concerning a dispute between Argentina and Uruguay in relation to the construction of pulp mills on a stretch of the River Uruguay which separates the two states, the ICJ stated that the customary principle of prevention originates in notions of *due diligence* and a state's obligation to 'use all the means at its disposal in order to avoid activities which take place in its territory, or in any area under its jurisdiction, causing significant damage to the environment of another

---

[26] See also GA Res. 1803 on Permanent Sovereignty over Natural Resources (14 December 1962).

[27] *Trail Smelter* (n 3) 1965.

[28] See *Corfu Channel (UK v Albania)*, Judgment of 9 April 1949 [1949] ICJ Rep 4, 22; *Pulp Mills on the River Uruguay (Argentina v Uruguay)*, Judgment [2010] ICJ Rep 14, para. 101.

[29] *Pulp Mills* (n 28) para. 101. See also the International Law Commission's 2001 Draft Articles on Prevention of Transboundary Harm from Hazardous Activities, with commentaries, *Yearbook of the International Law Commission*, 2001, vol. II, Part Two: see commentary to art. 2, p. 152, para. 6 and commentary to art. 3, p. 153, para. 5.

[30] See also Principle 21 of the 1972 Stockholm Declaration. See also the overview of general principles of law in Chapter 2.

[31] *Nuclear Weapons* (n 5) para. 29. See also *Gabčíkovo-Nagymaros Project* (n 18) para. 140 and *Pulp Mills* (n 28) paras 101, 185 and 193.

[32] *Pulp Mills* (n 28) para. 101.

State'.[32] Due diligence is not an obligation of result but of conduct and concrete means required to fulfil the due diligence obligation will vary according to the circumstances.[33] Relevant factors include the timing of the potential damage, the type of activity and the capacities of the state. So activities that entail a more serious risk, such as nuclear energy, require a higher degree of diligence. In addition, measures that may have been considered sufficiently diligent at a certain point in time may gradually prove not to be diligent enough in the light of, for example, new scientific or technological knowledge.[34]

The ICJ and ITLOS have stated that a state must undertake an *environmental impact assessment* (EIA) before it initiates an activity if there is a risk of significant adverse impact in a transboundary context,[35] and the obligation also seems to be of a customary law character. EIAs are explicitly governed by the 1991 Convention on Environmental Impact Assessment in a Transboundary Context (also known as the ESPOO Convention).[36] If the EIA indicates that a planned activity poses a risk of significant transboundary harm, the state must notify potentially affected states and consult on remedies to prevent significant harm or minimize the risk.[37] The latter illustrates that cooperation on implementing and applying measures to protect the environment is also considered to be an important guiding principle in international environmental law.[38]

The so-called '*precautionary approach*' stipulates that a lack of scientific certainty about the negative effects of an activity must not prevent states from taking preventive measures. Notions of precaution are found in many treaties in international environmental law, including in the 1985 Vienna Convention for the Protection of the Ozone Layer[39] and the 1992 UNFCCC.[40] In *Tatar v Romania*, the ECtHR found that Romania had breached the principle of precaution by allowing a company to continue its industrial operations after a preliminary impact assessment had highlighted the risks entailed by the activity for the environment and human health.[41] The International Tribunal for the Law of the Sea has stated that the precautionary approach is 'an integral part of the due diligence obligation'[42] and that the incorporation of the approach into a growing number of treaties has 'initiated a trend towards making this approach part of customary international law'.[43] Currently, however, this would appear to be too optimistic.[44] The approach is fairly imprecise and hardly suitable to serve as anything other than an interpretational aid.[45]

---

[33] Ibid, paras 186–187.

[34] *Responsibilities and Obligations of States* (n 19) para. 117; *Pulp Mills* (n 28) para. 197. See also ILC Draft Articles (n 29) see commentary to art. 3, p. 154, paras 11, 17–18.

[35] *Pulp Mills* (n 28) paras 204–205 and *Responsibilities and Obligations of States* (n 19) para. 145. See also Principle 17 of the Rio Declaration and art. 7 in the ILC Draft Articles (n 29).

[36] See, inter alia, art. 2(3).   [37] See arts 8–9 in the ILC' Draft Articles (n 29).

[38] See also art. 4 in the ILC Draft Articles (n 29) and Principle 24 of the Stockholm Declaration and Principle 7 in the Rio Declaration.

[39] See the Preamble.   [40] Art. 3(3). See also Principle 15 of the Rio Declaration.

[41] *Tatar v Romania*, App. no. 67021/01.

[42] *Responsibilities and Obligations of States* (n 19) para. 131.   [43] Ibid, para. 135.

[44] See the debate in Dupuy and Viñuales (n 4) 61–64.   [45] See also *Pulp Mills* (n 28) para. 165.

10.4.3 **Principles that seek to ensure a balanced approach to environmental protection**

The second group of principles are concerned with a 'fair' and sensible balance between environmental protection and a host of other considerations. The first is the so-called *'polluter-pays'* principle, whereby a state should ensure that it is the actor responsible for pollution that bears both the more immediate and the longer term costs thereof.[46] While the principle is hardly reflective of customary international law, it features as an important guiding principle in a wide range of conventions and legal instruments, including in EU law.[47]

The principle of *'common but differentiated responsibilities'* (CBDR) is derived from more overarching principles of equity and seeks to take account of the special needs of developing states and the fact that developed states generally hold greater responsibility for existing environmental damage and are better equipped to deal with the consequences than developing states.[48] There is, in other words, both an element of *contribution* or responsibility for the creation of an environmental problem and an element of *ability* to offer a remedy inherent in the principle. CBDR is reflected in a number of important conventions, including, as already mentioned, the 1992 UNFCCC. Thus, although all state parties to the UNFCCC are deemed to hold responsibilities, the burden is primarily laid on the developed countries.[49] In the (infamous) 1997 Kyoto Protocol to the UNFCCC, which we shall return to later, CBDR was translated into a system whereby omission targets only applied to developed states on the basis of historical contributions and capabilities.[50] In the 1987 Montreal Protocol to the 1985 Vienna Convention on the Protection of the Ozone Layer, CBDR led to delayed compliance with particular requirements by some developing states.[51] The CBDR principle has been a major impediment to reaching agreement on important environmental issues, most notably climate change.

The principle *of inter-generational equity* seeks to ensure a sensible balance between the needs of the present and future generations. The need to preserve the environment for future generations is noted in, inter alia, the 1946 International Whaling Convention.[52] Article 3 of the Rio Declaration states that the 'right to development must be fulfilled so as to meet developmental and environmental needs of present and future generation'.[53] The principle is closely tied to the concept of *sustainable development*, which was coined in the 1987 Brundtland Report.[54] It has been referred to as a 'comprehensive and integrated approach to economic, social and political processes, which aims at the sustainable

---

[46] See the 1972 OECD Council Recommendation on Guiding Principles Concerning the International Economic Aspects of Environmental Policies. See also art. 16 of the 1992 Rio Declaration and see the overview in Sands and Peel (n 4) 228–233.

[47] See, inter alia, art. 191 of the EU Treaty as amended by the Treaty of Lisbon.

[48] The principle is reflected in art. 7 of the Rio Declaration. For an overview, see Sands and Peel (n 4) 233–236 and Philippe Cullet, 'Common but Differentiated Responsibilities' in Malgosia Fitzmaurice and others (eds), *Research Handbook on International Environmental Law* (Edward Elgar Publishing, 2010) 161–180.

[49] UNFCCC art. 3(1).   [50] See the Kyoto Protocol's annexes.   [51] See art. 5(1).

[52] Preamble.

[53] See also *Gabčíkovo-Nagymaros Project* (n 18) para. 140 and *Nuclear Weapons* (n 5) para. 29.

[54] Report of the World Commission on Environment and Development, 'Our Common Future', 10 March 1987.

use of natural resources of the Earth and the protection of the environment …'[55] The ICJ referred to sustainable development in the *Gabčíkovo-Nagymaros Project* case.[56] Although the principle is hard to define in very precise terms, it is generally considered to encompass (at least) four elements.[57] Apart from the principle of inter-generational equity mentioned above, it covers 'sustainable' exploitation of natural resources that may entail setting limits on exploitation; a balanced and 'sustainable' use of resources where states take account of the needs of other states and, finally, a need to ensure the integration of environmental considerations in economic and other forms of development plans.

The *principle of participation* imposes on all states a duty to ensure that various groups and individuals affected by environmental matters are heard and are able to participate in important environmental projects and processes.[58] Among other things, the requirement of so-called 'prior informed consent' obliges a state to consult with and seek the informed consent of indigenous peoples before the displacement or relocation of those peoples.[59] The 1998 Aarhus Convention on Access to Information, Public Participation in Decision-Making and Access to Justice in Environmental Matters contains a number of important rights for the public, such as rights to receive environmental information held by public authorities, to participate in environmental decision-making and to challenge decisions that have been taken without regard to the other two rights. The ECtHR has found that the authorities of a state must ensure public access to the conclusions of investigations and studies on the consequences of environmental incidents.[60]

10.5 Substantive regulation

10.5.1 Introduction

International environmental law covers a wide array of both public and private law topics and the substantive regulation is enormous. We begin our overview of the most important areas of the law with the legal efforts to protect the atmosphere (Section 10.5.2). We then examine the protection of the marine environment (Section 10.5.3), conservation of nature and species (Section 10.5.4) and, finally, the regulation of hazardous substances (Section 10.5.5).[61]

10.5.2 Protection of the atmosphere

The protection of the air and overall atmosphere is one of the most important areas in international environmental law and it is certainly one of the topics to which most public attention is devoted. In practice, the regulation can be divided into three legal regimes.

---

[55] International Law Association, 2002 New Delhi Declaration on the Principles of International Law Related to Sustainable Development, see the Preamble.

[56] *Gabčíkovo-Nagymaros Project* (n 18) para. 140.   [57] Sands and Peel (n 4) 206–217.

[58] See Principle 10 in the 1992 Rio Declaration.

[59] GA Res. 61/295 Declaration on the Rights of Indigenous Peoples (13 September 2007), see art. 10. See also art. 8(j) of the Convention on Biodiversity.

[60] *Tatar v Romania* (n 41) para. 69.   [61] Conservation of marine life was covered in Section 8.4.

10.5.2.1 Limiting air pollution

Transboundary air pollution caused by industrialization has been a concern among states for a substantial period of time, in particular in North America and Europe. In fact, the *Trail Smelter* case mentioned earlier arose from a dispute about air pollution back in the 1930s. However, it was not until the 1970s that international awareness of the dangers to health and the environment associated with emissions of various toxic substances into the air led to the first legally binding international measures. In 1979, the Convention on Long-Range Transboundary Air Pollution (LRTAP) was adopted in order to limit and 'as far as possible, gradually reduce and prevent air pollution including long-range transboundary air pollution'.[62] LRTAP is a framework convention creating an institutional structure consisting of an executive body, a secretariat and a scientific body. The substantive regulation is found in eight protocols.

10.5.2.2 Protecting the ozone layer

Efforts to combat ozone depletion have resulted in one of the most successful legal regimes in international environmental law. At an altitude of around 25 km, the planet is surrounded by a thin layer of ozone that absorbs the vast majority of the ultraviolet radiation from the sun. Depletion of ozone has an adverse effect on environmental and human health and, in the 1980s, scientists began to link a gradual weakening of, and in some areas a 'hole' in, the ozone layer with a number of substances from the production and consumption of a limited range of products. The 1985 framework Vienna Convention on the Protection of the Ozone Layer was adopted to protect the 'layer of atmospheric ozone above the planetary boundary line'.[63] The Convention was built around a precautionary approach[64] and the institutional structure tasked with adopting the relevant substantive obligations was a Conference of the Parties (COP).[65] The 1987 Montreal Protocol introduced a sophisticated system of obligations, including provisions on trade in controlled substances and a flexible system for the transfer of production capacities. This system influenced the system created later for limiting damaging emissions in the efforts to combat climate change. The Montreal Protocol's approach to non-compliance would also later become a general characteristic of international environmental law. Instead of punishing non-compliance, the Protocol took the approach of offering to non-complying states both technical and economic assistance in order to improve performance.

10.5.2.3 Fighting climate change

Reaching international agreement on how to combat climate change has turned out to be one of the most pressing—and difficult—political issues of the 21st century. Scientific evidence indicates that an increase in certain greenhouse gases in the atmosphere is directly related to the so-called 'greenhouse effect' and a change in the global climate.[66] The increase in temperature is linked to an already visible decrease

---

[62] LRTAP art. 2.   [63] Art. 1(1).   [64] See also the Preamble to the Convention.   [65] Art. 6.

[66] See, inter alia, Intergovernmental Panel on Climate Change, *Climate Change 2013: The Physical Science Basis, Summary for Policymakers*: see sections B.1. and D.3.

in the area of sea ice and snow cover in arctic regions[67] as well as a potential rise in sea levels and more extreme weather events, such as heat waves, heavy precipitation and storms.[68] Concerns about climate change emerged in the late 1980s and resulted in the adoption in 1992 of the *UNFCCC* at the 1992 Rio Conference. Today, the Convention has an impressive 197 parties. The primary purpose of the Convention is to stabilize 'greenhouse gas concentrations in the atmosphere at a level that would prevent dangerous anthropogenic interference with the climate system' and overall agreement has gradually settled on the ambition of holding the increase in global average temperature to below 2 °C from pre-industrial levels.[69] The UNFCCC only contains limited substantive provisions and instead established a COP to adopt the specific measures required.[70] The Convention is guided by the principle of CBDR,[71] a precautionary approach, cost-effectiveness, the promotion of sustainable development and overall cooperation.[72] Based on these principles and the premise that the developed world should take the lead in combating climate change, the Kyoto Protocol was adopted in 1997, setting binding greenhouse gas reduction and limitation commitments[73] for developed countries.[74] The Protocol introduced some flexibility mechanisms to facilitate compliance with the targets in a cost-effective manner. Crucially, an emissions trading system for emissions units was established where countries can sell their Assigned Amounts Units, i.e. the division of the allowed country emissions under Kyoto, to other countries that need them for compliance,[75] and two project-based mechanisms were created,[76] whereby credits could be obtained in countries with economies in transition[77] and developing countries[78] for reducing emissions or enhancing removals and sinks of greenhouse gases. The first commitment period of Kyoto expired in 2012, and a second commitment period (2013–2020) was negotiated through the Doha Amendment although it is not yet in force.

By the time the Protocol entered into force in 2005, it was already clear that Kyoto was insufficient to keep greenhouse gas emissions in check, since major states with some of the highest emission levels, such as China, India and Brazil, were under no limitation or reduction obligations under the Protocol. Efforts then turned towards reaching a comprehensive climate agreement at the 2009 COP 15 in Copenhagen,

---

[67] Ibid, section B.3.   [68] Ibid, section B.1.

[69] Decision 1/CP.16, Cancun Agreement: Outcome of the Work of the Ad Hoc Working Group on Long-Term Cooperative Action under the Convention, see section I.4.

[70] See art. 7.

[71] Rowena Maguire, 'The Role of Common but Differentiated Responsibility in the 2020 Climate Regime' (2013) 4 *Carbon & Climate Law Review* 260–269.

[72] See arts 2–4.

[73] Kyoto Protocol, art. 3(1) and Annex B set the Quantified Emissions Limitation and Reduction Commitments for the parties.

[74] 'Developed country' in this respect is determined by OECD membership in 1992.

[75] Kyoto Protocol, art. 17.

[76] Ibid, art. 6 (Joint Implementation) and art. 12 (Clean Development Mechanism).

[77] Joint implementation is a mechanism that allows for project activities to be implemented by Annex I parties. These projects produce Emission Reduction Units, which can be used for compliance.

[78] The Clean Development Mechanism allows for project activities to be carried out in developing countries. These projects produce Certified Emission Reduction credits, which can then be used for compliance.

Denmark. But the negotiations in Copenhagen failed and the 'Copenhagen Accords' were merely a political agreement where countries pledged their mitigation ambitions.[79] But Copenhagen became a turning point towards a 'bottom-up' international climate change regime, which was reflected in the Paris Agreement adopted in 2015. At COP 21 in December 2015 in Paris, France, the *Paris Agreement* was adopted to keep the increase in 'the global average temperature to well below 2 °C above pre-industrial levels and to pursue efforts to limit the temperature increase to 1.5 °C above pre-industrial levels'. It also seeks to enhance states' abilities to 'adapt to the adverse impacts of climate change and foster climate resilience' and to make 'finance flows consistent with a pathway towards low greenhouse gas emissions and climate-resilient development'.[80] The Agreement allows each state to determine for itself what contribution it should make—so-called 'nationally determined contributions' (NDCs)—to fulfil the purposes of the Agreement,[81] but the contributions must represent a progression over time.[82] There is no enforcement mechanism for non-compliance. The Paris Agreement entered into force in November 2016 and by October 2018, it had reached 195 signatories and 184 ratifying parties.[83] On 1 June 2017, US President Trump announced that the United States would withdraw from the agreement.

10.5.3 Protection of the marine environment

It was not until the late 1960s and early 1970s that marine protection became a key priority for the international society. Up until that time, the law had almost exclusively focused on the exploitation of the sea and not its protection. But marine protection features prominently in the 1982 United Nations Convention on the Law of the Sea (UNCLOS), which devotes an entire Part of the Convention—Part XII—to the issue. In many ways, UNCLOS reflected a paradigm shift away from a general freedom to pollute to an obligation to prevent pollution.[84] Among other things, article 192 contains a general obligation on all states to 'protect and preserve the marine environment'.

In practice, the substantive regulation for the protection of the marine environment focuses on the source of the pollution.[85] *Land-based sources of pollution* are the greatest source of marine pollution, but due to the obvious tension between limiting pollution

---

[79] The agreement is available in Report of the Conference of the Parties on its fifteenth session, held in Copenhagen from 7 to 19 December 2009 (30 March 2010), UN Doc. FCCC/CP/2009/11/Add.1.

[80] See art. 2(1).

[81] Art. 4(2).

[82] Arts 3 and 4(3). The Paris Agreement has a binding obligation for states to prepare NDCs every five years. In order to ensure that ambition is increased over time, there is an expectation of progression reflected in the agreement and a review process through a global stocktake, where the NDCs have to be informed by outcomes of the global stocktake.

[83] https://treaties.un.org/Pages/ViewDetails.aspx?src=TREATY&mtdsg_no=XXVII-7-d&chapter=27&clang=_en (accessed 20 October 2018).

[84] Yoshifumi Tanaka, *The International Law of the Sea* (2nd edn, Cambridge University Press, 2015) 276.

[85] The source-based regulation is supplemented by a number of regional treaties adopted to protect the marine environment in certain regions of the world. Examples include the 1976 Convention for the Protection of the Mediterranean Sea against Pollution and the 1992 Convention for the Protection of the Marine Environment of the North-East Atlantic (OSPAR).

and economic and industrial growth, international regulation is weak. The general obligations to prevent pollution, including article 192 mentioned above, are essentially the only substantive obligations of a universal character that apply. However, a number of initiatives have been proposed under the UN Environment Programme (UNEP), including the non-binding 1985 Montreal Guidelines for the Protection of the Marine Environment against Pollution from Land-Based Sources. The—limited— regulation of land-based pollution is supplemented by regional conventions.

Dumping is the deliberate disposal at sea of waste or other matters from vessels, aircraft, platforms or other man-made structures.[86] The regulation of dumping has gone from an approach which generally allowed dumping unless it was explicitly prohibited, to the current approach where dumping is prohibited unless explicitly allowed. The 1972 London Dumping Convention, which has since been amended, most importantly in 1996 with the adoption of a London Protocol, obliges states to prohibit and prevent dumping of certain waste listed in a number of annexes.

Vessels may pollute the marine environment through the release of oil or other harmful substances in the course of normal operations or as a result of an accident. The primary legal instruments are the so-called 'MARPOL' instruments that consist of the 1973 International Convention for the Prevention of Pollution from Ships and a 1978 Protocol thereto.[87] MARPOL seeks to limit the discharge of oil and to assist in the management of an accident at sea and applies to discharges by 'ships' (including submarines or fixed or floating platforms).[88] Substantive regulation is found in a number of annexes.

Accidents such as the 1989 *Exxon Valdez* oil spill in Alaska and the 2010 *Deep Water Horizon* oil spill in the Gulf of Mexico illustrate the devastating effects major accidents may have on the marine environment. In response to the *Exxon Valdez* oil spill, the 1990 International Convention on Oil Pollution Preparedness, Response and Cooperation (OPRC) was adopted in the framework of the International Maritime Organization. As we shall see in Section 10.6, oil spills are also governed by a special regime of liability for environmental damage.

Mention should also be made of the efforts to develop an international legally binding instrument on the conservation and sustainable use of marine biodiversity in areas beyond national jurisdiction under UNCLOS. In December 2017, the General Assembly adopted a resolution that sought to initiate such a process.[89] According to the resolution, the new legal instrument should be 'fully consistent with' UNCLOS. Efforts to reach common legal ground are very much overdue as the general principle of the freedom of the high seas discussed in Chapter 8 is outdated for the purposes of conservation and regulation of the sustainable use of biodiversity in areas beyond national jurisdictions. As we saw in Chapter 8, marine genetic resources are not covered by the concept of 'resources' in the Area and UNCLOS does not specifically refer to biodiversity or sustainability.

---

[86] London Convention, art. 3(1)(a).

[87] See also the earlier 1954 International Convention for the Prevention of Pollution of the Sea by Oil (OILPOL).

[88] MARPOL, art. 3(1).   [89] GA Res. 72/249 (19 January 2018) See also GA Res. 69/292 (19 June 2015).

10.5.4 **Conservation of nature and species**

10.5.4.1 Protection of Antarctica

Antarctica is governed by a system of international instruments known as the Antarctic Treaty System (ATS), which seeks to ensure that Antarctica is used solely for peaceful purposes with due regard to the interests of all humankind.[90] The 1959 Antarctic Treaty specifies that no state can make claims of territorial sovereignty over Antarctica as long as the treaty is in force[91] and that military activities are prohibited.[92] The same holds for the disposal of radioactive waste.[93] The Treaty is supplemented with a range of protocols, including a 1991 Madrid Protocol that preserves all of Antarctica as a natural reserve 'devoted to peace and science'.[94] All activities relating to Antarctic mineral resources, except for scientific research, are prohibited.[95]

10.5.4.2 Protection of wetlands

The 1971 Convention on Wetlands of International Importance especially as Waterfowl Habitat—also known as the Ramsar Convention—provides a legal framework for the conservation and wise use, including 'sustainable' use, of wetlands and their resources. Wetlands are generally considered among the most diverse ecosystems and they are under threat in many regions of the world. The Convention's most important feature is the listing of sites that must be protected under national law.[96] By October 2018, it had designated 2,332 sites on a list maintained by a Secretariat.[97] Of these, some are also listed under the WHC (see below). It is the state itself that designates suitable wetlands within its territory for listing,[98] and the selection should consider the 'international significance in terms of ecology, botany, zoology, limnology or hydrology'.[99] The territorial state retains exclusive sovereign rights to the territory where the listed wetland is situated,[100] but once listed, the territorial state must conserve and ensure 'wise' use of the wetlands and 'formulate and implement their planning' accordingly.[101] If it fails to do so, the site may be listed on another list—the Montreux Record—of sites that require priority attention.[102]

10.5.4.3 Protection of 'World Heritage'

The 1972 Convention Concerning the Protection of the World Cultural and Natural Heritage—also known as the 'World Heritage Convention' (WHC)—seeks to promote international cooperation to protect heritage of outstanding universal value.[103] It is

---

[90] See the Preamble to the 1959 Antarctic Treaty. For a full overview, see Francesco Francioni and Tullio Scovazzi (eds), *International Law for Antarctica* (Martinus Nijhoff, 1996).

[91] Art. IV.   [92] Antarctic Treaty, art. I.

[93] Art. V. See also art. 27(1) of the IAEA Joint Convention on the Safety of Spent Fuel and Radioactive Waste Management.

[94] See Protocol, art. 2.   [95] Protocol, art. 7.   [96] See art. 2.

[97] https://www.ramsar.org/ (accessed 20 October 2018).   [98] Art. 2(1).   [99] Art. 2(2).

[100] Art. 2(3).   [101] Art. 3(1).

[102] The list is available at http://archive.ramsar.org/cda/en/ramsar-documents-montreux-montreux-record-23759/main/ramsar/1-31-118%5E23759_4000_0_ (accessed 20 October 2018).

[103] See also Francesco Francioni (ed.), *The 1972 World Heritage Convention: A Commentary* (Oxford University Press, 2008).

administered by a World Heritage Committee that keeps a World Heritage List of both cultural and natural sites or properties of outstanding universal value. By October 2018, the list had 1,092 sites of which 209 were natural properties.[104] Criteria for what qualifies as 'outstanding universal value' are set up in Operational Guidelines regularly updated by the World Heritage Committee.[105] The state on whose territory a natural heritage site is located must ensure the 'identification, protection, conservation, presentation and transmission to future generations' of the heritage site.[106] It retains full sovereignty over the site but recognizes that it constitutes a part of world heritage for 'whose protection it is the duty of the international community as a whole to co-operate'.[107] It also accepts that it will not 'take any deliberate measures which might damage directly or indirectly' the natural heritage located on the territory of another state.[108] It is up to the states themselves to nominate potential sites for listing by the World Heritage Committee.[109] If a site is under threat, it will be referred by the Committee to a List of World Heritage in Danger.

10.5.4.4 Protection of endangered species

The 1973 Convention on International Trade in Endangered Species of Wild Fauna and Flora (CITES) aims to limit and control the international trade in specimens of wild animals and plants in order to ensure their survival.[110] CITES—which has been fairly successful—adopts a 'list technique' that takes the form of three annexes with varying obligations with regard to international trade. Annex I contain a list of thousands of animal species and plants that are so endangered by extinction that trade is essentially prohibited, especially for commercial purposes.[111] Examples include the Siberian tiger, the panda, gorillas, orangutans, the African lion and most African elephants and rhinos. Annex II lists species that are not necessarily threatened with extinction at present, but that may become so unless trade is closely controlled. Such species include the hippopotamus, the African elephant in certain African countries, rhinos in South Africa and Swaziland, the great white shark, cobras and coral snakes. Trade in these species may be authorized by the exporting state without permission from the importing state but an authorization should only be given if the relevant authorities are satisfied that trade will not be detrimental to the survival of the species in the wild.[112] Annex III lists species that are included at the request of a party that already regulates trade in the species and that needs the cooperation of other countries to prevent unsustainable or illegal exploitation. International trade in such species (merely) requires the appropriate permits or certificates.[113] Species in Annex III include certain forms of squirrel, toucans, geckos, freshwater stingrays and salamanders. Species may be added to or removed from Appendices I and II, or moved

---

[104] Thirty-two properties were listed as fulfilling both cultural and natural criteria. The updated list is available at http://whc.unesco.org/en/list/ (accessed 20 October 2018).

[105] For the most recent 2012 guidelines, see United Nations Educational, Scientific and Cultural Organisation Intergovernmental Committee for the Protection of the World Cultural and Natural Heritage, *Operational Guidelines for the Implementation of the World Heritage Convention* (8 July 2015) WHC.15/01.

[106] Art. 4.   [107] Art. 6(1).   [108] Art. 6(3).   [109] See art. 11(1)–(3).

[110] As we saw in Chapter 8, the Convention covers certain marine mammals.

[111] See Art. II(1) and Art. III.   [112] Art. II(2) and Art. IV.   [113] Art. II(3) and Art. V.

between them, only by the Conference of the Parties.[114] Species may be added to or removed from Appendix III at any time and by any party unilaterally. As the overview reflects, one of the key features of the Convention is its permit system. To fulfils its obligations under the Convention, states must establish a 'Management Authority' responsible for issuing permits, a 'Scientific Authority' to give advice on environmental considerations and a 'Rescue Centre' that must take care of living specimens in cases of, for example, confiscation.

10.5.4.5 Fighting desertification

The threat posed by desertification and the ensuing loss of productivity of arid land led to the adoption of the 1994 UN Convention to Combat Desertification in those Countries Experiencing Serious Drought and/or Desertification, Particularly in Africa.[115] The Convention primarily obliges the parties to adopt national action programmes with longer term strategies with international assistance. It is a framework convention whose broad obligations are implemented through reliance on a set of annexes that form an integral part of the Convention. Since the problems associated with desertification are particularly acute in Africa, priority is given to that region.[116]

10.5.4.6 Protection of biodiversity

The 1992 Convention on Biological Diversity (CBD) was adopted at the 1992 Rio Summit as the first international convention to protect the diversity of the species and spaces in the environment and their complex interaction. It affirms that the conservation of biological diversity is a 'common concern to humankind'.[117] It seeks to conserve biological diversity, the sustainable use of its components and a fair and equitable sharing of the benefits arising out of the utilization of genetic resources.[118] Importantly, the CBD is not merely focused on conservation but seeks to balance it with sustainable use of the biological resources. The CBD leaves much of the responsibility on the states and their practical implementation of the aims of the Convention. Implementation is scrutinized through a process of reporting to a Conference of Parties (COP). A key provision is article 6, which obliges states to develop—in accordance with their circumstances and capabilities—national strategies, plans or programmes for the conservation and sustainable use of biological diversity and to integrate the conservation and sustainable use of biological diversity into relevant sectoral or cross-sectoral plans, programmes and policies.

It has been a core priority of the CBD to control the risks associated with genetically modified organisms (GMOs) resulting from modern biotechnology.[119] To that end, much progress was made with the 2000 Cartagena Protocol on Biosafety, which focuses on the transboundary movement of Living Modified Organisms (LMOs), which may have an adverse effect on diversity and health. The Protocol essentially adopts an

---

[114] Art. XV.

[115] The Convention defines desertification as: 'land degradation in arid, semi-arid and dry sub-humid areas resulting from various factors, including climatic variations and human activities', see art. 1(a).

[116] See also art. 7.   [117] Preamble.   [118] Art. 1.

[119] See, inter alia, arts 8(g) and 19(3) of the CBD.

advanced information agreement procedure that seeks to ensure that importing states receive the information about the LMOs required to make an informed decision.

Another important area is access to genetic resources—an issue that has been fraught with contention.[120] Due to technological advances, the potential use of—and rights over—modified seeds have grown in importance and agreement on benefit sharing and access has been hard to reach. Progress was made, however, with the 2010 Nagoya Protocol on Access to Genetic Resources and the Fair and Equitable Sharing of Benefits Arising from their Utilization. Among other things, the Protocol facilitates interstate access to genetic resources for environmentally sound uses and improves benefit sharing through the adoption of more predictable conditions for access.

10.5.5 The regulation of hazardous substances

10.5.5.1 Nuclear energy

Environmentally sound management of dangerous and hazardous substances is another important part of international environmental law. The potentially catastrophic international consequences of nuclear accidents have made the nuclear energy sector an obvious target for elaborate international regulation.[121] The International Atomic Energy Agency (IAEA) was created in 1957 to promote peaceful development and use of nuclear energy and prevent its military use. One of the main tasks of the IAEA is to assist states in balancing the many benefits of sound civilian exploitation of nuclear technology and the health and environmental hazards. The IAEA makes recommendations and designs programmes for the safe development and use of nuclear technology and nuclear materials and has been instrumental in the adoption of a number of relevant conventions. The 1986 Chernobyl disaster led to the adoption of the 1986 Convention on Early Notification of a Nuclear Accident or Radiological Emergency and the Convention on Assistance in the Case of a Nuclear Accident or Radiological Emergency. In 1994, the Convention on Nuclear Safety was adopted to give effect to some of the IAEA's standards on nuclear safety, waste management and fuel disposal and reprocessing. While the Convention affirmed that 'responsibility for nuclear safety rests with the State having jurisdiction over a nuclear installation',[122] it obliges states to, inter alia, 'take appropriate steps' to ensure that safety is given due priority,[123] that radiation is 'as low as reasonably achievable'[124] and that adequate emergency plans are developed.[125] The terms used are vague, however, and enforcement is weak and merely based on periodic reviews of reports on implementation measures taken.[126] In 1997, IAEA members adopted the Joint Convention on the Safety of Spent Fuel and Radioactive Waste Management to improve the management and disposal of nuclear waste. A noticeable feature of the Convention is the reference to the principle of inter-generational equity and the aim to 'avoid imposing undue

---

[120] See Dupuy and Viñuales (n 4) 192–196.

[121] For an overview, see Patricia Birnie and others, *International Law and the Environment* (Oxford University Press, 2009) ch. 9. The secondary rules on responsibility and liability for nuclear damage have been a particular point of focus: see ibid, 516–534.

[122] Preamble.   [123] Art. 6.   [124] Art. 15.   [125] Art. 16.   [126] Art. 20.

burdens on future generations'.[127] On a regional level, the 1957 *Euratom Treaty* sets up European standards for nuclear energy.[128] In response to the 11 March 2011 accident at the Fukushima nuclear power plant in Japan, the IAEA adopted an Action Plan on Nuclear Safety and, in 2015, the parties to the Convention on Nuclear Safety adopted the Vienna Declaration on Nuclear Safety with the aim of strengthening relevant nuclear procedures.[129]

The regulation of the *military use of nuclear energy* has generally followed a separate track from the one just described, with the law reflecting the paramount national security concerns and power politics associated with the advent and potential use of nuclear weapons. In the *Nuclear Weapons* opinion, the ICJ did note, however, that 'the use of nuclear weapons could constitute a catastrophe for the environment'.[130] The legality of *testing nuclear explosions* has been a cause of decades-long contention. The practical effect of the 1963 Nuclear Test Ban Treaty is that test explosions must be conducted outside Antarctica, underground, and cause no pollution. However, not all 'nuclear relevant states' are parties to the treaty and its status under customary international law is unclear. In the *Nuclear Tests* case, the ICJ refrained from ruling on whether or not atmospheric tests carried out by France were in violation of customary international law.[131] A number of regional agreements prohibit the testing of nuclear weapons in regions of Latin America, the South Pacific, South-East Asia and Africa. As we shall see in Section 10.6, like environmental damage caused by oil, nuclear damage is governed by a special liability regime.

10.5.5.2 Chemical substances

Many of the chemicals used in industrial processes pose substantial risks to the environment and public health, and as scientific understanding of the detrimental effects of various chemicals has increased, so has international regulation. For the most part, however, regulation remains fairly fragmented and different treaties regulate different stages/phases of the management of the substances. In 2001, the Stockholm Convention on Persistent Organic Pollutants was adopted on the basis of Agenda 21, which developed from the 1992 Rio Summit, with a view to restricting and, in many cases, eliminating the most harmful chemical substances.[132] It obliges state parties to eliminate or severely restrict the production and use of a set of persistent organic

---

[127] Arts 4(iv) and 11(iv).　　　[128] See Birnie and others (n 121) 505–507.

[129] Vienna Declaration on Nuclear Safety on principles for the implementation of the objective of the Convention on Nuclear Safety to prevent accidents and mitigate radiological consequences (9 February 2015) CNS/DC/2015/2/Rev.1.

[130] *Nuclear Weapons* (n 5) para. 29. The legality of using nuclear weapons is discussed in Chapter 14. Efforts by the IAEA to prevent military use of nuclear energy were enhanced substantially with the adoption in 1968 of the Nuclear Non-Proliferation Treaty (NPT), which obliges state parties to accept certain non-proliferation safeguards by bilateral agreement with the IAEA and to permit periodic verification inspections.

[131] The Court held instead that France had made a unilateral commitment to refrain from conducting such tests, see *Nuclear Tests Case (New Zealand v France)* [1974] ICJ Rep 457, paras 51–53 and *Nuclear Test Case (Australia v France)* [1974] ICJ Rep 253, paras 49–51. See also Chapter 2.

[132] For an overview, see Peter L. Lallas, 'The Stockholm Convention on Persistent Organic Pollutants' (2001) 95 *American Journal of International Law* 692–708.

pollutants (POP) and to take a range of measures to prevent or control the release of certain POPs that are created as an unintentional by-product of certain activities. The Convention is based on a precautionary approach[133] as well as on principles of CBDR.[134] It adopts a 'list technique' and establishes three annexes that are governed by different obligations.

The Basel Convention on the Control of Transboundary Movements of Hazardous Wastes and Their Disposal is a framework convention that was adopted to limit the transfer of hazardous waste from developed states to developing states for disposal— 'toxic transfers'.[135] The Convention seeks to reduce the generation of hazardous waste, ensure environmentally sound disposal of the waste as close to the source of the generation as possible, prohibit the export of hazardous waste to certain states and to ensure that the export of hazardous waste in all other situations is carried out in an environmentally sound manner. The definition of what constitutes 'hazardous waste' is tied to a list contained in an annex to the Convention.[136] Another annex lists waste that is presumed to be non-hazardous and therefore not subject to the regulation of the Convention.[137] Both export and import of hazardous waste to and from non-parties to the Convention is prohibited.[138] Parties are allowed to enter into other agreements on the transboundary movement of hazardous waste with both parties and non-parties as long as such agreements are no less 'environmentally sound', in particular with regard to the 'interests of developing countries'.[139] Transport and trade in hazardous substances is also regulated by the Rotterdam Convention on Prior Informed Consent Procedure for Certain Hazardous Chemicals and Pesticides. It too grew out of Agenda 21, a product of the 1992 Rio Summit, and it seeks to ensure that importing states— usually developing states—understand the risks associated with the import of a harmful substance and are in a position to make an informed decision about whether or not to allow it.[140] It sets up a system for the compulsory exchange of relevant information and relies on lists found in a number of annexes.

Unlike the fragmented approach to the handling and management of hazardous substances in the Stockholm, Basel and Rotterdam Conventions, the 2013 Minamata Convention on Mercury adopts an integrated approach to the regulation of hazardous substances.[141] The purpose of the Convention is to protect human health and the environment from the emission and release of mercury and mercury compounds, and it regulates the entire life cycle of mercury and thus contains obligations in relation to the extraction, use, trade, storage and disposal of mercury.

---

[133] See the Preamble and art. 1. See also arts 8(7)(a) and 8(9).   [134] See the Preamble.

[135] A comprehensive overview is available in Katharina Kummer, *International Management of Hazardous Wastes: The Basel Convention and Related Legal Rules* (Oxford University Press, 1999).

[136] Annex VIII.   [137] Annex IV.   [138] Art. 4(5).

[139] Art. 11(1). For a list of such agreements, see http://www.basel.int.

[140] See Katharina Kummer, 'Prior Informed Consent for Chemicals in International Trade: The 1998 Rotterdam Convention' (1999) 8(3) *Review of European, Comparative & International Environmental Law* 323–330.

[141] For an overview, see Jessica Templeton and Pia Kohler, 'Implementation and Compliance under the Minamata Convention on Mercury' (2014) 23(2) *Review of European, Comparative & International Environmental Law* 211–220.

10.6 Implementation and enforcement

A few points are worth noting about implementation and enforcement of international environmental law. The first point is that the *traditional approaches to state responsibility and reparation for damage* in international law are often ill-suited to environmental damage. In part, this is due to the difficulties of drawing a causal link between an act (or omission) and the environmental damage that may or may not be the result thereof. A further complication is the fact that environmental damage is often the result of progressive acts or omissions by a plurality of states that may have contributed to the damage in an unequal manner. Climate change may be the best example of this. Then there is the question of appropriate compensation, in particular in relation to environmental damage that may be irreversible. What is, for example, the right way to compensate for the extinction of an endangered species or an otherwise negative effect on biological diversity? While the law is still grappling with such issues, a number of approaches and remedies are becoming increasingly relevant. One example is the concept of *erga omnes* obligations, discussed in Chapter 2, whereby a state need not always be 'injured' by a violation of an international obligation by another state to be entitled to invoke the responsibility of that state. Another example is the establishment of special funds for collective compensation for environmental damage where the source of the damage is unidentified. In relation to damage to the environment per se, a 1997 Declaration on Responsibility and Liability under International Law for Environmental Damage adopted by the Institut de Droit International stipulates that environmental regimes 'should provide for the reparation of damage to the environment as such separately from or in addition to the reparation of damage relating to death, personal injury or loss of property or economic value'[142] and that the 'fact that environmental damage is irreparable or unquantifiable shall not result in exemption from compensation'.[143] The traditional approaches to state responsibility and compensation may also be less than optimal when breaches of environmental obligations are not due to ill-will on the part of the responsible state but rather to a lack of technical or financial ability to prevent violations of the law. This, of course, is particularly the case for developing states with scarce resources. Rather than resorting to the more traditional means of enforcing violations of international law, non-compliance with international environmental standards by poorer states is therefore often met with various forms of financial and technical assistance intended to give the non-complying state the ability to create the infrastructure required for effectively implementing its environmental obligations.[144]

The second point to note about implementation and enforcement of international environmental law concerns *the mechanisms for judicial adjudication of disputes*. An

---

[142] Institut de Droit International, *Declaration on Responsibility and Liability under International Law for Environmental Damage* (Strasbourg, 1997) art. 23.

[143] Ibid, art. 25.

[144] An overview is available in Dupuy and Viñuales (n 4) 272–284.

international environmental law court has not (yet) been created[145] and the existing courts that specialize in environmental law disputes have so far been of limited significance. The ICJ's 1993 Chamber for Environmental Matters never heard any cases and is no longer convened. In 1997, ITLOS created a Chamber for Marine Environmental Disputes tasked with dealing with disputes relating to the protection and preservation of the marine environment but it has yet to hear a case. The PCA has, however, been involved in a number of disputes involving environmental matters[146] and in 2001 it adopted a set of Optional Rules for Arbitration of Disputes Relating to Natural Resources and/or the Environment. The rules have, however, only been relied upon in a few cases.

In practice, therefore, international environmental law disputes are for the most part dealt with before courts that either have general jurisdiction—such as the ICJ— or courts that specialize in other branches of international law, such as ITLOS,[147] the ECtHR[148] and the World Trade Organization's DSB.[149] In such cases, however, environmental law considerations may sometimes 'compete' with potentially conflicting legal norms of particular interest to the court in question.

The final point to note about implementation and enforcement of international environmental law is the importance played by special *liability regimes for the economic operator* (whether public or private) responsible for environmental damage. Such regimes are particularly relevant in the area of nuclear energy[150] and oil pollution[151] and to an increasing extent also in relation to the movement of some hazardous waste.[152] In general, the regimes establish strict liability for the operator (in most cases without fault), the requirement of insurance, the establishment of a multi-layered system of compensation and a prohibition on discrimination in relation to access to compensation.[153]

---

[145] For arguments in favour of such a court, see Amedeo Postiglione, 'A More Efficient International Law on the Environment and Setting Up an International Court for the Environment within the United Nations' (1990) 20 *Environmental Law* 321–328.

[146] See https://pca-cpa.org/en/services/arbitration-services/environmental-dispute-resolution/ (accessed 20 October 2018).

[147] *Responsibilities and Obligations of States* (n 19).

[148] See e.g. *López Ostra* (n 19).

[149] See Chapter 11.

[150] See the 1960 OECD (Paris) Convention on Third Party Liability in the Field of Nuclear Energy and the 1963 supplementary convention to the Paris Convention, the 1963 International Atomic Energy Agency (IAEA) Convention on Civil Liability for Nuclear Damage (the Vienna Convention) and the 1997 Protocol to amend the Vienna Convention and the 1997 Convention on Supplementary Compensation for Nuclear Damage. See also the 1988 Joint Protocol Relating to the Application of the Vienna Convention and the Paris Convention.

[151] See the 1969 International Maritime Organization (IMO) Convention on Civil Liability and the 1992 Protocol amending the convention and the International Convention on the Establishment of an International Fund for Compensation for Oil Pollution Damage (the FUND Convention) and the 1992 and 2003 Protocols to amend the FUND Convention. See also the 2001 International Convention on Civil Liability for Oil Pollution Damage.

[152] For hazardous waste, see the 1996 International Convention on Liability and Compensation for Damage in Connection with the Carriage of Hazardous and Noxious Substances and the 2003 Protocol on Civil Liability and Compensation for Damage Cause by the Transboundary Effects of Industrial Accidents on Transboundary Waters.

[153] Dupuy and Viñuales (n 4) 259–264.

Summary

International environmental law covers those parts of international law that relate to the environment. It is not a separate and independent legal discipline and the regulation is generally piecemeal and sectoral. The development of the law has been catapulted by major events and conferences, the most notable being the 1972 Stockholm Conference on the Human Environment and the 1992 Rio Conference on Environment and Development. International environmental law is guided by a range of principles that are focused on preventing damage to the environment and ensuring that environmental protection is balanced and—where necessary—distributed among states. The substantive regulation covers a wide array of topics such as efforts to protect the atmosphere, the conservation of nature and species and the regulation of hazardous substances.

Recommended reading

Solid introductions to international environmental law include Philippe Sands and Jacqueline Peel, *Principles of International Environmental Law* (3rd edn, Cambridge University Press, 2012); Pierre-Marie Dupuy and Jorge E. Viñuales, *International Environmental Law* (Cambridge University Press, 2015) and Patricia Birnie and others, *International Law and the Environment* (Oxford University Press, 2009).

For an overview of the tension between environmental protection and development, see Nico Schrijver, *Sovereignty over Natural Resources: Balancing Rights and Duties* (Cambridge University Press, 1997).

On CBDR, see Philippe Cullet, 'Common but Differentiated Responsibilities' in Malgosia Fitzmaurice and others (eds), *Research Handbook on International Environmental Law* (Edward Elgar Publishing, 2010) 161–180.

On contemporary nuclear energy, see Patrick Reyners, 'A New World Governance for Nuclear Safety after Fukushima?' (2013) 4(1) *International Journal of Nuclear Law* 63.

On the Stockholm Convention on POPs, see Peter L. Lallas, 'The Stockholm Convention on Persistent Organic Pollutants' (2001) 95 *American Journal of International Law* 692.

For the Basel Convention, see Katharina Kummer, *International Management of Hazardous Wastes: The Basel Convention and Related Legal Rules* (Oxford University Press, 1999).

On PIC, see the same author in 'Prior Informed Consent for Chemicals in International Trade: The 1998 Rotterdam Convention' (1999) 8(3) *Review of European Comparative & International Environmental Law* 323.

An introduction to the Minamata Convention is available in Jessica Templeton and Pia Kohler, 'Implementation and Compliance under the Minamata Convention on Mercury' (2014) 23(2) *Review of European, Comparative & International Environmental Law* 211.

On world heritage, see Francesco Francioni (ed.), *The 1972 World Heritage Convention: A Commentary* (Oxford University Press, 2008).

Questions for discussion

1. Why does international environmental law generally form part of the international law of cooperation? Can you think of some principles of international environmental law that could be said to be part of the international law of coexistence?

2. Can you think of some concrete examples of where environmental law overlaps with other fields of public international law?

3. Why is there often a tension between environmental protection and economic development? Can you think of some examples of where this tension is visible?

4. The chapter notes that some of the basic principles of international environmental law are merely guiding principles. Does this mean that they are not legally binding?

5. Can you provide some examples of the techniques used in the treaty-based regulation of international environmental law?

6. Why are the traditional principles on state responsibility and compensation sometimes ill-suited for enforcing international environmental law?

11

International economic law

CENTRAL ISSUES

1. This chapter discusses international economic law with a particular focus on the Bretton Woods institutions.

2. It introduces the World Trade Organization and the most important principles governing international trade, including those contained in the General Agreement on Tariffs and Trade.

3. The chapter also presents international monetary law with an emphasis on the role and the activities of the International Monetary Fund.

4. The chapter discusses the international regulation of international investments and the most important principles thereof, including those that govern expropriation of foreign property.

11.1 Introduction

International economic law covers a vast range of rules and principles on economic conduct and relations between states, international organizations and private actors, both individuals and corporations. While certain aspects of it are covered elsewhere in this book,[1] the present chapter deals with the most fundamental areas of the law: the international law of trade, international monetary law and international investment law.

International law generally leaves it up to states to regulate their own economic affairs. As the International Court of Justice (ICJ) stated in *Nicaragua*, every 'State possesses a fundamental right to choose and implement its own political, economic and social system'.[2] In addition, states are not required to have economic relations with other states. To quote the ICJ again: 'A State is not bound to continue particular trade relations longer than it sees fit to do so, in the absence of a treaty commitment or other

---

[1] The issue of extraterritorial application of economic legislation, such as antitrust laws, is discussed in Chapter 5. Aspects of state immunity are covered in Chapter 6. See also the overview of international environmental law in Chapter 10.

[2] *Military and Paramilitary Activities in and against Nicaragua (Nicaragua v United States)*, Merits, Judgment [1986] ICJ Rep 14, para. 258.

specific legal obligations.'[3] In practice, though, the vast majority of states have limited their freedom in economic affairs by becoming parties to a range of treaties.

The modern international economic system originates in the 1944 Bretton Woods conference in New Hampshire, the United States, where participating states planted the seeds for a liberal international economic order with free-flowing economic transactions and equal market access. Much of the inspiration came from the latter part of the 19th century when liberal domestic legislation, bilateral trade agreements and treaties on friendship, commerce and navigation had made international trade flourish. The positive trends had been reversed by the outbreak of the First World War and the widespread protectionism that followed in the interwar period.

The Bretton Woods conference created the three most important international organizations for the regulation of trade and monetary policy: the International Monetary Fund (IMF), the International Bank for Reconstruction and Development (the 'World Bank') and the General Agreement on Tariffs and Trade (GATT). While the GATT was created to liberalize world trade by reducing tariffs and other barriers to trade, the IMF ensures exchange stability and provides loans to states with economic difficulties. To supplement the IMF, the World Bank provides loans to developing countries. The GATT was meant to be an interim agreement but, as attempts to establish an elaborate international trade organization failed,[4] it became the 'organizational' structure for international trade agreements for nearly half a century. It was not until January 1995 that a new organization—the World Trade Organization (WTO)—replaced the GATT system.[5]

The Bretton Woods institutions are not the only players in the governance of global economic matters. In 1964, the General Assembly created the United Nations Conference on Trade and Development (UNCTAD), and in 1966 a United Nations Commission on International Trade Law (UNCITRAL) was established. A range of specialized agencies are also involved in economic-related activities. The International Labour Organization (ILO), for example, sets international labour standards and, among other things, seeks to counteract 'social dumping'. Mention should also be made of the Food and Agriculture Organization (FAO), the World Health Organization (WHO), the International Fund for Agricultural Development (IFAD), the International Maritime Organization (IMO) and the International Civil Aviation Organization (ICAO). Important informal networks include the Group of Twenty (G20) consisting of the 19 major world economies and the EU.[6] It emerged from the G7, which encompassed the six most important industrialized Western states and Japan.[7]

---

[3] Ibid, para. 275.

[4] See the Havana Charter for an International Trade Organization.

[5] For an overview, see Andreas F. Lowenfeld, *International Economic Law* (2nd edn, Oxford University Press, 2008) 25–28.

[6] The states are Argentina, Brazil, Canada, China, France, Germany, India, Indonesia, Italy, Japan, Mexico, Russia, Saudi Arabia, Spain, South Africa, South Korea, Turkey, the UK and the United States.

[7] Canada, France, Germany, Italy, Japan, the UK and the United States. In 1997, the G7 became the G8 when Russia joined. In March 2014, however, the latter was excluded after it annexed Crimea.

In recent years, in part due to frustration with what they perceive to be a lack of willingness among Western states to reform the 'old' institutions, the so-called 'BRICS' countries (Brazil, Russia, India, China and South Africa) have created a number of new—and potentially rival—international economic institutions. These include a Contingent Reserve Arrangement (CRA), which (like the IMF) provides financial protection to member states in economic difficulties and a New Development Bank (NDB), which (like the World Bank) funds infrastructure and development programmes in the BRICS countries. The latter is expected to work closely together with a new investment bank set up on China's initiative—the Asian Infrastructure Investment Bank (AIIB).

The big international actors are supplemented by important regional institutions, such as the EU. Historically, the Organisation for Economic Co-operation and Development (OECD) has also served as an important forum for economic cooperation between industrialized Western states.[8]

We begin in Section 11.2 with a brief introduction to the capitalist theory on which the international economic system is based. Section 11.3 discusses the international regulation of trade and the GATT and WTO. Section 11.4 focuses on international monetary law, most notably the IMF, and Section 11.5 discusses the core principles of international investment law.

11.2 The capitalist basis of the Bretton Woods system

The economic system created at Bretton Woods derives from theories of market capitalism as developed by, among others, Adam Smith (1723–1790). Of particular importance was the theory of *comparative advantage* advanced by economists like John Stuart Mill (1803–1873) and in particular David Ricardo (1772–1823).[9] In essence, the theory holds that the advantages of international trade and liberalization outweigh the disadvantages even when the needs of the poorest states are taken into account. To understand the theory, it is important to distinguish it from absolute advantage, which refers to an ability to produce more or better products or services than someone else. Comparative advantage refers to the ability to produce products and services at a lower opportunity cost and not necessarily at a greater volume. To illustrate, consider the case of an architect and a secretary. The architect is better at both producing architectural services and at administering and organizing. The architect therefore has an absolute advantage when it comes to producing both architectural services and secretarial work. However, both the architect and the secretary benefit from their exchange because of their comparative advantages and disadvantages. It is here that the role of opportunity costs enters the picture. Imagine that the architect produces the equivalent of €100 per hour in architectural services and €50 per hour in secretarial tasks.

---

[8] Convention on the Organisation for Economic Co-operation and Development, 14 December 1960.

[9] Adam Smith, *An Inquiry Into the Nature and Causes of Wealth of Nations* (1776); David Ricardo, *Principles of Political Economy and Taxation* (1817); John Stuart Mill, *The Principles of Political Economy: With Some of Their Applications to Social Philosophy* (1848).

The secretary can produce the equivalent of €0 in architectural services and €40 in secretarial duties per hour. To produce €40 in secretarial tasks, the architect will lose €100 because he or she has to abandon one hour of architectural production. So the opportunity cost of secretarial work is high and the architect is better off producing one hour's worth of architectural services and employing a secretary to do all the administration and organizing. The secretary is much better off administering and organizing for the architect because his or her opportunity costs are very low. This, of course, is where the comparative advantage is found. David Ricardo applied the theory of comparative advantage to international trade and showed how two states (England and Portugal) were both better off by specializing and trading according to their comparative advantages in wine (Portugal) and cloth (England).

The capitalistic origin of the international economic system has made it the object of much criticism, and during the Cold War most of the communist states remained outside the Bretton Woods institutions. In the 1960s and 1970s, developing states made persistent calls for the creation of what they perceived to be a more fair and equitable 'New International Economic Order'.[10] Since then, opposition has primarily come from the so-called 'Global Justice Movement', which argues that more attention should be paid to non-economic considerations, such as the reduction of global poverty and protection of the environment.[11]

11.3 The WTO and international trade

11.3.1 Introduction

The 1994 Agreement Establishing the World Trade Organization created the WTO as the principal international trade organization with a global reach. By October 2018, it had 164 members, including the EU. The principal organ of the WTO is the Ministerial Conference, where all members are represented.[12] Other important organs include three Special Councils in specific sectors (trade in goods, trade in services and trade-related aspects of intellectual property rights)[13] and a Secretariat headed by a Director-General.[14] Since September 2013, the post has been occupied by Roberto Azevédo (Brazil).

In general terms, the evolution of international trade law within the GATT and WTO revolves around a series of *rounds of multilateral trade negotiations*.[15] While the first such round focused on reducing tariffs on goods, attention was gradually also turned to non-tariff measures affecting trade, such as dumping and state subsidies. The breakthrough came at the highly successful Uruguay Round (1986–1993) where

---

[10] See, inter alia, GA Res. 1803 (XVII) Permanent Sovereignty over Natural Resources (14 December 1962) and GA Res. 3281 (XXIX) Charter of Economic Rights and Duties of States (12 December 1974). See also Robert W. Cox, 'Ideologies and the New International Economic Order: Reflections on some Recent Literature' (1979) 33(2) *International Organization* 257–302.

[11] See Marc Doucet, *Global Justice and Democracy: The Anti-Globalisation Movement* (Routledge, 2010).

[12] WTO Agreement art. IV:1.   [13] Ibid, art. IV:5.   [14] Ibid, art. VI:1.

[15] For an overview, see Lowenfeld (n 5) 48–71.

agreement on a host of contentious issues, such as trade in services and intellectual property as well as a new mechanism for the settlement of disputes, was reached. It was also at the Uruguay Round that the GATT system was replaced by the WTO. The ninth—and so far latest—round of negotiations was initiated in Doha in 2001, but by October 2018 it looked unlikely to be concluded in the foreseeable future. The major hurdle is the requirement that WTO agreements must be approved by all member states. The increase in the number of states when compared to the first rounds of trade negotiations and the emergence of a number of powerful regional actors have made the attainment of unanimity on controversial areas of international trade policy seemingly impossible. The deadlock has led to calls to abandon consensus-based decision-making and some of the major actors have turned their attention to bilateral and regional negotiations. In February 2016, 12 Pacific Rim states adopted the *Trans-Pacific Partnership Agreement* (TPPA). In January 2017, however, the United States under President Trump withdrew from the agreement. As a result, in March 2018 the other 11 TPP countries signed a revised version of the agreement for the creation of a *Comprehensive and Progressive Agreement for Trans-Pacific Partnership*. In 2013, the EU and the United States initiated negotiations for a highly ambitious *Transatlantic Trade and Investment Partnership* (TTIP),[16] but by October 2018 the fate of the TTIP was unclear as the negotiations had been put on hold after the election of President Trump. In June and July 2018, the United States introduced tariffs on steel and aluminium from a range of countries, including the EU.

The overview of the WTO begins with its core principles (Section 11.3.2) before the focus turns to the most important aspects of its regulation (Section 11.3.3). Brief mention is then made of the dispute settlement mechanism (Section 11.3.4) and of the primary forms of regional trade cooperation (Section 11.3.5).

11.3.2 **The principles of regulation in the WTO**

The overall purpose of the WTO is to further the liberalization of international trade and economic transactions by reducing and eliminating tariffs and other barriers to trade. In practice, the various WTO agreements are governed by a number of core principles, the most fundamental being the principle of *non-discrimination* that seeks to ensure that foreign goods and services compete with domestic goods and services on the same conditions ('a level playing field'). The non-discrimination principle is reflected in two obligations often found in the agreements. The first is an obligation of so-called '*most-favoured-nation (MFN) treatment*'. An MFN clause allows a party to a trade agreement treaty and its nationals to benefit from an advantage that is granted to another (third) state and its nationals pursuant to another agreement concluded between one of the parties to the first treaty and the third state. For example, an MFN clause in a trade agreement between state A and state B gives state A and its nationals the same advantages granted to state C in a treaty concluded between state C and state B.

---

[16] See further at http://ec.europa.eu/trade/policy/countries-and-regions/negotiations-and-agreements/ (accessed 20 October 2018).

The benefits of an MFN clause require identity in the subject matter of the clause and the advantage granted to the third state.[17] The non-discrimination principle is also reflected in an obligation of *national treatment* where an importing state must treat imported goods or services no less favourably than it treats like national products. The obligation requires, in other words, that state B does not subject goods or services imported from state A to less favourable conditions in relation to, for example, requirements of internal sale, transportation, distribution, use etc., than those governing goods or services from state B itself.

The trade relationship between the developed and the developing world is an issue of continuing contention, and allegations of unjust treatment of poorer states are frequent. However, there are principles in international trade law that seek to take account of the *special needs of developing states*. The Preamble to the WTO Agreement recognizes 'the need for positive efforts designed to ensure that developing countries, and especially the least developed among them, secure a share in the growth in international trade commensurate with the needs of their economic development'.[18] In practice, developing states benefit from a host of preferential treatments, including *preferential tariffs* and *exemptions from general obligations*. As we shall see later, developing states have, for example, benefited from preferential treatment in relation to the protection of intellectual property and patents. International trade law also seeks to take account of the special needs of developing states via the facilitation of *transfer of technological know-how and processes*.[19]

11.3.3 Substantive regulation in the WTO

11.3.3.1 Introduction

The 1994 WTO Agreement is a short document with a mere 16 articles that establish the WTO. Through its annexes, however, the 1994 Agreement incorporates all the agreements of the Uruguay Round of negotiations that form an integral part of the Agreement, binding on all members.[20]

11.3.3.2 The 1994 General Agreement on Tariffs and Trade

The GATT's primary purpose is to contribute to the liberalization of trade by substantially reducing tariffs and other barriers to trade and eliminating 'discriminatory treatment in international commerce'.[21] To that end, it is supplemented by a number of agreements on specific topics, such as agriculture, the application of sanitary and phytosanitary measures, technical barriers to trade, anti-dumping, subsidies and safeguards.[22] Two initial points are worth noting. First, the GATT does not prohibit tariffs

---

[17] See also arts 9–10 of the International Law Commission's 1978 Draft Articles on Most-Favoured-Nation Clauses.

[18] See also *Differential and More Favourable Treatment: Reciprocity and Fuller Participation of Developing Countries*, Decision of 28 November 1979 (L/4903).

[19] As noted in Chapter 10, the transfer of technology from the developed to the developing states also plays an important role in conventions on environmental protection, such as in the UN Convention on Biological Diversity (CBD).

[20] WTO Agreement art. II:2.   [21] GATT Preamble.   [22] See Annex 1A to the WTO Agreement.

on imported goods as such. Article II merely obliges states to commit to certain 'tariff ceilings' on imported goods as well as to only decrease—and not increase—the tariffs in the future. Secondly, the GATT seeks to ensure that tariffs are the *only* restrictions on trade employed by states, and quantitative restrictions, such as quotas, are generally prohibited.[23]

As a legal instrument, the GATT is based on the principle of non-discrimination and the principle of MFN. Thus, article 1(1) of the 1994 GATT specifies:

> With respect to customs duties and charges of any kind imposed on or in connection with importation or exportation or imposed on the international transfer of payments for imports or exports, and with respect to the method of levying such duties and charges, and with respect to all rules and formalities in connection with importation and exportation, and with respect to all matters referred to in paragraphs 2 and 4 of Article III, any advantage, favour, privilege or immunity granted by any contracting party to any product originating in or destined for any other country shall be accorded immediately and unconditionally to the like product originating in or destined for the territories of all other contracting parties.

The principle of national treatment also forms an integral part of the GATT. This is reflected in article III. For example, according to the first part of article III:4:

> The products of the territory of any contracting party imported into the territory of any other contracting party shall be accorded treatment no less favourable than that accorded to like products of national origin in respect of all laws, regulations and requirements affecting their internal sale, offering for sale, purchase, transportation, distribution or use.[24]

Article III:2 prohibits discriminatory 'internal taxes or other internal charges of any kind in excess of those applied, directly or indirectly, to like domestic products'. In practice, of course, it may be difficult to determine if an imported and a domestic products are 'like'.[25] As noted previously, the purpose of the requirements of national treatment is to eliminate all forms of protectionist regulations and practices and secure equal market access for imported and domestic products.[26]

Certain *exceptions* to the MFN and national treatment principles exist. For one thing, as we shall return to later, the MFN principle does not apply to customs unions and free-trade areas, such as the EU.[27] Exceptions also exist for developing states.[28] Article XX stipulates that a state may be entitled to adopt measures that deviate from its obligations under the GATT if they fulfil certain aims, such as the protection of

---

[23] See GATT art. XI(1). Exceptions may be applied to certain imports of agricultural or fisheries products: see art. XI(2)(c). See also art. XII(1) relating to restrictions due to safeguards concerning external financial positions and balance of payments.

[24] See also art. III:1.

[25] See, inter alia, WTO, *Philippines: Taxes on Distilled Spirits—Report of the Appellate Body*, WT/DS396/AB/R; WT/DS403/AB/R, 21 December 2011, see para. 125, and WTO, *European Communities: Measures Affecting Asbestos and Asbestos-Containing Products—Report of the Appellate Body*, WT/DS135/AB/R, para. 99. See also the discussion in Matthias Herdegen, *Principles of International Economic Law* (Oxford University Press, 2013) 198–203 and 214–218.

[26] WTO, *Japan—Taxes on Alcoholic Beverages—AB-1996-2—Report of the Appellate Body*, WT/DS8/AB/R; WT/DS10/AB/R; WT/DS11/AB/R, 4 October 1996, paras 16–18.

[27] See GATT art. XXIV.   [28] Ibid, Part IV (Trade and Development).

public morals or human, animal or plant life or health, if they are adopted to ensure compliance with laws that protect patents, trademarks and copyrights, or if they are essential to the acquisition or distribution of products in general or local short supply. Trade restricting measures must not constitute a means of arbitrary or unjustifiable discrimination between states where the same conditions prevail or constitute a disguised restriction on international trade.[29] In addition, article XXI authorizes states to make certain security-related exceptions to their GATT obligations. The Trump administration has—somewhat dubiously—sought to justify its 2018 decision to impose tariffs on the import of steel and aluminium on an alleged need to protect the national security of the United States. Article XIX stipulates that a state may take 'emergency action on imports of particular products' if 'as a result of unforeseen developments … any product is being imported into the territory of that contracting party in such increased quantities and under such conditions as to cause or threaten serious injury to domestic producers in that territory of like or directly competitive products'.[30] Agreement on the application and implementation of safeguard measures was reached at the Uruguay Round of negotiations.[31]

11.3.3.3 The General Agreement on Trade in Services

Until the Uruguay Round of negotiations, the GATT regime only dealt with goods and not the increasingly important area of trade in services. This changed with the adoption of the General Agreement on Trade in Services (GATS) that covers all forms of measures affecting trade in services and all sectors, with the exclusion of services 'supplied in the exercise of governmental authority'.[32] Like the GATT, the GATS incorporates the MFN principle,[33] but it also goes further by prohibiting certain non-discriminatory but restrictive measures.[34] The obligation of national treatment, on the other hand, only applies when a state has made special commitments in a certain sector.[35] A key feature of the Agreement is the prohibition of quantitative restrictions.[36] Like the GATT, the GATS lists a number of general and security-related exceptions to the obligations of the Agreement, including references to the protection of public morals or the maintenance of public order, the protection of human, animal or plant life or health, the protection of the privacy of individuals etc.[37] All restrictions must be 'necessary'. In the *US Gambling* case, for example, the United States was found to be in violation of the GATS for prohibiting gambling and betting services on the US market supplied by actors outside the United States because it had not demonstrated that the prohibition was necessary in order to protect public morals and maintain public order given that it simultaneously permitted remote betting on horse racing.[38]

Special rules apply for telecommunication services and financial services.[39] With regard to the former, an annex stipulates that service suppliers must be 'accorded

---

[29] See also Herdegen (n 25) 203–211.   [30] Art. XIX:1(a).   [31] See Agreement on Safeguards.
[32] GATS art. I:3(b).   [33] Art. II:1.   [34] Art. VI.   [35] See Part III, art. XVII.
[36] Art. XVI:2   [37] Art. XIV(a), (b) and (c)(ii). See also art. XIV*bis*.
[38] WTO, *United States: Measures Affecting the Cross-Border Supply of Gambling and Betting Services— Report of the Appellate Body*, WT/DS285/AB/R, 7 April 2005, para. 369.
[39] See Annex on Financial Services.

access to and use of public telecommunications transport networks and services on reasonable and non-discriminatory terms and conditions'.[40]

11.3.3.4 The Agreement on Trade-Related Aspects of Intellectual Property Rights

The Agreement on Trade-Related Aspects of Intellectual Property Rights (TRIPS) introduces substantial protection of patents, trademarks and other forms of intellectual property rights. The Agreement generally provides for both national treatment and MFN treatment.[41] It covers trademarks,[42] geographical indications,[43] industrial designs,[44] layout designs[45] and undisclosed information.[46] TRIPS specifies that patents must be available in all fields of technology and only limited exceptions can be made.[47] The relationship between intellectual property rights for expensive pharmaceuticals and the provision of vital health care in developing states with limited financial resources is a matter of contention.[48] Although the issue is not yet resolved, a few points are worth noting. First, the least developed states have been exempted for a certain period of time from some of the obligations under TRIPS.[49] Secondly, TRIPS may allow a state to issue compulsory licences when required.[50] Recently, controversy has also emerged in relation to patents for inventions in biotechnology, such as DNA.[51] The transfer of technology is a key component of TRIPS and it explicitly specifies that developed states shall 'provide incentives to enterprises and institutions in their territories for the purpose of promoting and encouraging technology transfer to least-developed country Members in order to enable them to create a sound and viable technological base'.[52]

In its practical application, TRIPS is supplemented by a range of other international treaties for the protection of intellectual property, including the 1883 Paris Convention for the Protection of Industrial Property, the 1886 Berne Convention for the Protection of Literary and Artistic Works and the 1952 Universal Copyright Convention.

11.3.4 Dispute settlement in the WTO

One of the major achievement of the Uruguay Round of negotiations was the establishment of a permanent Dispute Settlement Body (DSB).[53] In general, the settlement

---

[40] See art. 5(a) of Annex on Telecommunications.   [41] See TRIPS arts 3 and 4.   [42] Arts 15–21.
[43] Arts 22–24.   [44] Arts 25–26.   [45] Arts 35–38.   [46] Art. 39.
[47] Art. 27. Accepted exceptions are covered in art. 27(2) and (3).
[48] See also *Declaration on the TRIPS Agreement and public health*, WT/MIN(01)/DEC/2, 20 November 2001. For a discussion, see Madhavi Sunder, 'IP3' (2006) 59(2) *Stanford Law Review* 257–332.
[49] TRIPS art. 66(1) exempted the least-developed states from the relevant obligations of the agreement for a period of ten years. See also *Declaration on the TRIPS Agreement and public health* (n 48). On 11 June 2013, the Council for Trade-Related Aspects of Intellectual Property Rights extended the transitions period until 1 July 2012, see *Decision of the Council for TRIPS of 11 June 2013*, Doc. IP/C/64.
[50] Art. 31.   [51] See the overview in Herdegen (n 25) 239–241.   [52] Art. 66(2).
[53] See also WTO Agreement art. IV:3. The Understanding on Rules and Procedures Governing the Settlement of Disputes (DSU) constitutes Annex 2 to the WTO Agreement.

system applies to all WTO agreements. The DSB refers disputes to a Panel that makes a binding decision in a report and subsequently supervises proper implementation.[54] The Panels are composed of 'well-qualified governmental and/or non-governmental individuals'[55] selected in order to ensure the 'independence of the members, a sufficiently diverse background and a wide spectrum of experience'.[56] An Appellate Body reviews the Panel reports.[57] The procedure at the DSB is governed by fairly tight time limits in order to ensure both prompt dispute settlement and subsequent implementation.[58] If a measure by a member violates a WTO obligation, it must be withdrawn[59] and compliance achieved within a reasonable period of time.[60] If a state does not comply with the decision of the DSB, the latter may authorize the complaining state to take proportionate countermeasures.[61] The countermeasures should preferably be of a symmetrical nature but they can also be applied to other areas under the agreement that has been violated. In the *Beef Hormones* case, for example, the European Community (EC) was found to be in violation of its obligations under the WTO's Agreement on the Application of Sanitary and Phytosanitary Measures (SPS Agreement) for imposing a ban on the sale or importation of meat and meat products from farm animals to which a number of specified hormones had been administered.[62] When the EC failed to comply with the decision, the DSB authorized the United States and Canada to initiate countermeasures.[63] Although the EC later revised its regulations, the United States and Canada maintained that it had still not complied with the decision and upheld their countermeasures.[64] In 2013, the DSB also authorized Antigua and Barbuda to proceed with countermeasures in response to the lack of compliance by the United States in the *US Gambling* case mentioned earlier.[65] By October 2018, a number of states, including China, Russia, Canada and the EU, had requested consultations with the United States before the DSB due to President Trump's decision to introduce tariffs on certain imported goods and steel and aluminium on grounds of national security. Bilateral consultations between the parties are the first stage of the dispute settlement process and they aim to give the parties an opportunity to discuss the matter and to find a satisfactory solution without resorting to litigation.

[54] DSU art. 2.1. See also arts 6, 11 and 21.
[55] Art. 8(1).   [56] Art. 8(2).
[57] Art. 17.   [58] See art. 20.   [59] Art. 3(7).   [60] Art. 21.
[61] Art. 22. In practice, states tend to comply: see Bruce Wilson, 'Compliance by WTO Members with Adverse WTO Dispute Settlement Rulings: The Record To Date' (2007) 10(2) *Journal of International Economic Law* 397–403.
[62] WTO, *European Communities—EC Measures Concerning Meat and Meat Products (Hormones)— Report of the Appellate Body*, WT/DS26/AB/R; WT/DS48/AB/R, 16 January 1998, para. 208.
[63] See WTO, *Decision by the Arbitrators, European Communities—Measures Concerning Meat and Meat Products (Hormones)*, WT/DS26/ARB, 12 July 1999, para. 84.
[64] WTO, *United States: Continued Suspension of Obligations of the EC—Hormones Dispute—Report of the Appellate Body*, WT/DS320/AB/R, 16 October 2008. The prolonged dispute was brought to a close in May 2009 with an agreement that provided for a phased reduction of US sanctions and a gradual increase in the EU tariff quota for high-quality, hormone-free beef.
[65] See WTO, *Authorization to Retaliate Granted, United States: Measures Affecting the Cross-Border Supply of Gambling and Betting Services*, WT/DS285/AB/R, 28 January 2013.

11.3.5 **Regional economic cooperation**

The WTO encourages regional integration of economic markets as a means of gradually eliminating barriers to international trade and investment.[66] The GATT explicitly exempts the application of the MFN principle from customs unions and free-trade areas.[67] By far the most advanced form of regional economic integration is found in the *European Union* (EU). The EU was founded on a customs union without internal customs duties on imports and exports and a common external customs tariff.[68] The Single European Act created an internal market with free movement of goods, persons, services and capital to be established by 31 December 1992. Within that market, quantitative restrictions on both the import and export of goods as well as all 'measures having equivalent effect' are prohibited unless justified on the basis of an explicitly mentioned interest and applied in a non-discriminatory and proportionate manner.[69] Similar restrictions apply to services.[70] Over the years, the EU has developed common rules on competition and in the very politically sensitive area of agricultural policy. As we shall see in Section 11.4.5, in 1999 the EU introduced a single common currency—the euro.

The *North American Free Trade Agreement* (NAFTA) was adopted in 1992 to establish a free trade area between the United States, Canada and Mexico. Among other things, NAFTA sought to eliminate internal barriers to trade and facilitate the cross-border movement of goods and services, to promote conditions of fair competition and to increase investments in the member states. On 1 October 2018, the United States, Mexico and Canada announced that they had reached agreement on a new trade agreement—the United States–Mexico–Canada Agreement (USMCA) that will replace NAFTA. In South America, *Mercado Común del Sur* (MERCOSUR) was created in 1991 by Argentina, Brazil, Paraguay and Uruguay to promote trade and the free movement of goods, people and currency.[71] Over time, it has developed into a tentative customs union. In 1996, Bolivia, Colombia, Ecuador and Peru created the *Andean Community of Nations* (CAN) on the basis of the 1969 Cartagena Agreement on Sub-Regional Integration (the Andean Pact). Although the Cartagena Agreement abolishes internal tariffs, CAN is not yet a proper customs union. In May 2008, the constitutive treaty of the *Union of South American Nations* (UNASUR) was signed in Brasilia with the aim of integrating the policies of MERCOSUR and CAN.[72] In Africa, the *Economic Community of West African States* (ECOWAS) was formed in 1975 as an ambitious customs union involving 15 West African states. In Asia, the most significant regional organization for the purposes of economic cooperation is the *Association of Southeast Asian Nations* (ASEAN).

---

[66] GATT art. XXIV:4. See also arts V and V*bis* of the GATS Agreement.

[67] See GATT art. XXIV.   [68] Treaty on the Functioning of the European Union (TFEU), art. 28(1).

[69] Ibid, art. 26(2). See also arts 34–36 and the seminal ECJ *Cassis de Dijon* case: Case 120/78 *Rewe-Zentral AG v Federal Monopoly Administration for Spirits* [1979] ECR 649.

[70] See TFEU arts 56–62. The free movement of workers is covered by arts 45–48, the right of establishment by arts 49–55 and capital and payments by arts 63–66.

[71] See also the 1994 Protocol of Ouro Preto. Venezuela joined in July 2012 and efforts to incorporate Bolivia were initiated in July 2015.

[72] Aside from the members of MERCOSUR and CAN, initial membership of UNASUR included Chile, Guyana and Suriname.

11.4 International monetary law

11.4.1 Introduction—the IMF

The *International Monetary Fund* (IMF) was established to introduce a monetary legal regime—overseen by an international organization of global reach—that would prevent a repetition of the interwar policies of competitive and manipulative devaluation of currencies.[73] In the 1920s and 1930s, when economies started to contract and unemployment began to increase, individual states resorted to a variety of measures, including devaluation, trade restrictions and subsidies, with a disastrous effect on the global economy and monetary stability. The primary purposes of the IMF are to promote international monetary cooperation, promote exchange stability and make resources available to members with balance of payments difficulties. Today, it has 189 member states. The daily operations of the IMF are conducted by an *Executive Board* composed of 25 directors appointed by member states or groups of states. The Board is led by a *Managing Director* who serves in an independent capacity. The Managing Director has always been a European, and since July 2011 the position has been held by Christine Lagarde (France). The practice of always appointing a European to direct the organization has, however, now been abandoned. The *Board of Governors* consists of one governor appointed by each member state, who meet at least once a year.

The money in the IMF comes from the member states on the basis of a system of quotas. In practice, each member is assigned a quota based on its relative share of the world economy. The quota determines the state's maximum contribution to the financial resources of the Fund. The biggest quotas are held by the United States (17.46 per cent), China (6.41 per cent), Germany (5.6 per cent) and the UK and France (both hold 4.24 per cent). When joining the IMF, a state generally pays up to a quarter of its quota with widely accepted currencies (US dollars, euros, yen or pound sterling) and the remaining quota in its own currency. The quotas are revised periodically and in 2010 the IMF's members decided to double the Fund's resources as of January 2016.[74] The total value of the quotas is now around $650 billion. The Fund has additional pledges or committed resources of around the same amount and also has one of the largest gold reserves in the world. In April 2018, the Fund had committed $189 billion under existing lending arrangements of which $134 billion had been drawn. The biggest borrowers were Greece, Ukraine, Pakistan and Egypt.[75]

Since voting on both the Executive Board and the Board of Governors is based on the quota system, the most powerful states in the IMF are those which hold the largest quotas. The IMF has been criticized for a lack of reform, in particular from the BRICS countries. Although these five states comprise more than one-fifth of the global economy, they only possess around 14 per cent of the votes at the IMF. In part as a result, they have established a $100 billion Contingent Reserve Arrangement (CRA),

---

[73] See Articles of Agreement of the International Monetary Fund, art. 1.

[74] See the Fourteenth General Review of Quotas.

[75] The International Monetary Fund, 'The IMF at a Glance, April 19, 2018' (4 July 2018), available at http://www.imf.org/en/About/Factsheets/IMF-at-a-Glance (accessed 20 October 2018).

which provides financial protection to member states facing balance of payments problems.[76] Around 40 per cent of the funding for the CRA comes from China. The loans offered under the CRA would also seem to take account of some of the criticism (typically by poorer states) of the IMF's often very stringent loan conditions (on the issue of 'conditionality', see Section 11.4.3).

In this section, we will focus on the IMF's approach to exchange rate policy (Section 11.4.2) and lending arrangements, including the controversial issue of conditionality (Section 11.4.3). Brief attention will also be turned to the World Bank (Section 11.4.4) and the monetary system in the EU (Section 11.4.5).

11.4.2 Exchange rate policies

In its original form, the 1944 IMF Agreement created a regime of fixed exchange rates by which each member state was obliged to set the value of its currency in relation to gold or the US dollar (which was tied to gold) and maintain that value.[77] The system lasted until 1971 when the United States abandoned the Gold Standard and exchange rates began to float freely.[78] However, states are still under obligations in relation to their exchange arrangements. Thus, under article IV(1) of the 1976 Amended Articles of Agreement, each member state shall:

(i) endeavor to direct its economic and financial policies toward the objective of fostering orderly economic growth with reasonable price stability, with due regard to its circumstances;

(ii) seek to promote stability by fostering orderly underlying economic and financial conditions and a monetary system that does not tend to produce erratic disruptions;

(iii) avoid manipulating exchange rates or the international monetary system in order to prevent effective balance of payments adjustment or to gain an unfair competitive advantage over other members; and

(iv) follow exchange policies compatible with the undertakings under this Section.

Of the obligations listed, requirement (iii)—to desist from exchange rate manipulation in order to gain an unfair competitive advantage—is the most specific. For many years, Western states, and in particular the United States, have accused China of violating the provision by intentionally keeping its currency, the yuan, at a low value in order to reap trade benefits.[79]

The IMF oversees compliance with article IV and states are obliged to provide the Fund with the necessary information. While the IMF conducts regular consultations with the member states and issues country reports,[80] it does not have any means of enforcing violations of article IV. In 2007, the Executive Board adopted a decision that

---

[76] Treaty for the Establishment of a BRICS Contingent Reserve Arrangement, Fortaleza, Brazil, 15 July 2014.

[77] See art. IV of the original Articles of Agreement.

[78] Under the Amended Articles of the IMF Agreement, states can arrange their exchange rates as they choose. Some states, including a number of European states such as Denmark, decided to link their currencies to each other.

[79] See, inter alia, Wei Gu, 'Is Yuan Undervalued or Overvalued?', *Wall Street Journal* (11 August 2015).

[80] See art. IV(3).

provides additional guidance on the obligations of the member states and the surveillance regime.[81] The extent of the Fund's surveillance of the domestic affairs of its
members has been a matter of contention. While article IV(3) stipulates that the IMF
'shall respect the domestic social and political policies of members' and shall 'pay due
regard to the circumstances of members', the exact line between justified and unjusti-
fied surveillance is hard to distinguish.[82] In general terms, basic monetary and fiscal
policies are appropriate objects of inquiry and comment by the IMF while detailed
policy choices are for the state itself to make.[83]

11.4.3 Lending arrangements and the issue of 'conditionality'

One of the core functions of the IMF is to provide loans to states with acute balance of
payments problems. In fact, to many states the IMF serves as a 'lender of last resort'.[84]
Drawing funds is governed by article V of the Amended Articles of the IMF. Under
section 3(b) of that article, a state is entitled to funds under the following conditions:

(i)   the member's use of the general resources of the Fund would be in accordance with
      the provisions of this Agreement and the policies adopted under them;

(ii) the member represents that it has a need to make the purchase because of its balance
      of payments or its reserve position or developments in its reserves;

(iii) the proposed purchase would be a reserve tranche purchase, or would not cause the
      Fund's holdings of the purchasing member's currency to exceed two hundred percent
      of its quota;

(iv) the Fund has not previously declared ... that the member desiring to purchase is
      ineligible to use the general resources of the Fund.

The first condition (i) refers to the highly politicized principle of so-called 'conditionality' where issuing a loan to a member state is subject to conditions set by the IMF. Unlike
some of the other conditions,[85] conditionality cannot be waived. In fact, article V(3)
(c) explicitly states that the IMF shall examine whether a request for a loan 'would be
consistent with the provisions of this Agreement and the policies adopted under them'.

In practice, the IMF issues loans on the basis of a 'letter of intent' to the Executive
Board that has been prepared by the lending state after consultation with the IMF.
The purpose of the letter is to commit the lending state to adopt certain economic and
financial policies and concrete programmes for addressing its underlying economic
problems. The content of a letter of intent is not legally binding but is instead tied to the
IMF's political commitment to continue lending money to the state. Since its creation,
the lending policies and practices of the IMF have evolved substantially as the Fund has
sought to learn from its experiences. The economic crises in states in South-East Asia
and in Russia in the mid to late 1990s, as well as the collapse of the economy in Argentina
in the early 2000s, posed major challenges to the Fund's approach to conditionality.[86]

---

[81] Bilateral Surveillance over Members' Policies, Executive Board Decision, 15 June 2007.
[82] See the overview and discussion in Lowenfeld (n 5) 639–643.   [83] Ibid, 640.
[84] Herdegen (n 25) 450.   [85] See art. V(4).
[86] For a historical account, see Lowenfeld (n 5) 667–733.

More recently, it has been the economic crisis in Greece that has tested the IMF and other international creditors. In October 2009, as the global economic crisis was still unfolding, Greece announced that its public deficit was higher than previously stated.[87] As a result, Greece was unable to borrow money on the financial markets and quickly drifted towards bankruptcy. To assist Greece, a 'troika' consisting of the IMF, the European Central Bank (ECB) and the EU Commission provided Greece with the first of two 'bailout' programmes totalling €220 billion. True to the principle of conditionality, the bailouts were conditional on tough austerity measures, including cuts in public spending, tax increases, as well as measures aimed at improving Greece's overall and more long-term economic conditions. On 30 June 2015, however, Greece became the first developed state to default on a payment to the IMF. At that time, its debt was estimated to be in the vicinity of an astounding €240 billion.[88]

The troika's approach and the general politics of 'austerity' have been heavily criticized for being counter-productive in getting the Greek economy back on track and for forcing the Greek government to impose overly severe conditions on the Greek population. Like Argentinean politicians in the early 2000s, many Greek politicians protested against what they perceived to be the international financial institutions' unwarranted interference in the domestic affairs of their state. Defenders of austerity, on the other hand, stressed how institutions such as the IMF are not charitable organizations and that the money Greece has received was provided by other states, including developing states, which expect to have their money returned. Defenders also argue that a number of the austerity measures should have been adopted many years earlier by the state itself, and they question why it required outside 'intervention' from institutions such as the IMF before the Greek government began to collect taxes in a modern and organized manner and to reform a pension system that allowed employees in the public sector to retire on taxpayer-funded pensions in their late 50s. In the autumn of 2018, the Greek economy finally began to show signs of slight recovery. In 2017, the economy grew by 1.5 per cent and in 2018 unemployment was expected to fall below 20 per cent for the first time since 2011.[89]

11.4.4 The World Bank—and debt assistance to the poorest states

The *International Bank for Reconstruction and Development*—also known as the World Bank—was created alongside the IMF to reduce poverty by providing loans to developing countries for the purpose of reconstruction and development.[90] While it was the original intention that the IMF would render short- and medium-term aid to states with payment difficulties and the World Bank would provide longer-term

---

[87] In 2008, the deficit was around 10 per cent and in 2009 the deficit was estimated to be roughly 15 per cent.

[88] Reuters, 'How Much Greece Owes to International Creditors' (28 June 2015), available at http://www.reuters.com/article/us-eurozone-greece-debt-factbox-idUSKCN0P80XW20150628 (accessed 30 July 2016).

[89] European Commission, 'Economic Forecast for Greece' (Autumn 2018), available at: https://ec.europa.eu/info/business-economy-euro/economic-performance-and-forecasts/economic-performance-country/greece/economic-forecast-greece_en (accessed 20 October 2018).

[90] See IBRD Articles of Agreement, art. 1.

assistance, this division of functions has become somewhat blurred in recent decades. Like the IMF, the World Bank has a board of 25 Executive Directors and an independent staff headed by a President. The latter has always been an American. The voting system is also similar to that used by the IMF in the sense that voting is allocated on the basis of shares. The five largest pools of shares belong to the United States, Japan, Germany, France and China. In recent years, processes have been initiated to increase the representation of developing states. In contrast to the IMF, the Bank does not receive its resources from the governments of states but primarily via the capital markets of industrial states.

The World Bank has adopted a number of initiatives and programmes aimed at assisting the poorest states in the world. In 1960, for example, the International Development Association (IDA) was created as a subsidiary of the World Bank to provide loans on very generous terms to the weakest and poorest of the developing states. In 1996, the IMF and the World Bank initiated a Heavily Indebted Poor Countries Initiative, which provides extensive debt relief for poor countries that fulfil certain conditions.

The World Bank is not the only institution to focus on providing financial assistance to poor countries. In 2005, for instance, the Group of Eight (G8) adopted a Multilateral Debt Relief Initiative. Mention should also be made of the so-called 'Paris Club'[91] and the 'London Club'.[92] While the former is composed of creditor states, the latter consists of commercial banks. Both 'clubs' negotiate sovereign debt restructuring for highly indebted countries. In 2015, the BRICS countries established the New Development Bank (NDB) with headquarters in Shanghai, China, to fund infrastructure and development programmes in BRICS countries. Every BRIC member contributes $10 billion and there is equity in power sharing and no member has a right of veto. The NDB aims to gradually broaden its membership irrespective of geography and it will work closely with a new (2016) Asian Infrastructure Investment Bank (AIIB) headquartered in Beijing, China, in areas of mutual interest, such as infrastructure and sustainable development projects.[93] By October 2018, the AIIB had 87 member states. China held approximately 26 per cent of the voting power. Unlike the major European economies, the United States is not a member of the AIIB.

11.4.5 **The monetary system in the EU**

Any discussion of the basic aspects of the international monetary system must include a brief overview of the monetary system in the EU. From AIIB 1979 until 1992, members of the European Community (with the exception of the UK) were parties to the European Monetary System (EMS) and an Exchange Rate Mechanism (ERM) that ensured all currencies were fixed in relation to each other. The system created reasonable stability in exchange rates and was a means to create greater convergence in the economics of the participating states. The EMS paved the way for the creation in the

[91] See Lowenfeld (n 5) 756–760.   [92] Ibid and Herdegen (n 25) 465.
[93] See Asian Infrastructure Investment Bank, Articles of Agreement, art. 1, Beijing, 29 June 2015.

1992 Treaty of Maastricht of a European Monetary Union (EMU) with a common currency and a single European Central Bank (ECB). In 1999, the euro was introduced in 11 of the EU member states.[94] The UK, Denmark and Sweden, however, decided to stay outside the EMU. The introduction of the euro in Greece was delayed until 2001 because its public deficit and debt did not fulfil the criteria for joining the EMU. The EU member states that did not join the EMU and the common currency became (optional) parties to an updated version of the ERM.[95]

After joining the common currency, states are no longer able to change their interest rates, devalue their currency or control the supply of money, all of which are now controlled by the ECB. So, in contrast to other states, an EU state with the euro cannot respond to an economic crisis by, for example, printing more money. Importantly, however, the EMU is based on exclusive individual liability in the sense that each member is responsible for its own financial commitments. The principle is also known as the 'no-bail out principle'.[96] To prevent the participating states from diverting too far from each other in their economic policies, they are bound by certain conditions relating to fiscal discipline and the avoidance of excessive public debt.[97] The 1998 Stability and Growth Pact (SGP) authorizes the imposition of sanctions on a state that exceeds certain limits relating to public deficit and debt.[98] In 2005, the requirements were relaxed.[99] As the debt crisis in states like Greece illustrates, the construction of a monetary union without centralized economic governance and with great disparity in economic growth and fiscal discipline between the members is far from flawless.

11.5 International investment law

11.5.1 Introduction

Foreign investments are a vital element in achieving sustainable economic growth and overall improvements in social conditions. As a general rule, however, states are free to decide whether they want to accept foreign investment in their territories, and they are also free to set their own conditions for admitting foreign investment. But once an investment has been permitted and established, international law protects the investor. As the ICJ stated in *Barcelona Traction*, when 'a State admits into its territory foreign investments or foreign nationals, whether natural or juristic persons, it is bound to extend to them the protection of the law and assumes obligations concerning the treatment to be afforded them'.[100] The purpose of international investment law

---

[94] See TFEU art. 128.

[95] See Resolution of the European Council on the establishment of an exchange-rate mechanism in the third stage of economic and monetary union, Amsterdam, 16 June 1997.

[96] TFEU art. 125.   [97] Art. 126(1).

[98] See European Council Regulation Nos 1466/97 and 1467/97 and Resolution of the European Council on the Stability and Growth Pact, 17 June 1997. See also ECJ, Case C-27/04 *Commission of the European Union v Council of the European Union* [2004] ECR I-6649, paras 80–81 and 97.

[99] European Council Regulation No. 1055/2005 amending Regulation 1466/97, and European Council Regulation No. 1056/2005 amending Regulation 1467/97, 27 June 2005.

[100] *Barcelona Traction, Light and Power Co., Ltd*, Judgment [1970] ICJ Rep 3, para. 33.

is to balance the sovereign rights of the host state to govern its own economic affairs with the legitimate rights of foreign investors. For political and ideological reasons, this balancing act has been an issue of ongoing contention. The following discussion is limited to the question of expropriation of foreign investments (Section 11.5.2), treaties on investment protection (Section 11.5.3) and dispute settlement (Section 11.5.4).

11.5.2 Expropriation and protection of foreign investors under customary international law

Expropriation of foreign property is one of the few areas in international economic law that is governed by both treaties and customary law principles.[101] As a legal term, 'expropriation' generally refers to the taking by the state of private property for public purposes. The term 'nationalization' is used when the state takes control over entire sectors, such as the banking sector or oil sector, by statute or decree. The term 'property' includes alienable rights with a market value, such as title to real and movable property, intellectual property rights, claims to payment and stocks. While goodwill is included, it does not cover more volatile expectations.[102] As a legal concept, expropriation also covers instances where the property in question is subject to such severe legal restrictions that its economic benefit is essentially destroyed—also known as *de facto* or *indirect* expropriation.[103] Expropriation is termed *creeping* when it consists of the gradual imposition of measures that destroy the economic benefit of the property. What is decisive is the *effect* of the governmental measures imposed on the property, and the motives of the government are immaterial. Expropriation does not, therefore, require the state to obtain control of the property. General regulatory action, such as the introduction of new and tougher legislation in a certain sector, may in principle suffice. The threshold is high, though, and expropriation requires that the investor is no longer in 'control of its business operation, or that the value of the business has been virtually annihilated'.[104] The relationship between environmental regulation and expropriation is particularly controversial and case law is not uniform.[105]

Customary international law grants foreign investors a certain *minimum standard of protection*.[106] But the actual content of the standard is not clear. A classic articulation is found in the 1926 *Neer* case, in which an arbitral tribunal stated that investors are

---

[101] See also the discussion in Lowenfeld (n 5) 469–494. For a—generous—enumeration of customary law principles applicable to foreign investments, see Surya P. Subedi, 'International Investment Law' in Malcolm D. Evans (ed.), *International Law* (4th edn, Oxford University Press, 2014) 740–741. See also Lowenfeld (n 5) 586. Expropriation of property owned by the state's own nationals is governed by the national laws of the state: in practice, constitutional law.

[102] Herdegen (n 25) 360.

[103] *Starrett Housing Corp. v Islamic Republic of Iran* (1987 III) 16 Iran–USCTR 112, 154.

[104] ICSID, *Sempra Energy International v Argentine Republic*, Case No. ARB/02/16, para. 285.

[105] Lowenfeld (n 5) 559–564. See e.g. ICSID, *Técnicas Medioambientales Tecmed SA v United Mexican States*, Case No. ARB(AF)/00/2, 29 May 2003, para. 116 and *S.D. Myers, Inc. v Government of Canada*, Partial Award, 13 November 2000, paras 281–286.

[106] It should be noted, however, that some Latin American states applied the so-called 'Calvo Doctrine' according to which foreign investors were not entitled to any greater protection than that offered to the nationals of the home state.

protected against authorities behaving 'in an outrageous way, in bad faith, in wilful neglect of their duties, or in a pronounced degree of improper action'.[107] In *Mondev International v United States*, the International Centre for Settlement of Investment Disputes (ICSID, see Section 11.5.4) noted that the minimum standard today cannot 'be limited to the content of customary international law as recognized in arbitral decisions in the 1920s'.[108]

Customary international law allows a state to expropriate foreign property subject to certain conditions. The expropriation must serve public—and not private—purposes and it must be non-discriminatory. Therefore, once accepted, a foreign investment must benefit from the same protection against expropriation as an investment made by a national of the host state. In addition, expropriation is subject to compensation. The most politicized issue relates to the standard of compensation. In essence, while Western states have generally stressed rigorous protection for investors and *full* compensation for expropriation,[109] developing states and communist states have been more willing to lower their standards of compensation. Non-Western resistance to full compensation was particularly noticeable in the 1960s and 1970s in the calls for a 'New International Economic Order'. The 1962 Resolution 1803 on Permanent Sovereignty over Natural Resources, for example, calls not for 'full' but merely 'appropriate' compensation in the event of nationalization and expropriation.[110] The same—ambivalent—wording was inserted in the 1974 Charter of Economic Rights and Duties of States.[111] In recent decades, however, states are generally in agreement that expropriation triggers full compensation. In part, this is due to the collapse of communism after the end of the Cold War and the realization in the developing world that uncertainty about compensation has a negative impact on a state's ability to attract much needed foreign investment. As we shall see in the next section, just and full compensation is also the general standard adopted in the large number of bilateral investment treaties concluded over the years. International jurisprudence generally supports full compensation. Already in 1928, for example, in the *Factory at Chorzów* case, the Permanent Court of International Justice (PCIJ) stated that reparation for unlawful conduct 'must, as far as possible, wipe out all the consequences of the illegal act and re-establish the situation which would have existed if that act had not been committed'.[112] The rich jurisprudence of the Iran–US Claims Tribunal relating to Iran's expropriation of US assets after the 1979 revolution also supports full compensation.[113]

---

[107] *L.F.H. Neer and Pauline Neer (USA) v United Mexican States* (1926) IV RIAA 60–66, para. 5.

[108] ICSID, *Mondev International Ltd v United States*, Case No. ARB(AF)/99, 11 October 2002, para. 123.

[109] See e.g. the so-called 'Hull Formula' named after Cordell Hull, US Secretary of State and the overview in Lowenfeld (n 5) 475–481.

[110] GA Res. 1803 (XVII) Permanent Sovereignty over Natural Resources (14 December 1962) and GA Res. 3281 (XXIX), para. 4.

[111] Charter of Economic Rights and Duties of States, 12 December 1974, para. 2(2)(c).

[112] *Factory at Chorzów*, 1928, PCIJ, Series A, No. 17, 47. See also *Norwegian Shipowners' Claims (Norway v United States)* (1922) I RIAA 307, 338.

[113] See, inter alia, *American International Group, Inc. v Islamic Republic of Iran* (1983 III) 4 Iran–USCTR 96, see 105ff and *Sola Tiles Inc. v Islamic Republic of Iran* (1987 I) 14 Iran–USCTR 223, 234ff. For a thorough account, see George H. Aldrich, *The Jurisprudence of the Iran–United States Claims Tribunal* (Oxford University Press, 1996).

In practice, full compensation refers to the *market value of the asset* in question. In *Starrett Housing Corp. v Islamic Republic of Iran*, the Iran–US Claims Tribunal determined that the concept of market value should be determined on the basis of the price a 'willing buyer would pay to a willing seller in circumstances in which each had good information, each desired to maximize his financial gain, and neither was under duress or threat'.[114]

11.5.3 Treaties on investment protection

A *bilateral investment treaty* (BIT) is concluded between two states in order to introduce clear safeguards and guarantees under international law to foreign investors. As such, a BIT complements the level of protection offered to the foreign investment by the national laws of the host state. Germany was the first state to conclude BITs with developing states but the practice quickly spread and, by June 2018, UNCTAD had registered 2,954 such treaties.[115] While the content of individual BITs differs, they generally follow a fairly standardized format and structure. In practice, the treaties seek to offer as many incentives as possible to foreign investors, and these are reflected in the level of protection. The concept of an 'investment' is generally defined as broadly as possible in order to attract all possible forms of foreign investment.

The standard BIT contains the following elements. First, BITs generally offer '*fair and equitable treatment*' as well as '*full protection and security*'. In practice, this is translated not only into protection from discrimination with regard to access to courts and administrative bodies and with regard to taxes and other regulations, but also into a certain international standard of protection even in the absence of discrimination. 'Security' refers primarily to physical protection from attacks by not just the government but also various non-state actors, such as rebel groups.[116] In practice, it is a due diligence obligation. Secondly, BITs regulate *expropriation*, including *de facto* expropriation. In general, expropriation is permitted as long as it is carried out for public purposes, is non-discriminatory, accords with principles of due process and is accompanied by payment of compensation, usually of a 'prompt, adequate and effective' nature. The latter refers to full compensation according to the market value of the property, the effect of which should be to put the investor in a position similar to that which would have existed had the expropriation or breach not taken place. Thirdly, as we will see in Section 11.5.4, BITs generally also make provisions for dispute settlement in the event of a dispute between the investor and the host state. In cases where the treaty provides for arbitration pursuant to ICSID, it serves as consent to the exercise of jurisdiction by ICSID.

Many investment treaties also contain provisions on extraordinary circumstances, including severe economic crises. Protection of foreign investments in times of economic crises became a contentious issue in connection with Argentina's economic

---

[114] *Starrett Housing Corp.* (n 103) 201.

[115] See the overview at http://investmentpolicyhub.unctad.org/IIA (accessed 20 October 2018).

[116] ICSID, *Asian Agricultural Products Ltd v Republic of Sri Lanka*, Case No. ARB/87/3, 27 June 1990.

collapse in 2000–2003.[117] After Argentina had defaulted on its foreign debt and adopted a range of controversial 'emergency' financial measures (including abandoning a policy where the local peso was tied one-to-one with the US dollar and also freezing US dollar deposits), many foreign investors brought cases against Argentina alleging violation of the BITs and the principle of fair and equitable treatment. Argentina, for its part, defended its policies on the ground of the existent financial emergency that left it with no other choice. The ICSID tribunals did not agree on whether Argentina could invoke necessity as a ground for precluding the wrongfulness of the acts, either on the basis of customary international law or pursuant to provisions in the BITs. In *LG&E v Argentine Republic*, a tribunal found in favour of Argentina,[118] but other tribunals reached opposite results. The latter found that Argentina had not shown that it did not have other options and that it contributed to the situation that gave rise to the state of necessity.[119]

Investments secured through corruption are not protected.[120] Depending on the circumstances, protection may also be absent if an investment does not conform with the laws of the host state.[121]

Although BITs are the primary instrument for the regulation and protection of foreign investments, a number of *regional investment treaties* have also been concluded. Within the EU, investments between member states are protected by the freedom of establishment and the free movement of capital as well as by the fundamental rights protection in EU law. Investments may also be protected under the European Convention on Human Rights, which protects the right to property in a 1952 Protocol to the Convention.[122] Thus, expropriation must be 'in the public interest' and duly compensated. In practice, the European Court of Human Rights applies a principle of proportionality.[123] The EU plays an increasing role in relation to international investments with non-EU states. Under the Treaty of Lisbon, it holds exclusive competence to conclude agreements on foreign investment.[124] In 2013, the EU initiated negotiations with China on a comprehensive investment agreement that aims at removing market access barriers to investment and provides a high level of protection to investors and investments in EU and Chinese

---

[117] See also Alberto Alvarez-Jiménez, 'Foreign Investment Protection and Regulatory Failures as States' Contribution to the State of Necessity under Customary International Law' (2010) 27(2) *Journal of International Arbitration* 141–177.

[118] ICSID, *LG&E Energy Corp., LG&E Capital Corp., and LG&E International, Inc. v Argentine Republic*, Case No. ARB/02/1, 25 July 2007, para. 238. For support in the literature, see Lowenfeld (n 5) 581–582.

[119] See ICSID, *CMS Gas Transmissions Co. v Argentine Republic*, Case No. ARB/01/8, 12 May 2005, paras 354–355. See also ICSID, *Sempra Energy International v Argentine Republic*, Case No. ARB/02/16, paras 351–354. In the latter case, the Tribunal found that the conditions for necessity in the BIT were identical to those found in customary international law, see para. 388. For an overview, see also Herdegen (n 25) 467–472. It bears noting that the investors generally also claimed that their investments had been expropriated. This was, however, rejected by all tribunals.

[120] ICSID, *World Duty Free Co. Ltd v Republic of Kenya*, Case No. ARB/00/7, 4 October 2006, para. 157.

[121] ICSID, *Fraport AG Frankfurt Airport Services Worldwide v Republic of the Philippines*, Case No. ARB/03/25, 16 August 2007, para. 402. See also *Tokios Tokeles v Ukraine*, Case No. ARB/02/18, Decision on Jurisdiction, 29 April 2004, para. 182.

[122] See art. 1.

[123] ECtHR, *James and Others v UK*, App. no. 8793/79, 21 February 1986. See also *Jahn and Others v Germany*, App. no. 46720/99, 22 January 2004.

[124] TFEU art. 207(1).

markets. It will replace the existing BITs between individual EU Member States and China with one single comprehensive investment agreement.[125]

Mention should also be made of the 1994 Energy Charter Treaty (ECT), which seeks to enhance energy cooperation and promote energy security by operating open and competitive energy markets. It has 54 members, including the EU and Euratom. The ECT primarily offers protection to foreign investment on the basis of the principles of national treatment and MFN status.

In recent years, dissatisfaction with the existing investment regime has spread and a growing number of states have criticized the system for a lack of respect for concerns associated with development and sustainable development. As a result, some states have decided to disengage with the investment regime while others have made adjustments in order to address specific concerns.[126] Notably, calls have been made for more systematic reforms that will comprehensively address the system's alleged challenges.[127]

11.5.4 Settlement of investment disputes

There are different avenues for arbitration in investment disputes. The primary international dispute settlement organ is the *International Centre for Settlement of Investment Disputes* (ICSID) based in Washington DC. It was created pursuant to the 1965 Convention on the Settlement of Investment Disputes between States and Nationals of Other States. ICSID is competent to hear a case if the state party to the dispute and the home state of the investor are contracting parties and the parties to the dispute have consented to submit the dispute to ICSID.[128] Jurisdiction covers 'any legal dispute' arising directly out of an investment dispute.[129] The decisions ('awards') are binding on the parties and generally not subject to appeal.[130] They are also directly enforceable. The arguably most important ICSID decision to date was *Abaclat v Argentine Republic* where the arbitral tribunal found that it had jurisdiction to deal with claims by around 60,000 Italian nationals in a case brought against Argentina after its financial collapse and debt restructuring.[131] Alternatives to ICSID include arbitration under a legal regime created under the auspices of the UN Commission on International Trade Law (UNCITRAL). Dispute settlement is also available under the ECT.[132]

Summary

International economic law covers a vast range of rules and principles on economic conduct and relations between states, international organizations and private actors, both individuals and corporations. The most important areas are those that relate to international trade, international monetary law and international investment law.

---

[125] On EU negotiations, see http://ec.europa.eu/trade/policy/countries-and-regions/negotiations-and-agreements/.
[126] See also UNCTAD, 'Reform of the IIA Regime: Four Paths of Action and a Way Forward', June 2014, 4–5.
[127] Ibid.   [128] ICSID art. 25(1).   [129] Art. 25(1).   [130] Art. 53.
[131] ICSID, *Abaclat and Others v Argentine Republic*, Case No ARB/07/5, Award, 2011.
[132] See ECT arts 26–27.

The primary institutions governing the global economic system are the WTO and the IMF. The purpose of the WTO is to further the liberalization of international trade and economic transactions through the reduction and elimination of tariffs and other barriers to trade. Its trade agreements are governed by a number of core principles, including the principle of non-discrimination. The IMF promotes international monetary cooperation and exchange stability and makes resources available to members with balance of payments difficulties. IMF loans are subject to certain conditions. Foreign investments—including the expropriation of foreign property—are governed by a number of basic principles derived from both customary international law and treaty law. The purpose of the law is to find a balance between the sovereign rights of the host state to govern its own economic affairs with the legitimate rights of foreign investors. A host state may expropriate foreign property if the expropriation serves public purposes, is non-discriminatory and is subject to full compensation.

Recommended reading

For an excellent presentation of international economic law, see Andreas F. Lowenfeld, *International Economic Law* (2nd edn, Oxford University Press, 2008) and Matthias Herdegen, *Principles of International Economic Law* (Oxford University Press, 2013).

An introduction to investment law is also available in Surya P. Subedi, 'International Investment Law' in Malcolm D. Evans (ed.), *International Law* (4th edn, Oxford University Press, 2014) 727.

Politics plays a major role in international economic law. See, inter alia, the contributions in Tomer Broude and others, *The Politics of International Economic Law* (Cambridge University Press, 2011).

A discussion of economic crises and necessity is available in Alberto Alvarez-Jiménez, 'Foreign Investment Protection and Regulatory Failures as States' Contribution to the State of Necessity under Customary International Law' (2010) 27(2) *Journal of International Arbitration* 141.

Questions for discussion

1. Can you think of some concrete examples where international economic law overlaps with other fields of public international law? What role do the Bretton Woods institutions play in the international economic system?

2. The international economic system is frequently the object of criticism. Can you give some examples?

3. What is the difference between the MFN principle and the principle of national treatment? Why is it necessary for the GATT to exempt the application of the MFN principle in the EU?

4. Why is the IMF vital to the maintenance of a stable international economic order?

5. In what way does the monetary system in the EU differ from the system created under the IMF?

6. Under what conditions does international law allow a host state to expropriate foreign property?

12

The peaceful settlement of disputes

CENTRAL ISSUES

1. This chapter examines the most important methods for the peaceful settlement of disputes in international society.

2. It introduces a number of non-adjudicatory settlement mechanisms and provides a brief overview of the role played by the UN.

3. The chapter also discusses the adjudicatory means of settling disputes, including international arbitration.

4. It discusses the competences and powers of the International Court of Justice and analyses issues of access to the Court and the Court's jurisdiction in contentious cases and competence to issue advisory opinions.

12.1 Introduction

At its core, the purpose of international law is to provide the answers required to separate the powers of sovereign states and, to that end, help avoid undue friction between states. The maintenance of international peace and stability through the peaceful settlement of disputes therefore occupies a central place in international law. In order to further the chances of maintaining peace and stability, the international system must be able to point adversaries to viable options that will assist them in de-escalating and hopefully resolving destabilizing disputes.

International law does not generally *oblige* states to settle their disputes, and all forms of dispute settlement are based on the consent of the states involved. It is a well-known fact that disagreements between states may linger and simmer for years. States disagree with each other all the time and fairly persistent disagreements continue to exist on many important issues, such as drawing territorial boundaries or maritime zones. Denmark and Canada have, for example, for many years agreed to disagree about entitlement to Hans Ø—an uninhabited piece of land situated in the middle of the Kennedy Canal in the Nares Strait between Canada and Greenland.[1] But what international law requires is that states find peaceful solutions to the disputes they seek to resolve. Article 2(3) of the UN Charter stipulates that members must resolve their disputes by 'peaceful means' so that 'international peace and security, and justice are not endangered'. The obligation in article 2(3)—also found in customary international law[2]—is closely tied to the prohibition on the threat or use of force in article 2(4) that we shall examine in more detail in Chapter 13.[3] The Charter also requires states to seek a peaceful resolution to disputes that are likely to endanger international peace and security.[4]

We saw in Chapter 1 that there is no centralized body to enforce international law and that it is primarily up to the states themselves to interpret and apply the law. Since disagreements about interpretation and application can lead to legal disputes, a range of dispute settlement methods exist. This chapter discusses the most relevant. Conceptually, there is a distinction between adjudicatory settlement and settlement by other means. The majority of the chapter is devoted to international legal adjudication, in particular the role of the International Court of Justice (ICJ). But we begin in Section 12.2 with non-adjudicatory means/diplomatic dispute settlement and the role played by the UN. Section 12.3 discusses international arbitration before Section 12.4 looks at the competences of the ICJ. Section 12.5 provides an overview of a number of permanent international courts with special jurisdiction.

12.2 Non-adjudicatory means of settling international disputes

State are generally free to decide how they will try to resolve their international disputes.[5] The preferred method is for the parties themselves to directly try to *negotiate* a suitable solution.[6] There are no established procedures or firm practices for when and how negotiations must be conducted. Sometimes, states commit themselves legally to initiate negotiations if a dispute arises. Members of the UN, for example, must seek a resolution by negotiation or other peaceful means of their own choice if they are parties to a dispute the continuance of which may endanger international peace and security. In *Georgia v Russia*, the ICJ stated that the

[1] The Kingdom of Denmark includes the island of Greenland and the Faroe Islands.
[2] *Military and Paramilitary Activities in and against Nicaragua (Nicaragua v United States)*, Merits [1986] ICJ Rep 14, para. 290.
[3] See also the 1982 Manila Declaration on the Peaceful Settlement of International Disputes, GA Res. 37/10 (15 November 1982).
[4] UN Charter art. 33.
[5] *Status of Eastern Carelia*, Advisory Opinion, 1923, PCIJ, Series B, No. 5, 27. See also GA Res. 2625 (XXV) Declaration on Principles of International Law concerning Friendly Relations and Co-operation among States in accordance with the Charter of the United Nations (24 October 1970) and Manila Declaration (n 3) para. 3.
[6] See also the overview in Yoshi Tanaka, *The Peaceful Settlement of International Disputes* (Cambridge University Press, 2018) 19–24.

concept of negotiation requires—at the very least—a genuine attempt by one of the disputing parties to engage in discussions with the other with a view to resolving the dispute.[7]

The term '*good offices*' is used when a third party—usually someone deemed neutral and trustworthy by the parties—offers to facilitate and support potential efforts to enter into direct negotiations. A noteworthy example was Iceland's facilitation of the 1986 Reykjavik Summit on US and Soviet arms reduction. 'Good offices' evolve into *mediation* when the third party assumes a more direct role in the negotiations and suggests terms for settlement or offers solutions for compromise.[8] In practice, of course, the line separating the two functions is a thin one. In many cases, the introduction of a powerful and/or trusted state into difficult negotiations will facilitate a dispute settlement process. This is particularly the case when the third party is also interested in peaceful settlement of the dispute. A well-known example is the role played by the United States in the efforts—often frustrated—to find a peaceful solution to the dispute between Israel and the Palestinians in the Middle East. In practice, mediation is highly relevant to successful conflict resolution, and it was, for instance, the tough and firm intervention of the United States that led to the conclusion of the 1995 Dayton Agreement that brought an end to the civil war in Bosnia. As a mode of settling disputes, mediation is not governed by any specific rules or principles and the mediator is generally free to approach the negotiations as he or she prefers. But successful mediation usually requires the mediator to play an active role and seek to identify the underlying interests of the parties to the dispute. In many cases, it requires both common and separate—often confidential—meetings with the parties. The solutions offered by a mediator are not binding.

When parties disagree about factual circumstances surrounding a dispute, they can appoint an impartial *commission of inquiry* or *a fact-finding mission* to ascertain the relevant facts. In 1961, for example, a commission of inquiry was established by the UK and Denmark in the 'Red Crusader incident', which involved the arrest by a Danish frigate of a British vessel for alleged illegal fishing in the waters off the Faroe Islands.[9] To be trusted, the inquiring entity must be independent and impartial. A commission of inquiry may also be established by an international organization or a supervisory organ to determine if a state has breached a relevant treaty obligation and additional steps may be warranted. The UN Human Rights Council, for example, often sets up commissions tasked with investigating potential human rights violations in individual states. In August 2011, for instance, the Council established an Independent International Commission of Inquiry on the Syrian Arab Republic to investigate alleged violations of international human rights in Syria since March 2011.[10] At

---

[7] *Application of the International Convention on the Elimination of All Forms of Racial Discrimination (Georgia v Russian Federation)*, Preliminary Objections, Judgment [2011] ICJ Rep 70, para. 157.

[8] See also GA Res. 70/304 Strengthening the Role of Mediation in the Peaceful Settlement of Disputes, Conflict Prevention and Resolution (26 September 2016).

[9] *Investigation of Certain Incidents affecting the British Trawler Red Crusader* (1962) XXIX RIAA 521.

[10] HRC Res. S-17/1 (22 August 2011). For some of the findings of the Commission, see '"They came to destroy": ISIS Crimes Against the Yazidis' (16 June 2016).

times, it may be difficult for the fact-finding mission not to become embroiled in the politics of the facts it has been set up to investigate. A well-known example was the fact-finding mission undertaken by Richard Goldstone, who headed the mission set up by the Human Rights Council to investigate alleged violations of international law committed in the January 2009 Gaza War. Goldstone's conclusions—the 'Goldstone Report'—was heavily criticized by Israel for being biased against it. Commissions of inquiry are often established to investigate incidents at sea or air crashes. A recent example was the team of experts set up to investigate the circumstances surrounding the shooting down of a Malaysia Airlines passenger plane over the eastern part of Ukraine in July 2014. In October 2015, the team concluded that the plane had been brought down by a surface-to-air-missile[11] and in May 2018, the Netherlands and Australia held Russia responsible for the incident. The states also asked Russia to 'enter into talks aimed at finding a solution that would do justice to the tremendous suffering and damage caused by the downing of MH17' and indicated that they considered bringing the case to a suitable international court or organization.[12]

The term *conciliation* refers to the production of a report with non-legally binding recommendations by a third party trusted by the parties on the proper settlement of a dispute. The report of the conciliatory body will present all the relevant aspects of the dispute. The purpose of the report is not to determine who is wrong or right but merely to offer a tentative solution to the dispute. An example was the 1981 conciliation between Iceland and Norway on the boundaries of the continental shelf between Iceland and Jan Mayen (Norway). The commission adopted a report with recommendations accepted by both parties as the foundation for the subsequent negotiations that eventually led to an agreement.[13] A more recent example was the successful conciliation commission, headed by the Danish ambassador to India, established under the 1982 UN Convention on the Law of the Sea in relation to delimiting a permanent boundary between the maritime zones of East Timor and Australia.[14] As a potential form of dispute settlement, conciliation is increasing in importance and a number of conventions, in particular in international environmental law, explicitly refer to conciliation. Examples include the 1992 UN Convention on Biological Diversity[15] and the 1998 Rotterdam Convention on the Prior Informed Consent Procedure for Certain Hazardous Chemicals and Pesticides in International Trade.[16] Mention should also be made of the 1980 conciliatory rules of the UN Commission on International Trade Law (UNCITRAL) for the purpose of settling disputes on international commercial relations[17] and the adoption by the Permanent Court of Arbitration (PCA) (see Section 12.3 below) of its own Optional Conciliation Rules and Optional Rules for Conciliation of Disputes Relating to Natural Resources and/or the Environment. Both sets of rules are based on the

---

[11] Dutch Safety Board, *Crash of Malaysia Airlines MH17*, 22 October 2015.

[12] Government of the Netherlands, Press Release, 'MH17: The Netherlands and Australia hold Russia responsible' (25 May 2018).

[13] *Conciliation Commission on the Continental Shelf area between Iceland and Jan Mayen: Report and recommendations to the governments of Iceland and Norway*, Decision of June 1981 (1981) XXVII RIAA 1.

[14] PCA Case No. 2016-10, *In the Matter of the Maritime Boundary Between Timor-Leste and Australia* ('The 'Timor Sea Conciliation'), 9 May 2018.

[15] See Annex II, Part 2.   [16] See Annex VI, B.   [17] GA Res. 35/52 (4 December 1980).

UNCITRAL Conciliation Rules.[18] Conciliation is also offered in the framework of the International Centre for Settlement of Investment Disputes (ICSID).

Dispute settlement is well developed within the *United Nations*. While we shall return to adjudicatory settlement by the ICJ in Section 12.4, it bears noting that the UN Security Council, the UN Secretary-General and the UN General Assembly all have roles to play in efforts to settle disputes peacefully. The *Security Council* has primary responsibility for the maintenance of international peace and security and possesses wide-ranging powers. As we will see in Chapter 13, the Council even has the authority under Chapter VII of the UN Charter to take enforcement measures if they are required 'to maintain or restore international peace and security'.[19] Chapter VI of the Charter concerns the Council's power in relation to the pacific and therefore non-coercive settlement of disputes the continuance of which are 'likely to endanger the maintenance of international peace and security'. According to article 33, the parties to such a dispute shall first seek a solution by means of their own choice (negotiation, mediation, arbitration etc.) but the Council may also 'call upon the parties to settle their disputes by such means'. Article 34 stipulates that the Council may investigate any dispute or situation 'which might lead to international friction or give rise to a dispute' and under article 36 the Council may, at any stage, 'recommend appropriate procedures or methods of adjustment'. Articles 37 and 38 specify that the parties shall refer the dispute to the Security Council if they fail to settle it themselves and that the Council may then make recommendations with a view to reaching a pacific settlement. A well-known recommendation is found in Resolution 242 from November 1967, after the Six Day War. The Resolution concerned the settlement of the Israeli/Palestinian dispute, which included the withdrawal of Israeli armed forces from the occupied territories as well as acknowledgement of the sovereignty of all states in the area and their right to live in peace with secure and recognized boundaries free from threats or acts of force.[20] Recommendations by the Council under Chapter VI are not legally binding on the parties.

The *UN General Assembly* also fulfils an important role in peaceful dispute solution. Since all members of the UN are represented in the Assembly, it offers a crucial institutional setting for all sorts of debates, negotiations and interstate dialogue. In addition, the Assembly may discuss and make recommendations on any issue within the scope of the UN Charter, and under article 14 it may 'recommend measures for the peaceful adjustment of any situation ... which it deems likely to impair the general welfare or friendly relations among nations'.[21] Two things must be noted, however. First, the Assembly is subordinate to the Security Council and it cannot make any recommendation with regard to a 'dispute or situation' while the Security Council is 'exercising ... the functions assigned to it' in the Charter.[22] Secondly, unlike the Security Council, the Assembly does not have the authority to issue binding decisions or resolutions and states are therefore under no legal obligation to comply with its decisions and recommendations.

---

[18] See more at https://pca-cpa.org/en/services/mediation-conciliation/ (accessed 1 June 2018).
[19] Art. 42.   [20] SC Res. 242 (22 November 1967).
[21] See also *Certain Expenses of the United Nations*, Advisory Opinion, 20 July 1962, 16.
[22] Art. 12(1).

The *Secretary-General of the UN* also plays an increasing role in the peaceful settlement of disputes. Among other things, the Secretary-General often offers his 'good offices' as a method of trying to pave the way for the negotiation of peaceful solutions to ongoing disputes.[23] According to article 99, the Secretary-General may bring any matter to the attention of the Security Council which 'in his opinion may threaten the maintenance of international peace and security'.

12.3 Arbitration

Arbitration is a form of international *adjudicatory* dispute settlement where the parties to a dispute create their own arbitral tribunal. Arbitration has a long history in international law. In fact, it was the experiences and practices of arbitration that led to the creation of the Permanent Court of International Justice (PCIJ) in 1921. The modern history of international arbitration is generally traced back to the 1794 Jay Treaty between Britain and the United States and the establishment of mixed commissions for resolving, inter alia, issues arising from the American War of Independence (1775–1783).[24] Another example was the *Alabama* arbitration, which resolved US claims against Britain stemming from the American Civil War (1861–1865) and border issues with newly created Canada.[25] In 1899, the first Hague Peace Conference adopted the Hague Convention for the Pacific Settlement of International Disputes, which created the *Permanent Court of Arbitration* (PCA), an important mechanism that still exists. The PCA—seated at The Hague in the Netherlands—has a secretariat and a roster of judges who may be appointed by the parties to a dispute. It has rendered assistance to numerous important arbitral bodies, including two bodies created in 2000 by Eritrea and Ethiopia after the conclusion of the armed conflict between those states.[26] International arbitration is not limited to disputes between states and the term 'mixed arbitration' is used for the settling of disputes between states, on the one side, and individuals or corporations, on the other. The Iran–US Claims Tribunal, for example, dealt with nationalization of US property and assets after the 1979 revolution in Iran.

Like other means of dispute settlement, arbitration is based on the consent of the disputing parties. Consent to arbitration can take different forms, First, by becoming a party to a 'dispute settlement treaty' a state may agree/consent to submit some or all future disputes under a bilateral or multilateral treaty to arbitration. Secondly, a state may become party to one of the many conventions that stipulate that disputes concerning the interpretation of the convention shall be solved by arbitration. An example of such a treaty is the 1982 United Nations Convention on the Law of the Sea (UNCLOS), discussed in

---

[23] Thomas M. Franck, *Fairness in International Law and Institutions* (Oxford University Press, 1995) 173–217.

[24] Treaty of Amity, Commerce and Navigation between Great Britain and the United States, 19 November 1794. For a historical overview, see Cornelis G. Roelofsen, 'International Arbitration and Courts' in Bardo Fassbender and Anne Peters (eds), *The Oxford Handbook of the History of International Law* (Oxford University Press, 2012) 151–168.

[25] Treaty of Washington, 8 May 1871.

[26] Agreement on Cessation of Hostilities between the Government of the Federal Democratic Republic of Ethiopia and the Government of the State of Eritrea, 18 June 2000.

Chapter 8.[27] UNCLOS was, for example, the basis for the 2016 award in *South China Sea* concerning a maritime dispute between the Philippines and China regarding the latter's activities and controversial sovereign claims in the South China Sea.[28] The third way whereby parties can consent to submit a dispute to arbitration is by special agreement, also known as *compromis*, concluded after the dispute has arisen.

Arbitration differs from the procedure before a permanent court, such as the ICJ (see Section 12.4), because the parties maintain substantial control over the arbitration process. First, the composition, including the number and identity of the judges, of the arbitral tribunal is decided by the parties. In highly technical disputes, for example, the parties may decide to appoint one or more technical experts, such as scientists, as arbitrators. Secondly, the parties may require the arbitral tribunal to apply particular rules that are not necessarily binding under international law. Thirdly, the parties may establish procedural rules that are more flexible than those relied upon by other courts, such as the ICJ. Fourthly, the parties may decide to keep the proceedings confidential, often a desirable choice in politically sensitive disputes. Finally, arbitration is often a much faster way to resolve a dispute than resorting to a permanent court, such as the ICJ.

The judgments/final decisions—termed 'awards'—are final and binding on the parties to the dispute.

12.4 The International Court of Justice

12.4.1 Introduction

The ICJ is the only court in international law with a *general* jurisdiction to deal with interstate disputes, and as we see throughout this book, the Court has made many contributions to the development of international law. It was established in 1945 as a principal organ of the UN and its Statute is attached to the UN Charter. All members of the UN are automatically parties to the ICJ Statute. The ICJ replaced the PCIJ, which had been established in 1921 pursuant to article 14 of the 1919 Covenant of the League of Nations as the first permanent international tribunal with general jurisdiction. Between 1922 and 1940, the PCIJ dealt with 29 contentious interstate cases and rendered a total of 27 advisory opinions.[29]

The ICJ is based in The Hague in the Netherlands and it is composed of 15 judges elected by the Security Council and the General Assembly for terms of nine years. The judges elect its President and Vice-President who sit for three-year terms.[30] In practice, most of the ICJ judges are men, and it was not until the appointment of Rosalyn Higgins in 1995 that a female judge was introduced to the Court. The five permanent members

---

[27] See UNCLOS art. 287(1) and Annex VII.

[28] *The Republic of the Philippines and the People's Republic of China*, Award, PCA Case No. 2013-19, 12 July 2016.

[29] For a thorough discussion of the PCIJ, see Ole Spiermann, *International Legal Argument in the Permanent Court of International Justice* (Cambridge University Press, 2005). All cases and opinions are available via the homepage of the ICJ, see http://www.icj-cij.org/pcij/?p1=9.

[30] Art. 21.

of the Security Council each appoint a judge and the remainder (ten judges) are chosen with regard to a reasonable distribution between geographical and political groups within the UN. The judges must be 'persons of high moral character, who possess the qualifications required in their respective countries for appointment to the highest judicial offices' as well as being representative of 'the main forms of civilization and of the principal legal systems of the world'.[31] The judges are independent and in principle elected without consideration of their nationality.[32] If, however, one of the parties to a dispute before the Court does not have a judge of its nationality on the Court, it may appoint an ad hoc judge who will sit on the bench in the case in question.[33] While the disputes are generally heard by all 15 regular judges (and potentially one or two specially appointed ad hoc judges), the Court has since 1982 made use of an authority contained in article 26 of the Statute to form chambers of three or more judges for dealing with particular categories of cases. In total, six such ad hoc chambers have been created, the first being a chamber of five judges in *Gulf of Maine* concerning delimitation of a maritime boundary between Canada and the United States.[34] As at October 2018, however, there were no active ad hoc chambers.[35] In 1993, the Court created a Chamber for Environmental Matters, but since no state ever sought to utilize it, the Court decided in 2006 to stop appointing judges to its bench.[36]

The ICJ decides disputes submitted to it and it can deal with both contentious cases and issue advisory opinions. Its judgments are binding on the parties and not subject to appeal. Decisions are made by majority vote and the judges may attach individual views/ positions in the form of either a 'Separate' or a 'Dissenting' Opinion to the decision. The legal sources available to the Court are found in article 38(1) of the ICJ Statute and were discussed in Chapter 2. It should be noted that article 38(2) of the Statute specifies that the Court may decide a case on the basis of what it considers fair and right—*ex aequo et bono*—if the parties to a case agree. This, however, has yet to occur.

The remainder of this section is devoted to a presentation of the competences of the ICJ. We begin with access to the Court in contentious cases (Section 12.4.2) and then discuss the role of consent to the jurisdiction of the Court (Section 12.4.3). We then examine the Court's competence to issue provisional measures (Section 12.4.4) and the legal effect of the Court's decisions (Section 12.4.5). Attention then briefly turns to the relationship between the Court and the Security Council (Section 12.4.6), before we provide an overview of the Court's competence to issue advisory opinions (Section 12.4.7).

12.4.2 **Access to the Court in contentious cases**

According to article 34 of the ICJ Statute, only states can be parties to a contentious case before the Court.[37] Access to the Court is dealt with in article 35 and it is important to note that access to the Court is separate from the Court's jurisdiction

---

[31] See arts 2 and 9 respectively.   [32] Art. 2.   [33] Art. 31(2).
[34] *Delimitation of the Maritime Boundary in the Gulf of Maine Area*, Judgment [1984] ICJ Rep 246.
[35] http://www.icj-cij.org/en/chambers-and-committees (accessed 20 October 2018)
[36] http://www.icj-cij.org/court/index.php?p1=1&p2=4 (accessed 1 June 2018).
[37] Art. 34(1).

over a particular dispute.[38] *Access* concerns who may bring or be brought before the Court while *jurisdiction* concerns whether the Court has the power to settle a dispute that is brought before it (by parties with access). So although the Court will only have jurisdiction over a case if the parties to it have access to the Court, jurisdiction does not follow automatically from access. As we shall see in Section 12.4.3, for the Court to have jurisdiction over a dispute the parties involved must have given their consent. Logically, the question of access is resolved prior to the issue of jurisdiction.

Article 35(1) specifies that the Court is open to the state parties to the Statute. Since the Statute is an integral part of the UN Charter to which the vast majority of states are party, article 35(1) therefore serves as the primary method for obtaining access to the Court. The almost universal membership of the UN makes it of limited relevance that article 93(2) provides that a state may become a party to the ICJ Statute without joining the UN. Article 35(2) is concerned with access to the Court for *other states* and stipulates that there are two ways non-state parties may gain access. First, the Security Council may provide a non-party state with access to the Court[39] and, although this option is no longer of any practical relevance, it was relied on in *Corfu Channel*, where Albania was not a member of the UN or a party to the ICJ Statute.[40] Secondly, a non-party state may gain access to the Court by 'special provisions contained in treaties in force'. As we shall return to below, the ICJ has stated that this option only refers to treaties already in force when the Statute was adopted in October 1945.

Although access is rarely a contentious issue, it was debated in relation to the dis-integration of Yugoslavia in the 1990s. In the 2004 *Legality of Use of Force* case, the Court found that the former Federal Republic of Yugoslavia (FRY) (later Serbia and Montenegro) could not bring a case against a number of NATO states for alleged breaches of the prohibition on the use of force during the 1999 'humanitarian inter-vention' because the FRY did not have access to the Court when it filed the application in April 1999. According to the Court, the FRY did not have access in accordance with article 35(1) because it was not considered a UN member state from 1992 until 2000.[41] As discussed in Chapter 4, the FRY did not automatically continue the membership of the former Yugoslavian state at the UN after secession.[42] Furthermore, the FRY could not gain access pursuant to article 35(2) and the existence of a 'special provision' in a treaty because this only covered treaties already in force when the Statute entered into force on 24 October 1945.[43] The relevant treaty was the 1948 Genocide Convention,[44] which did not enter into force until 12 January 1951.

---

[38] See also *Legality of Use of Force (Serbia and Montenegro v Belgium)*, Preliminary Objections, Judgment [2004] ICJ Rep 279, para. 36.

[39] See also SC Res. 9 (15 October 1946).

[40] *Corfu Channel (UK v Albania)*, Judgment on Preliminary Objection [1948] ICJ Rep 15.

[41] *Legality of Use of Force* (n 38) paras 79 and 91.

[42] Ibid, paras 58–64. See SC Res. 757 (30 May 1992), SC Res. 777 (19 September 1992) and GA Res. 47/1 (22 September 1992). For a discussion, see Chester Brown, 'Access to International Justice in the *Legality of Use of Force* Cases' (2005) 64 *Cambridge Law Journal* 267–271.

[43] *Legality of Use of Force* (n 38) paras 113–114. For a critique of the majority decisions, see Joint Declaration of Vice-President Ranjeva, Judges Guillaume, Higgins, Kooijmans, Al-Khasawneh, Buergenthal and Elaraby.

[44] See art. IX of the Convention on the Prevention and Punishment of the Crime of Genocide, 9 December 1948.

The Court's conclusions in the *Legality of Use of Force* case were, however, hard to reconcile with its earlier decisions. In a 1996 decision in *Genocide*, the Court had found that the Genocide Convention *could* serve as the basis for jurisdiction in a case brought by Bosnia and Herzegovina against the FRY in relation to, among other things, the 1995 Srebrenica massacres.[45] When the Court was confronted with its inconsistent practice, it applied the principle of *rex judicata*—where a matter already resolved by a court cannot be raised again—and found that it was bound by its 1996 decision.[46] In 2008, the Court's practice concerning the FRY became even more confusing when it concluded that it had jurisdiction in a case brought by Croatia against the FRY even though the application was filed in July 1999 and thus at a time when the FRY was not a party to the UN.[47] This seemed to contradict the Court's conclusions in *Legality of Use of Force*. The Court defended its zigzag course by noting that it had earlier shown a certain degree of 'realism and flexibility' in its interpretations of the formal provisions of the Statute.[48] The Court's 'flexibility' meant that while the FRY was denied the opportunity to bring other states before the ICJ, it could be brought before the ICJ itself.

12.4.3 Consent to jurisdiction in contentious cases

12.4.3.1 Introduction

The Court's jurisdiction is conditioned on the *consent* of the parties to a dispute. Thus, even though the parties may have access to the Court, it can only deal with a dispute if the parties involved have consented to the jurisdiction of the Court in the specific case or in a category of disputes of which the existing case is part.

12.4.3.2 The expression of consent

According to article 36 of the ICJ Statute, consent to the Court's jurisdiction can be expressed in different ways. First, it can take the form of an explicit agreement—also referred to as a *compromis*—whereby parties agree to submit a particular dispute to the Court. Such voluntary referrals by the parties generally raise few jurisdictional problems.

---

[45] *Application of the Convention on the Prevention and Punishment of the Crime of Genocide*, Preliminary Objections, Judgment [1996] ICJ Rep 595. See also *Application for Revision of the Judgment of 11 July 1996 in the Case concerning Application of the Convention on the Prevention and Punishment of the Crime of Genocide (Bosnia and Herzegovina v Yugoslavia), Preliminary Objections (Yugoslavia v Bosnia and Herzegovina)*, Judgment [2003] ICJ Rep 7.

[46] *Application of the Convention on the Prevention and Punishment of the Crime of Genocide (Bosnia and Herzegovina v Serbia and Montenegro)*, Judgment [2007] ICJ Rep 43, para. 140.

[47] *Application of the Convention on the Prevention and Punishment of the Crime of Genocide (Croatia v Serbia)*, Preliminary Objections, Judgment [2008] ICJ Rep 412.

[48] See paras 81–82 and the references to the judgments by the PCIJ in *Mavrommatis Palestine Concessions*, Judgment No. 2, 1924, PCIJ, Series A, No. 2, 34 and *Certain German Interests in Polish Upper Silesia*, Jurisdiction, Judgment No. 6, 1925, PCIJ, Series A, No. 6, 14. For a critique, see Yehuda Z. Blum, 'Consistently Inconsistent: The International Court of Justice and the Former Yugoslavia (*Croatia v Serbia*)' (2009) 103(2) *American Journal of International Law* 264–271. See also the overview and discussion in Fernando Lusa Bordin, 'Continuation of Membership in the United Nations Revisited: Lessons from Fifteen Years of Inconsistency in the Jurisprudence of the ICJ' (2001) 10 *Law and Practice of International Courts and Tribunals* 315–350.

Secondly, a state consents by becoming a party to a dispute settlement treaty where the parties agree to submit future disputes between them to the ICJ or a treaty that specifies that disputes in relation to the application or interpretation of that particular treaty can be brought before the Court, sometimes contingent on the inability of the parties to resolve the dispute by other means, such as arbitration. In *Great Belt*, Finland initiated proceedings against Denmark partly on the basis of a 1958 Optional Protocol of Signature concerning the Compulsory Settlement of Disputes adopted in the field of the law of the sea.[49] Article 30(1) of the 1984 Convention against Torture stipulates that:

> Any dispute between two or more States Parties concerning the interpretation or application of this Convention which cannot be settled through negotiation shall, at the request of one of them, be submitted to arbitration. If within six months from the date of the request for arbitration the Parties are unable to agree on the organization of the arbitration, any one of those Parties may refer the dispute to the International Court of Justice by request in conformity with the Statute of the Court.[50]

The third way whereby a state can consent to the jurisdiction of the Court is by making a declaration under article 36(2) of the ICJ Statute and accepting the Court's jurisdiction in relation to international legal disputes that may arise in the future with another state 'accepting the same obligation'. This is the so-called 'optional clause' system that enables states to accept the compulsory jurisdiction of the Court. Nothing precludes a state from withdrawing a declaration under article 36(2), as the United States did in 1985 after its defeat in *Nicaragua*. A state cannot, however, prevent the Court from dealing with a case by withdrawing its declaration *after* the Court has seised a case. Also, under the so-called 'Nottebohm rule', the Court will keep jurisdiction of a case that it has seised even after the date a declaration that was limited in time has expired.[51] Since many states have made reservations to article 36, the optional clause system is a detailed patchwork of various bilateral obligations.[52]

The fourth and final form of consent is based on the doctrine of *forum prorogatum* whereby a state that has not consented to the jurisdiction of the Court at the time an application is filed against it subsequently does so. In *Case Concerning Certain Criminal Proceedings in France*, the Republic of Congo in December 2002 brought a case against France for measures of investigation and prosecution by French authorities in relation to a complaint concerning crimes against humanity and torture allegedly committed in the Congo by Congolese nationals. France no longer accepts the Court's compulsory jurisdiction and the Republic of Congo instead based its claim on the expectation that France would subsequently give its consent to the jurisdiction

---

[49] See ICJ, *Passage Through the Great Belt (Finland v Denmark)*, Application Instituting Proceedings, 17 May 1991, paras 9–10.

[50] See also *Questions relating to the Obligation to Prosecute or Extradite (Belgium v Senegal)*, Judgment [2002] ICJ Rep 422, para. 63. See also *LaGrand (Germany v United States)*, Provisional Measures, Order of 3 March 1999 [1999] ICJ Rep 9 and *Avena and Other Mexican Nationals (Mexico v United States)*, Provisional Measures, Order of 5 February 2003 [2003] ICJ Rep 77.

[51] *Nottebohm*, Preliminary Objection [1953] ICJ Rep 122–123.

[52] For an overview, see Tanaka (n 6) 149–163.

of the Court in the case. In April 2003, France did exactly that.[53] The Court will only base its jurisdiction on *forum prorogatum* if it can be proven that the state showed 'an unequivocal indication' of a wish to accept the Court's jurisdiction in a 'voluntary and indisputable' manner.[54] The mere fact that a state has participated in the proceedings of a case and has not refused to appear before the Court or to make submissions cannot be interpreted as consent to the Court's jurisdiction over the merits.[55]

If the state against which the case is brought—the respondent state—disputes that it has consented to the jurisdiction of the Court, it will raise it as a preliminary matter that must be dealt with by the Court before dealing with the merits of the dispute. Article 36(6) of the Statute stipulates that the Court has competence to rule on its own jurisdiction—also known as *compétence de la compétence* or *Kompetenz-Kompetenz*—and the decision by the Court is binding on the parties.

12.4.3.3 Third states

The consensual nature of jurisdiction means that the Court will decline to exercise its jurisdiction in a dispute between two consenting states if it finds that the rights and obligations of a non-consenting third state form the subject matter of the dispute. In *Monetary Gold Removed from Rome in 1943*, the Court concluded that it could not decide a dispute between Italy and the UK in the absence of consent from Albania because the Court would have to determine if Albania had committed an international wrong against Italy and, on that basis, was obliged to pay compensation.[56] In *East Timor*, the Court also declined to exercise its jurisdiction in a case brought against Australia by Portugal because it would not be possible for the Court to decide on the Portuguese claims without having to rule, as a prerequisite, on the legality of Indonesia's actions. Indonesia had not given its consent to the Court's jurisdiction.[57] The Court will, however, only decline to exercise jurisdiction if the interest of the third party is central to the case, and there are many examples where it has dealt with disputes that have at least *some* effect on a non-consenting third state. In *Frontier Dispute*, for example, the Court did not find that it should refrain from delimiting the frontier between Mali and Burkina Faso just because the delimitation was of interest to Niger, which was not a party to the proceedings. The Court noted that its decisions are only binding on the parties to the dispute (see Section 12.4.5) and that Niger's rights could be considered at a later stage.[58]

Article 62 of the Statute stipulates that a state with a legal interest in a case to which it is not a party may request permission to intervene. The intervening state

---

[53] In 2010, the case was removed by the Court, see *Certain Criminal Proceedings in France (Republic of the Congo v France)*, Order of 16 November 2010 [2010] ICJ Rep 635.

[54] *Armed Activities on the Territory of the Congo (New Application: 2002) (Democratic Republic of the Congo v Rwanda)*, Jurisdiction and Admissibility, Judgment [2006] ICJ Rep 6, para. 21. See also *Corfu Channel* (n 40) 27.

[55] *Armed Activities* (n 54) para. 22.

[56] *Case of the Monetary Gold Removed from Rome in 1943*, Preliminary Question, Judgment of 15 June 1954 [1954] ICJ Rep 19, 32.

[57] *East Timor (Portugal v Australia)*, Judgment [1995] ICJ Rep 90, para. 35.

[58] *Frontier Dispute*, Judgment [1986] ICJ Rep 554, paras 46–50. See also *Certain Phosphate Lands in Nauru (Nauru v Australia)* [1992] ICJ Rep 240, para. 55. See also *Continental Shelf (Libyan Arab Jamahiriya v Malta)*, Judgment [1985] ICJ Rep 13, para. 21.

need not have a jurisdictional link to the case and the right to intervene is not made conditional on the acceptance of the parties to the dispute.[59]

12.4.4 **The power of the ICJ to indicate provisional measures**

Article 41 of the ICJ Statute stipulates that the Court has the 'power to indicate, if it considers that circumstances so require, any provisional measures which ought to be taken to preserve the respective rights of either party'. The purpose of such provisional or interim measures is to call a temporary halt to conduct that would make the final outcome of the case futile. It is, in other words, tied to notions of effective decision-making. The purpose of provisional measures is to 'preserve the respective rights of the parties pending the decision of the Court'.[60]

The Court's power to issue provisional measures is subject to a number of conditions. First, it must appear that the Court has jurisdiction in relation to the merits of the case. Importantly, though, the Court does not have to 'satisfy itself in a definitive manner' that it has jurisdiction and a prima facie determination is sufficient.[61] In *Fisheries Jurisdiction (Germany v Iceland)*, the Court stated that it should not act under article 41 if the 'absence of jurisdiction on the merits is manifest'.[62] Secondly, the rights asserted by the requesting party must be at least 'plausible'.[63] There must also be a link between the rights which form the substance of the merits of the case and the provisional measures sought.[64] The third requirement is an urgent need for action. There must be 'a real and imminent risk that irreparable prejudice will be caused to the rights in dispute before the Court gives its final decision'.[65]

---

[59] *Land, Island and Maritime Frontier Dispute (El Salvador v Honduras)*, Application to Intervene, Judgment [1990] ICJ Rep 92, para. 100. See also *Land and Maritime Boundary between Cameroon and Nigeria (Cameroon v Nigeria: Equatorial Guinea intervening)*, Judgment [2002] ICJ Rep 303, para. 15.

[60] *Anglo-Iranian Oil Co.*, Order of 5 July 1951 [1951] ICJ Rep 89, 93; *Fisheries Jurisdiction (Federal Republic of Germany v Iceland)*, Interim Protection, Order of 17 August 1972 [1972] ICJ Rep 30, para. 22, and *Questions relating to the Seizure and Detention of Certain Documents and Data (Timor-Leste v Australia)*, Provisional Measures, Order of 3 March 2014 [2014] ICJ Rep 147, para. 22.

[61] See, inter alia, *Questions relating to the Seizure and Detention of Certain Documents and Data* (n 60) para. 18; *Certain Activities Carried Out by Nicaragua in the Border Area (Costa Rica v Nicaragua)*, Provisional Measures, Order of 8 March 2011 [2011] ICJ Rep 6, para. 49. *Questions relating to the Obligation to Prosecute or Extradite (Belgium v Senegal)*, Provisional Measures, Order of 28 May 2009 [2009] ICJ Rep 139, para. 40.

[62] *Fisheries Jurisdiction (Federal Republic of Germany v Iceland)* (n 60) para. 16.

[63] *Questions relating to the Seizure and Detention of Certain Documents and Data (Timor-Leste v Australia)* (n 60) para. 22; *Construction of a Road in Costa Rica along the San Juan River (Nicaragua v Costa Rica); Certain Activities Carried Out by Nicaragua in the Border Area (Costa Rica v Nicaragua)*, Provisional Measures, Order of 13 December 2013 [2013] ICJ Rep 398, para. 15. See also *Certain Activities Carried Out by Nicaragua in the Border Area (Costa Rica v Nicaragua)*, Provisional Measures, Order of 8 March 2011 (n 61) para. 53; *Questions relating to the Obligation to Prosecute or Extradite (Belgium v Senegal)*, Provisional Measures, Order of 28 May 2009 (n 61) para. 57; *Pulp Mills on the River Uruguay (Argentina v Uruguay)*, Provisional Measures, Order of 13 July 2006 [2006] ICJ Rep 113, para. 57.

[64] *Questions relating to the Seizure and Detention of Certain Documents and Data (Timor-Leste v Australia)* (n 60) para. 23. *Certain Activities Carried Out by Nicaragua in the Border Area (Costa Rica v Nicaragua)*, Provisional Measures, Order of 13 December 2013 (n 63) para. 54.

[65] *Fisheries Jurisdiction (Federal Republic of Germany v Iceland)* (n 60) para. 22. See also *Questions relating to the Seizure and Detention of Certain Documents and Data (Timor-Leste v Australia)* (n 60) para. 32. *Certain Activities Carried Out by Nicaragua in the Border Area (Costa Rica v Nicaragua)*, Provisional Measures, Order of 13 December 2013 (n 63) para. 64.

Issuing provisional measures has so far been an exceptional step for the Court. In *Great Belt*, the Court did not grant a request for provisional measures because the case would be settled by the time the construction of the bridge proved to be a hindrance to passage through the Great Belt.[66] In *Questions Relating to the Obligation to Prosecute or Extradite*, the Court did not find it necessary to ask Senegal to keep an individual wanted for extradition under control and surveillance because Senegal had on numerous occasions assured the Court that it would not allow the individual to leave the territory before the Court had given its final decision.[67] The Court has, however, granted requests for provisional measures in cases involving the potential infringement of individuals' rights rights. In both the *LaGrand* and *Avena* cases, it asked the United States to ensure that non-American nationals on death row were not executed before the Court could determine if their rights under the Vienna Convention on Consular Rights had been violated.[68] With regard to the provisional measures to be adopted, article 75 of the Rules of the Court stipulates that the Court is not bound by the measures requested by the party to the dispute. This has also been noted by the Court in its case law.[69]

Practice by the ICJ shows that an order for provisional measures under article 41 is legally binding on the parties. In *LaGrand*, the Court noted that the object and purpose of the Statute of the Court is to enable the ICJ to fulfil its function as an organ that settles international disputes by binding decisions, and that article 41 is meant to prevent the Court from being hampered in exercising that function.[70]

12.4.5 **The effects of the Court's decisions**

Article 60 of the ICJ Statute expresses the fundamental rule that a judgment by the Court is 'final and without appeal'. As we saw earlier, the same principle applies to the Court's decisions on jurisdiction and provisional measures. But the Court's judgments are only binding on the parties to the dispute and they cannot oblige third parties. Article 60 also provides that disputes about 'the meaning and scope of the judgment' will be settled by the Court on the request of one of the parties. In 2008, for example, Mexico requested the

---

[66] See *Passage through the Great Belt (Finland v Denmark)*, Provisional Measures, Order of 29 July 1991 [1991] ICJ Rep 12, para. 27.

[67] *Questions relating to the Obligation to Prosecute or Extradite (Belgium v Senegal)*, Provisional Measures, Order of 28 May 2009 (n 61) paras 72–73. See also *Pulp Mills on the River Uruguay (Argentina v Uruguay)*, Provisional Measures (n 63) paras 73–77 and *Pulp Mills on the River Uruguay (Argentina v Uruguay)*, Provisional Measures, Order of 23 January 2007 [2007] ICJ Rep 3, para. 50.

[68] *LaGrand*, Provisional Measures, Order of 3 March 1999 (n 50) para. 28 and *Avena*, Provisional Measures, Order of 5 February 2003 (n 50) para. 55.

[69] See, inter alia, *Certain Activities Carried Out by Nicaragua in the Border Area (Costa Rica v Nicaragua)*, Provisional Measures, Order of 8 March 2011 (n 61) para. 76 and *Request for Interpretation of the Judgment of 15 June 1962 in the Case concerning the Temple of Preah Vihear (Cambodia v Thailand)*, Provisional Measures, Order of 18 July 2011 [2011] ICJ Rep 537, para. 58.

[70] *LaGrand (Germany v United States)*, Judgment [2001] ICJ Rep 466, para. 102. See also *Request for Interpretation of the Judgment of 31 March 2004 in the Case concerning Avena and Other Mexican Nationals (Mexico v United States)*, Provisional Measures, Order of 16 July 2008 [2008] ICJ Rep 311; *Request for Interpretation of the Judgment of 15 June 1962 in the Case concerning the Temple of Preah Vihear (Cambodia v Thailand)*, Provisional Measures, Order of 18 July 2011 [2011] ICJ Rep 537, para. 67; *Questions relating to the Seizure and Detention of Certain Documents and Data (Timor-Leste v Australia)* (n 60) para. 53

ICJ to interpret certain aspects of its 2004 judgment in *Avena* and to clarify the extent of the US obligations.[71] Article 61 provides for the possibility of a review of a judgment if the application for such a revision is based on the 'discovery of some fact of such a nature as to be a decisive factor' that was previously unknown to the Court.

According to article 94 of the UN Charter, members of the UN are obliged to comply with the decisions of the Court and, if a party does not comply, the other party may bring the matter before the UN Security Council, which may, 'if it deems necessary, make recommendations or decide upon measures to be taken to give effect to the judgment'. Though this aspect of article 94(2) is seldom relied on, the Security Council did become involved after the ICJ's 2007 judgment in *Genocide*.[72]

12.4.6 **The relationship between the Court and the Security Council**

Since the UN Charter grants both the ICJ and the Security Council a role in efforts to resolve disputes peacefully, the two organs may become involved in the same dispute. Unlike the General Assembly, however, the Court is not subordinate to the Council and it has consistently found that it is not bound to dismiss a case that is being considered by the Council.[73] Since the Council (like the Assembly) has political functions and the Court only exercises functions of a judicial nature, the functions of the two organs do not overlap but rather complement each other. In *Lockerbie*, Libya instituted proceedings against the UK and the United States and argued that a request by those states—subsequently endorsed by a binding resolution of the Security Council[74]—that Libya surrender to trial two nationals suspected of bombing a civilian airliner in December 1998 violated Libya's rights under the 1971 Convention for the Suppression of Unlawful Acts against the Safety of Civil Aviation. Libya also requested the Court to order provisional measures that would prevent the UK and the United States from taking any action that would coerce Libya into surrendering the two nationals.[75] Although the Court dismissed the applications for provisional measures, it did *not* do so because the Security Council had become involved but because Libya's obligations under the UN Charter pursuant to article 103 of the Charter prevailed over obligations under other international agreements, which meant that, since the Council had ordered Libya to surrender its nationals, its obligation to comply with that order trumped its rights under the 1971 Convention.[76]

---

[71] *Request for Interpretation of the Judgment of 31 March 2004 in the Case concerning Avena and Other Mexican Nationals (Mexico v United States)*, Judgment [2009] ICJ Rep 3. See also *Request for Interpretation of the Judgment of 15 June 1962 in the Case concerning the Temple of Preah Vihear (Cambodia v Thailand)*, Judgment [2013] ICJ Rep 281 and *Application for Revision and Interpretation of the Judgment of 24 February 1982 in the Case concerning the Continental Shelf (Tunisia v Libyan Arab Jamahiriya)*, Judgment [1985] ICJ Rep 192.

[72] S/PV.5675, pp. 3–17, S/PV.5697, p. 19.

[73] See, inter alia, *United States Diplomatic and Consular Staff in Tehran (United States v Iran)* [1980] ICJ Rep 3, para. 40 and *United States Diplomatic and Consular Staff in Tehran*, Judgment [1980] ICJ Rep 3, para. 37.

[74] SC Res. 748 (31 March 1992).

[75] *Case Concerning Questions of Interpretation and Application of the 1971 Montreal Convention arising from the Aerial Incident at Lockerbie*, Request for the Indication of Provisional Measures, Order of 14 April 1992.

[76] Ibid, paras 42–43.

12.4.7 **Advisory opinions**

Article 65(1) of the ICJ Statute provides that the Court may give an advisory opinion on 'any legal question' at the request of a body authorized to make such a request. According to article 96 of the UN Charter, the General Assembly and the Security Council may make requests for advisory opinions. The same goes for other organs and specialized agencies if so authorized by the General Assembly. In *Legality of the Use by a State of Nuclear Weapons in Armed Conflict*, the Court declined to issue an advisory opinion because the subject of the request did not fall within the 'scope of activities' of the requesting organ—the World Health Organization.[77] It subsequently found that the General Assembly was entitled to make a more or less similar request.[78] The purpose of an advisory opinion is not to settle a particular dispute but instead to assist the requesting organ in *its* efforts to deal with an issue. The opinions are not binding but since they express the view of the ICJ on a particular issue, they provide important contributions to identifying the status of international law.[79]

Over the years, the Court has issued opinions on a number of politically sensitive issues, including the situation in Namibia[80] and, in more recent times, the legality of the use of nuclear weapons,[81] the legality of Israel's construction of a wall in the occupied Palestinian territories[82] and the legality of Kosovo's declaration of independence.[83] While the Court possesses a discretionary power to decline to give an advisory opinion, it has so far been unwilling to decline jurisdiction due to the political character of the situation.[84] It has expressly stated that the fact that a legal question also has political aspects 'does not deprive it of its character as a "legal question" [nor does it] "deprive the Court of a competence expressly conferred on it by its Statute".[85] In practice, of course, it will often be in situations where 'political considerations are prominent' that it may be particularly useful for a UN organ to request an advisory opinion.[86] The motives for requesting an opinion are irrelevant,[87] and the Court has noted that a request for an advisory opinion should, in principle, 'not be refused'.[88] The decisive issue is whether the questions asked are legal questions in the sense

---

[77] *Legality of the Use by a State of Nuclear Weapons in Armed Conflict* [1996] ICJ Rep 66, paras 25–26.

[78] *Legality of the Use by a State of Nuclear Weapons* [1996] ICJ Rep 226.

[79] See also the discussion in Chapter 2.

[80] *Legal Consequences for States of the Continued Presence of South Africa in Namibia (South West Africa) notwithstanding Security Council Resolution 276 (1970)* [1971] ICJ Rep 16.

[81] *Legality of the Use by a State of Nuclear Weapons* (n 78).

[82] *Legal Consequences of the Construction of a Wall in Occupied Palestinian Territory* [2004] ICJ Rep 136.

[83] *Accordance with International Law of the Unilateral Declaration of Independence in respect of Kosovo*, Advisory Opinion of 22 July 2010 [2010] ICJ Rep 403.

[84] For PCIJ practice, see *Status of Eastern Carelia*, Advisory Opinion, 1923, PCIJ, Series B, No. 5.

[85] *Application for Review of Judgment No. 158 of the United Nations Administrative Tribunal*, Advisory Opinion [1973] ICJ Rep 172, para. 14. See also *Legality of the Use by a State of Nuclear Weapons* (n 78) para. 13, *The Wall* (n 82) para. 41 and *Accordance with International Law of the Unilateral Declaration of Independence in respect of Kosovo*, Advisory Opinion of 22 July 2010 (n 83), para. 27.

[86] *Interpretation of the Agreement of 25 March 1951 between the WHO and Egypt* [1980] ICJ Rep 87, para. 33. See also *Legality of the Use of Nuclear Weapons* (n 78) para. 13.

[87] *Legality of the Use of Nuclear Weapons* (n 78) para. 13. See also *The Wall* (n 82) para. 41.

[88] *Interpretation of Peace Treaties with Bulgaria, Hungary and Romania, First Phase*, Advisory Opinion [1950] ICJ Rep 71. *Certain Expenses of the United Nations*, Advisory Opinion (n 21). See also *Legality of the Use of Nuclear Weapons* (n 78) para. 14.

that they are 'framed in terms of law and [raise] problems of international law'.[89] As it stated in *Legality of the Use of Nuclear Weapons*, the Court 'may give an advisory opinion on any legal question, abstract or otherwise'.[90]

An advisory opinion does not require consent from a state whose actions may be the object of the Court's attention. In *The Wall*, Israel argued that the Court should decline to exercise its jurisdiction because the request in practice related to a contentious matter between Israel and Palestine and Israel had not consented to the Court's exercise of jurisdiction.[91] In refusing Israel's argument, the Court noted that its opinions are merely of an advisory nature, and thus without any binding force, and that its opinions are given not to states but to the requesting organ.[92] It also noted that the subject matter of the request (the legality of Israel's wall) could not be regarded 'as only a bilateral matter between Israel and Palestine', but was also 'deemed to be directly of concern to the United Nations' due to the powers and responsibilities of the UN in questions relating to international peace and security.[93]

With regard to the procedure before the Court, article 68 of the ICJ Statute provides that 'the exercise of its advisory functions ... shall be guided by the provisions ... which apply in contentious cases to the extent to which it recognizes them to be applicable'. In applying article 68, the Court has been reluctant to grant states with a special interest the right to appoint a judge ad hoc.

12.5 International courts and tribunals with a specialized mandate

One of the most important developments in international law in the last couple of decades has been the creation of a number of specialized international courts and tribunals competent to adjudicate legal disputes within a specific area of international law. A particularly important example is that of the *International Tribunal for the Law of the Sea* (ITLOS) discussed in Chapter 8. As noted there, ITLOS was set up as a permanent judicial organ by the 1982 United Nations Convention on the Law of the Sea (UNCLOS), and it is competent to deal with contentious disputes as well as to issue advisory opinions. Decisions by ITLOS in contentious cases are final and binding on the parties and the tribunal may order provisional measures if required to preserve the rights of the parties or to prevent serious environmental harm. In Chapter 11 we also saw that permanent adjudicatory dispute settlement mechanisms have been established in international economic law. The Uruguay Round of trade negotiations, for example, paved the way for the creation of the *Dispute Settlement Body* (DSB).[94] A permanent mechanism for adjudicatory dispute settlement has also been created in international investment law with the establishment

---

[89] *Western Sahara*, Advisory Opinion [1975] ICJ Rep 18, para. 15. See also *The Wall* (n 82) para. 37.
[90] *Legality of the Use of Nuclear Weapons* (n 78) para. 15.   [91] *The Wall* (n 82) para. 46.
[92] Ibid, para. 47.   [93] Ibid, para. 59.
[94] See also WTO Agreement art. IV:3. The Understanding on rules and procedures governing the settlement of disputes (DSU) constitutes Annex 2 to the WTO Agreement.

of the International Centre for the Settlement of Investment Disputes (ICSID). As we shall return to in Chapter 15, specialized courts have also been created in international criminal law, where the 1998 Rome Statute created the permanent *International Criminal Court* (ICC) based in The Hague in the Netherlands. The ICC is meant to supplement national prosecutions of international crime, and the Court is competent to criminally prosecute the most serious offences under international law. The area of international law in which most specialized and permanent adjudicatory bodies have been created is international human rights law. As Chapter 9 discussed, the UN has created a highly elaborate system for resolving disputes about the interpretation and application of human rights, including a range of Special Procedures and committees. In practice, the many bodies primarily deal with 'disputes' that involve complaints by individuals against their own states, but treatment of disputes between states is also possible. Human rights dispute settlement is also available at a regional level, in particular in Europe where the European Court of Human Rights plays a pivotal role. On a final note, mention must also be made of the dispute settlement system in the EU and in particular of the Court of Justice of the European Union (CJEU) in Luxembourg.

Summary

The international legal system contains a range of methods by which states can resolve their disputes in a peaceful manner. While some mechanisms are of a diplomatic and non-adjudicatory nature, there are also a number of adjudicatory methods of dispute settlement available. Diplomatic methods include negotiation, mediation and conciliation. The most important adjudicatory means of settling disputes are arbitration and reliance on a number of permanent international courts and tribunals. The most important of the latter is the ICJ, which is the only international court with general jurisdiction to deal with interstate disputes. The ICJ deals with contentious cases and has the competence to issue advisory opinions. The jurisdiction of the Court in contentious cases is based on consent from the state parties involved. A number of more specialized international courts and tribunals also exist.

Recommended reading

For peace settlement of disputes in general, see Yoshi Tanaka, *The Peaceful Settlement of International Disputes* (Cambridge University Press, 2018) and John Merrills, 'The Means of Dispute Settlement' in Malcolm D. Evans (ed.), *International Law* (4th edn, Oxford University Press, 2014).

On the UN and peaceful dispute settlement, see Thomas M. Franck, *Fairness in International Law and Institutions* (Oxford University Press, 1995).

For peacekeeping, see Christine Gray, *International Law and the Use of Force* (3rd edn, Oxford University Press, 2008) chs 7–9, and the United Nations, *The Blue Helmets: A Review of United Nations Peacekeeping* (3rd edn, United Nations, 1997).

For the history of international arbitration, see Cornelis G. Roelofsen, 'International Arbitration and Courts' in Bardo Fassbender and Anne Peters (eds), *The Oxford Handbook of the History of International Law* (Oxford University Press, 2012) 151.

The most thorough discussion of the PCIJ is Ole Spiermann, *International Legal Argument in the Permanent Court of International Justice* (Cambridge University Press, 2005).

For the ICJ, see Andreas Zimmermann and others (eds), *The Statute of the International Court of Justice: A Commentary* (2nd edn, Oxford University Press, 2012).

A more concise overview is available in Hugh Thirlway, 'The International Court of Justice' in Malcolm D. Evans (ed.), *International Law* (4th edn, Oxford University Press, 2014).

Questions for discussion

1. Why is arbitration often a more tempting choice than the ICJ for states that seek to settle their disputes in a peaceful manner?

2. What are the conditions that must be fulfilled before a state can successfully bring proceedings against another state before the ICJ?

3. The text notes that a state is entitled to make reservations to a declaration under article 36(2). Is that problematic with regard to making states utilize the ICJ?

4. What is the interpretative value of an advisory opinion issued by the ICJ?

13

The international regulation of the use of force

CENTRAL ISSUES

1. This chapter discusses the regulation of when and for what purpose a state may use force against another state—*jus ad bellum*.

2. It provides an overview of the legal framework in the 1945 UN Charter and the prohibition on the use of force in article 2(4).

3. The chapter also examines the role of the Security Council and its competences for the maintenance of international peace and security and under Chapter VII of the Charter.

4. It analyses the unilateral use of force in accordance with the right to self-defence under article 51 of the Charter and a selected number of contentious examples of use of force.

13.1 Introduction

The initiation of war has always been one of the most debated—and politicized—topics of international relations and public international law. The answers to the questions of when, for what reasons and how a member of a community may forcibly submit another to its will is of paramount importance for the maintenance of peaceful relations between the members. Hence, the international rules and principles governing force constitute a vital component of the international law of coexistence.

International law distinguishes between rules regulating *when* and *for what purpose* a state may use force against another state—termed *jus ad bellum*—and those relating to how *military hostilities must be conducted*—*jus in bello*.[1] While the first primarily relates to a state's political decision to use international force, the latter concerns how that political decision is implemented. To illustrate, the legality under international law of the 2003 decision of the US-led coalition to invade Iraq is a matter for *jus ad bellum*. But once the invasion commenced and hostilities were initiated, the focus

---

[1] Christopher Greenwood, 'The Relationship Between *Ius ad Bellum* and *Ius in Bello*' (1983) 9 *Review of International Studies* 221–234.

turned to the requirements for the proper conduct of military operations under *jus in bello*. In practice, therefore, the legal regimes potentially implicate different actors of a state. They are independent of one another and must be so applied.

In this chapter, we discuss *jus ad bellum* while Chapter 14 focuses on *jus in bello*. Here, we begin in Section 13.2 with the framework in the UN Charter and the prohibition on the use of force in article 2(4). In Section 13.3, we turn to the Security Council and in Section 13.4 we examine the unilateral use of force, including the use of force in self-defence. Section 13.5 discusses whether a state can rely on a plea of necessity to use force and Section 13.6 examines some examples of particularly contentious uses of unilateral force.

13.2 The UN Charter and the prohibition on the use of force

13.2.1 Introduction

It was not until the very end of the 19th century that legal attempts were made to curtail the freedom of states to use force internationally. Initially, the endeavour took the form of *procedural* limitations[2] and in the 1919 post-First World War Covenant of the League of Nations member states agreed to submit a dispute 'likely to lead to a rupture' to either arbitration, judicial settlement or inquiry by the League's Council and agreed that resort to war had to wait 'until three months after the award by the arbitrators or the judicial decision, or the report by the Council'.[3] The first effort to limit the *substantive* right of states to resort to war was the 1928 *General Treaty for Renunciation of War as an Instrument of National Policy*—also known as the Kellogg–Briand Pact—in which the parties renounced war as an instrument of dispute settlement.[4]

As discussed in Chapter 1, the UN Charter was created in 1945 with the primary purpose of upholding international peace and security and avoiding yet another major conflict. It entered into force on 24 October 1945. At its core, the UN is concerned with securing stability, preventing unilateral force and saving 'succeeding generations from the scourge of war'.[5] All other considerations remain secondary. But the Charter is not an inherently pacifistic document and states were well aware in 1945 that, at times, to win the peace one had to be prepared to fight the war. Rather than completely outlawing the use of force, the Charter *collectivizes* it and sets up a system whereby the international community, acting through the Security Council, can take the measures required to keep or restore international peace and security. The 1945 vision was that, from then on, save in the case of self-defence in response to very serious attacks on a state ('armed attacks'), international force should be used only in the common interests of the international community.

---

[2] See art. 2 of the 1899 Convention for the Pacific Settlement of International Disputes.
[3] Covenant of the League of Nations (1919), art. 12.
[4] General Treaty for the Renunciation of War as an Instrument of National Policy (1928), art. 2.
[5] Preamble to the UN Charter (1945).

We begin the discussion in this section with the prohibition against the use of force in article 2(4) (Section 13.2.2), before we turn to the legality of interferences that fall below the threshold of 'force' (Section 13.2.3).

13.2.2 The prohibition on the use of force

The starting point is the prohibition on the use of force contained in article 2(4) of the UN Charter, which stipulates that all members of the UN:

> shall refrain in their international relations from the threat or use of force against the territorial integrity or political independence of any state, or in any other manner inconsistent with the Purposes of the United Nations.

The concept of '*force*' has been debated ever since the adoption of the Charter in 1945, but the prevailing view is that it is limited to *armed* measures.[6] This is supported by the General Assembly's 1970 Declaration on Friendly Relations[7] and its 1987 Declaration on the Non-Use of Force.[8] According to the *2017 Tallinn Manual 2.0 on the International Law Applicable to Cyber Operations*, a cyber operation constitutes a use of force when its 'scale and effects are comparable to non-cyber operations rising to the level of a use of force'.[9] While some have argued that the wording 'against the territorial integrity and political independence … or any other manner inconsistent with the Purposes of the United Nations' in Article 2(4) implies that only use of force directed at territorial integrity and political independence is covered by the prohibition,[10] the better view is that the prohibition covers *all* uses of force.[11] The *travaux préparatoires* of the Charter testify to the efforts of the drafters to limit, to the extent possible, the use of non-Security Council-sanctioned force.[12]

In *Nicaragua*, the International Court of Justice (ICJ) stated that the use of force is regulated in both the UN Charter and in customary international law[13] and that the content of the two sources of law is not identical in all relevant aspects.[14] In practice,

---

[6] Bruno Simma (ed.), *The Charter of the United Nations: A Commentary* (Oxford University Press, 2012) 208–209.

[7] GA Res. 2625 (XXV) Declaration on Principles of International Law concerning Friendly Relations and Co-operation among States in accordance with the Charter of the United Nations (24 October 1970).

[8] GA Res. 42/22 Declaration on the Enhancement of the Effectiveness of the Principles of Refraining from the Threat or Use of Force in International Relations (18 November 1987).

[9] Michael N. Schmitt (ed.), *The Tallinn Manual 2.0 on the International Law Applicable to Cyber Operations* (Cambridge University Press, 2017) Rule 69.

[10] See e.g. Derek W. Bowett, *Self-Defence in International Law* (Frederik A. Praeger, 1958) 152; see also *Legality of Use of Force (Serbia and Montenegro v Belgium)*, Provisional Measures, Order of 10 May 1999, 12.

[11] Yoram Dinstein, *War, Aggression and Self-Defence* (6th edn, Cambridge University Press, 2017) 93–94; Ian Brownlie, *International Law and the Use of Force by States* (Oxford University Press, 1963) 265–268; Thomas Franck, *Recourse to Force: State Action Against Threats and Armed Attacks* (Cambridge University Press, 2002) 12; see also *Corfu Channel (UK v Albania)*, Merits [1949] ICJ Rep 4, 35. But see Rosalyn Higgins, *Problems & Process: International Law and How We Use It* (Oxford University Press, 1994) 245–246.

[12] See the overview in Simma (n 6) 216–217.

[13] *Military and Paramilitary Activities in and against Nicaragua (Nicaragua v United States)*, Merits [1986] ICJ Rep 14, para. 174.

[14] Ibid, para. 181.

however, it is hard to imagine the existence of a substantial material difference between the prohibition on the use of force deriving from these two sources.[15]

Using force on the basis of valid consent (invitation) from a host state is not prescribed by article 2(4). As we saw in Chapter 7, consent is a circumstance that precludes the wrongfulness of an act otherwise in violation of an international obligation.[16] There are many uncontroversial instances where international force is based on consent from the territorial state, the most obvious example being UN peacekeeping operations. Other examples include NATO's military presence in Afghanistan from December 2001 onwards and the international military campaign against the so-called 'Islamic State' (ISIL) in Iraq.[17] More doubtful cases are where consent is given by a government that has lost effective control over substantial parts of its territory due to civil war. Some argue that consent cannot be relied upon in such circumstances, because there will be doubt as to which of the contending parties can give valid consent to the intervention.[18] That, however, does not seem to be supported by state practice. For instance, remarkably few states have questioned whether Syrian President Bashar al-Assad' was in a position to invite Iran and Russia to conduct military operations in Syria, even though there were years when his regime did not control major parts of Syria. In addition, with regard to the civil war in Yemen, there seems to be broad international consensus that President Abdrabbuh Hadi, despite being ousted from the capital Sana'a, can validly consent to the military operations conducted by a coalition led by Saudi Arabia against Houthi rebels. The legitimacy of consent to the use of force seems to be influenced by the extent to which the consenting government is seen as representative of the will of the population and/or if the government has previously been recognized by the international community and not yet been replaced by another entity.[19]

13.2.3 Interferences that fall below the threshold for constituting force under article 2(4)

A state's interference in another state that does not constitute force under article 2(4) may still violate international law. First, as discussed in Chapter 5, the principle of territorial sovereignty dictates that a state may not exercise its physical power in any form in the territory of another state.[20] A violation of that principle constitutes a *breach*

---

[15] Ibid. See also *Legal Consequences of the Construction of a Wall in the Occupied Palestinian Territory*, Advisory Opinion [2004] ICJ Rep 136, para. 87, and GA Res. 2625 (n 7).

[16] ILC, Draft Articles on State Responsibility, Report of the International Law Commission, 53rd Session (2001), art. 20.

[17] *Letter dated 25 June 2014 from the Permanent Representative of Iraq to the United Nations addressed to the Secretary-General* (25 June 2014), UN Doc. S/2014/440. Of course, ISIL is not a 'state' for the purposes of international law.

[18] See, inter alia, the debate in Louise Doswald-Beck, 'The Legal Validity of Military Intervention by Invitation of the Government', *British Yearbook of International Law 1985* (1986) 189–252 and Christine Gray, *International Law and the Use of Force* (3rd edn, Oxford University Press, 2008) 80–81.

[19] See the discussion in Gregory H. Fox, 'Intervention by Invitation' in Marc Weller (ed.), *The Oxford Handbook of the Use of Force in International Law* (Oxford University Press, 2015) 816–840 and Benjamin Nussberger, 'Military Strikes in Yemen in 2015: Intervention by Invitation and Self-Defence in the Course of Yemen's "Model Transitional Process"' (2017) 4(1) *Journal on the Use of Force and International Law* 110–160.

[20] *Island of Palmas (Netherlands v United States)* (1928) II RIAA 829, 838.

of sovereignty. The obligation to respect the sovereignty of other states is reflected in article 2(1) of the Charter. Peacetime espionage does not *as such* violate international law but the methods whereby the espionage is conducted may constitute breaches of sovereignty.[21] While the principle of sovereignty also applies in cyberspace,[22] the regulation of cyber-espionage has turned out to be contentious. According to the 2017 *Tallinn Manual 2.0,* cyber-espionage conducted by state A against state B (only) violates the sovereignty of the latter if the agents of state A are physically present on the territory of state B or if the cyber operation causes injury, physical damage or a loss of functionality, or if it interferes with the inherently governmental functions of state B.[23]

Secondly, an interference that falls below the threshold of force may also violate the principle of *non-intervention,* according to which a state may not intervene in the internal affairs of another state. While the principle is not explicitly mentioned in the UN Charter, like the principle of sovereignty, it springs from the sovereign equality of states and is reflected in article 2(1) of the Charter. The ICJ has referred to the principle as being 'part and parcel of customary international law'.[24] The prohibition against interventions consists of two elements: (1) an *intervention* aimed at (2) *a matter in which each state is permitted to decide freely.*[25] The key to the first element is an attempt to 'coerce', and it is therefore only acts that are intended to cause *a change in policy* in another state that can violate the principle.[26] While coercion does not have to be physical, it must be distinguished from persuasion, criticism and propaganda.[27] In *Nicaragua,* the ICJ found that US support to the military and paramilitary activities of the Nicaraguan *contras,* including financial support, training, weapons supply and intelligence and logistical support, violated the principle of non-intervention.[28] As to the second element, an intervention only violates international law if it seeks to coerce a state on such matters 'which must remain free ones'.[29] Most importantly, states are entitled to freely determine their own political, economic, cultural and social systems, to develop their own foreign policies and to exercise permanent sovereignty over their natural resources.[30] For example, the use of cyber operations by a state to remotely alter electronic actions and manipulate an election constitutes an unlawful intervention.[31]

We saw in Chapter 7 that a state is generally entitled to respond to another state's violations of international law by resorting to countermeasures.[32] As a point of departure, therefore, a state that is the victim of a breach of sovereignty or an

---

[21] *Tallinn Manual 2.0* (n 9) Rule 32, para. 6.

[22] Ibid. Rules 1–5. See also the report by the United Nations Group of Governmental Experts on Developments in the Field of Information and Telecommunications in the Context of International Security (UN GGE), UN Doc. A/68/98 (24 June 2013), para. 20 and UN Doc. A/70/174 (22 July 2015), para. 28.

[23] See the discussion in *Tallinn Manual 2.0* (n 9) Rule 4, paras 7–22.

[24] *Nicaragua* (n 13) para. 202. See also *Armed Activities on the Territory of the Congo (Democratic Republic of the Congo v Uganda),* Judgment [2005] ICJ Rep 168, paras 164–165 and GA Res. 2625 (n 7) and GA Res. 36/103 Declaration on the Inadmissibility of Intervention and Interference in the Internal Affairs of States (9 December 1981).

[25] *Nicaragua* (n 13) para. 205.   [26] See also GA Res. 2625 (n 7).

[27] *Tallinn Manual 2.0* (n 9) Rule 66, paras 20–21.   [28] *Nicaragua* (n 13) para. 228.

[29] Ibid, para. 205.   [30] GA Res. 36/103 (n 24) para. 2(b). See also *Nicaragua* (n 13) para. 205.

[31] *Tallinn Manual 2.0* (n 9) Rule 66, para. 2.

[32] See Section 7.5.4.

unlawful intervention may initiate countermeasures against the responsible state.[33] A countermeasure cannot, however, take the form of use of force unless it is a response to an armed attack (see Section 13.4).

13.3 The Security Council and the maintenance of international peace and security

13.3.1 Introduction

As already noted, the Security Council has the primary responsibility for the maintenance of international peace and security. Use of force authorized by the Council does not, therefore, violate the prohibition in article 2(4). Only 15 states have a seat on the Council, and the five most powerful states in the 1945 world—China, France, the Soviet Union (today Russia), the UK and the United States—are permanent members ('the permanent five').[34] All decisions of a non-procedural nature are made by an affirmative vote of nine members including the concurring votes of the permanent members.[35] In practice, therefore, any of 'the permanent five' can block significant initiatives by the Council. This, of course, can hardly be said to be 'democratic' and numerous suggestions for reform of the Council have been advanced. However, the whole point of the Security Council is that states are not all of equal importance. The permanent members have a right of veto not just because they won the Second World War but also because it was the belief in 1945 that the efforts to maintain international peace and security are best served by ensuring that the five big powers agree on resort to the use of force. In addition, for many years, 'the permanent five' were the only states that possessed nuclear weapons.

The Charter gives the Security Council wide-ranging powers. As we saw in Chapter 12, the Council can adopt non-coercive and non-binding measures under Chapter VI of the Charter to settle disputes that may lead to a situation where international peace and security are threatened. If the Council determines that an ongoing dispute is a threat to the peace, however, it can also authorize binding and potentially *forcible* measures under Chapter VII. As discussed in Chapter 2, article 25 of the Charter stipulates that member states agree to carry out the decisions of the Council. Also, under article 103, obligations undertaken under the Charter—including those stemming from Security Council resolutions—prevail over other international obligations.

We start by examining the Council's determination of a threat to the peace in article 39 (Section 13.3.2) and then we briefly look at provisional measures (Section 13.3.3). We then discuss non-forcible measures (Section 13.3.4) before examining forcible measures (Section 13.3.5). Attention is then turned to the limits to the Council's authority

---

[33] See also Anders Henriksen, 'Lawful State Responses to Low-Level Cyber-Attacks' (2015) 84(2) *Nordic Journal of International Law* 323–351.
[34] UN Charter art. 23.   [35] Ibid, art. 27.

(Section 13.3.6), interpretation of the Council's resolutions (Section 13.3.7) and the Council's use of regional organizations (Section 13.3.8).

13.3.2 Determinations under article 39

Article 39 of the Charter specifies that the Security Council shall initially determine the existence of 'any threat to the peace, breach of the peace, or act of aggression'. The Council enjoys considerable discretion and the concept of a 'threat to the peace' has evolved substantially. In the last few decades, the Council has found that everything from internal conflicts, humanitarian crises, violations of democratic principles, acts of terrorism, piracy, arms control issues, the outbreak of Ebola to the prevention of 'foreign terrorist fighters' falls within the concept of a threat to the peace under article 39. In practice, as long as a matter can be reasonably tied to international peace and security, the Council has the authority to find that its powers under Chapter VII are triggered.[36]

13.3.3 Provisional measures under article 40

Article 40 authorizes the Security Council to call on the parties to a dispute to comply with such provisional measures as it may deem necessary to 'prevent an aggravation of the situation'. The Council may, for example, call for a ceasefire and/or for the withdrawal of troops from foreign territory. The measures in question must, however, be temporary in nature and leave the legal positions of the parties to the dispute unaffected. Practice illustrates that, although the wording of article 40 ('may … call upon') indicates that provisional measures are only recommendations, such measures may be binding.[37]

13.3.4 Non-forcible measures under article 41

According to article 41, the Security Council may take legally binding non-forcible measures, such as 'complete or partial interruption of economic relations and of rail, sea, air, postal, telegraphic, radio, and other means of communications, and the severance of diplomatic relations'. The list is not exhaustive. The Council often responds to a crisis by imposing economic sanctions on the parties, such as an arms embargo. The most comprehensive sanctions regime was imposed on Iraq after its invasion of Kuwait in August 1990 and its subsequent refusal to cooperate fully with the UN weapons inspectors.[38] The sanctions led to a widespread humanitarian crisis in the country and to the introduction of more targeted—or 'smart'—sanctions that focus on individuals or institutions that are the primary cause of the threat to the peace.[39] For example, when the Security Council in 2006 imposed sanctions on Iran

---

[36] ICTY, *Tadić (Jurisdiction)*, Appeals Chamber Judgment (2 October 1995), paras 28–29.

[37] Simma (n 6) 1303. See e.g. SC Res. 660 (2 August 1990).

[38] See, among others, SC Res. 661 (6 August 1990), SC Res. 665 (25 August 1990), SC Res. 687 (3 April 1991).

[39] See also GA Res. 51/242 (26 September 1997), Annex II. See also Matthew Craven, 'Humanitarianism and the Quest for Smarter Sanctions' (2002) 13 *European Journal of International Law* 43–50.

for its failure to cooperate with the International Atomic Energy Agency (IAEA), it also targeted individuals and entities in Iran involved with the nuclear programme.[40] The nuclear-related elements of the sanctions (but not an arms embargo) began to be lifted in January 2016 after Iran had completed certain steps agreed to with 'the permanent five' and Germany ('P5+1') in the July 2015 Joint Comprehensive Plan of Action (JCPOA) ('Iran Nuclear Deal').[41] In May 2018, however, US President Trump declared that the United States would abandon the agreement. North Korea has also been under an increasingly tough sanctions regime, as it has continued to ignore international demands to stop its nuclear programme.[42]

The Security Council has generally become more creative in how it applies its powers under article 41. As we shall see in Chapter 15, the Council has, for example, relied on article 41 to establish international tribunals to prosecute international crimes, and to refer situations to the International Criminal Court (ICC). It has also used article 41 to restrict trade in certain goods, such as so-called 'conflict diamonds' from African conflict zones.[43] Article 41 is also utilized to adopt 'legislative' resolutions, where general and more abstract obligations are imposed on states. Here, the Council does not focus on a particular country or entity but instead on a 'phenomenon' or a range of activities it deems inherently threatening to international peace.[44] Recently, with reference to the fight against terrorism, the Council has imposed general obligations on states in order to tackle the so-called 'foreign terrorist fighter phenomenon', where individuals travel to areas of armed conflict to join militant Islamist groups.[45] In Resolution 2396, adopted in December 2017, for example, the Council obliged member states to, inter alia, develop watch lists and gather biometric data on suspected foreign fighters.[46]

13.3.5 Enforcement under article 42

When non-forcible measures are insufficient to uphold or restore international peace and security, article 42 gives the Security Council the authority to mandate 'such action by air, sea, or land forces as may be necessary'. Hence, if required, the Council can authorize the initiation of military operations. While the original idea was that UN members would put forces at the disposal of the Security Council, which could then rely on such 'UN forces', this never materialized. Instead, the Council relies on 'coalitions of the willing' or, as we shall in Section 13.3.8, on regional organizations.

During the Cold War, the broad authority to use forcible measures lay mostly dormant,[47] and it was not until the 1990s that the Security Council began, to some degree, to live up to its responsibilities. In 1990, the Council responded to Iraq's invasion of Kuwait by authorizing member states to use 'all necessary means' to secure

---

[40] See, among others, SC Res. 1737 (23 December 2006) and SC Res. 1929 (9 June 2010).
[41] The 'Iran Deal' was endorsed by the Security Council in SC Res. 2231 (20 July 2015).
[42] For the latest resolutions, see SC Res. 2397 (22 December 2017) and SC Res. 2375 (11 September 2017).
[43] SC Res. 1306 (5 July 2000), SC Res. 1343 (7 March 2001).
[44] See, inter alia, SC Res. 1373 (28 September 2001) and SC Res. 1540 (28 April 2004).
[45] See, inter alia, SC Res. 2178 (24 September 2014).   [46] SC Res. 2396 (21 December 2017).
[47] But see SC Res. 83 (27 June 1950).

an Iraqi withdrawal and to restore international peace and security in the region.[48] Although the subsequent US-led First Iraq War liberated Kuwait and created optimism for the dawning of a New World Order centred on a revitalized Security Council, the following decades turned out to be fairly disappointing. The post-Cold War period has, however, seen an unprecedented level of activity in the Security Council with regard to enforcement under Chapter VII. Since the end of the First Iraq War, the Council has authorized the use of force in, among other places, Yugoslavia,[49] Somalia,[50] Haiti,[51] East Timor,[52] the Ivory Coast[53] and Libya.[54] It has also relied on article 42 to establish large multinational 'security' forces that have been deployed in the aftermath of the international interventions in Kosovo in 1999,[55] in Afghanistan in 2001[56] and in Iraq in 2003.[57] In 2013, the Council expanded the mandate for the large contingent of UN forces deployed to the Democratic Republic of Congo to include 'targeted offensive operations' against armed groups with a view to neutralizing and disarming them.[58]

One of the results of the Cold War paralysis of the Security Council was the emergence of peacekeeping operations.[59] The General Assembly took the early lead with the establishment in 1956–1967 of a major peacekeeping force (UNEF, the UN Emergency Force) in Egypt.[60] UNEF was created pursuant to a 1950 resolution on 'Uniting for Peace', in which the General Assembly declared its willingness to make 'appropriate recommendations … for collective measures including … the use of armed force' when the Security Council was unable to fulfil its role.[61] In the *Certain Expenses* case, the ICJ confirmed that the Assembly can establish peacekeeping operations on the basis of consent of the state or states concerned, but that only the Security Council may authorize the use of force.[62] Initially, peacekeeping was based on the consent of the territorial state, and peacekeepers were considered impartial, lightly armed and only authorized to use force in self-defence.[63] In addition, they were mostly deployed to interstate disputes where their main task was to monitor ceasefires and contested borders.[64] After the end of the Cold War, however, the Security Council assumed control over peacekeeping and began to deploy forces to places where there was little peace to keep. The character of UN operations evolved substantially and peacekeeping forces were gradually dragged

---

[48] SC Res. 678 (29 November 1990) referred to the earlier Res. 660 (2 August 1990).

[49] SC Res. 836 (4 June 1993).   [50] SC Res. 794 (3 December 1992).

[51] SC Res. 940 (31 July 1994).   [52] SC Res. 1264 (15 September 1999).

[53] SC Res. 1464 (4 February 2003) and SC Res. 1528 (27 February 2004).

[54] SC Res. 1973 (17 March 2011).   [55] SC Res. 1244 (10 June 1999).

[56] SC Res. 1386 (6 December 2001). See also SC Res. 1510 (13 October 2003).

[57] SC Res. 1511 (16 October 2003).

[58] SC Res. 2098 (28 March 2013). For the latest extension of the mandate, see SC Res. 2409 (27 March 2018).

[59] Elements of enforcement action were, however, visible in the peacekeeping operation in the Congo: see also Simma (n 6) 1333.

[60] SC Res. 998 (4 November 1956) and SC Res. 1000 (5 November 1956).

[61] GA Res. 377 (V) (3 November 1950).

[62] *Certain Expenses of the United Nations*, Advisory Opinion of 20 July 1962 [1962] ICJ Rep 151, 163–165.

[63] For an overview, see the United Nations, *The Blue Helmets: A Review of United Nations Peacekeeping* (3rd edn, United Nations, 1997).

[64] But see also SC Res. 161 (21 February 1961).

into the fighting.[65] The most notable examples were the UN missions in Yugoslavia (UNPROFOR) and Somalia (UNOSOM) in the early 1990s.[66] For a time, the experiences in the 1990s in Yugoslavia and Somalia led to a loss of appetite for major peacekeeping operations, and subsequent UN missions were much less ambitious. Since the turn of the century, however, there has been a massive increase in UN peacekeeping operations, and as at October 2018 the UN Department for Peacekeeping Operations (DPKO) was running 15 missions. The five largest were all in Africa: Congo (MONUSCO), Darfur (UNAMID), Mali (MINUSMA), the Central African Republic (MINUSCA) and South Sudan (UNMISS).[67] The year 2018 marked the 70th anniversary of UN peacekeeping. Over the years, a series of reviews and evaluations have been conducted and numerous suggestions for reform have been put forward.[68]

Although enforcement measures under article 42 do not depend on consent from the territorial state, consent is not uncommon. A Chapter VII resolution from the Security Council will ensure that a UN operation can continue even if consent is withdrawn.[69] By adopting a resolution under Chapter VII, the Council may also create binding obligations on other member states.

13.3.6 Limits on the Security Council's authority

The authority of the Security Council is not unlimited. First, article 24(2) stipulates that the Council is bound by the UN's general purposes and principles as formulated in articles 1 and 2. Secondly, as noted earlier, the Council can only deal with threats to international peace and security. Thirdly, as noted in Chapter 2, the Council cannot oblige states to disregard norms of a *jus cogens*/peremptory character. In response to the criticism by, most notably, the Court of Justice for the European Union (CJEU) of the Council's sanctions and listing regime, and its seeming lack of concern for due process guarantees, the Council modified its procedures for delisting individuals.[70] It has also stated that the implementation of sanctions must respect human rights law, refugee law and international humanitarian law.[71] In 2009, it created the Office of the Ombudsperson to serve as an independent and impartial entity for reviewing the cases of individuals on the sanctions list.[72] Its mandate is now found in Resolution 2368 of July 2017.[73]

---

[65] On post-Cold War peacekeeping, see Gray (n 18) 272–281.   [66] Ibid, 281–292.

[67] For an updated overview, see http://peacekeeping.un.org/en.

[68] See, inter alia, 'An Agenda for Peace', Report of the Secretary-General pursuant to the statement adopted by the Summit Meeting of the Security Council on 31 January 1992 (17 June 1992), UN Doc. A/47/277-S/24111 and the follow-up, 'An Agenda for Peace: Supplement' (3 January 1995), UN Doc. A/50/60-S/1995/1; Report of the Panel on United Nations Peace Operations ('Brahimi report') (21 August 2000), UN Doc. A/55/305-S/2000/809; and the Report of the High-Level Independent Panel on Peace Operations on uniting our strengths for peace: politics, partnership and people (17 June 2015), UN Doc. A/70/95-S/2015/446, 9.

[69] Simma (n 6) 1344.

[70] SC Res. 1730 (19 December 2006), SC Res. 1822 (30 June 2008), SC Res. 1904 (17 December 2009), SC Res. 1989 (17 June 2011).

[71] SC Res. 1456 (20 January 2003).   [72] SC Res. 1904 (17 December 2009).

[73] SC Res. 2368 (20 July 2017).

13.3.7 **Interpretation of Security Council resolutions**

There are few authoritative sources on the interpretation of Security Council resolutions.[74] Although the principles for treaty interpretation in the Vienna Convention on the Law of Treaties is a good place to start, the Council's resolutions and treaties differ in a number of ways. For one thing, the procedure for drafting resolutions is different from drafting treaties. In addition, the words and terms contained in a resolution often reflect hard-won political compromises and the end result may be that certain terms are intentionally left vague and open-ended. As with interpretation of a treaty, however, interpretation of a Security Council resolution should start with the ordinary meaning of the text of the resolution and the terms used. Interpretation should also take account of the context of the resolution, such as prior Council resolutions on the matter, statements by the representatives of the states in the Council, reports by the Secretary-General etc., as well as the object and purpose of the resolution and of the Charter as a whole. It may be difficult to ascertain if a resolution is intended to be binding. In *Namibia*, the ICJ stated that the determination often requires careful analysis of the language used.[75] In practice, the interpretation may be assisted by the wording used by the Council. Thus, terms like 'decide', 'demands' and 'acting under Chapter VII' will signal that the Council intends its resolution to be binding. When it wants to supplement a binding decision with the power to use force, it often authorizes the use of 'all necessary means'. In non-binding resolutions, the Council frequently uses terms like 'recommend' or 'appeal'. Some resolutions contain both binding and non-binding provisions. An example is Resolution 2396 of December 2017 on the threat from international terrorism/'foreign terrorist fighters', adopted under Chapter VII.[76] While the majority of the resolution's many operative paragraphs merely 'welcomes', 'encourages' states to take a range of measures, there are also certain measures the Council 'decides' that states must adopt.[77]

Some states have sought to justify the use of force on what can only be interpreted as *implied authority* from the Security Council.[78] The most noteworthy—and controversial—example was the US and British invasion of Iraq in March 2003. At the time of the invasion, Iraq had been under Security Council-imposed sanctions for more than a decade for its failure to cooperate with UN weapons inspectors. In November 2002, the Council adopted Resolution 1441, which recalled previous resolutions with regard to Iraq, including a 1990 resolution that had authorized the use of all necessary means to liberate Kuwait and restore international peace and security in the area, and gave Iraq 'a final opportunity' to comply with its disarmament obligations. It also sent the inspectors back to Iraq and obliged the Iraqis to fully cooperate and provide a complete declaration of their weapons programmes. Resolution 1441 did not, however, contain any express authorization for the use of (renewed) force against Iraq

---

[74] See the limited contributions in *Legal Consequences for States of the Continued Presence of South Africa in Namibia (South West Africa)* [1971] ICJ Rep 53 and *Prosecutor v Tadić*, Appeals Chamber Judgment, IT-94-1-A (15 July 1999), paras 293–304.

[75] *Namibia* (n 74) para. 114.   [76] SC Res 2396 (21 December 2017), para. 1.

[77] Ibid, paras 11–13, 15.   [78] For an overview, see Gray (n 18) 348–369.

if the latter did not comply with the renewed inspection regime. It merely noted that the 'Council has repeatedly warned Iraq that it will face serious consequences as a result of its continued violations of its obligations'. The United States and the UK subsequently interpreted the feedback from the weapons inspectors as evidence that Iraq had not cooperated and argued that a new resolution with an *express* authorization for invading Iraq was not necessary.[79] The three other permanent members of the Security Council—France, China and Russia—disagreed.[80] The reliance on implied authority is highly controversial, because it seems to be more consistent with the purposes of the Charter to conclude that a resolution should give a clear—rather than implicit—indication if it is to be interpreted as authorizing the use of force.[81]

After the Iraq controversy, the Council has gone to great lengths to make it very clear what it authorizes and what it does not.[82] This, however, did not prevent new controversies from arising. In March 2011, the Security Council responded to the civil war in Libya by authorizing the establishment and enforcement of a no-fly zone over Libya and the use of 'all necessary measures' to 'protect civilians and civilian populated areas under threat of attack'.[83] When NATO relied on that authorization to conduct a lengthy bombing campaign that eventually led to the collapse of Gaddafi's regime, a number of states—including Russia and China—accused NATO of using the mandate as a pretext for regime change.[84]

13.3.8 Regional organizations

Article 53 of the Charter stipulates that the Security Council may utilize 'regional arrangements or agencies for enforcement action under its authority'. For example, instead of authorizing member states to enforce its resolutions adopted under Chapter VII in their individual capacity, the Council may request states to do so under the framework of a regional organization.[85] Like states, regional organizations' use of force is contingent on Council authorization. In practice, regional organizations have become increasingly important to the Council, and article 53 has been relied on in many instances and by numerous regional organizations. As mentioned in Section

---

[79] See *Letter dated 20 March 2003 from the Permanent Representative of the United States of America to the United Nations Addressed to the President of the Security Council* (21 March 2003), UN Doc. S/2003/351 and *Letter dated 20 March 2003 from the Permanent Representative of the United Kingdom of Great Britain and Northern Ireland to the United Nations addressed to the President of the Security Council* (21 March 2003), UN Doc. S/2003/350. For a more elaborate British justification, see 'Iraq: legal basis for the use of force', UK Foreign and Commonwealth Office, 17 March 2003. For the Australian justification, see UN Doc. S/2003/352 (21 March 2003). In February and March 2003, the United States and the UK tried in vain to secure the adoption of a resolution that would legitimize the use of force against Iraq, see Sean D. Murphy, 'Contemporary Practice of the United States relating to International Law' (2003) 97 *American Journal of International Law* 419, 424.

[80] Murphy (n 79).   [81] Simma (n 6) 1342.

[82] SC Res. 1718 (14 October 2006) and SC Res. 1696 (31 July 2006).

[83] SC Res. 1973 (17 March 2011).

[84] Geir Ulfstein and Hege Føsund Christiansen, 'The Legality of the NATO Bombing in Libya' (2013) 62 *International and Comparative Law Quarterly* 159–171.

[85] See e.g. SC Res 816 (31 March 1993).

13.3.5, the African Union has begun to play a very active role in Council-mandated missions in Africa. NATO (in the former Federal Republic of Yugoslavia, Kosovo, Afghanistan, Iraq and Libya, and for counter-piracy off the Horn of Africa) and the Economic Community of West African States (ECOWAS) have also been willing contributors (in Liberia and the Ivory Coast).

13.4 The unilateral use of force by states

13.4.1 The right to self-defence

13.4.1.1 Introduction

The use of force in self-defence constitutes an exception to the prohibition on the use of force in article 2(4). Under article 51 of the Charter:

> Nothing in the present Charter shall impair the inherent right of individual or collective self-defence if an armed attack occurs against a Member of the United Nations, until the Security Council has taken measures necessary to maintain international peace and security. Measures taken by Members in the exercise of this right of self-defence shall be immediately reported to the Security Council and shall not in any way affect the authority and responsibility of the Security Council under the present Charter to take at any time such action as it deems necessary in order to maintain or restore international peace and security.

The scope of the right is one of the most contested areas of international law.[86] One of the matters of contention is the reference to the 'inherent' right to self-defence. In *Nicaragua*, the ICJ stated that the term testifies to the existence of a right to self-defence under customary international law that exists alongside article 51.[87] US scholars, in particular, have argued that the authority to resort to self-defence under customary law is wider than that under article 51.[88] Others are rightfully sceptical and hold that the material difference between the two 'rights' is very limited.[89] There is little indication that the pre-1945 customary right to self-defence differed in any significant extent from the content of the right adopted under article 51[90] and it is difficult to see how a potentially more expansive right to self-defence under customary international law could have survived the adoption of the Charter in 1945. In neither of the cases where the ICJ has dealt with the right to self-defence has it assumed that the content of the right to self-defence under article 51 should be anything but a manifestation of *the* right to self-defence.[91]

In this section, we discuss the concept of an 'armed attack' (Section 13.4.1.2), whether private actors can trigger a right to self-defence (Section 13.4.1.3), when self-defence can be initiated (Section 13.4.1.4), the dual requirements of necessity

---

[86] Jorg Kammerhofer, 'Uncertainties of the Law on Self-Defence in the United Nations Charter' (2004) 35 *Netherlands Yearbook of International Law* 143.

[87] *Nicaragua* (n 13) paras 193 and 176.

[88] See e.g. Bowett (n 10) 185–186 and ICJ, *Nicaragua* (n 13) Dissenting Opinion of Judge Schwebel, para. 173.

[89] Simma (n 6) 1403–1404.   [90] Brownlie (n 11) 271–274.

[91] *The Wall* (n 15) paras 87 and 109. See also *Armed Activities* (n 24) paras 118, 128, 130–131, 140–149.

and proportionality (Section 13.4.1.5), collective self-defence (Section 13.4.1.6), the relationship between the Security Council and the exercise of self-defence (Section 13.4.1.7) and the link between collective security and self-defence (Section 13.4.1.8).

13.4.1.2 An 'armed attack'

The right to self-defence is triggered by an 'armed attack'. To qualify, an attack *must be of a certain intensity* and not all uses of force prescribed by article 2(4) will trigger a right to self-defence. In *Nicaragua*, the ICJ distinguished between the 'the most grave forms of the use of force' and 'other less grave forms'.[92] The Court also noted that the 'provision of weapons or logistical or other support' to rebels[93] as well as 'a mere frontier incident' fall outside the ambit of article 51.[94] The latter conclusion was reiterated by the Eritrea Ethiopia Claims Commission.[95] Only acts producing or likely to produce very serious consequences, such as territorial invasions, human fatalities or massive destruction of property, will suffice to constitute an 'armed attack'. In *Oil Platforms*, the ICJ found that the 'mining of a single military vessel might be sufficient' to trigger a right to self-defence.[96] In *Nuclear Weapons*, the Court stated that the rules on the use of force in the Charter do not refer to any 'specific weapons', but 'apply to any use of force, regardless of the weapons employed'.[97] Thus, if an attack perpetrated through cyberspace leads to sufficiently serious consequences in a direct and foreseeable manner, it may also constitute an armed attack.[98]

Some argue that a series of small-scale attacks not individually sufficiently grave to constitute an armed attack may be weighed cumulatively. Israel, in particular, has been a strong advocate of such an *accumulation of events* doctrine. In the run-up to its 2006 military operation against Hezbollah in Lebanon, the Israeli government stressed that a Hezbollah operation killing three and leading to the abduction of two Israeli soldiers should not be considered in isolation but rather as one incident in an ongoing campaign by Hezbollah.[99] The ICJ has made a number of remarks that *could* be interpreted as an implicit endorsement of the doctrine,[100] and though it remains controversial in some circles, international legal opinion may well have shifted to such an extent that the doctrine now enjoys a fair amount of support.[101]

Attacks on objects or individuals located on the territory of a state or on a state's military installations and/or military personnel abroad may constitute an armed attack on the state.[102] In *Teheran Hostages*, the ICJ indicated that the same holds true

---

[92] *Nicaragua* (n 13) para. 191. See also *Oil Platforms (Islamic Republic of Iran v United States)*, Judgment [2003] ICJ Rep 161, para. 191. GA Res. 3314 (14 December 1974), para. 2.
[93] *Nicaragua* (n 13) para. 195. See also para. 230.
[94] Ibid, para. 195.
[95] Eritrea Ethiopia Claims Commission, Partial Award, *Jus ad Bellum*, Ethiopia's Claims 1–8, para. 11.
[96] *Oil Platforms* (n 92) para. 72.
[97] *Legality of the Threat or Use of Nuclear Weapons*, Advisory Opinion [1996] ICJ Rep 226, paras 38–39.
[98] *Tallinn Manual 2.0* (n 9) Rule 71.
[99] Yael Ronen, 'Israel, Hizbollah, and the Second Lebanon War' (2006) 9 *Yearbook of International Humanitarian Law* 362, 372.
[100] See *Nicaragua* (n 13) para. 231. See also *Oil Platforms* (n 92) para. 64.
[101] Tom Ruys, *'Armed Attack' and Article 51 of the UN Charter: Evolutions in Customary Law and Practice* (Cambridge University Press, 2010) 169–174. See also Simma (n 6) 1409; Dinstein (n 11) 206–207.
[102] See also GA Res. 3314 (XXIX) Definition of Aggression (14 December 1974), art. 3(c).

for attacks on a state's diplomatic missions and/or diplomatic representatives.[103] It is less clear, however, if attacks on civilian objects and individual citizens abroad, such as tourists, also qualify. While a traditional view holds that this is not the case,[104] there is no universal agreement. The United States and Israel argue that attacks on their citizens abroad *may* constitute an armed attack on their home state if the individuals are targeted because of their nationality.[105] In 1979, Israel relied on the right to self-defence as justification for a special operation in Entebbe, Uganda, which led to the successful evacuation of Israeli citizens held hostage in a French civilian airliner. The international reaction to the Israeli operation was mixed.[106]

13.4.1.3 Attacks by private actors

Traditionally, it was controversial to argue for the existence of a right to self-defence against private actors[107] and the prevailing view seemed to be that a territorial state would have to carry out an armed attack *itself* before it could be the target of legitimate self-defence aimed at the perpetrators of the attack.[108] In response to the terrorist attacks on the United States on 11 September 2001, however, the UN Security Council 'recognized' a right to self-defence without requiring that the attacks be attributed to any state.[109] Today, most agree that the international response to 9/11 shows that acts by private actors can indeed trigger a right to self-defence.[110] As discussed in Chapter 7, while the attacks on 9/11 did not lead to a lowering of the standard of attribution for acts of private individuals under the principles of state responsibility, it seems to have paved the way for an 'unable or unwilling' doctrine, whereby a state may be entitled to resort to measures of self-defence against a private actor, such as a terrorist organization, located in another state if the host state does not have the ability or willingness to stop the private actor's activities.[111] References to the 'unable and unwilling' doctrine are also found in some of the legal justifications by states that participate in the military campaign against 'the Islamic State'/ ISIL in Syria.[112] It should be noted, however, that the ICJ has so far been sceptical about the existence of a right to self-defence against private actors.[113]

---

[103] *United States Diplomatic and Consular Staff in Tehran*, Judgment [1980] ICJ Rep 3, para. 57.

[104] See also Simma (n 6) 1413.

[105] Bowett (n 10) 91–94 and Dinstein (n 11) 220.   [106] Franck (n 11) 84. See also Gray (n 18) 202.

[107] *The Wall* (n 15) Separate Opinion of Judge Kooijmans, para. 35.

[108] See Kammerhofer (n 86) 186. But see Bowett (n 10) 55–56.

[109] SC Res. 1368 (12 September 2001) and SC Res. 1373 (28 September 2001).

[110] Gray (n 18) 199; Dinstein (n 11) 227–230; Franck (n 11) 54. But see Eric P. J. Myjer and Nigel D. White, 'The Twin Towers Attack: An Unlimited Right to Self-Defence?' (2002) 7 *Journal of Conflict and Security Law* 5.

[111] See also the overview in Anders Henriksen, '*Jus ad Bellum* and American Targeted Use of Force to Fight Terrorism Around the World' (2014) 1 *Journal of Conflict and Security Law* 1–40. See also Dinstein (n 11) 289–294 and Ruys (n 101) 505. For a sceptical view, see Olivier Corten, 'The "Unwilling or Unable" Test: Has It Been, and Could It Be, Accepted?' (2016) 29 *Leiden Journal of International Law* 777–799.

[112] See, inter alia, *Letter dated 23 September 2014 from the Permanent Representative of the United States of America to the United Nations addressed to the Secretary-General* (23 September 2016), UN Doc. S/2014/695.

[113] *The Wall* (n 15) para. 139; *Armed Activities* (n 24) paras 146ff. But see *The Wall* (n 15) Separate Opinion of Judge Kooijmans, para. 35, Separate Opinion of Judge Higgins, para. 33, Declaration by Judge Buergenthal, para. 6. See also *Armed Activities* (n 24) Separate Opinion of Judge Kooijmans, para. 29; *Armed Activities* (n 24) Separate Opinion of Judge Simma, para. 8.

13.4.1.4 The initiation of self-defence

According to article 51, the right to self-defence is triggered when an armed attack 'occurs'. Hence, while a state that fears a potential attack from another state may make military preparations in anticipation of the attack and bring the matter to the attention of the Security Council, it may not resort to any measures of self-defence until the attack actually takes place. Despite the clear wording of the article, however, there appears to be overall agreement that a state may be entitled to resort to *anticipatory self-defence* against an expected assault when the threat is *imminent*.[114] Two things must be stressed, however. First, a right to anticipatory self-defence must be interpreted narrowly and only relied on in exceptional circumstances. The earlier a state is allowed to defend itself against potential threats, the harder it is to maintain international peace and stability. Secondly, anticipatory self-defence must be distinguished from so-called pre-emptive or preventive self-defence, which is not exercised in response to an imminent threat but instead to remove a less certain threat of attack or to eliminate the possibility of a future attack by another state. Pre-emptive/preventive self-defence clearly violates article 51. Thus, in the absence of any information that states like Iran or North Korea are on the verge of committing an armed attack on other state, military strikes against these states to prevent them from developing nuclear weapons are incompatible with article 51.

On several occasions, Israel has resorted to what can only be termed preventive—and therefore unlawful—self-defence. In 1981, Israel conducted an airstrike on an alleged Iraqi nuclear reactor that Israel feared would be used to develop nuclear weapons for use against it. The airstrike was criticized by the Security Council as a clear violation of international law.[115] In September 2007, Israel again bombed a suspected nuclear facility, this time in Syria. In the course of the war in Syria, Israel has apparently also conducted a range of airstrikes on targets in Syria allegedly tied to the shipment of sophisticated missiles from Iran to Hezbollah in Lebanon.[116] One of the ways in which the United States responded to the terrorist attacks on 9/11 was to proclaim a new *pre-emptive* or *preventive* self-defence doctrine (the 'Bush Doctrine'), according to which the United States would act against emerging 'threats before they are fully formed'.[117] Outside the United States, however, the attempt to rewrite the temporal dimension of article 51 did not find much support, and even the UK—the closest ally of the United States in the international fight against terrorism—objected.[118]

---

[114] See also Simma (n 6) 1324 and Report of the Secretary-General's High-Level Panel on Threats, Challenges and Change, *A More Secure World: Our Shared Responsibility* (2 December 2004), UN Doc. A/59/565, 188.

[115] SC Res. 487 (19 June 1981).

[116] See the discussion in Oona Hathaway, 'Recent Israeli Strikes in Syria and the Prohibition on the Unilateral Use of Force', Justsecurity.org (16 January 2018) https://www.justsecurity.org/51047/israeli-strikes-syria-prohibition-unilateral-force/ (accessed 1 June 2018).

[117] Covering letter of National Security Strategy of the United States (September 2002).

[118] See the statement of the UK Attorney General, Lord Goldsmith, on 21 April 2004.

13.4.1.5 Necessity and proportionality

To be lawful, self-defence must be necessary and proportionate.[119] The requirement of *necessity* means that a state must ascertain if other, more peaceful, means of redress are available before using force in self-defence. In the words of the US Secretary of State, Daniel Webster, in the famous *Caroline Case*, the state alleging a right to use self-defence is under an obligation to 'show a necessity of self-defence, instant, overwhelming, leaving no choice of means, and no moment for deliberation'.[120] In short, self-defence is use of force as a last resort. In addition, the response to an armed attack should be undertaken either while the attack is still in progress or at least not too long thereafter. This requirement of 'immediacy' must, however, be interpreted with a certain degree of flexibility. It may take time for a victim state to determine the perpetrator of an armed attack, the state may need time for preparation before launching a response and it must also be allowed some time to explore whether a peaceful resolution to the situation is possible. Furthermore, as noted earlier, self-defence against a private actor located in another state is conditional on the inability or unwillingness of the authorities in the host state to stop the private actor's activities. So *before* resorting to the use of force against a private actor in another state, the victim state should request the host state to intervene and stop the private actor's activities.[121]

The principle of *proportionality* requires the victim state to strike a fair balance between the armed attack and the measures taken to stop it. Under the *Caroline* formula, it is for the victim state to show that it 'did nothing unreasonable or excessive; since the act, justified by the necessity of self-defence, must be limited by that necessity, and kept clearly within it'.[122] Proportionality does not mean, however, that the victim state can never resort to more force than that used in the armed attack,[123] nor does it necessarily preclude a state from responding to an armed attack by exercising its right to self-defence in more than one state.[124] To properly assess the proportionality of use of force, it is first necessary to identify the legitimate aim of the use of force and then to determine if the amount of force is either necessary or excessive in order to achieve that aim. In practice, proportionality assessments of instances of alleged self-defence are difficult to make.[125] In part, this is due to a lack of consensus in the international community on the underlying purpose of the right to self-defence.[126] Under a traditional view, the purpose of self-defence is to offer a state under attack the legal justification to use force to halt and repel the attack until the UN Security

---

[119] *Nicaragua* (n 13) para. 14; *Nuclear Weapons* (n 97) para. 41; *Oil Platforms* (n 92) paras 76–77; *Armed Activities* (n 24) para. 147.

[120] The citation is quoted from R. Y. Jennings, 'The *Caroline* and *McLeod* Cases' (1938) 32 *American Journal of International Law* 82, 89.

[121] Ruys (n 101) 506.

[122] Jennings (n 120) 89.

[123] See also Ruys (n 101) 111ff.

[124] Noam Lubell, *Extraterritorial Use of Force Against Non-State Actors* (Oxford University Press, 2010) 66–68.

[125] Simma (n 6) 1426.

[126] Kammerhofer (n 86) 194. See also Ruys (n 101) 111–116.

Council gets the opportunity to take control of the situation and offer the victim state the protection needed. Accordingly, if there is a need for additional force beyond that deemed necessary to halt and repel the armed attack, such force must be authorized by the Security Council.

It is particularly difficult to assess the proportionality of self-defence against international terrorism.[127] Usually, the act of self-defence occurs *after* the terrorist attack has taken place and it is therefore open to criticism for a number of reasons. First, since the response comes after the attack it appears punitive rather than aimed at preventing a threat against the state. Hence, it may resemble an armed countermeasure ('reprisal'), which—as we saw in Chapter 7—is unlawful under international law.[128] Also in this regard, however, the attitude seems to have changed somewhat following the attacks on 9/11. The overwhelming international support for the US claim that it was entitled to rely on a right to self-defence in response to the terrorist attacks, illustrates that the international community may be willing to accept a delayed response in the exercise of necessary and proportionate self-defence against specific terrorist attacks. Secondly, the armed response may appear to be unlawful pre-emptive or even preventive use of force applied in order to protect against future attacks. Thirdly, the response may appear disproportionate if it is employed against a fairly small-scale terrorist attack.

13.4.1.6 Collective self-defence

Article 51 permits not only individual but also collective self-defence and, depending on the circumstances, a state may therefore be entitled to use force in the defence of another state that has been the victim of an armed attack. It is not necessary for the assisting state to also have been attacked or that the exercise of such collective self-defence is triggered by a treaty-based obligation, such as article 5 of the NATO Treaty. The assistance must, however, be given with the consent of the state under attack. According to the ICJ, resort to collective self-defence under customary international law requires the attacked state to declare itself under attack and make a request for assistance.[129] An example of collective self-defence is the use of force against ISIL in Syria by an international coalition of states. In September 2014, the Iraqi government notified the UN Secretary-General that it had asked the United States to lead an international effort to defend Iraq by using force against ISIL in Syria pursuant to the exercise of collective Iraqi self-defence.[130] Article 54 stipulates that the Security Council must be fully informed of activities undertaken by regional organizations for the maintenance of international peace and security.

---

[127] Henriksen, '*Jus ad Bellum* and American Targeted Use of Force to Fight Terrorism Around the World' (n 111).

[128] See also GA Res. 2625 (n 7); *Nuclear Weapons* (n 97) para. 46.

[129] *Nicaragua* (n 13) para. 199.

[130] *Letter dated 23 September 2014 from the Permanent Representative of the United States of America to the United Nations addressed to the Secretary-General* (23 September 2016), UN Doc. S/2014/695.

13.4.1.7 The relationship between the Security Council and the exercise of self-defence

According to article 51, the right to self-defence can only be exercised 'until the Security Council has taken measures necessary to maintain international peace and security'. Hence, collective security and the wish to centralize and collectivize the use of force overrides the exercise of unilateral measures in self-defence and even the right to self-defence is subject to the powers of the Security Council. Thus, if the Council adopts a binding decision that orders a state to cease using force in self-defence the latter must comply. If, however, the Council is unable to agree on a decision or merely adopts a decision that falls short of maintaining or restoring international peace and security, the state resorting to measures in self-defence is entitled to continue to do so.[131] In order to enable the Council to fulfil its role, article 51 requires member states to report any measures taken in self-defence to the Council. Although a lack of reporting may not rule out that the non-reporting state acted in legitimate self-defence, it may indicate that the state is not itself satisfied that it is acting in lawful self-defence.[132]

13.4.1.8 Collective security and self-defence

On a few occasions, the Security Council has responded to an armed attack on a member state by authorizing the use of force under Chapter VII. As mentioned earlier, in reaction to Iraq's 1990 invasion of Kuwait, for example, the Council authorized the member states to use all necessary measures to liberate Kuwait. If the state under attack also requests assistance from other states (see Section 13.4.1.6), two separate authorities for the use of force will then exist: one based on collective self-defence and one based on an authorization from the Security Council. The drafting and the terms adopted in the authorization from the Council generally determine if the material content of the two authorities differs.

13.5 A plea of necessity?

It has been argued that a plea of necessity may under exceptional circumstances serve as a justification for using force in another state.[133] As discussed in Chapter 7, necessity is listed in article 25 in the International Law Commission's (ILC) draft articles on state responsibility as one of several circumstances that may preclude the wrongfulness of an act otherwise in violation of international law.[134] In *Legality of Use of Force*, Belgium relied in part on an alleged state of necessity to justify its participation in the unilateral humanitarian intervention in Kosovo in 1999. According to Belgium, the

---

[131] Dinstein (n 11) 257.

[132] *Nicaragua* (n 13) para. 200. See also Eritrea Ethiopia Claims Commission, Partial Award, *Jus ad Bellum*, Ethiopia's Claims 1–8, para. 11.

[133] See, inter alia, Ole Spiermann, 'Humanitarian Intervention as a Necessity and the Threat or Use of *Jus Cogens*' (2002) 71 *Nordic Journal of International Law* 543.

[134] See n 16.

alleged violation of the prohibition on the use of force in article 2(4) of the UN Charter was justified because the intervention attempted to safeguard 'rights of *jus cogens*'.[135] Invoking necessity to justify breaches of article 2(4) is, however, problematic.[136] As we saw in Chapter 7, necessity cannot be invoked if the actions taken 'seriously impair an essential interest of the State or States to which the obligations exists' and it is difficult to imagine a more essential interest than non-use of force.[137] In addition, a plea of necessity is unavailable if the international obligation in question 'excludes the possibility of invoking necessity'. The Charter does not explicitly mention necessity but it seems logical to conclude that the Charter is the *exclusive* source of the international legal regulation of interstate force in the sense that it rules out the invocation of necessity.[138]

13.6 Contentious use of force

13.6.1 Introduction

In this last section, we shall discuss the legality of three forms of non-UN-authorized use of force that are subject to particular debate. We begin by examining the claim that states do not need an authorization from the Security Council to use force in order to rescue their own nationals in peril abroad (Section 13.6.2). We then discuss the legality of using non-Security Council-authorized force to stop mass atrocities perpetrated against nationals of other states—also known as 'humanitarian intervention' (Section 13.6.3). The final discussion concerns the legality of the US missile strikes in 2017 and 2018 against Syria to deter the Syrian regime from using chemical weapons (Section 13.6.4).

13.6.2 The use of force to rescue nationals abroad

There is no universal agreement on the legality of a state's use of force in another state to rescue its own nationals in imminent danger without the consent of the host state or a resolution from the Security Council.[139] There are essentially two ways such operations can be justified. The first is to argue that the threat posed to the nationals—even though they are located abroad—constitutes an armed attack on their home state that triggers a right to self-defence under article 51.[140] As we saw earlier, however, it is doubtful if attacks on the citizens of a state qualify as attacks on the state itself. Since a rescue operation must nevertheless always comply with the dual requirements of

---

[135] *Legality of Use of Force (Serbia and Montenegro v Belgium)*, Provisional Measures, Order of 10 May 1999, 13–14.

[136] Anders Henriksen and Marc Schack, 'The Crisis in Syria and Humanitarian Intervention' (2014) 1(1) *Journal on the Use of Force and International Law* 122.

[137] See also Jens Elo Rytter, 'Humanitarian Intervention without the Security Council: From San Francisco to Kosovo—and Beyond' (2001) 70 *Nordic Journal of International Law* 134.

[138] James Crawford, 'Second Report on State Responsibility' (1999), UN Doc. A/CN.4/498/Add.2, para. 287.

[139] For a discussion, see Mathias Forteau, 'Rescuing Nationals Abroad' in Weller (n 19) 947–961.

[140] See also Dinstein (n 11) 221, 275–279.

necessity and proportionality, an operation would seem to require not only a genuine threat to the nationals in question but also that the host state is unable or unwilling to secure the safety of the individuals. In addition, to be proportionate a rescue operation cannot pursue goals other than to evacuate the nationals.

The second way to justify a forcible unilateral rescue operation in the absence of consent from the host state or a Security Council authorization is to argue for the existence of a right in customary international law. In fact, some find that sufficient state practice and *opinio juris* exist.[141] It is certainly true that states generally react to the rescue operations of other states with a certain degree of pragmatism and sympathy.[142] The alleged criteria for a customary right to conduct forcible rescue operations appear to be more or less identical to those that would be relevant if an operation were based on a right to self-defence. Thus, to be lawful, there must be a genuine threat to the safety of the nationals, the host state must not offer the protection needed and the sole purpose of the operation must be to rescue the nationals.[143]

Russia has sought to defend the legality of its use of force and subsequent annexation of Crimea by claiming that it was necessary to defend Russian citizens from a genuine threat in the region. That justification must, however, be forcefully rejected. Regardless of one's position on the principled legality of forcible rescue operations abroad, Russia has never proved the existence of any real threat to Russians citizens in Crimea. In addition, Russia's alleged 'rescue' measures have gone far beyond what anyone would consider to be reasonable if they had in fact been taken only to protect the citizens in question.[144]

13.6.3 Unilateral humanitarian intervention

A particularly contentious issue in international law concerns the legality of using force in another state, without consent from the territorial state or a mandate from the Security Council, to stop massive human rights violations perpetrated against the local population, also referred to as 'unilateral humanitarian interventions'. The legality of such interventions was yet again debated in 2013, when a number of Western states, including the United States, asserted in broad terms that the use of force against the Syrian government for its alleged policy of using chemical weapons against its own population did not necessarily require an authorization from the Security Council.[145]

While it is hard not to sympathize with the underlying humanitarian impulses that may drive the proponents of a right to humanitarian intervention, it is difficult to see how such interventions can be lawful.[146] First, as already noted, all uses of force, including force for humanitarian purposes, are covered by the prohibition in article 2(4). Secondly, neither state practice nor *opinio juris* supports the claim that a non-UN-mandated

---

[141] Simma (n 6) 226–228. See also Higgins (n 11) 245–248.

[142] Forteau (n 139) 956–958; Gray (n 18) 159–160. See also Franck (n 11) 76–96.

[143] Simma (n 6) 228. See also Franck (n 11) 96.

[144] See also Veronika Bilkova, 'The Use of Force by the Russian Federation in Crimea' (2015) 75 *ZaöRV* 46–47.

[145] See the overview in Henriksen and Schack (n 136) 122–147.   [146] See also Dinstein (n 11) 76.

right to humanitarian intervention has emerged in customary international law.[147] While the proponents of a right to unilateral humanitarian intervention usually rely on NATO's 1999 intervention in Kosovo, a closer look at the events in 1999 reveals that the intervention only provides very limited support for their argument. In fact, NATO itself was fundamentally divided on the legal basis for the operation, and in the end the operation was primarily justified on moral rather than legal grounds. By October 2018, only three states (the UK, Belgium and Denmark) have *explicitly* argued for the existence of a *right* to humanitarian intervention.[148]

Those who argue in favour of the existence of a customary right to unilateral human-itarian intervention also overlook the fact that major non-Western states—such as Russia, China and India—found the intervention in Kosovo to be in clear violation of the Charter and international law.[149] Furthermore, both the G77[150] and the Non-Aligned Movement have stated their opposition to unilateral humanitarian interventions.[151]

In the debate about humanitarian intervention, reference is often made to the doctrine of 'Responsibility to Protect' (R2P), which was invented in the early 2000s in response to the debates in the 1990s about the legality of humanitarian intervention and the momen-tous moral failures of the international community in Rwanda in 1994 and Bosnia in 1995. R2P later found its way into UN documents, including the 2005 World Summit Outcome Document. The doctrine is based on the premise that sovereignty comes with an obliga-tion to protect civilian populations from atrocities and that all states—both territorial states as well as other members of the international community—have a responsibility to prevent atrocities. But whatever merits R2P has as a common framework for preventing mass atrocity crimes and for highlighting (as well as limiting) the forms of grave breaches of international law a potential right to humanitarian intervention should seek to coun-ter, it does not justify the unilateral use of force.[152] Although the doctrine holds that the international community has a responsibility to help protect populations from atrocities and that 'we are prepared to take collective action' if peaceful means are inadequate, the 2005 World Summit Outcome Document explicitly refers to the existing framework in the Charter and clearly states that military measures shall be taken 'through the Security Council, in accordance with the Charter, including Chapter VII'.[153] In a 2009 report on the implementation of the R2P doctrine, the UN Secretary-General also stated that actions are to be undertaken only in 'conformity with the provisions, purposes and principles of

---

[147] Simma (n 6) 224–226.

[148] For the UK position, see Prime Minister's Office, 'Chemical Weapon Use by Syrian Regime—UK Government Legal Position' (29 August 2013). See also the UK's position in relation to Kosovo in UN Doc. S/PV.3988 (24 March 1999). The Danish position can be found in UPN, Alm.del. Bilag 298, 30 August 2013. As mentioned earlier, Belgium argued for the legality of a right to humanitarian intervention in *Legality of Use of Force (Serbia and Montenegro v Belgium)* (n 10).

[149] UN Doc. S/PV.3988 (24 March 1999), 2, 12 and 15, and UN Doc. S/PV.3989 (26 March 1999), 3, 4, 9 and 16.

[150] Group of 77 South Summit, 'Declaration of the South Summit', Havana, Cuba, 10–14 April 2000, para. 54.

[151] Non-Aligned Movement, 'Comments of the Non-Aligned Movement on the Observations and Recommendations Contained in the Report of the High-Level Panel on Threats, Challenges and Change' (n 114) para. 14.

[152] Henriksen and Schack (n 136) 132–133.

[153] UN Doc. A/Res/60/1 (24 October 2005), para. 139.

the Charter of the United Nations. In that regard, the responsibility to protect does not alter, indeed it reinforces, the legal obligations of Member States to refrain from the use of force except in conformity with the Charter.'[154]

13.6.4 Using force to deter chemical warfare

In April 2017 and April 2018, the United States (in 2018 with the UK and France) launched military strikes against military installations belonging to the Assad regime in response to its alleged use of chemical weapons in the Syrian civil war. Although most commentators seem to consider the strikes as examples of unilateral humanitarian intervention, statements by the United States and the reaction of other states reveal that they had the more limited purpose of (merely) seeking to deter the Syrian regime from continuing its use of chemical weapons in the civil war.[155] Is a state entitled to use force to deter another state from using chemical weapons in times of armed conflict without an authorization from the Security Council?[156]

As we shall see in Chapter 14, there is a very strong international norm against any use of chemical weapons. In fact, the legal prohibition against chemical warfare dates all the way back to the 1899 Peace Conference in The Hague.[157] Furthermore, the 1993 Chemical Weapons Convention (CWC) bans not just the use of chemical weapons but also a host of other activities involving development, stockpiling etc. The Security Council has on numerous occasions stated that the 'proliferation of ... chemical ... weapons, as well as their means of delivery, constitutes a threat to international peace and security'[158] and in September 2013 it responded to a chemical attack in Syria by stressing how 'those responsible for any use of chemical weapons must be held accountable'.[159] In August 2015, it established an investigative mechanism to identify those responsible for the use of chemical weapons in Syria.[160] Before the mandate of the mechanism expired in November 2017 (Russia blocked an extension of the mandate), it had concluded in its reports that both the Syrian Armed Forces (belonging to Assad) and the 'Islamic State' (ISIL) had used chemical weapons in Syria.[161] The international reaction to the missile strikes in

---

[154] UN Doc. A/63/677 (12 January 2009), para. 3.

[155] D. Trump, 'Statement by President Trump on Syria' (6 April 2017) https://www.whitehouse.gov/the-press-office/2017/04/06/statement-president-trump-syria (accessed 30 November 2017). See also Statement by Secretary James N. Mattis on Syria (13 April 2018). An overview of states' reactions can be found in Alonso Gurmendi Dunkelberg and others, 'Mapping States' Reactions to the Syria Strikes of April 2018—A Comprehensive Guide', Justsecurity.org, https://www.justsecurity.org/55835/mapping-states-reactions-syria-strikes-april-2018-a-comprehensive-guide/ (accessed 1 June 2018).

[156] See also Anders Henriksen, 'Trump's Missile Strike on Syria and the Legality of Using Force to Deter Chemical Warfare' (2018) 23(1) *Journal of Conflict and Security Law* 33–48.

[157] Declaration (IV, 2) concerning Asphyxiating Gases, The Hague, 29 July 1899.

[158] See, inter alia, SC Res. 1540 (28 April 2004).

[159] SC Res. 2118 (27 September 2013). See also SC Res. 2235 (7 August 2015).

[160] SC Res. 2235, para. 5.

[161] See, inter alia, Third Report of the Organisation for the Prohibition of Chemical Weapons–United Nations Joint Investigative Mechanism (24 August 2016), UN Doc. S/2016/738/Rev.1 and Seventh Report of the Organisation for the Prohibition of Chemical Weapons–United Nations Joint Investigative Mechanism (26 October 2017), UN Doc. S/2017/904.

2017 and 2018 illustrates the strength of the norm against chemical warfare. This is particularly the case with regard to the military operation in April 2017, when many states offered strong support.[162] The international reaction to the strike in 2018 was less positive.[163]

To some, the strikes on Syria could signal 'the slow and rather painful birth of a nascent right in customary international law allowing States to act forcefully to put an end to the use of particularly repugnant weaponry against a civilian population'.[164] While it cannot be ruled out that the law may gradually move in that direction, we are still far from such a reality. State practice is too scarce and *opinio juris* not sufficiently supportive.[165] A limited right to use force to deter a state from using chemical weapons—if it was ever to develop—would, however, be more clearly demarcated and thus, one would hope, not as prone to potential abuse as a potential and more diffuse right to humanitarian intervention.

Summary

The answers to the questions of when, for what reason and how a member of a community may forcibly submit another to its will is of paramount importance for the maintenance of peaceful relations among the members. *Jus ad bellum* regulates when a state is entitled to resort to the use of force against another state. The relevant rules are found in both the 1945 UN Charter and in customary international law. In practice, however, the content of the rules and principles in question is identical. The 1945 ambition to create a framework for collective security is the key to understanding the legal framework of the Charter. One of the main provisions of the Charter is article 2(4), which bans the member states from using force in their international relations. Under the Charter, only two exceptions to the prohibition in article 2(4) exist. The first exception is the competence of the UN Security Council to authorize the use of force. The second is the inherent right of all states to defend themselves against an armed attack. Since the primary purpose of the UN is to limit the use of unilateral force and collectivize the use of force that may be required to maintain international peace and security, it is hard to see how unilateral use of force that falls outside the use of self-defence and that is not sanctioned by the Council can be lawful under international law.

---

[162] For an overview, see Madison Park, 'Who's with the US on Syria strike and who isn't', CNN (9 April 2017) http://edition.cnn.com/2017/04/07/world/syria-us-strike-world-reaction/ (accessed 2 March 2018) and Chiara Palazzo and Peter Foster, '"Assad bears full responsibility": how the world reacted to Donald Trump's missile strike on Syria', *The Telegraph* (7 April 2017) http://www.telegraph.co.uk/news/2017/04/07/us-air-strike-syria-world-reacted-donald-trumps-decision-intervene/ (accessed 2 March 2018).

[163] See Gurmendi Dunkelberg and others (n 155).

[164] Michael Schmitt and Chris Ford, 'The Use of Force in Response to Syrian Chemical Attacks: Emergence of a New Norm?', Justsecurity.org (8 April 2017) https://www.justsecurity.org/39805/force-response-syrian-chemical-attacks-emergence-norm/ (accessed 2 March 2018).

[165] Henriksen, 'Trump's Missile Strike on Syria and the Legality of Using Force to Deter Chemical Warfare' (n 156) 33–48.

Recommended reading

Classic works on the use of force include Ian Brownlie, *International Law and the Use of Force by States* (Oxford University Press, 1963) and D. W. Bowett, *Self-Defence in International Law* (Frederik A. Praeger, 1958).

More recently see, Yoram Dinstein, *War, Aggression and Self-Defence* (6th edn, Cambridge University Press, 2017); Thomas Franck, *Recourse to Force: State Action Against Threats and Armed Attacks* (Cambridge University Press, 2002); Christine Gray, *International Law and the Use of Force* (3rd edn, Oxford University Press, 2008); and Marc Weller (ed.), *The Oxford Handbook of the Use of Force in International Law* (Oxford University Press, 2015).

Bruno Simma's edited version of *The Charter of the United Nations: A Commentary* (Oxford University Press, 2012) contains an impressive and meticulous discussion of the UN Charter.

Other useful works include Tom Ruys, *'Armed Attack' and Article 51 of the UN Charter: Evolutions in Customary Law and Practice* (Cambridge University Press, 2010).

Questions for discussion

1. How does the tension between, on the one hand, considerations of order and stability and, on the other, overall notions of justice manifest itself in the international regulation of the use of force?

2. The UN Security Council has primary responsibility for the maintenance of international peace and security and has therefore been vested with certain powers. Are there any limits to what the Council can authorize?

3. What legal authority does a regional organization, such as NATO, possess with regard to the use of force?

4. Why is the notion of 'implied authority' of the use of force in Security Council resolutions controversial?

5. According to the text, the so-called 'accumulation of events' doctrine is controversial. Why is that the case?

6. In what regard has the threat from terrorism led to uncertainty about the applicability of the right to self-defence under article 51?

7. How could one argue for the legality of humanitarian intervention in the absence of an authorization from the UN Security Council?

14

The law of armed conflict

CENTRAL ISSUES

1. This chapter examines the international regulation of the conduct of military operations (*jus in bello*).

2. It introduces the relevant sources of law and discusses the application of the law of armed conflict in the different forms of armed conflict.

3. The chapter provides an overview of the issue of battlefield status and presents the distinction between combatants and civilians. It

also examines the basic principles of the conduct of hostilities, including the principle of distinction and the prohibition against causing unnecessary suffering to combatants.

4. It discusses the regulation of both international armed conflict (including belligerent occupation) and non-international armed conflict as well as the interplay between the application of the law of armed conflict and international human rights law in times of armed conflict.

14.1 Introduction

This chapter examines those parts of international law that regulate *how military operations must be conducted—jus in bello*. The identification of norms for proper conduct in times of war has been a topic of interest for thousands of years and some of the most important works in international law have been devoted to the regulation of war.[1] It is, naturally, a field of international law that is of vital importance for the maintenance of peaceful and well-organized relations among states, and it thus constitutes an inherent part of the international law of coexistence. *Jus in bello* is also referred to as the 'law of armed conflict' or 'international humanitarian law', and in the following these terms are used interchangeably. The term 'war' has rarely been used since the 1945 adoption of the UN Charter.

At the outset it is important to reiterate that *jus ad bellum* and *jus in bello* are conceptually distinct and must be applied independently. *All* parties to an armed conflict

---

[1] Christopher Greenwood, 'Historical Development and Legal Basis' in Dieter Fleck (ed.), *The Handbook of International Humanitarian Law* (2nd edn, Oxford University Press, 2008) 15–20.

must comply with the law of armed conflict, regardless of who is considered to have violated its obligations under *jus ad bellum* and who is the victim of aggression.[2]

The law of armed conflict is an inherently pragmatic discipline that accepts that war is a recurring feature of human existence. Rather than outlawing war, it merely offers balanced solutions that take account of both military necessity and humanitarian sentiments. It seeks to limit human suffering to the greatest extent possible without negating the rights of the warring parties to pursue their military objectives.

The chapter begins in Section 14.2 with an overview of the most important legal sources, before Section 14.3 discusses when the law of armed conflict applies. Section 14.4 examines the issue of battlefield status and the distinction between combatants and civilians and Section 14.5 provides an overview of some of the most basic principles governing the conduct of hostilities. Section 14.6 discusses the regulation of belligerent occupation, before Section 14.7 deals with non-international armed conflicts. Section 14.8 explores the relationship between international humanitarian law and human rights law in times of armed conflict.

14.2 The sources of international humanitarian law

The law of armed conflict has developed incrementally in response to often bitter experience of past conflicts and the invention of new means and methods of warfare. As states have continued to develop new modes and forms of killing and maiming other human beings in war, so has the need for revision of and addition to the relevant legal framework.[3] The 'modern' history of international humanitarian law starts with the introduction in the American Civil War (1861–1865) of a manual on existing rules and principles for the conduct of war developed by a German–American professor, Francis Lieber—the 'Lieber Code'.[4] Also, in 1863 the Swiss national Henry Dunant founded the *International Committee of the Red Cross* (ICRC) in Geneva, which has since played a vital role in the development of international humanitarian law.

The arguably most important conventions are the four 1949 Geneva Conventions (GC I–IV), which have 196 parties and are the most ratified treaties in the world. The Conventions cover the Condition of the Wounded and Sick in Armed Forces in the Field (I), the Condition of Wounded, Sick and Shipwrecked Members of Armed Forces at Sea (II), the Treatment of Prisoners of War (III) and the Protection of Civilian Persons in Time of War (IV). In 1977, two important additional protocols to the four Geneva Conventions were adopted: The Additional Protocol Relating to the Protection of Victims of International Armed Conflicts (AP I) and the Additional

---

[2] See also the preamble to the 1977 Additional Protocol Concerning the Protection of Victims of International Armed Conflict.

[3] For a debate about contemporary armed conflicts and some of the challenges they pose, see, inter alia, Steven Haines, 'The Nature of War and the Character of Contemporary Armed Conflict' in Elizabeth Wilmshurst (ed.), *International Law and the Classification of Conflicts* (Oxford University Press, 2012) 9–31.

[4] Gary Solis, *The Law of Armed Conflict* (Cambridge University Press, 2010) 39–46.

Protocol Relating to the Protection of Victims of Non-International Armed Conflicts (AP II). Certain conventions focus on the means and methods of warfare. An example is Hague Convention IV and the annex thereto—also known as the Hague Regulations—which is of vital importance to the regulation of belligerent occupation. Other examples include the 1954 Convention for the Protection of Cultural Property in the Event of Armed Conflict, the 1972 Convention on Biological Weapons, the 1980 Conventional Weapons Convention, the 1993 Chemical Weapons Convention (CWC), the 1997 Ottawa Land Mines Convention on anti-personnel mines and the 2008 Convention on Cluster Munitions.

Some older conventions contain 'general participation' clauses—*clausula si omnes*—whereby the convention only applies if *all* belligerents are parties to the convention.[5] Although such clauses are based on the prima facie sensible assumption that all parties to an armed conflict should be bound by the same sets of rules and obligations, they may preclude the application of a convention in a conflict that involves a group of states simply because one of the parties is not a party to the convention. More recent conventions, therefore, stipulate that contracting parties are bound by the conventions in their *mutual relations* even if one of the parties to the conflict is not a party to the convention.[6] The basic rules in the major treaties in the law of armed conflict generally reflect customary international law binding on all states.[7] This is certainly the case with regard to the central provisions of the 1907 Hague Regulations,[8] 1949 GC I–IV[9] and the weapons conventions listed above, with the exception of the 1997 Ottawa Convention[10] and the 2008 Convention on Cluster Munitions. The 1977 additional protocols contain a number of provisions that were so controversial that certain states, including the United States, Israel, India and Pakistan,[11] decided not to ratify them. These are therefore not binding under customary international law. The International Court of Justice (ICJ) has referred to the fundamental rules of the law of armed conflict as constituting a 'minimum yardstick' that reflects 'elementary considerations of humanity'.[12] In *The Wall*, the Court found that these rules are of an *erga omnes* character.[13]

---

[5] See, inter alia, art. 2 of the 1907 Hague Convention IV.

[6] See Common Art. 2.

[7] For an overview of relevant customary international law, see Jean-Marie Henckaerts and Louise Doswald-Beck, *Customary International Humanitarian Law*, Vol. I (Cambridge University Press, 2005).

[8] See, inter alia, *Legal Consequences of the Construction of a Wall in the Occupied Palestinian Territory*, Advisory Opinion [2004] ICJ Rep 136, para. 89. See also HCJ 769/02, *Public Committee Against Torture in Israel v Government of Israel*, 13 December 2006, para. 20.

[9] See *Legality of the Threat or Use of Nuclear Weapons*, Advisory Opinion [1996] ICJ Rep 226, para. 79.

[10] Henckaerts and Doswald-Beck (n 7) 282.

[11] See the overview in Yves Sandoz, Christophe Swinarski and Bruno Zimmermann (eds), *Commentary on the Additional Protocols of 8 June 1977 to the Geneva Conventions of 12 August 1949* (ICRC/Martinus Nijhoff, 1987) 39–56. The US position is available in *Letter of Transmittal from President Ronald Reagan, Protocol II Additional to the 1949 Geneva Conventions, and Relating to the Protection of Victims of Non-International Armed Conflict* (1987) 81 *American Journal of International Law* 910.

[12] *Military and Paramilitary Activities in and against Nicaragua (Nicaragua v United States)*, Merits [1986] ICJ Rep 14, para. 218. See also *Nuclear Weapons* (n 9) para. 79.

[13] *The Wall* (n 8) para. 157.

14.3 The application of international humanitarian law

14.3.1 Introduction

International law used to distinguish clearly between a 'state of peace' and a 'state of war' and the relations between two or more states were governed by either of the two. In addition, the outbreak of war was governed by formal criteria, most notably by issuing declarations of war. In the 21st century, however, the line separating war and peace is rarely so easily discernible and the application of the law of armed conflict does not depend on the subjective intentions of the parties and a declaration of war. In fact, since the adoption of the 1945 UN Charter, declarations of war are rare.

The law of armed conflict applies in times of armed conflict, but none of the conventions define 'armed conflict'. In *Tadić*, the International Criminal Tribunal for the former Yugoslavia (ICTY) stated that an armed conflict exists 'whenever there is a resort to armed force between States or protracted armed violence between governmental authorities and organized armed groups or between such groups within a State'.[14] This '*Tadić* definition' reflects the treaty-based differentiation between 'international armed conflicts', involving the armed forces of two or more states, and 'non-international armed conflicts', which involve fighting between either a state and a private organized armed group or between two or more such groups.

We begin by examining 'international armed conflict' (Section 14.3.2), before we discuss 'non-international armed conflict' (Section 14.3.3). We then turn our attention to the thorny question of classification of so-called 'transnational armed conflict' (Section 14.3.4) and to changes in conflict status (Section 14.3.5).

14.3.2 International armed conflict

According to Article 2 of the Geneva Conventions, the Conventions apply in 'all cases of declared war or of any other armed conflict which may arise between two or more of the High Contracting Parties, even if the state of war is not recognized by one of them'. They thereby cover 'classic' interstate armed conflicts, where two or more states fight each other, and it is towards the regulation of such conflicts that the majority of the law of armed conflict is aimed. An international armed conflict arises in relation to 'any difference arising between two States and leading to the intervention of members of the armed forces' and it makes 'no difference how long the conflict lasts, how much slaughter takes place, or how numerous are the participating forces'.[15] In principle, therefore, Turkey's downing of a Russian fighter jet in Turkish airspace in December 2015 was sufficient to initiate an international armed conflict between Turkey and Russia. To the present author, however, the limited use of force by one state directed

---

[14] ICTY, *Prosecutor v Tadić*, Appeals Chamber, Decision on the Defence Motion for Interlocutory Appeal on Jurisdiction, ICTY-94-1 (2 October 1995), para. 70.

[15] ICRC, *Commentary on the First Geneva Convention* (Cambridge University Press, 2016) paras 236–44. See also Yoram Dinstein, including his *The Conduct of Hostilities under the Law of International Armed Conflict* (2nd edn, Cambridge University Press, 2010) 28–29.

against private individuals on the territory of another state (without the latter's consent) will not always be sufficient to conclude that an international armed conflict has arisen 'between' the two states.[16] The determination is nevertheless *factual* and it is immaterial whether the involved states recognize the existence of an armed conflict. It is also immaterial if one of the parties involved is not formally recognized as a 'state'. As long as two or more parties can be said to satisfy the conditions for statehood that we visited in Chapter 4, the armed conflict is 'international'.[17] Under AP I, an 'international armed conflict' includes certain armed conflicts involving a state and a non-state actor. Thus, according to article 1(4) of AP I, armed conflict in which 'peoples are fighting against colonial domination and alien occupation and against racist régimes in the exercise of their right of self-determination' is also deemed to be of an international character. The Protocol has yet to be applied to such a conflict and does not reflect customary international law.

The area of war in an international armed conflict includes all the territories of the parties to the conflict, including territorial waters and the airspace above the territories, the high seas, including the airspace above and the sea floor, as well as the exclusive economic zones (EEZs) of neutral states.[18] Unless a neutral state allows one of the belligerents to conduct military operations on its territory, the latter shall not be made part of the conflict. Historically, international armed conflicts came to an end with the conclusion of a peace treaty—or at least an express declaration—but, like declarations of war, peace treaties are now rare. In practice, hostilities may be terminated on either a temporary or a permanent basis. A *ceasefire* is a temporary suspension of military operations, generally serving humanitarian purposes such as collecting the wounded, delivering aid or facilitating the removal of civilians, often agreed to by local commanders. An *armistice*, on the other hand, is usually intended to prepare for the permanent termination of the conflict.[19] The conflict cannot generally be considered to have ended unless there is evidence that neither of the parties *intends* to resume hostilities. The conflict must have ended in a 'general, definitive and effective way'.[20] An intention to permanently suspend hostilities may sometimes be inferred from the overall circumstances. For example, although the 2011 international armed conflict between a number of Western states and Gaddafi's Libya did not end with the conclusion of a formal peace treaty, it is generally assumed that the conflict

---

[16] See also the discussion in Noam Lubell, 'Fragmented Wars: Multi-Territorial Military Operations against Armed Groups' (2017) 93 *International Law Studies* 234. If this reading is correct, neither the sinking of the *Rainbow Warrior* by French agents in 1985 in New Zealand nor Russia's alleged attempt to poison and assassinate a former Russian intelligence officer in Salisbury, UK, in March 2018 initiated an international armed conflict between, respectively, France and New Zealand, and Russia and the UK. For a different position on the incident in Salisbury, see Ryan Goodman and Alex Whiting, 'Salisbury Response Options: Take Putin to Int'l Criminal Court', Justsecurity.org (13 March 2018) https://www.justsecurity.org/53713/salisbury-response-options-putin-intl-criminal-court/ (accessed 20 October 2018).

[17] Dinstein (n 15) 29.

[18] For an overview, see also Katja Schöberl, 'The Geographical Scope of Application of the Conventions' in Andrew Clapham, Paola Gaeta and Marco Sassòli (eds), *The 1949 Geneva Conventions: A Commentary* (Oxford University Press, 2015) 67–83.

[19] See the overview in Greenwood (n 1) 66–72.

[20] ICRC, *Commentary on GC I* (n 15), art. 2, paras 277–283.

was brought to an end with the fall of Gaddafi and the general conclusion of the aerial bombing campaign.[21] Importantly, certain obligations arise as soon as active hostilities have ended regardless of the existence of a formal peace treaty. Under GC III, for example, prisoners of war 'shall be released and repatriated without delay after the cessation of active hostilities'.

International armed conflicts include cases of *belligerent occupation*. According to Common Article 2 of GC I–IV, the Conventions also apply in situations of total or partial occupation, 'even if the said occupation meets with no armed resistance'. A territory is 'occupied' when it is actually placed under the authority of the hostile army[22] and the occupation extends only to the territory where such authority has been established and can be exercised.[23] Thus, 'effective control' is an indispensable condition of belligerent occupation.[24] A well-known example was the 2003–2004 US/UK-led occupation of Iraq following the March 2003 invasion and subsequent fall of the Saddam Hussein regime. A more recent one is that of Crimea, which remains *de jure* part of Ukraine despite Russia's March 2014 annexation of the territory. In *The Wall*, the ICJ found that Israel is an occupying power in the Palestinian territories 'situated between the Green Line and the former eastern boundary of Palestine under the Mandate', including in East Jerusalem.[25] With the exception of East Jerusalem, this is recognized by Israel.[26] The key to belligerent occupation is the lack of consent from the territorial state to the presence of the foreign troops, and occupation may therefore result not only from an outright invasion, but also from a state's refusal to withdraw its military from the territory of a state that no longer consents to the troops' presence. In *Armed Activities*, for example, Uganda became an occupying power in the Ituri region in the DRC when its forces remained on Congolese territory after the DRC had asked all foreign troops to leave.[27] The occupying power remains bound by its obligations 'for the duration of the occupation'.[28] In most cases, occupation ends when the occupying power no longer exercises effective control over the occupied territory, either because it withdraws or is driven out. Israel's status as an occupying power in Gaza after its 2005 disengagement is less clear.[29] The occupation of Iraq is so far the only instance in which occupation was brought to an end not by the withdrawal of the foreign troops but by the adoption of a resolution by the UN Security Council and the formation of a new local government.[30] Since the new government invited the US and UK

[21] A discussion of the war in Libya is available in Louise Arimatsu and Mohbuda Choudhury, 'The Legal Classification of the Armed Conflicts in Syria, Yemen and Libya', Chatham House, March 2014, 34–41.

[22] See art. 42 of the 1907 Hague Regulations.

[23] *Armed Activities on the Territory of the Congo (Democratic Republic of the Congo v Uganda)*, Judgment [2005] ICJ Rep 168, para. 172.

[24] See also the criteria listed in ICTY, *Prosecutor v Naletilić et al.*, Trial Chamber, Judgment (31 March 2003), para. 217. For an overview, see Yoram Dinstein, *The International Law of Belligerent Occupation* (Cambridge University Press, 2009) 38–45.

[25] *The Wall* (n 8) para. 78.

[26] *Public Committee Against Torture* (n 8) paras 19–20. Israel is also an occupying power in the Golan Heights, which were occupied by Israeli forces in June 1967, see SC Res. 497 (17 December 1981).

[27] *Armed Activities* (n 23) paras 53 and 172.   [28] GC IV art. 6. But see also art. 6(3).

[29] A discussion is available in Iain Scobbie, 'Gaza' in Wilmshurst (n 3) 280–316.

[30] SC Res. 1546 (8 June 2004).

forces to remain in Iraq, the presence of the foreign troops after 28 June 2004 was based on Iraq's consent.

14.3.3 Non-international armed conflict

International humanitarian law also covers armed conflicts not involving two or more states—also known as non-international armed conflict. Common Article 3 of GC I–IV contains a number of minimum guarantees that must be applied by all parties in 'the case of armed conflict not of an international character occurring in the territory of one of the High Contracting Parties'. Common Article 3 conflicts have traditionally been referred to as 'internal' armed conflicts or 'civil wars'.[31]

A non-international armed conflict is distinguished from 'acts of banditry or unorganized and short-lived insurrections' that fall outside Common Article 3.[32] Two conditions must be fulfilled for violence to qualify as non-international armed conflict. First, *the level of violence must surpass a certain minimum threshold*. Thus, a non-international armed conflict is in many respects similar to an international war, but it takes place within the confines of a single country.[33] The second condition is that both parties to the conflict must be *militarily organized*. Since the forces of a state party are usually sufficiently organized the requirement is mostly relevant for private actor(s).[34] According to the ICRC, 'the group does not need to have the level of organisation of state armed forces', but it 'must possess a certain level of hierarchy and discipline and the ability to implement the basic obligations of IHL'.[35] The requirement of military organization may be difficult to fulfil. In the civil war in Syria, for example, it took a substantial amount of time before the opposition became sufficiently militarily organized.[36] Conceptually, it is not impossible for a state to be engaged in an armed conflict with a terrorist organization provided the *Tadić* conditions are fulfilled.[37]

The category of non-international armed conflict was expanded with the adoption of AP II in 1977. In practice, however, the protocol has only been applied in a limited number of armed conflicts. It merely applies to armed conflicts between a state and an organized armed group under responsible command that is capable of exercising 'such control over a part of its territory as to enable them to carry out sustained and concerted military operations and to implement this Protocol'.[38] The protocol seems to have become applicable during the 2011 armed conflict in Libya, when the armed insurgents assumed control of parts of Libyan territory.[39] The protocol also appears to apply in the civil war in Yemen[40] and in the armed conflict in Ukraine, where

---

[31] See also art. 8(2)(f) of the Rome Statute of the International Criminal Court.

[32] See also the discussion in ICRC, *Commentary on GC I* (n 15) paras 414–445. See also *Tadić*, Trial Judgment, para. 562 and *Prosecutor v Akayesu*, Judgment, ICTR-96-4-T (2 September 1998), para. 619.

[33] See also art. 8(2)(b) of the Rome Statute of the International Criminal Court.

[34] See also ICTY, *Prosecutor v. Đorđević*, Judgment, IT-05-87/1 (23 February 2011), paras 1523–1526.

[35] ICRC, *Commentary on GC I* (n 15) para. 429.

[36] See the discussion in Arimatsu and Choudhury (n 21) 15.

[37] Noam Lubell, 'The War (?) against Al-Qaeda' in Wilmshurst (n 3) 434–437.   [38] AP II art 1.

[39] Arimatsu and Choudhury (n 21) 34–38.   [40] Ibid, 29–30.

pro-Russian militants control parts of Eastern Ukraine.[41] Russia may, however, be so involved in the armed conflict in Ukraine that it qualifies as an 'international' rather than 'non-international' conflict (see Section 14.3.5). In a non-international armed conflict, the area of war in principle covers the entirety of the state's territory. For a specific act to be regulated by the law of armed conflict it must, however, be closely related to the hostilities in the armed conflict.

According to the ICTY, the law of armed conflict applies in a non-international armed conflict until 'a peaceful settlement is achieved'.[42] In practice, though, violence may cease to qualify as a non-international armed conflict if it falls below the minimum threshold or if it no longer involves two parties that can be said to be sufficiently organized. A non-international armed conflict may also be brought to an end if the conflict evolves into an international armed conflict (see Section 14.3.5).[43]

14.3.4 Classification of so-called 'transnational armed conflicts'

It is not clear how one should classify an armed conflict between a state and a private actor that is not confined to the territory of one state—sometimes referred to as 'transnational armed conflict'. The question is relevant, for example, in relation to the hostilities between a coalition of states and the so-called Islamic State (ISIL) in Syria and Iraq as well as to the decade-long US policy of targeted killings—often with the use of unmanned aerial vehicles—of suspected terrorists in states such as Pakistan, Yemen and Somalia. As is well known, the US government adopts the position that the United States is engaged in an armed conflict with members of al Qaida and associated forces.[44] In the wake of the 9/11 attacks, the US claimed that the conflict was a new and different form of armed conflict that was not governed by the conventions of international humanitarian law.[45] That position has been discarded and the debate is now focused on determining whether a 'transnational' armed conflict should be classified as an international armed conflict or a non-international armed conflict.[46] To the present author, hostilities between a state and a private actor not limited to the territory of one state should be considered a non-international armed conflict as long as the actual hostilities only involve the state and the non-state actor and the state does not occupy foreign territory. Classification would thereby focus on the nature of the parties rather than the geographical location of

---

[41] Robert Heinsch, 'Conflict Classification in Ukraine: The Return of the "Proxy War"?' (2015) 91 *International Law Studies* 356.

[42] *Tadić* (n 14) para. 70.

[43] See also the view in ICRC, *Commentary on GC I* (n 15) paras 483–502 and Yoram Dinstein, *Non-International Armed Conflicts in International Law* (Cambridge University Press, 2014) 47–50.

[44] Harold H. Koh, 'The Obama Administration and International Law', Remarks at the Annual Meeting of the American Society of International Law, Washington DC, 25 March 2010.

[45] *Memorandum From Alberto R. Gonzales, Counsel to the President, to President Bush*, 25 January 2002. See also *Salim Ahmed Hamdan, Petitioner v Donald H. Rumsfeld et al., Brief for Respondents*, 38 and 48.

[46] Some argue that transnational armed conflict should be accepted as a third and novel form of conflict, see Geoffrey Corn, 'Hamdan, Lebanon and the Regulation of Armed Hostilities: The Need to Recognize a Hybrid Category of Armed Conflict' (2006) 40 *Vanderbilt Journal of Transnational Law* 295.

the fighting.[47] This also seems to be the position of the International Criminal Court (ICC) in the *Lubanga* case[48] and the US Supreme Court.[49] While the ICRC agrees that hostilities between a foreign state and a private actor are a non-international armed conflict, it finds that the relationship between the foreign state and the territorial state must be classified as an international armed conflict if the territorial state has not consented to the foreign state's use of force on its territory.[50] This conclusion is supported by the ICJ's judgment in *Armed Activities*.[51] According to the ICRC, the international armed conflict will run parallel to the non-international armed conflict between the foreign state and the private actor.[52]

The geographical scope of a conflict between a state and a non-state actor that is not limited to the territory of one state is uncertain. The present author agrees with the position that the conflict involves not only the territory of the state that is a party to the conflict but in principle also any state whose territory is being used by the private actor to commit acts that are connected to the conflict. The purpose of the law of armed conflict is not to set geographical limits on an armed conflict (that is for the *jus ad bellum* to do) but rather to regulate the hostilities wherever they occur.[53] In practice, then, the armed conflict goes where the hostilities go. As we shall see in Section 14.8, however, the simultaneous application of human rights law in non-international armed conflict will often impact the questions if and how a state can use deadly force against a civilian who is participating directly in the hostilities.

14.3.5 Changes of conflict status

It is not infrequent that armed conflicts develop and require new classification. First of all, a non-international armed conflict can be 'internationalized' and attain an international character if another state becomes a party to the conflict. This may occur if a foreign state intervenes and begins to exercise 'overall control' over the private actor. According to the ICTY, the traditional 'effective control' test for state attribution for acts of private individuals that we visited in Chapter 7 is replaced with an 'overall control' test, whereby attribution occurs as soon as a state 'has a role in organizing, coordinating or planning the military actions' of a militarily organized group in addition to financing, training and equipping or providing operational support.[54] While the ICJ has rejected the 'overall control' test for the purposes of state attribution under general international law,[55] it has left open the possibility that it could be 'suitable'

---

[47] See also Noam Lubell, *Extraterritorial Use of Force Against Non-State Actors* (Oxford University Press, 2010) 100–104 and the same author in n 16.

[48] *Prosecutor v Thomas Lubanga Dyilo*, Judgment, ICC-01/04-01/06 (14 March 2012), para. 539.

[49] *Hamdan v Rumsfeld*, 548 US 557 (2006), see pp. 65–69 of the judgment.

[50] ICRC, *Commentary on GC I* (n 15) art. 3, see paras 465–477. See also Dapo Akande, 'Classification of Armed Conflicts: Relevant Legal Concepts' in Wilmshurst (n 3) 73–79.

[51] *Armed Activities* (n 23) paras 163–165.

[52] ICRC, *Commentary on GC I* (n 15) art. 3, see para. 477.   [53] Lubell (n 16) 244–247.

[54] ICTY, *Tadić* (n 14) Appeals Chamber, Judgment, para. 137. See also ICRC, *Commentary on GC I* (n 15) art. 2, paras 271–273.

[55] See Section 7.3.6.

for determining whether or not an armed conflict is international.[56] A non-international armed conflict may also evolve into one or more international armed conflicts if the state in which the conflict occurs disintegrates and is replaced by new sovereign states. In *Tadić*, the ICTY concluded that the Federal Republic of Yugoslavia's continued participation in the armed conflict in Bosnia after the latter acquired status as an independent state in 1992 ignited an international armed conflict between those two states.[57]

An international armed conflict may be 'internalized' if a state ceases to exercise 'overall control' over a private actor involved in an armed conflict with a state or if the private actor in question succeeds in replacing the former government and subsequently gives its consent to the continued foreign intervention. The latter occurred in 2001 in Afghanistan, when the international armed conflict between Afghanistan and a number of states in an international US-led coalition evolved into a non-international armed conflict once the Taleban had been ousted and replaced with a new Afghan government led by Hamid Karzai.[58]

The 2011 armed conflict in Libya is an interesting case study of conflict classification. As we saw earlier, the armed conflict between pro- and anti-government forces constituted a non-international armed conflict governed by Common Article 3 and—after the rebels' successful seizure of substantial parts of Libyan territory—seemingly also AP II to the Geneva Conventions. Following the initiation of an aerial bombing campaign by an international coalition against the Libyan regime in March 2011, the non-international armed conflict was supplemented by an international armed conflict. It also bears noting that a number of states rendered extensive support to the rebels, and that the support would have had the effect of 'internationalizing' the non-international armed conflict between the rebels and the government forces if it equated to exercising 'overall control' of the rebels.[59] The Libyan case is complicated even further by the French decision to recognize the rebels as the legitimate representatives of the Libyan people *before* the launch of the air campaign and the physical ousting of Gaddafi and the government forces. This raises the question of whether the recognition transformed the international armed conflict between France and the pro-Gaddafi forces into one of a non-international character.[60] The relationship between classification of armed conflict and the role of recognition is complicated and the law may be far from settled. The war in Syria also illustrates how a state may be the scene of separate armed conflicts raging at the same time. By October 2018, for example, the Syrian war appeared to still consist of at least (and arguably more) three separate armed conflicts: First, with the assistance of Russia and Iran, the Assad regime is involved in a non-international armed conflict with a range of armed groups with diverging objectives. Secondly, there is seemingly still a non-international armed conflict between ISIS and the international coalition, which has yet to be brought to an end. Thirdly, in the north of Syria, Turkish forces are involved in an 'on and off' armed conflict with various Kurdish militias. That conflict may be classified as either an international or a non-international armed conflict depending on the level of control that Turkey

---

[56] *Application of the Convention on the Prevention and Punishment of the Crime of Genocide (Bosnia and Herzegovina v Serbia and Montenegro)*, Judgment [2007] ICJ Rep 43, para. 404.

[57] ICTY, *Tadić* (n 14) para. 162.

[58] For a discussion, see Françoise J. Hampson, 'Afghanistan 2001–2010' in Wilmshurst (n 3) 242–258.

[59] For a discussion, see Arimatsu and Choudhury (n 21) 39–40.   [60] Ibid, 40.

exercises over Syrian territory and thus its status as an occupying power.[61] Furthermore, aside from these conflicts, Syria has been a party to very brief international armed conflicts with the United States when the latter launched cruise missiles at Syrian military bases in April 2017 and April 2018.

14.4 Battlefield status in international armed conflict

14.4.1 Introduction

The protection offered to individuals in times of armed conflict depends on the classification of the armed conflict and on the specific status of the individuals. International humanitarian law offers a much more detailed regime of protection in times of international armed conflict than in non-international armed conflict and the overview in this section is limited to regulation in international armed conflict (including cases of belligerent occupation). Non-international armed conflict is dealt with in Section 14.7. In international armed conflict, everyone has a status and an accompanying level of legal protection. The most relevant categories are those of 'combatants' and 'civilians'.

14.4.2 Combatants

Combatants consist of members of the armed forces, including organized armed groups belonging to the parties to the armed conflict and other individuals who take a direct part in the hostilities. All remaining individuals are civilians.[62] Since they take part in the armed conflict, combatants can lawfully be the object of lethal force at all times and in all circumstances[63] or detention until the end of hostilities. Importantly, detention of enemy combatants, known as internment, is not a punishment but simply a way of preventing the combatant from continued participation in combat. In a sense, the combatant trades his liberty for the safety of his life. Internment is therefore not conditional on criminal prosecution. If, however, a combatant becomes 'hors de combat' he shall not be made the object of attack. A combatant is hors de combat if he is in the power of an adverse party, if he clearly expresses an intention to surrender, or if he has been rendered unconscious or is otherwise incapacitated by wounds or sickness, and is therefore incapable of defending himself. Also, the individual must abstain from any hostile act and must not attempt to escape.

Conceptually, one can distinguish between lawful/privileged and unlawful/unprivileged combatants.[64] A combatant may be considered lawful if he is entitled to take part in the hostilities and unlawful if he is not so entitled. Entitlement to participate

---

[61] 'Military Occupation of Syria by Turkey', RULAC, Geneva Academy, http://www.rulac.org/browse/conflicts/military-occupation-of-syria#collapse4accord (accessed 1 June 2018). For a discussion, see Terry D. Gill, 'Classifying the Conflict in Syria' (2016) 92 *International Law Studies* 353.

[62] AP I art. 50(1). See also Henckaerts and Doswald-Beck (n 7) rule 5.

[63] For the regulation of the use of deadly force during belligerent occupation, see Section 14.6.

[64] Dinstein (n 15) 33–35. Some presentations of battlefield status use a different terminology and desist from relying on two categories of combatant (lawful/unlawful) in order to operate with two categories of civilians (privileged/unprivileged), see e.g. *Public Committee Against Torture* (n 8) remarks by Vice President E. Rivlin, para. 2. In practical terms, the differences in approach lead to the same results.

in the hostilities is crucial, because lawful and unlawful combatants are treated very differently. A lawful combatant possesses so-called 'combatant's privilege', which means that the individual is offered immunity by international law from prosecution for merely participating in the hostilities.[65] In addition, if a lawful combatant is captured by the enemy, the individual benefits from protection as a prisoner of war under GC III.[66] An unlawful combatant, on the other hand, does not have 'combatant's privilege' and may therefore be criminally prosecuted under the national laws of the detaining state for acts perpetrated during the hostilities. Unlike a lawful combatant, then, an unlawful combatant may be prosecuted for murder if the individual has used deadly force against a member of the enemy's armed forces. Furthermore, an unlawful combatant does not benefit from protection as a prisoner of war under GC III. But unlawful combatants are not devoid of protection in the law of armed conflict. Unlawful combatants are protected under GC IV[67] and, if applicable in the conflict, AP I.[68] In addition, article 75 of AP I lists a number of fundamental guarantees, which protect individuals 'who do not benefit from a more favourable protection' and which are generally considered to reflect customary international law.

The requirements for being a lawful combatant have undergone historical changes. For those states that are (still) not parties to AP I, the law operates with three main types of lawful combatants, reflected in GC III. The first category is that of 'members of the armed forces of a state as well as members of militias or volunteer corps forming part of such forces'.[69] The second type is 'members of other militias and members of other volunteer corps, including those of organized resistance movements' that fulfil four cumulative conditions. They must be 'commanded by a person responsible for his subordinates', have 'a fixed distinctive sign recognizable at a distance', carry 'their arms openly' and conduct their 'operations in accordance with the laws and customs of war'.[70] The third and final category is the rare case of *levée en masse*, where the inhabitants of a non-occupied territory 'spontaneously take up arms' to resist an invading force 'without having had time to form themselves into regular armed units, provided they carry arms openly and respect the laws and customs of war'.[71]

AP I erases the formal distinction between regular and irregular forces in GC III and introduces a less stringent standard for lawful combatancy. First, article 43(1) of AP I stipulates that the armed forces 'consist of all organized armed forces, groups and units which are under a command responsible to that Party for the conduct of its subordinates'. Secondly, although article 44(3) states that combatants must distinguish themselves from the civilian population when engaged in an attack or in a military operation preparatory to an attack, it also notes that 'the nature of the hostilities' may

---

[65] AP I art. 43(2).   [66] AP I art. 44(1).

[67] Jean S. Pictet, *Commentary to the IV Geneva Convention Relative to the Protection of Civilian Persons in Time of War* (ICRC, 1958) 51. See also *Prosecutor v Delalić et al.*, Judgment, IT-96-21-T (16 November 1998), para. 271. *Public Committee Against Torture* (n 8) para. 28.

[68] See, inter alia, arts 44(4) and 45(3).   [69] GC III art. 4(1).

[70] GC III art. 4(2)(a)–(d). See also art. 1 of Annex to the 1907 Hague Convention IV Concerning the Laws and Customs of War on Land.

[71] GC III art. 4(6). See also art. 2 of the 1907 Hague Convention IV Concerning the Laws and Customs of War on Land.

make that requirement hard to comply with. Thus, an individual will remain a lawful combatant as long as he, 'in such situations', carries his arms openly: (1) 'during each military engagement' and (2) 'during such time as he is visible to the adversary while he is engaged in a military deployment preceding the launching of an attack in which he is to participate'. The more relaxed standards in article 44(3) have been criticized for reducing '*ad absurdum* the conditions for lawful combatancy'[72] and do not reflect customary international law.

The law of armed conflict contains a number of provisions that are meant to ensure that an individual is not deprived of the rightful status of lawful combatant. For parties who are not bound by AP I, the relevant provision is article 5 in GC III, according to which a person who has 'committed a belligerent act' and 'has fallen into the hands of the enemy' shall be protected by the Convention 'until such time as their status has been determined by a competent tribunal'. In AP I, the protection against 'mistaken' status is contained in article 45(1), which stipulates that anyone who has taken part in hostilities and fallen into the 'power of an adverse Party shall be presumed to be a prisoner of war … if he claims the status of prisoner of war, or if he appears to be entitled to such status'.

14.4.3 Civilians

All individuals who are not combatants (or other members of the armed forces) are deemed to be civilians. Civilians enjoy general protection from the dangers of military operations and shall not be the object of attack unless they take a direct part in hostilities; conceptually, when a civilian participates in the fighting he or she ceases to be considered a 'civilian'.[73] Thus, while the law does not prohibit civilians from taking part in hostilities, they do so at their own risk. If civilians fall into the hands of the enemy in an international armed conflict, they enjoy protection under GC IV and—if applicable—AP I.[74]

Since civilians lose protection from direct attack when they take a direct part in hostilities, it is important to know when, exactly, an activity constitutes 'direct/active participation'. The ICRC lists three cumulative conditions that must be met for an act to amount to 'direct participation'. First, the act must be 'likely to adversely affect the military operations or military capacity of a party to an armed conflict or, alternatively, to inflict death, injury, or destruction on persons or objects protected against direct attack'. There is, in other words, a threshold regarding the damage or harm that results from the act in question. Secondly, there needs to be a 'direct causal link between the act and the harm likely to result either from that act, or from a coordinated military operation of which that act constitutes an integral part'. Thirdly, the act must be linked to the armed conflict by being 'specifically designed to directly cause the required threshold of harm in support of a party to the conflict and to the detriment of another'.[75] In most cases, of course, in their practical application, the

---

[72] See e.g. the critique in Dinstein (n 15) 54.   [73] AP I art. 51(2) and (3).
[74] See in particular Part IV.
[75] *Interpretive Guidance on the Notion of Direct Participation in Hostilities under International Humanitarian Law* (ICRC, 2009), see 46.

three elements may be interlinked. A particular cause of contention among states relates to the question of the point in time when a civilian loses his right to protection. According to article 51(3) of AP I, civilian protection is only lost 'for such time' as an individual takes a direct part in the hostilities. Thus, as the ICRC notes in its interpretive guidance, 'suspension of protection lasts exactly as long as the corresponding civilian engagement in direct participation in hostilities'. In effect, civilians lose and regain protection against direct attack in parallel with the intervals of their engagement.[76] The law thereby seems to acknowledge the existence of a so-called 'revolving door' in international armed conflict, where a civilian can cross in and out between protection and non-protection from direct attack.[77] As we will see in Section 14.7, the temporal aspect of direct participation thereby differs between international and non-international armed conflict.

14.5 The basic principles of the conduct of hostilities

14.5.1 Introduction

In *Nuclear Weapons*, the ICJ referred to two 'cardinal' principles of international humanitarian law: the principle of distinction and the prohibition against causing unnecessary suffering to combatants.[78] In fact, both principles are derived from the even more basic premise in international law that the 'right of belligerents to adopt means of injuring the enemy is not unlimited'.[79]

14.5.2 The principle of distinction

The principle of distinction dictates that when launching an attack belligerents are obliged to distinguish between, on the one hand, combatants and military objectives and, on the other, civilians and civilian objects. The principle is reflected in articles 48 and 52(1) and (2) of AP I and is a well-established principle in customary international law.[80] We saw earlier that combatants in an international armed conflict consist of members of the armed forces of a party to the conflict as well as other individuals who take a direct part in the hostilities. Article 52(2) of the Protocol defines a military objective as 'objects which by their nature, location, purpose or use make an effective contribution to military action and whose total or partial destruction, capture or neutralization, in the circumstances ruling at the time, offers a definite military advantage'. Thus, whereas some objectives are deemed to be military objectives by

---

[76] Ibid, 70.   [77] For a critique, see, inter alia, Dinstein (n 15) 147–149.

[78] *Nuclear Weapons* (n 9) para. 78.

[79] See 1899 Convention (II) with Respect to the Laws and Customs of War on Land and its annex: Regulations concerning the Laws and Customs of War on Land, art. 22 and 1907 Convention (IV) respecting the Laws and Customs of War on Land and its annex: Regulations concerning the Laws and Customs of War on Land, art. 22. See also Dinstein (n 15) 8–10.

[80] Henckaerts and Doswald-Beck (n 7) rules 1 and 7.

nature, such as the enemy's combatants, military aircraft and warships, others will only qualify if they are used in a manner in which they make an effective contribution to military action. If there is doubt about the military character of an objective, it must be presumed to be civilian.[81] This definition of military objective is derived from a doctrine of 'limited warfare', which was developed to limit the range of potential military objectives. Among other things, article 52(2) prohibits the practice of so-called 'strategic air warfare', known from the Second World War, where an objective would be considered a military objective as long as its destruction would lower the enemy's determination to fight.[82] Another important provision is article 51(2), which prohibits attacks designed to spread terror among the civilian population. In 2003, the ICTY convicted a commander of the Bosnian Serb armed forces on this basis for shelling and sniping the civilian population during the siege of Sarajevo in the early 1990s.[83] Also prohibited are 'indiscriminate attacks', which are attacks not 'directed at a specific military objective', attacks 'which employ a method or means of combat which cannot be directed at a specific military objective' or attacks that 'employ a method or means of combat the effects of which cannot be limited'.[84] Firing rockets blindly into enemy territory, for example, or resorting to the Second World War practice of treating clearly separate objectives in a target area as one single military objective ('area bombardment') is unlawful.[85]

Although *direct* attacks against civilians or civilian targets are prohibited, the law of armed conflict accepts civilian casualties and civilian destruction that are the result of attacks on military targets. As already noted, international humanitarian law is a pragmatic legal regime that balances military necessity and humanitarian considerations.[86] The law of armed conflict stipulates that even though states must seek to spare civilians and civilian objects, they may attack military objectives as long as the expected 'incidental loss of civilian life, injury to civilians, damage to civilian objects, or a combination thereof' is not 'excessive in relation to the concrete and direct military advantage anticipated'—also referred to as 'collateral damage'.[87] Like all tests of proportionality, the assessment of acceptable 'collateral damage' is context-specific and takes account of the operational realities of the battlefield. Thus, there is no fixed formula for determining when civilian casualties are excessive. Importantly, the assessment is based on information available to the decision-maker *at the time of the decision* to launch an attack and not when the consequences of the attack materialize.

14.5.3 **The prohibition against causing unnecessary suffering**

The prohibition against causing unnecessary suffering to combatants is primarily reflected in treaties that outlaw the use of certain weapons[88] and is well established

---

[81] AP I art. 52(3).

[82] See the discussion in H. Parks, 'Air War and the Law of War' (1990) 32 *Air Force Law Review* 139, n 412.

[83] *Prosecutor v Stanislav Galić*, Judgment, IT-98-29-T (5 December 2003).   [84] AP I art. 51(4).

[85] See also AP I art. 51(5)(a).   [86] Dinstein (n 15) 5–8.   [87] AP II arts 51(5)(b) and 57(2).

[88] See also the 1868 St Petersburg Declaration. For a thorough overview, see William H. Boothby, *Weapons and the Law of Armed Conflict* (Oxford University Press, 2009) 55–68.

in customary international law.[89] In practice, of course, suffering is an inherent feature of armed conflict and the prohibition only extends to suffering that is deemed 'unnecessary' or 'superfluous'.[90] What is prohibited are weapons the effects of which go beyond those required to put a combatant out of action (generally referred to as rendering a combatant *hors de combat*). Or, as the ICJ has formulated it, weapons that cause 'a harm greater than the unavoidable'.[91] The decisive factor is the nature and not the intention of the weapon and the prohibition against causing unnecessary suffering has played a role in banning the use of certain projectiles, poison, poisonous gases, non-detectable fragments, booby-traps, incendiary weapons, blinding laser weapons, cluster munitions as well as chemical and biological weapons.[92]

The horrific use of chemical gas in the war in Syria has brought increased attention to the ban on chemical warfare. Although the original objection to using chemical weapons was derived from the difficulty of controlling the release of chemical substances and the risk that both combatants and civilians would be exposed,[93] chemical warfare appears to violate ancient ethical objections to the use of poison as a weapon in war.[94] The ICTY has referred to chemical weapons as inherently inhumane.[95] The first prohibition on chemical warfare is contained in a 1899 treaty proscribing 'the use of projectiles the sole object of which is the diffusion of asphyxiating or deleterious gases'.[96] In 1925, the 'Gas Protocol' banned the use of biological and chemical warfare. The more recent 1993 Chemical Weapons Convention (CWC) prohibits not only the use of chemical weapons in times of armed conflict but also their development and storing, as well as military preparations for chemical warfare.[97] It also obliges states to destroy chemical weapons they may be in possession of, to dismantle their facilities for producing chemical weapons[98] and to comply with a verification and inspection regime.[99] As at October 2018, the Convention had 193 parties.[100] The ban on the use of chemical weapons reflects customary international law in both international and non-international armed conflicts[101] and chemical warfare is a war crime within the jurisdiction of the International Criminal Court (ICC).[102]

14.5.4 Nuclear weapons

The legality of using nuclear weapons has been debated since the invention of the atomic bomb in the 1940s. In *Nuclear Weapons*, the ICJ concluded that neither the

---

[89] Henckaerts and Doswald-Beck (n 7) rule 70.

[90] AP II art. 35(2). For a debate, see Dinstein (n 15) 63–67.   [91] *Nuclear Weapons* (n 9) para. 78.

[92] For a full overview and discussion, see Boothby (n 88).

[93] Richard Price, 'A Genealogy of the Chemical Weapons Taboo' (1995) 49 *International Organizations*, Winter, 82–83.

[94] See also the 1874 Brussels Declaration, which sought to outlaw the use of poison or poisoned weapons and the *1880 Manual on The Laws of War on Land*, Oxford.

[95] *Tadić* (n 14) paras 120–124.

[96] Declaration (IV, 2) concerning Asphyxiating Gases, The Hague, 29 July 1899.

[97] CWC art. I.   [98] Ibid, art. I(2)–(4).   [99] Ibid, art. IV.

[100] Organisation for the Prohibition of Chemical Weapons, *Status of Participation in the Chemical Weapons Convention as at 17 October 2015*, https://www.opcw.org/about-opcw/member-states/ (accessed 20 October 2018).

[101] Henckaerts and Doswald-Beck (n 7) rule 74.   [102] Rome Statute art. 8(2)(b)(xviii).

treaties that specifically deal with nuclear weapons nor customary international law as such prohibits the use of such weapons.[103] It did find, however, that the existing rules and principles, including the principle of distinction and the prohibition on inflicting unnecessary suffering to combatants, apply to nuclear weapons. It also noted that 'the unique characteristics of nuclear weapons' seem to make 'the use of such weapons ... scarcely reconcilable with respect for such requirements'.[104] Since the legality of nuclear weapons essentially depends on the risk of excessive collateral damage, the deployment of such weapons probably only complies with the law of armed conflict if they are used as a tactical weapon against a military target located far from a civilian population (such as in a desert or on the high seas).[105]

14.5.5 Emerging technologies

There has recently been much discussion about the legality of a number of emerging technologies that increasingly find their way into the military arsenal of states. For example, the use of *armed unmanned aerial vehicles* ('combat drones') has garnered a lot of attention, and in 2009 a former judge of the UK House of Lords suggested that drones could potentially be outlawed as a particularly cruel weapon.[106] It is, however, hard to follow the logic of such a statement. The combat drones currently in use fire conventional missiles and as such do not differ from other conventional weapon systems, such as manned fighter jets, battleships, submarines, helicopter gunships etc. While the introduction of remotely operated vehicles may raise both strategic and ethical issues,[107] they pose few of an international legal character. What is of interest to international law is not that a drone is operated from the ground but, rather, how (where and against whom) the drone and its missiles are used.[108]

Another issue of modern technology that has drawn substantial attention is the emergence of cyber-related means of warfare and the compatibility with the law of armed conflict of *computer network operations*. While there is certainly room for debate about the likelihood of so-called 'cyberwar',[109] it seems fairly straightforward to conclude that the ordinary principles in the law of armed conflict apply to cyber operations conducted in conjunction with more classic military operations.[110] The extent to which the law of armed conflict also applies when cyber operations are the only hostile interaction between two states is less certain. As the ICRC has noted, that remains to

---

[103] *Nuclear Weapons* (n 9) paras 62–63 and 67.   [104] Ibid, para. 95.

[105] See also Boothby (n 88) 222–223 and Dinstein (n 15) 86.

[106] British Institute of International and Comparative Law, 'Joshua Rozenberg's interview with Lord Bingham on the rule of law' (2009), http://www.biicl.org/files/4415_bingham_interview_transcript.pdf (accessed 9 October 2013).

[107] Paul W. Kahn, 'The Paradox of Riskless Warfare' (2002) 22(3) *Philosophy & Public Policy Quarterly* 2; Christopher Coker, *Waging War Without Warriors? The Changing Culture of Military Conflict* (Lynne Rienner, 2002).

[108] See also Philip Alston, 'The CIA and Targeted Killings Beyond Borders' (2011) 2 *Harvard National Security Journal* 282, 325.

[109] See, inter alia, Thomas Rid, *Cyber War Will Take Place* (Oxford University Press, 2013).

[110] Michael N. Schmitt (ed.), *The Tallinn Manual 2.0 on the International Law Applicable to Cyber Operations* (Cambridge University Press, 2017) Part IV, Rules 80–154.

be seen.[111] Even more profound challenges may be posed by the invention and subsequent introduction of *autonomous weapons systems* which, once activated, will be able to select and strike targets without human intervention.[112] Like the technology, the legal debate is only gradually gaining momentum. While some adopt a pragmatic view and argue that there need not be anything particularly disconcerting about the introduction of automated weapons,[113] others are more critical.[114] The question has even been raised whether the law of armed conflict is the proper lens through which autonomous weapons should be viewed.[115]

Article 36 of AP I specifies that contracting parties, in 'the study, development, acquisition or adoption of a new weapon, means or method of warfare', must determine 'whether its employment would, in some or all circumstances, be prohibited' by the Protocol or any other rule of international law applicable to the party.[116] Since not all states are parties to AP I, it bears noting that a general obligation to ensure that new weapons comply with the law of armed conflict has also been derived from article 3 of the 1907 Hague Convention IV.[117]

14.6 The regulation of belligerent occupation

As noted in Section 14.3.2, belligerent occupation is a form of international armed conflict governed by the law of armed conflict. In the law of armed conflict, belligerent occupation is primarily governed by the 1907 Hague Regulations, GC IV and customary international law. In general, the Regulations are based on the basic principle (discussed in Chapter 4) that occupation is meant to be of a temporary nature that does not alter *de jure* title to the territory. The primary duty on the occupying power is therefore that it ensures stability and protects both the economic and social life of the inhabitants.[118]

According to article 43 of the 1907 Hague Regulations, the occupying power 'shall take all the measures in his power to restore, and ensure, as far as possible, public order and safety, while respecting, unless absolutely prevented, the laws in force in the country'. While the first part of the article seeks to protect the inhabitants from a decline in law and order, even if it entails a risk to the occupying forces, the second part specifies that the occupying power must maintain existing laws and not replace

---

[111] ICRC, *Commentary on GC I* (n 15) art. 2, para. 256.

[112] For a debate, see Nehal Bhuta and others (eds), *Autonomous Weapons Systems: Law, Ethics, Policy* (Cambridge University Press, 2016).

[113] See Kenneth Anderson, Daniel Reisner and Matthew Waxman, 'Adapting the Law of Armed Conflict to Autonomous Weapon Systems' (2014) 90 *International Law Studies* 386–411.

[114] Human Rights Watch, 'Losing Humanity: The Case Against Killer Robots', Human Rights Watch and International Human Rights Clinic, 2012.

[115] See Hin-Yan Liu, 'Refining Responsibility: Differentiating Two Types of Responsibility Issues Raised by Autonomous Weapons Systems' in Bhuta and others (n 112).

[116] See also *A Guide to the Legal Review of New Weapons, Means and Methods of Warfare, Measures to Implement Article 36 of Additional Protocol I of 1977*, ICRC, January 2006.

[117] Boothby (n 88) 341.   [118] Dinstein (n 24) 94.

them with their own legislation unless it deems it absolutely necessary. Article 43 is supplemented by article 64 of GC IV, according to which the occupying power is only allowed to legislate when necessary to: (1) remove threats to the security of the occupying power; (2) implement the Convention; or (3) ensure the needs and welfare of the inhabitants.[119] Certain changes to meet human rights standards can also be made.[120] The restriction on introducing new laws may prove problematic in cases of prolonged occupation, and it may well be sensible to give more leeway to the occupying power when occupation drags on for many years and the new laws serve the welfare of the inhabitants.[121] However, the law of armed conflict does not generally allow fundamental transformations of the political institutions of government in the occupied territory. To be lawful, the sort of 'transformative occupations' the United States sought to impose on Iraq following the 2003 invasion would need a legal basis in resolutions from the UN Security Council.[122]

In order to protect the inhabitants of an occupied territory, article 49(6) of GC IV prohibits the deportation or transfer of 'parts of its own civilian population into the territory it occupies'. Article 8(2)(b)(viii) of the Rome Statute of the ICC also lists this as a war crime. The extent of the prohibition has primarily been discussed in relation to the Israeli settlements in the West Bank, which has been occupied by Israel since 1967. In *The Wall*, the ICJ concluded that the Israeli settlements in the Occupied Palestinian Territories (including East Jerusalem) 'have been established in breach of international law'.[123]

The final point worth making about the regulation of belligerent occupation concerns the basis for the use of force by the occupying forces. Here, occupation law is not entirely clear.[124] As a point of departure, however, when the use of force by the occupying power occurs in the course of maintaining general law and order and 'policing' the inhabitants of the occupied territory, it must be governed by law enforcement standards. If, on the other hand, the occupying power is confronted with active hostilities of the sort that characterize an active armed conflict, it may rely on the standards found in the conduct of hostilities. Depending on the circumstances, fighting between an occupying power and an independent organized armed group may amount to a non-international armed conflict that exists alongside the international armed conflict/the belligerent occupation.[125] Importantly, the use of deadly force by the occupying forces against insurgents or other civilians who directly participate in hostilities would seem to require that arrest is not possible without undue risk to the occupying forces.[126]

---

[119] See the discussion in Dinstein (n 24) 112–116.

[120] Tristan Ferraro (ed.), *Expert Meeting on Occupation and Other Forms of Administration of Foreign Territory* (ICRC, 2009) 68–69.

[121] Ibid, 72. See also Dinstein (n 24) 120.

[122] Ferraro (n 120) 71. See also David J. Scheffer, 'Beyond Occupation Law' (2003) 97 *American Journal of International Law* 842.

[123] *The Wall* (n 8) para. 120. See also SC Res. 465 (1 March 1980), para. 5.

[124] See the discussion in Ferraro (n 120) 110–130.		[125] Ibid, 124–127.

[126] *Public Committee Against Torture* (n 8) para. 40. See also Dinstein (n 24) 104. Interestingly, the Israeli Supreme Court and Dinstein seem to arrive at this conclusion without *explicitly* recognizing the application of human rights in times of belligerent occupation. For a discussion of the relationship between the law of armed conflict and human rights, see Section 14.8.

14.7 Non-international armed conflict

On the face of it, the vast majority of legal instruments in international humanitarian law are limited in their application to international armed conflict, including belligerent occupation.[127] This, of course, stands in stark contrast to the increase in non-international armed conflicts since the end of the Second World War and to the fact that civil wars may be just as bloody (at times even more so) than those of an interstate character. Currently, treaty-based regulation of non-international armed conflict is limited to Common Article 3 of GC I–IV, AP II, the 1954 Hague Convention for the Protection of Cultural Property in the Event of Armed Conflict, the 1993 Chemical Weapons Convention, the 1996 Protocol II on Prohibitions or Restrictions on the Use of Mines, Booby-Traps and Other Devices and the 1997 Ottawa Landmine Convention.

It is therefore of paramount importance that there has been a gradual movement in the direction of *greater application of customary international law* in times of non-international armed conflict.[128] As a rule of thumb at least, the limits imposed by customary international law on the conduct of international armed conflict are equally applicable to non-international armed conflict.[129] In a study of customary international humanitarian law, the ICRC found that the vast majority of the customary rules developed for regulating international armed conflict also apply in non-international armed conflict.[130] In *Tadić*, the ICTY stated that 'the distinction between interstate wars and civil wars is losing its value as far as human beings are concerned'.[131] Surely, what 'is inhumane, and consequently proscribed, in international wars, cannot but be inhumane and inadmissible in civil strife'.[132] The expansion of customary legal principles into the domain of non-international armed conflict has led to what some term a 'unification' of the regulation of armed conflict.[133]

There are, however, (still) notable differences in the regulation of international and non-international armed conflicts. First, the regime of belligerent occupation is inapplicable in non-international armed conflicts. Secondly, while the conceptual distinction between 'combatants' and 'civilians' also applies in non-international armed conflict in the sense that some individuals will participate in the fighting (and therefore may be liable to targeting and/or detention) and some will not, captured 'combatants' cannot benefit from protection as prisoners of war. Insurgents do not benefit from 'combatants' privilege' and upon apprehension by government forces are liable to criminal prosecution before national courts for participating in hostilities. A third difference between the regulation of international and non-international armed conflicts concerns the interaction between the law of armed conflict and international

---

[127] For a thorough analysis, see Sandesh Sivakumaran, *The Law of Non-International Armed Conflict* (Oxford University Press, 2012).

[128] See the debate in Dinstein (n 24) 205–223.   [129] Henckaerts and Doswald-Beck (n 7) xxix.

[130] See ibid.   [131] *Tadić* (n 14) para. 97.

[132] Ibid, para. 119. See also *Prosecutor v Blaškić*, Appeals Chamber (2004), para. 157.

[133] Lindsay Moir, 'Towards the Unification of International Humanitarian Law' in Richard Burchill and Nigel D. White (eds), *International Conflict and Security Law* (Cambridge University Press, 2005) 108–127. But see also Rogier Bartels, 'Timelines, Borderlines and Conflicts' (2009) 91 *International Review of the Red Cross* 35–67.

human rights law, which we will discuss in Section 14.8 below. Here, reference should also be made to the practical application of the temporal aspect of 'direct participation in hostilities' in non-international armed conflict. By virtue of their 'continuous combat function', members of an organized armed group which belongs to a private actor in an armed conflict can be targeted at all times, including in situations where the individual is not actively engaged in acts that are harmful to the enemy.[134] While the concept of continuous combat function exists in all armed conflicts, it is primarily of relevance in non-international armed conflict where at least one of the parties to the conflict is a non-state actor.[135]

14.8 The relationship between international humanitarian law and human rights law

As we saw in Chapter 9, it is now well established that human rights law—with due regard to its territorial limitations—applies alongside international humanitarian law in times of armed conflict. With regard to the practical application of the two regimes, the ICJ has stated that some rights may be governed exclusively by either international humanitarian law or human rights law, whereas other rights 'may be matters of both these branches of international law'.[136] In most situations, the simultaneous application of the two branches of law is unproblematic. After all, as the ICTY has noted, both human rights law and the law of armed conflict seek to protect the human dignity of every person and the 'general principle of respect for human dignity is the basic underpinning and indeed the very raison d'être' of the two legal regimes.[137] Thus, where possible, the relationship between the two legal regimes is one of coexistence.[138] One of the ways in which the application of human rights law in times of armed conflict may have practical significance is in relation to the interpretation of terms and standards contained in the law of armed conflict. Thus, when interpreting a provision in the law of armed conflict reference is often made to similar provisions in human rights law. In *Delalić et al.*, for example, the ICTY found that the definition of torture in the Convention against Torture was helpful when defining torture for the purposes of the law of armed conflict.[139]

When it comes to the application of human rights law in times of armed conflict, two things must be stressed, though. First, the application of human rights norms into the law of armed conflict must take account of the 'specificities of the latter body of law'.[140] Secondly, in certain circumstances, the norms contained in human rights law and the law of armed conflict differ fundamentally. Most pertinently, international

---

[134] ICRC, *Interpretive Guidance* (n 75) 70–73.   [135] Ibid, 71–72.

[136] *The Wall* (n 8) para. 106. See also *Armed Activities* (n 23) para. 216.

[137] *Prosecutor v Furundžija*, Judgment, IT-95-17/1-T (10 December 1998), para. 183. See also *Prosecutor v Kunarac et al.*, Trial Chamber (2001), para. 467.

[138] For a debate, see Sivakumaran (n 127) 87–99.   [139] *Delalić* (n 67) para. 459.

[140] *Kunarac* (n 137) para. 471.

humanitarian law allows substantial room for military necessity.[141] When the norms of human rights law and international humanitarian law cannot be reconciled, one must be given priority over the other.

The interaction between human rights law and the law of armed conflict is most relevant in relation to the use of deadly force and detention for security purposes/ internment, where the norms differ substantially. In *international armed conflict* the standards in international humanitarian law generally function as the *lex specialis*, informing the content of the human rights to life and liberty. Thus, in *Nuclear Weapons*, the ICJ stated that while 'the right not arbitrarily to be deprived of one's life applies also in hostilities', the 'test of what is an arbitrary deprivation of life … falls to be determined by the applicable *lex specialis*, namely, the law applicable in armed conflict which is designed to regulate the conduct of hostilities'.[142] As noted in Section 14.6, the Israeli Supreme Court has indicated that the law on belligerent occupation dictates that in times of *belligerent occupation*, if feasible, arresting an individual directly participating in hostilities is preferable to using deadly force.[143] To the present author, such a result will also follow from a reasonable application of human rights standards. In *non-international armed conflict*, the relationship between human rights law and international humanitarian law is less clear. The problem is the limited treaty-based regulation of non-international armed conflict and the absence of any explicit authority for the use of deadly force and/or preventive detention in Common Article 3 and AP II. Some argue that the gap in the treaty-based regulation of non-international armed conflict in international humanitarian law must be filled by human rights law, in particular with regard to detention.[144] In *Hassan v UK*, the European Court of Human Rights stated that 'the taking of prisoners of war and the detention of civilians who pose a threat to security' are 'only accepted features of international humanitarian law' in international armed conflict and that it is therefore only in such armed conflict that the right to liberty in article 5 of the European Convention on Human Rights could be 'interpreted as permitting the exercise of such broad powers'.[145] In the UK, both a High Court and an appeal court reached a similar decision in relation to the detention by British forces of a suspected member of the Taleban in Afghanistan.[146]

Other sources—including the ICRC[147] and the US Supreme Court[148]—adopt the view that the gap in the treaty-based regulation of non-international armed conflict in

---

[141] See also Kenneth Watkin, 'Controlling the Use of Force: A Role for Human Rights Norms in Contemporary Armed Conflict' (2004) 98 *American Journal of International Law* 10.

[142] See also *Nuclear Weapons* (n 9) para. 25 and ECtHR, *Hassan v UK*, App. no. 29750/09, Judgment, 16 September 2014, paras 102–104.

[143] See also *Public Committee Against Torture* (n 8) para. 40.

[144] See the overview and positions reflected in Sivakumaran (n 127) 93–99.

[145] *Hassan* (n 142) para. 102.

[146] *Serdar Mohammed v Ministry of Defence* [2014] EWHC 1369 (QB) [239]-[268] and *Serdar Mohammed and Others v Secretary of State for Defence* [2015] EWCA Civ 843, [242]. The UK Supreme Court left the issue unanswered, see [2017] UKSC 2, on appeal from [2014] EWHC 2714 (QB) and [2015] EWCA Civ 843.

[147] On the use of deadly force, see ICRC, *Interpretive Guidance* (n 75) 27–36. On security detention, see ICRC, 'Strengthening Legal Protection for Persons Deprived of their Liberty in relation to Non-International Armed Conflict', Background Paper, Regional Consultations 2012–2013, see 3 and 10.

[148] On security detention, see US Supreme Court, *Hamdan* (n 49) 12–15.

international humanitarian law is filled by customary international law and principles derived from international armed conflict.[149] The identification of the legal norms that govern non-international armed conflict is thus by and large an exercise in 'analogical or deductive reasoning' according to which states are generally deemed to have the authority to undertake the same practices in non-international conflict as they are in international armed conflict.[150] Since the law of armed conflict permits a state to use deadly force against combatants and detain civilians in international armed conflict, the law also permits a state to do the same in a non-international armed conflict.

The present author is inclined to side with the latter approach. The proposition— seemingly advanced by the UK High Court—that the authority to detain for security purposes can somehow be disentangled from an authority to use deadly force appears misguided. The two authorities must go together in the sense that it can only be demanded of soldiers that they accept surrender by the enemy if they can be certain that the latter can be kept in detention and thus removed from the battlefield until the fighting is over. In the practical application of force, however, a state may be obliged to take account of the overall circumstances that surround the armed conflict, including the ability of government forces to exercise physical control over an area. The ICRC has stressed that government forces should refrain from using deadly force if capture is possible without undue risk to government officials.[151]

Summary

The law of armed conflict regulates *how military operations must be conducted*. It is an inherently pragmatic discipline offering balanced solutions that take account of both military necessity and humanitarian sentiments. The law of armed conflict applies in times of armed conflict and the law differentiates between 'international armed conflict', involving the armed forces of two or more states, and 'non-international armed conflict', which involves fighting between either a state and a private organized armed group or between two or more such groups. International armed conflict includes belligerent occupation. All individuals have a status in times of armed conflict and the two most notable categories are those of civilians and combatants. While civilians must be protected from the effects of the conflict, combatants may generally be targeted and detained until the end of hostilities. The conduct of hostilities is governed by a number of basic principles, the most important being the principle of distinction and the prohibition against causing unnecessary suffering to combatants. While human rights law also applies in times of armed conflict, its practical application will sometimes be informed by the content of the law of armed conflict.

---

[149] See, inter alia, Dinstein (n 15) 226–230 and Sivakumaran (n 127) 98–99. See also Jelena Pejic, 'Procedural Principles and Safeguards of Violence' (2005) 87 *International Review of the Red Cross* 377.

[150] Ryan Goodman, 'The Detention of Civilians in Armed Conflict' (2009) 103 *American Journal of International Law* 50.

[151] *Interpretive Guidance* (n 75) 81–82. It must be noted, however, that the ICRC derives the duty from the laws of armed conflict and not human rights law.

Recommended reading

There is an extensive literature on the law of armed conflict. Solid comprehensive works include the contributions by Yoram Dinstein, including his *The Conduct of Hostilities under the Law of International Armed Conflict* (2nd edn, Cambridge University Press, 2010), *The International Law of Belligerent Occupation* (Cambridge University Press, 2009) and *Non-International Armed Conflicts in International Law* (Cambridge University Press, 2014). See also Dieter Fleck, *The Handbook of International Humanitarian Law* (2nd edn, Oxford University Press, 2008), Gary Solis, *The Law of Armed Conflict* (Cambridge University Press, 2010) and Andrew Clapham, Paola Gaeta and Marco Sassòli (eds), *The 1949 Geneva Conventions: A Commentary* (Oxford University Press, 2015).

On non-international armed conflict, see Sandesh Sivakumaran, *The Law of Non-International Armed Conflict* (Oxford University Press, 2012).

For treatment of relevant customary international law, see Jean-Marie Henckaerts and Louise Doswald-Beck, *Customary International Humanitarian Law*, Vol. I (Cambridge University Press, 2005), also available online: https://ihl-databases.icrc.org/customary-ihl/eng/docs/v1_rul.

On weaponry, see William H. Boothby, *Weapons and the Law of Armed Conflict* (Oxford University Press, 2009).

On the interplay between human rights and the law of armed conflict, see Kenneth Watkin, 'Controlling the Use of Force: A Role for Human Rights Norms in Contemporary Armed Conflict' (2004) 98 *American Journal of International Law* 1.

Questions for discussion

1. Why may one reasonably consider the law of armed conflict as a pragmatic discipline?

2. Has the international armed conflict between North and South Korea been brought to an end?

3. Are Ukraine and Russia engaged in an international armed conflict?

4. In 2011, US Special Forces killed the leader of al Qaida, Osama bin Laden, in Pakistan. Did the killing of bin Laden violate international humanitarian law?

5. In November 2015, individuals with alleged ties to the Islamic State perpetrated a series of terrorist attacks in Paris, France. Could the attacks be considered part of an armed conflict?

6. When it comes to the use of deadly force against individuals who are not members of the armed forces of a state, why does it matter if the armed conflict is classified as an international and not a non-international armed conflict?

7. How is the right to liberty regulated in a non-international armed conflict?

15

International criminal law

CENTRAL ISSUES

1. This chapter presents and discusses the purposes and principles of international criminal law.

2. It discusses the concept of an 'international crime' and the basic principles of international criminal liability as well as some of the relevant grounds for excluding criminal responsibility.

3. The chapter examines the prosecution of international crimes before international criminal courts, including the conditions for prosecuting suspected international criminals before the International Criminal Court (ICC).

4. The chapter also discusses the national prosecution of international crimes and the obligation found in a number of conventions to criminalize and prosecute certain conduct.

15.1 Introduction

International criminal law seeks to ensure that perpetrators of certain heinous acts are criminally liable for their acts before either national or international criminal courts or tribunals.[1] It is a fairly recent addition to international law and it was not until after the end of the Second World War that it became accepted that international law authorizes the criminal prosecution of individual perpetrators of certain serious offences. As illustrated in Chapter 1, the Nuremberg trials famously established that international law imposes obligations *directly* on individuals without the need for the interposition of national law. After the successful establishment and operation of two ad hoc criminal tribunals—the International Criminal Tribunal for the former Yugoslavia (ICTY) and the International Criminal Tribunal for Rwanda (ICTR)—in the 1990s, international criminal law has developed at an impressive pace and is now well on the way to becoming a legal regime in its own right. A noteworthy accomplishment was the adoption in 1998 of the Rome Statute for a permanent International Criminal Court. At the current stage of its development, international law limits criminal responsibility to individuals,

---

[1] In the following, the term 'international court' will cover both international tribunals and international courts.

and an effort by the International Law Commission to introduce 'state crimes' did not find support among states. Corporate criminal responsibility has not been established.

International law does not authoritatively define an 'international crime' and there are numerous ways of arriving at a definition. One approach is to limit the concept to four 'core' offences directly criminalized under international law: genocide, crimes against humanity, certain war crimes and aggression.[2] However, this book adopts a more expansive view and also includes in the definition a range of offences that international law obliges states to criminalize and in most cases also prosecute before their national courts, such as piracy, torture and a number of terrorism-related offences.[3] While the legal basis for prosecuting the four 'core' international crimes is customary international law directly, prosecution for other international crimes is based on the national laws of the states.

International criminal law is heavily influenced and informed by other branches of international law. For example, due to its original focus on prosecuting war crimes, it draws extensively on the law of armed conflict discussed in Chapter 14 and the definitions and distinctions contained therein. It is also influenced by international human rights law, discussed in Chapter 9, which helps define some of the international crimes, such as crimes against humanity and torture and provides the procedural guarantees afforded to individuals prosecuted for international crimes. Other relevant branches of international law include the principles of state responsibility discussed in Chapter 7 and those relating to immunity from national jurisdiction discussed in Chapter 6.

We begin in Section 15.2 with the most important sources of international criminal law. Section 15.3 discusses prosecution of international crimes before *international* criminal courts before Section 15.4 examines prosecutions before *national* criminal courts.

Before proceeding, it is important to clarify the distinction between 'international' and 'national' courts. Despite frequent references to so-called 'hybrid' or 'internationalized' criminal courts, in this chapter only two types of criminal court exist. A criminal court is either 'international' or 'national' depending on *the legal nature of its founding document*. Thus, if a court derives its existence and legal authority from an instrument of international law, it is an international court, and it is a national court if its existence is derived from an instrument of national law.[4] For present purposes, then, it is immaterial whether the court is composed of a mix of national and international judges or if it has jurisdiction to deal with violations of both international and national law. Because the International Military Tribunal (IMT) at Nuremberg was created

---

[2] See, inter alia, Antonio Cassese and others, *Cassese's International Criminal Law* (3rd edn, Oxford University Press, 2013) 18–21 and Robert Cryer, 'International Criminal Law' in Malcolm D. Evans (ed.), *International Law* (4th edn, Oxford University Press, 2010) 752, 754.

[3] For this approach, see Roger O'Keefe, *International Criminal Law* (Oxford University Press, 2015) 56–57. See also *Questions relating to the Obligation to Prosecute or Extradite (Belgium v Senegal)*, Judgment [2012] ICJ Rep 422, para. 75. International criminal law would thus include what some scholars (for lack of a better term) call 'transnational criminal law': see Neil Boister, 'Transnational Criminal Law?' (2003) 14 *European Journal of International Law* 953.

[4] See Astrid Kjeldgaard-Pedersen, 'What Defines an International Criminal Court? A Critical Assessment of "the Involvement of the International Community" as a Deciding Factor' (2015) 28 *Leiden Journal of International Law* 113. See also O'Keefe (n 3) 85–114.

pursuant to a treaty between the UK, the United States, France and the Soviet Union, it was an international court. The same goes for the International Criminal Court (ICC) set up by the 1998 Rome Statute (a treaty). The ICTY and the ICTR, the International Residual Mechanism for the International Criminal Tribunals (MICT) and the Special Tribunal for Lebanon (STL) were created by the Security Council under its treaty-based powers in Chapter VII of the UN Charter, and they are therefore also international courts. Similarly, the Special Court for Sierra Leone (SCSL) and the Residual Court for Sierra Leone (RCSL), created under a treaty between Sierra Leone and the UN. In contrast, the Extraordinary Chambers of the Courts of Cambodia for the Prosecution of Crimes Committed during the Period of Democratic Kampuchea (ECCC) derive their existence and authority from the national laws of Cambodia and are therefore 'national courts'. The many military criminal courts set up by the occupying powers in Germany after the end of the Second World War were also national criminal courts.

15.2 Sources of international criminal law

The primary sources of international criminal law are the treaties that establish the international courts, such as the 1945 London Agreement that created the IMT at Nuremberg and the 1998 Statute of the ICC. While the statutes only apply to the tribunal or court they establish and not to other courts, at least parts of the statutes reflect customary international law or may assist in the creation of such law.

In fact, customary international law is a very important source of international criminal law and, as we shall see later, prosecution of international crimes before international criminal courts is based on the premise that the crimes are prescribed under customary international law. Customary international law is also frequently relied upon when determining how to define an international crime.[5]

International courts also typically rely on 'general principles of international law', typically derived from domestic legal systems and over time recognized as principles of the international legal system. Noteworthy examples include the principle of legality and the disallowance of the application of ex post facto law whereby an individual is punished for an act that was not criminalized when the act was performed (*nullum crimen sine lege*).[6] Another general principle is the presumption of innocence, according to which the burden of proof rests upon the prosecution. As a supplement to general principles of international criminal law, courts have also referred to legal principles that are 'borrowed' from the national criminal systems of states.[7] Both international and national courts often make extensive references to relevant case law, and judicial decisions play an important interpretative role in the development of international

---

[5] *Prosecutor v Anto Furundžija*, Judgment, ICTY-95-17/1-T (10 December 1998), paras 137–138, 168–169. See also the lengthy discussion of how to define the crime of persecution as a crime against humanity in *Prosecutor v Kupreškić et al.*, Judgment, ICTY-95-16-T (14 January 2000), paras 567–626.

[6] For an overview, see Cassese and others (n 2) 22–36.

[7] *Prosecutor v Anto Furundžija* (n 5) paras 177–178.

criminal law. Seminal cases include the judgment in the trial of the major German war criminals at the IMT at Nuremberg,[8] the *Tadić* case from the ICTY,[9] the *Akayesu* case from the ICTR[10] and the *Lubanga* case from the ICC.[11]

15.3 Prosecution of international crimes before international courts

15.3.1 Introduction

This section provides an overview of prosecution of international crimes before international courts. We begin with a brief introduction to the international courts so far established, including the ICC (Section 15.3.2). Attention then turns to individual crimes that have been included in the jurisdiction of the international courts (Section 15.3.3) and a selected number of issues concerning criminal liability (Section 15.3.4) and possible defences (Section 15.3.5). We conclude with relevant due process guarantees (Section 15.3.6) and the extent to which immunity serves as a bar to criminal prosecution before international courts (Section 15.3.7).

15.3.2 International criminal courts

15.3.2.1 Ad hoc international criminal courts

The modern history of international criminal prosecution starts with the August 1945 London Charter establishing the *IMT in Nuremberg*, which criminally prosecuted some of the major war criminals of the Nazi regime.[12] The Tribunal had jurisdiction over crimes against peace, crimes against humanity and war crimes and, as already noted, it famously articulated the principle that individuals may be held criminally responsible directly under international law. The IMT has also been criticized, however, for allegedly violating the prohibition against applying ex post facto law in relation to (at least) crimes against peace.[13] The 1946 *Tokyo International Military Tribunal* was created to prosecute those with the greatest responsibility for the Japanese atrocities in the Eastern theatre of the Second World War.[14] Like the IMT in Nuremberg, the Tokyo

---

[8] *Judgment of the Nuremberg International Military Tribunal 1946* (1947) 41 *American Journal of International Law* 172.

[9] See in particular *Prosecutor v Tadić*, Decision on the Defence Motion for Interlocutory Appeal on Jurisdiction, ICTY-94-1 (2 October 1995).

[10] *Prosecutor v Akayesu*, Judgment, ICTR-95-4 (2 September 1998).

[11] *Prosecutor v Thomas Lubanga Dyilo*, Judgment, ICC-01/04-01/06 (14 March 2012).

[12] Agreement for the Prosecution and Punishment of the Major War Criminals of the European Axis, and Charter of the International Military Tribunal, London, 8 August 1945.

[13] For an overview and debate about Nuremberg, see Kevin Jon Heller, *The Nuremberg Military Tribunals and the Origins of International Criminal Law* (Oxford University Press, 2011).

[14] Special Proclamation, Establishment of an International Military Tribunal for the Far East, 19 January 1946. For a thorough overview, see Neil Boister and Robert Cryer, *The Tokyo International Military Tribunal: A Reappraisal* (Oxford University Press, 2008).

Tribunal had jurisdiction over crimes against peace, crimes against humanity and war crimes. On most of the principle legal issues, the Tokyo Tribunal reached conclusions that were similar to those of the Nuremberg Tribunal. The Tokyo Tribunal has been criticized as a particularly clear example of 'victor's justice'.[15]

After the Nuremberg and Tokyo trials, no international courts were created until after the end of the Cold War. In 1993, the UN Security Council reacted to the atrocities committed in the war in Yugoslavia by establishing the ICTY in The Hague, the Netherlands.[16] The ICTY—which ceased its operations in 2017—had jurisdiction over a range of war crimes, the crime of genocide and crimes against humanity and afforded primacy over national courts in the sense that it could oblige states to defer criminal proceedings to it.[17] Although the Court got off to a slow start, it ended up indicting all the main culprits of the worst atrocities in the Balkan war. The high-water mark was the indictment and subsequent surrender to the Court of the former Yugoslavian President Slobodan Milošević[18] and former President of the Bosnian Serbs Radovan Karadžić.[19] Although Milošević died in his prison cell before the Tribunal could render its judgment in the case against him, in 2016 Karadžić was found guilty of genocide, crimes against humanity and war crimes and sentenced to 40 years' imprisonment.[20] In general, the ICTY was a success and many of its rulings have had a noticeable impact on international criminal law.[21] In 1994, the Security Council set up the International Criminal Tribunal for Rwanda (ICTR) in Arusha, Tanzania, for prosecuting the horrendous crimes committed in Rwanda.[22] The Court—which operated until the end of 2015—had jurisdiction over genocide, crimes against humanity and certain war crimes, namely violations of Common article 3 of the Geneva Conventions and of Additional Protocol II. Like the ICTY, the ICTR was given primacy over national courts. Lack of cooperation on the part of Rwanda was an obstacle from the beginning and the ICTR has generally been less successful than its sister court in The Hague.[23] The ICTR and the ICTY shared an appeals chamber in order to ensure consistency in their interpretation and application of the law.

In 2010, the Security Council established the International Residual Mechanism for Criminal Tribunals (IRMCT) (also known as the Mechanism for International

---

[15] See, inter alia, Richard Minear, *Victor's Justice: The Tokyo War Crimes Trial* (Princeton University Press, 1971).

[16] SC Res. 827 (25 May 1993), UN Doc. S/RES/827.   [17] Ibid, art. 9(2).

[18] For the initial indictment (concerning Kosovo), see *Prosecutor v Slobodan Milošević et al.*, Initial Indictment, ICTY-99-37 (22 May 1999).

[19] For the initial indictment (concerning Bosnia and Herzegovina), see *Prosecutor v Radovan Karadžić*, Initial Indictment, ICTY-95-5-I (24 July 1995).

[20] *Prosecutor v Radovan Karadžić*, Judgment, ICTY-95-5/18 (24 March 2016). On 22 November 2017, in the last high-profile case, the former general in the Bosnian Serb Army, Ratko Mladić, was convicted of genocide, crimes against humanity and war crimes and sentenced to life imprisonment: see *Prosecutor v Ratko Mladić*, Judgment, ICTY-IT-09-92-T (22 November 2017).

[21] For a debate see, inter alia, Mohamed Shahabuddeen, *International Criminal Justice at the Yugoslav Tribunal: A Judge's Recollection* (Oxford University Press, 2012). Following the arrest and subsequent surrender to the ICTY in 2011 of Goran Hadžić (former president of the self-proclaimed Republic of Serbian Krajina) and Ratko Mladić, none of the 161 individuals indicted by the ICTY remain at large.

[22] SC Res. 935 (1 July 1994), UN Doc. S/RES/935.

[23] The ICTR indicted a total of 98 individuals of whom nine remain at large.

Criminal Tribunals—MICT) to finish the work of the ICTY and the ICTR.[24] While the MICT cannot issue new indictments, it prosecutes already indicted individuals arrested after the completion of the mandates of the 'old' courts. It also supervises the enforcement of the sentences rendered and makes decisions on pardons.

The *Special Court for Sierra Leone* (SCSL) was set up in 2002 to prosecute crimes committed in Sierra Leone from 1996.[25] The Court had jurisdiction over crimes against humanity and certain war crimes, namely violations of Common article 3 of the Geneva Conventions and of Additional Protocol II as well as certain other serious violations of international humanitarian law.[26] It operated from July 2002 until December 2013 when its essential functions were taken over by a Residual Special Court for Sierra Leone (RSCSL).[27] Apart from successfully prosecuting the former president of Liberia, Charles Taylor,[28] the Court primarily contributed to the development of international criminal law by concluding that the enlistment of child soldiers is a war crime under customary international law.[29]

The *Special Tribunal for Lebanon* (STL) was set up in Leidschendam, the Netherlands, by the UN Security Council to prosecute those responsible for the February 2005 assassination of former prime minister of Lebanon, Rafiq Hariri, and a number of other individuals.[30] As an international court, the STL is noteworthy because its jurisdiction covers crimes under Lebanese criminal law, most notably certain acts of terrorism.[31]

15.3.2.2 The International Criminal Court

The international courts listed in the previous section were established to prosecute crimes committed within a certain predefined context. The International Criminal Court (ICC), on the other hand, is a permanent international court for criminally prosecuting the 'most serious crimes of international concern'.[32] The Statute of the Court was adopted in Rome in 1998 and it entered into force on 1 July 2002. By November

---

[24] SC Res. 1966 (22 December 2010), UN Doc. S/RES/1966. See also Statute of the International Residual Mechanism for Criminal Courts in Annex I of the aforementioned resolution.

[25] Agreement between the United Nations and the Government of Sierra Leone on the Establishment of a Special Court for Sierra Leone, 16 January 2002, http://www.rscsl.org/Documents/scsl-agreement.pdf (accessed 20 November 2018). For a general discussion of the SCSL, see Jalloh C. Chernor (ed.), *The Sierra Leone Special Court and Its Legacy: The Impact for Africa and International Criminal Law* (Cambridge University Press, 2014).

[26] The SCSL also had jurisdiction over certain crimes under Sierra Leonean law but never relied on that jurisdiction.

[27] See Agreement between the United Nations and the Government of Sierra Leone on the Establishment of a Residual Special Court for Sierra Leone (n 25).

[28] *Prosecutor v Charles Taylor*, Judgment, SCSL-03-01-T (18 May 2012). For the sentencing, see *Prosecutor v Charles Taylor*, Sentencing Judgment, SCSL-03-01-T (30 May 2012).

[29] *Prosecutor v Norman (Fofana intervening)*, Decision on Preliminary Motion Based on Lack of Jurisdiction, SCSL-2003-04-14 AR72 (E) (31 May 2004), para. 25.

[30] SC Res. 1757 (30 May 2007), UN Doc. S/RES/1757.

[31] See art. 2 of the Statute of the Special Tribunal for Lebanon annexed to SC Res. 1757 (n 30). By August 2018, the Court had indicted a total of nine individuals, four of whom remained at large and one of whom was presumed dead. Two of the defendants were acquitted and the Court has yet to issue a conviction.

[32] Rome Statute of the International Criminal Court (adopted 17 July 1998, entered into force 1 July 2002), 2187 UNTS 90, art. 1. See generally William Schabas, *An Introduction to the International Criminal Court* (4th edn, Cambridge University Press, 2011).

2018, it had 123 state parties.[33] The Court is based in The Hague, the Netherlands, and its primary legal instruments are the Statute, the Elements of Crime and the Rules of Procedure and Evidence. The Statute of the ICC explicitly lists the sources available to the Court.[34] The primary organs of the ICC are the three divisions (the Pre-Trial Division, the Trial Division and the Appeals Division), the Office of the Prosecutor (OTP) and the Registry. The Court has jurisdiction over genocide, crimes against humanity, war crimes and—as of 17 July 2018—aggression, but the jurisdiction of the Court is limited to crimes committed after the entry into force of the Statute (1 July 2002).[35] With regard to states that have subsequently become parties to the Statute, the Court can only exercise jurisdiction for crimes committed *after* the Statute entered into force for that state unless the latter has declared its acceptance of the Court's exercise of jurisdiction in relation to a particular crime.[36]

From the outset, the ICC has been embroiled in high politics. The attitude of the United States has been particularly delicate and it has been critical of the Court from the beginning.[37] Along with only seven other states, the United States voted against the Rome Statute in 1998. Although then-US President Bill Clinton signed the Rome Statute on 31 December 2000, he recommended that his successor did not move forward with the ratification process until US 'fundamental concerns' were satisfied.[38] On 6 May 2002, the administration of President George W. Bush famously 'withdrew' the US signature to the Statute and informed the UN Secretary-General that the United States did not intend to become a party to the treaty.[39] Although US–ICC relations improved to some degree during the Obama administration,[40] they have worsened under the presidency of Donald Trump.[41]

In recent years, a number of African states have criticized the Court and its Prosecutor for focusing too much on crimes committed in Africa, including on prosecuting acting African heads of state. In response to the ICC's indictment of Kenyan president Kenyatta, in 2013 members of the African Union (AU) issued strong protests and even threatened to withdraw from the ICC.[42] Tension flared again in reaction to

---

[33] https://asp.icc-cpi.int/en_menus/asp/states%20parties/pages/the%20states%20parties%20to%20 the%20rome%20statute.aspx (accessed 20 November 2018).

[34] Art. 21.   [35] Art. 11(1).   [36] See arts 11(2) and 12(3).

[37] For an overview of the US position on the Court, see John P. Cerone, 'Dynamic Equilibrium: The Evolution of US Attitudes toward International Criminal Courts and Tribunals' (2007) 18 *European Journal of International Law* 277.

[38] 'Statement by US President Bill Clinton, authorizing the US signing of the Rome Statute of the International Criminal Court', Camp David, Maryland (31 December 2000) www.iccnow.org/documents/ USClintonSigning31Dec00.pdf (accessed 20 August 2018).

[39] John R. Bolton, Under Secretary of State for Arms Control and International Security, 'International Criminal Court: Letter to UN Secretary General Kofi Annan', Washington DC (6 May 2002) http://2001– 2009.state.gov/r/pa/prs/ps/2002/9968.htm (accessed 20 August 2018).

[40] Harold Hongju Koh, 'US Engagement With the ICC and the Outcome of the Recently Concluded Review Conference', Special Briefing (15 June 2010).

[41] Owen Bowcott, Oliver Holmes and Erin Durkin, 'John Bolton Threatens War Crimes Tribunal with Sanctions in Virulent Attack', *The Guardian* (10 September 2018) https://www.theguardian.com/us-news/2018/sep/10/john-bolton-castigate-icc-washington-speech (accessed 20 November 2018).

[42] See, inter alia, African Union, Extraordinary Session of the Assembly of the African Union: Decisions and Declarations (12 October 2013), Ext/Assembly/AU/Dec.1–2, Ext/Assembly/AU/Decl.a-1, Addis Ababa, Ethiopia.

the commencement of the trial against former president of the Ivory Coast, Laurent Gbagbo, and in October 2016 South Africa, Burundi and Gambia declared their intention to withdraw.[43] On 27 October 2017, Burundi became the first state to leave the ICC. In March 2018, the Philippines also notified the Court that it will withdraw and by March 2019 it, too, will have ceased to be a party to the Court.

Only a few points about the ICC will be noted here. First, in contrast to the ICTY and the ICTR, the ICC has not been given primacy over national courts and the Court cannot therefore oblige states to defer criminal proceedings to it. According to article 17 of the Statute, a case is inadmissible if it is being investigated or prosecuted by a state that has jurisdiction over it 'unless the State is unwilling or unable genuinely to carry out the investigation or prosecution'.[44] This principle of so-called 'complementarity' in practice means that national criminal jurisdiction takes precedence over the jurisdiction of the ICC.[45] Insufficient willingness may be found to exist if national proceedings do not seem consistent with a genuine intention to bring the person concerned to justice.[46]

Another interesting feature of the ICC is *the competence of the Office of the Prosecutor (OTP) to initiate an investigation* of potential crimes under the Court's jurisdiction. According to article 13 of the Statute, the Prosecutor may initiate an investigation in three situations.[47] First, a state party may refer a 'situation' to the Prosecutor and request the latter to investigate (art. 13(a)). Secondly, the UN Security Council may rely on its powers under Chapter VII of the UN Charter and refer a situation to the Prosecutor (art. 13(b)). Thirdly, the OTP may initiate an investigation on his or her own initiative—*proprio motu*—provided it obtains authorization from a pre-trial chamber (art. 13(c)).[48] By November 2018, the Prosecutor had initiated a total of 11 investigations.[49] Five of these had been referred to the Court by a state party and two by the Security Council. The Prosecutor has opened four *proprio motu* investigations, the most recent concerning alleged crimes against humanity committed in Burundi.[50] Four trials have so far been completed. On 14 March 2012, Thomas Lubanga was the first individual convicted by the ICC.[51] Since then, three more individuals have been

---

[43] Sewell Chan and Marlise Simons, 'South Africa to Withdraw from International Criminal Court', *New York Times* (21 October 2016) http://www.nytimes.com/2016/10/22/world/africa/south-africa-international-criminal-court.html?_r=1 (accessed 20 November 2018).

[44] Art. 17(1)(a). Article 17(1)(b) stipulates that a case is inadmissible if it 'has been investigated by a State which has jurisdiction over it and the State has decided not to prosecute the person concerned, unless the decision resulted from the unwillingness or inability of the State genuinely to prosecute'.

[45] See also *Prosecutor v Katanga and Ngudjolo*, Judgment on the Appeal of Mr Germain Katanga against the Oral Decision of Trial Chamber II of 12 June 2009 on the Admissibility of the Case, ICC-01/04-01/07-1497 (25 September 2009), para. 85. On the principle of complementarity, see Jann K. Kleffner, *Complementarity in the Rome Statute and National Criminal Jurisdictions* (Oxford University Press, 2008).

[46] Art. 17(2). See also O'Keefe (n 3) 556–562 and *Prosecutor v Saif Al-Islam Gaddafi and Abdullah Al-Senussi*, Judgment on the appeal of Mr Abdullah Al-Senussi against the decision of Pre-Trial Chamber I of 11 October 2013 entitled 'Decision on the admissibility of the case against Abdullah Al-Senussi', ICC-01/11-01/11-565 (24 July 2014), para. 2.

[47] Art. 13.   [48] Art. 15(4).

[49] https://www.icc-cpi.int/pages/situation.aspx (accessed 20 November 2018).

[50] See the overview at: https://www.icc-cpi.int/pages/situation.aspx (accessed 20 August 2018).

[51] *Prosecutor v Thomas Lubanga Dyilo* (n 11).

convicted, while one has been acquitted. By August 2018, the OTP was conducting ten preliminary examinations (the stage before a decision is made to open up an investigation) concerning, among others, alleged war crimes committed in Afghanistan since May 2003; alleged war crimes committed by UK nationals in Iraq during the 2003–2008 occupation; and alleged crimes committed in the Occupied Palestine Territories, including in East Jerusalem, since 13 June 2014.[52]

In practice, the jurisdiction of the Court depends on the manner in which a situation has been referred to it. Thus, when a case has been referred by a state party or if the Prosecutor has initiated an investigation on his or her own initiative, article 12(2) states that the Court may exercise its jurisdiction over conduct:

(a) that has occurred on the territory of, or on board a vessel or aircraft registered in, a state that is a party to the Statute or that has accepted the jurisdiction of the Court with respect to the crime; or

(b) when the accused individual is a national of a state party or a state that has accepted the jurisdiction of the Court.[53]

If, however, the case is referred to the Prosecutor by the Security Council, the Court may exercise its jurisdiction *regardless* of where the alleged crime was committed and the nationality of the suspected offender. The rationale for the absence of the limitations in these cases stems from the Security Council's powers under Chapter VII of the UN Charter to uphold international peace and security.

15.3.3 Crimes in international criminal law

15.3.3.1 Introduction

The legal basis for criminal prosecutions before international courts is that the prosecuted crimes are directly applicable to individuals in customary international law without the need for the interposition of national law. In fact, it is of no relevance if the offence in question is prescribed under national criminal law.[54] Four crimes are generally considered to be directly binding on individuals under customary international law: genocide, crimes against humanity, certain war crimes and aggression.[55] In the following, we will discuss each in turn. Before proceeding, it is important to note that a crime always consists of both a physical and a mental element. The physical element—known by its Latin term *actus reus*—is the conduct itself, such as the physical act of killing another human being. The metal element—in Latin, *mens rea*—is the psychological state of mind of the offender required for the conduct to be subject to punishment (the 'guilty mind').

---

[52] See the overview at: https://www.icc-cpi.int/pages/pe.aspx (accessed 20 November 2018).

[53] Special rules apply with regard to the crime of aggression, see Section 15.3.3.5.

[54] See also ILC, Draft Code of Crimes against the Peace and Security of Mankind, art. 1 and the commentaries to the article in *Yearbook of the International Law Commission*, 1996, vol. II, Part Two, 17, paras 6–10.

[55] Some include the crimes of torture and terrorism, see Cassese and others (n 2) 131–135, 146–158. See also Claus Kress, 'International Criminal Law' in Rüdiger Wolfrum (ed.), *Max Planck Encyclopedia of Public International Law* (Oxford University Press, 2009) para. 10. The ILC Draft Code of Crimes (n 54) includes crimes against UN and associated personnel, see art. 19.

Brief mention must also be made of the unusual case of the crime of piracy. Piracy is not a crime under customary international law, but as we saw in Chapters 5 and 8, there is a treaty-based rule in the 1982 UN Convention on the Law of the Sea and a customary international legal principle whereby all states may assert universal pre-scriptive jurisdiction over the crime of piracy.[56]

15.3.3.2 Genocide

As an international crime, genocide is part of customary international law and the prohi-bition against genocide is recognized as *jus cogens*.[57] Although genocide was not included in the jurisdiction of the IMT at Nuremberg, it was prosecuted as a form of persecution contained in the wider notion of crimes against humanity.[58] Genocide was included in the jurisdiction of the ICTY, the ICTR and the ICC. The definition of genocide is authori-tatively put forward in article II of the 1948 Genocide Convention according to which:

genocide means any of the following acts committed with intent to destroy, in whole or in part, a national, ethnical, racial or religious group, as such:

(a) Killing members of the group;

(b) Causing serious bodily or mental harm to members of the group;

(c) Deliberately inflicting on the group conditions of life calculated to bring about its physical destruction in whole or in part;

(d) Imposing measures intended to prevent births within the group;

(e) Forcibly transferring children of the group to another group.

With regard to the element of conduct (*actus reus*), the intentional killing of other human beings is the most straightforward way to perpetrate the crime of genocide. It may, however, be committed by other means, such as causing serious bodily harm or deliberately inflicting conditions that may bring about the destruction of life.[59] It is the subjective or mental element of the crime of genocide (*mens rea*) that sets it apart from other crimes. Thus, the distinguishing feature is the 'genocidal intent' and the intention to 'destroy, in whole or in part', one of the groups listed in the definition 'as such'.[60] The intention to destroy the group need not be realized—the intention suffices. Also, the intention need only be to destroy the group 'in part', such as within a limited geographi-cal area. Both the International Court of Justice (ICJ) and the ICTY concluded that the massacre of around 7,000 Muslim men at Srebrenica constituted genocide.[61] The victims

---

[56] For an overview, see also O'Keefe (n 3) 17–21.

[57] *Reservations to the Convention on Genocide*, Advisory Opinion [1951] ICJ Rep 15, 23. See also *Application of the Convention on the Prevention and Punishment of the Crime of Genocide (Bosnia and Herzegovina v Serbia and Montenegro)*, Judgment [2007] ICJ Rep 43, para. 161. See also *Prosecutor v Goran Jelisić*, Judgment, ICTY-95-10-T (14 December 1999) and ICTR, *Prosecutor v Akayesu* (n 10) para. 495.

[58] See also commentary to art. 17 of the ILC Draft Code of Crimes (n 54) 44, paras 1–2.

[59] See also the discussion in *Prosecutor v Akayesu* (n 10) para. 731. See also the Elements of Crimes for the International Criminal Court (adopted 9 September 2002), UN Doc. PCNICC/2000/1/Add.2, art. 6(c).

[60] See also *Prosecutor v Jean Kambanda*, Judgment, ICTR 97-23-S (4 September 1998), para. 16.

[61] *Application of the Convention on the Prevention and Punishment of the Crime of Genocide* (n 57) para. 297. *Prosecutor v Radislav Krstić*, Judgment, ICTY-98-33-T (2 August 2001), para. 598. See also *Prosecutor v Vidoje Blagojević and Dragan Jokić*, Judgment, ICTY-02-60-T (17 January 2005), paras 670–677.

must be chosen due to their membership of the group whose destruction is sought. In most cases, intent must be inferred from the factual circumstances surrounding the case.[62] In addition, what is important is not whether an individual actually belongs to the groups in question, but whether the perpetrator believes that that is the case.[63]

15.3.3.3 Crimes against humanity

One of the novelties of the Nuremberg trials was the inclusion in the Statute of the IMT of 'crimes against humanity'.[64] At the time, the crime sought to make up for the fact that the laws of armed conflict only covered acts perpetrated against enemy forces or enemy populations and not Germany's atrocities against its own population. It is questionable if crimes against humanity existed as an international crime at the time.[65] But that is no longer the case, and crimes against humanity can be committed both in times of armed conflict and in peacetime. The ICTY, the ICTR, the ICC and the SCSL all include jurisdiction over crimes against humanity, but the definition of the crime is not identical for each court.[66]

The physical element (*actus reus*) of 'crimes against humanity' are acts of serious violence committed during a large-scale or systematic attack against a civilian population. Under the Rome Statute, the physical element consists of any of the following acts: murder, extermination, enslavement, deportation or forcible transfer of populations, imprisonment or other severe deprivation of physical liberty in violation of fundamental rules of international law, torture, rape, sexual slavery, enforced prostitution, forced pregnancy, enforced sterilization, or any other form of sexual violence of comparable gravity, persecution, enforced disappearance of persons, the crime of apartheid or other inhumane acts of a similar character intentionally causing great suffering, or serious injury to body or to mental or physical health.[67] The physical act must form part of a more widespread or systematic pattern of violent acts against a civilian population. It is, in other words, the *context* in which the acts occur that elevates the acts to crimes against humanity under international law.[68] The term 'civilian population' refers to *any* civilian population and neither the nationality nor the geographic location of the population is decisive. The term 'civilian' is defined in accordance with the law of armed conflict and it thus excludes members of the armed forces of a state and members of certain organized resistance movements.[69] The requirement that the act of violence form part of a wider pattern of violence means that the perpetrator of the act must be aware of the existence of the widespread or systematic practice of violence against a civilian

---

[62] See also *Prosecutor v Akayesu* (n 10) para. 523. See also *Prosecutor v Radovan Karadžić* (n 20) para. 550.

[63] *Prosecutor v Radislav Krstić* (n 61) paras 556–557.

[64] See art. 6(c) of the Statute of the Tribunal (n 12).

[65] For a discussion, see Cassese and others (n 2) 86–88. It is worth noting that the crime had to be committed in connection with one of the other crimes within the jurisdiction of the IMT.

[66] The ICTY Statute limited crimes of humanity to acts committed in times of armed conflict.

[67] Rome Statute art. 7(1)(a)–(k). For a discussion of the status of art. 7 under customary international law, see Cassese and others (n 2) 105–108.

[68] See also *Prosecutor v Kunarac et al.*, Judgment, ICTY-96-23 and IT-96-23/1-A (12 June 2002), paras 93–94, 98.

[69] For the distinction in the laws of armed conflict, see Chapter 14.

population and that his or her acts constitute a part thereof.[70] In practice, therefore, there are two relevant mental elements (*mens rea*) that must be fulfilled. The first is the element required for the underlying offence (murder, torture, rape etc.) and the second is an awareness of the context of which the offence is part. However, although the perpetrator must be aware of the context, he or she need not agree with the underlying policy that provides the rationale for the overall attack on the civilian population. A crime against humanity may therefore be committed for purely personal ends.[71]

15.3.3.4 War crimes

A war crime is the 'classic' international crime and it has been included in the jurisdiction of all the international criminal courts with the exception of the Special Tribunal for Lebanon. As a legal concept, the term is linked to the relevant provisions in the law of armed conflict discussed in Chapter 14. However, it is not all violations of the many provisions in international humanitarian law that constitute war crimes covered by individual criminal responsibility under customary international law. As the ICTY Appeals Chamber noted in *Tadić*, a war crime 'must constitute a breach of a rule protecting important values'.[72] There is no authoritative list of which acts constitute war crimes and the content of the jurisdictional clauses of the international courts are not identical. It is, however, well settled that the term covers the so-called 'grave breaches' of the four 1949 Geneva Conventions and the 1977 Additional Protocol I[73] and other serious violations of the regulation of means and methods of warfare in international armed conflict, such as the 1899 and 1907 Hague Regulations as well as the 1977 Additional Protocol I.[74]

Certain acts committed in non-international armed conflicts may also constitute war crimes giving rise to individual criminal responsibility under customary international law.[75] In *Tadić*, the Appeals Chamber of the ICTY concluded that customary international law imposes criminal liability for 'serious violations of common Article 3, as supplemented by other general principles and rules on the protection of victims of internal armed conflict, and for breaching certain fundamental principles and rules regarding means and methods of combat in civil strife'.[76] The recognition that acts committed in times of non-international armed conflict may also constitute war crimes for the purposes of international criminal law has made the proper classification of an armed conflict as one of an 'international' or a 'non-international' character less important.

15.3.3.5 Aggression

The crime of aggression was prosecuted as a 'crime against the peace' at the Nuremberg and Tokyo IMTs. Like crimes against humanity, however, it was doubtful if aggression constituted a crime under customary international law at the time. As an international

---

[70] *Prosecutor v Kunarac et al.* (n 68) para. 102.   [71] Ibid, para. 103.

[72] *Prosecutor v Tadić* (n 9) 94. See also art. 20 of the ILC Draft Code of Crimes (n 54) and the requirement that a crime be 'committed in a systematic manner or on a large scale'.

[73] See, inter alia, the Rome Statute art. 8(2)(a) and (b). See also ILC Draft Code of Crimes (n 54) art. 20(a)–(c).

[74] See ILC Draft Code of Crimes (n 54) arts 8(2)(c) and 20(e).   [75] See also ibid, art. 20(f).

[76] *Prosecutor v Tadić* (n 9) para. 134. See also ILC Draft Code of Crimes (n 54) art. 8(2)(c)–(e).

crime, aggression has always been controversial and it was not included in the Statutes of the ICTY, the ICTR or the SCSL.[77] It was inserted in the Rome Statute, however, but agreement on a definition and the Court's jurisdiction over the crime was not reached until 2010 when a new article was inserted into the Rome Statute.[78] The new article defines aggression in accordance with the General Assembly's 1974 Definition of Aggression but includes a higher threshold for criminal conduct.[79] Thus, the *crime of aggression* is defined as the 'planning, preparation, initiation or execution' 'of an act of aggression which, by its character, gravity and scale, constitutes a manifest violation of the Charter of the United Nations'.[80] A violation of the 1974 General Assembly Definition must therefore be 'manifest' in order to be prosecuted.[81] The crime is limited to the absolute leadership of a state. Special provisions and procedures were inserted in relation to the Court's exercise of jurisdiction over aggression, including with regard to Security Council referrals.[82] The Court's jurisdiction over the crime of aggression was activated by the Assembly of States Parties on 17 July 2018.[83] After tough negotiations, the Assembly decided that, in cases of a state referral or a *proprio motu* investigation, the Court should not exercise jurisdiction regarding aggression when committed by a national or on the territory of a state party that has not ratified or accepted these amendments.

15.3.4 **Criminal liability**

The majority of the principles of criminal liability in international criminal law are familiar to a national lawyer. According to article 2 of the 1996 Draft Code of Crimes against the Peace and Security of Mankind, an individual shall be held responsible for an international crime when he or she:

(a) intentionally commits such a crime;

(b) orders the commission of the crime;

(c) under certain circumstances fails to prevent or repress the crime;

(d) knowingly aids, abets or otherwise assists in the commission of the crime;

(e) directly participates in the planning or conspiring to commit the crime;

(f) directly and publicly incites another individual to commit the crime which then in fact occurs; or

(g) attempts to commit such a crime.[84]

One of the more interesting forms of international criminal liability is the concept of *joint criminal enterprise* (JCE) applied in cases where more than one person is involved

---

[77] But see ILC Draft Code of Crimes (n 54) art. 16.   [78] See art. 8*bis*.

[79] GA Res. 3314 (XXIX) (14 December 1974), UN Doc. A/RES/3314(XXIX).

[80] Rome Statute art. 8*bis*(2).

[81] See also commentary to art. 16 of the ILC Draft Code of Crimes (n 54) 43, para. 5.

[82] See Rome Statute arts 15*bis* and 15*ter*.   [83] See ICC-ASP/16/L.10 (14 December 2017).

[84] ILC Draft Code of Crimes (n 54) art. 2(3)(a)–(g).

in the commission of an offence.[85] The rationale of JCE is that anyone who takes part in a common criminal act with an awareness of its purpose and who shares its requisite criminal intent must share the criminal liability. The core elements of JCE were discussed and articulated by the ICTY Appeals Chamber in *Tadić*.[86] Conceptually, conviction for a JCE requires:

(1) the existence of more than one individual involved in the commission of the crime;

(2) a common plan; and

(3) that the accused made a significant contribution to the crime.

In practice, three forms of JCE have been created. The first, JCE I, is where all the accused individuals act under a common design possessing the same criminal intention, such as an intention to kill.[87] The second form is JCE II—also referred to as the 'concentration camp' cases—where JCE is applied to offences committed by members of military or administrative units, such as those who run concentration camps and in that regard can be considered to be acting according to a concerted plan.[88] JCE II is a variant of JCE I. The third and last category of JCE is the controversial JCE III. Here, an individual is found criminally liable for participation in a 'common design to pursue one course of conduct where one of the perpetrators commits an act which, while outside the common design, was nevertheless a natural and foreseeable consequence of the effecting of that common purpose'.[89] When JCE III is applied, all participants in 'the common design' are held responsible for the crime regardless of the role they have played.[90] JCE III is controversial because it paves the way for prosecution for offences that did not form an explicit part of the common design but were merely a 'foreseeable' result thereof. Most cases against high-ranking political and military officials have relied on JCE III.[91]

Liability may arise not only due to the commission of a positive act but also due to a failure to take action—an omission. Under *the principle of superior responsibility*, for example, international law imposes criminal liability on a superior if he or she has failed to prevent or punish the criminal acts of a subordinate. In *Yamashita*, the US Supreme Court famously convicted a Japanese general for large-scale atrocities perpetrated by his subordinates in the Philippines during the Second World War even though it had not been proven that the general had any knowledge of the atrocities.[92] The doctrine of superior responsibility was subsequently extended to civilian leaders and supplemented with a requirement that the superior knew or had reason to know

---

[85] For an overview, see the discussion in Cassese and others (n 2) 163–178.

[86] *Prosecutor v Tadić*, Judgment, IT-94-1-A (15 July 1999), paras 195–220.

[87] Ibid, paras 196–201.   [88] Ibid, paras 202–203.   [89] Ibid, paras 204–219.

[90] See also the debate in Antonio Cassese, 'The Proper Limits of Individual Responsibility under the Doctrine of Joint Criminal Enterprise' (2007) 5 *Journal of International Criminal Justice* 109.

[91] See, inter alia, *Prosecutor v Radovan Karadžić* (n 20) para. 3524. See also *Prosecutor v Radovan Karadžić*, Second Amended Indictment, ICTY-02-54-T (23 October 2002), para. 8.

[92] US Supreme Court, *Yamashita v Styer*, 327 US 1 (1946). The principle of superior responsibility is reflected in Additional Protocol to the Geneva Conventions of 12 August 1949, Relating to the Protection of Victims of International Armed Conflicts (API) (adopted 8 June 1977, entered into force 7 December 1978), 1125 UNTS 3, art. 86.

about the criminal acts of the subordinates.[93] In *Delalić et al.*, the Trial Chamber of the ICTY listed three essential elements to command responsibility for failure to act:

(i) the existence of a superior–subordinate relationship

(ii) the superior knew or had reason to know that the criminal act was about to be or had been committed, and

(iii) the superior failed to take the necessary and reasonable measures to prevent the criminal act or punish the perpetrator thereof.[94]

The superior–subordinate relationship can be either an official (*de jure*) relationship or one based on effective (*de facto*) subordination.[95] Regardless of the relationship, however, the control of the superior must be effective.[96] International law thereby recognizes that a situation may arise in which a superior is aware that unlawful conduct occurs but is incapable of preventing or repressing the conduct. Conviction of a superior is conditional on the existence of information available which would have put him or her 'on notice of offences committed by subordinates'.[97]

15.3.5 **Defences**

As with national criminal law, international criminal law recognizes that the existence of certain grounds may exclude criminal responsibility. Under the Rome Statute, for example, a person shall not be criminally responsible if, at the time of the conduct, the person was mentally incapacitated and did not know that what they were doing was wrong.[98] Other grounds for excluding criminal responsibility include intoxication, self-defence, the defence of others and the defence of certain property.[99] Mention should also be made of 'duress', which refers to those situations where a person defends their conduct by claiming that it followed from 'a threat of imminent death or of continuing or imminent serious bodily harm against that person or another'.[100] Duress was recognized as a possible defence in some of the trials after the Second World War.[101] In the *Erdemović* case, the Trial Chamber of the ICTY accepted that fear for an accused's own life and that of his wife and child could constitute a valid defence, but it also found that the general duty to disobey manifestly illegal orders only receded in 'the face of the most extreme duress'.[102]

---

[93] See, inter alia, *United States v Soemu Toyoda* cited in *Prosecutor v Zejnil Delalić et al.*, Judgment, IT-96-21-T (16 November 1998), para. 339. See also the ILC Draft Code of Crimes (n 54) art. 6 and the Rome Statute art. 28.

[94] *Prosecutor v Zejnil Delalić et al.* (n 93) para. 346.

[95] Ibid, paras 377–378. See also the decision from the Appeals Chamber in the same case, *Prosecutor v Zejnil Delalić et al.*, Judgment, ICTY-96-21-A (20 February 2001), paras 197–198.

[96] *Prosecutor v Zejnil Delalić et al.* (n 93) para. 192. See also *Fofana and Kondewa*, Judgment, SCSL-04-14-A (28 May 2008), para. 175.

[97] *Prosecutor v Radovan Karadžić et al.* (n 91) para. 393 and *Prosecutor v Zejnil Delalić et al.* (n 93) para. 214.

[98] Rome Statute art. 31(1)(a). See also *Prosecutor v Zejnil Delalić et al.* (n 93) para. 582.

[99] Rome Statute art. 31(1)(b) and (c).   [100] Ibid, art. 31(1)(d).

[101] See the overview in the commentary to art. 14 of the ILC Draft Code of Crimes (n 54) 40, para. 10.

[102] *Prosecutor v Erdemović*, Sentencing Judgment No. 1, ICTY-96-22-T (29 November 1996), para. 18. It must be noted, however, that some of the Chamber's statements could be read to the effect that a plea of duress cannot be advanced in relation to crimes against humanity, see para. 19. For a debate, see Cassese and others (n 2) 218–219.

It has been a contentious issue whether an individual can defend their unlawful conduct by pleading that the acts or omissions were mandated by an order from a superior.[103] Although a plea of superior orders was generally accepted historically, things changed after the end of the Second World War, when it became generally accepted that an individual who receives an unlawful order is under a duty to disobey rather than obey.[104] The Statute of the IMT explicitly states that the 'fact that the defendant acted pursuant to the order of his Government or of a superior shall not free him from responsibility, but may be considered in mitigation of punishment'.[105] Similar provisions have since been concluded in the Statutes of the ICTY, the ICTR and the SCSL. In contrast, the Statute of the ICC seems to leave a small window open to a plea of superior orders. Thus, under article 33(1) an individual may be relieved of criminal responsibility if the individual was legally obliged to obey 'orders of the Government or the superior in question', if he or she 'did not know that the order was unlawful' and the order 'was not manifestly unlawful'. The article also stipulates, however, that an order to commit genocide or crimes against humanity is always considered 'manifestly unlawful'.[106] In practice, pleas of superior orders are rarely successful.[107]

15.3.6 Due process guarantees

It is well established that criminal proceedings must comply with the overall fair trial guarantees and principles of due process contained in human rights law.[108] The right to a fair trial was recognized in article 14 of the Statute of the IMT, and both the Statutes of the ICTY and the ICTR contained a number of fair trial provisions. Procedural protection is particularly strong in the Rome Statute, where article 21(3) provides that the ICC's application and interpretation of law 'must be consistent with internationally recognized human rights'.[109] The protection offered in the Statute is modelled on article 14 of the UN Covenant on Civil and Political Rights and the rights contained therein. Thus, international criminal law protects the well-established rights of an accused, including protection from self-incrimination,[110] the presumption of innocence,[111] the right to be informed of the charges and the opportunity to challenge them,[112] the right to trial without delay,[113] a public hearing[114] and the right to be present at trial.[115]

15.3.7 The question of immunity as a procedural bar to prosecution before international criminal courts

The statutes of international criminal courts generally specify that the official capacity of an accused individual is no bar to criminal prosecution and that the court may

---

[103] See Cassese and others (n 2) 228–240.

[104] See, inter alia, *Trial of Wilhelm List and Others*, US Military Tribunal, Nuremberg, 8 July 1947–19 February 1948, LRTWC, Case No. 47, Vol. VIII, pp. 50–52.

[105] See Nuremberg Charter (n 12) art. 8.   [106] See also *Prosecutor v Erdemović* (n 102) para. 15.

[107] For a brief overview of relevant case law, see Cassese and others (n 2) 232–237.

[108] See also art. 11 of the ILC Draft Code of Crimes (n 54). For an overview and discussion of the protections offered, see Cassese and others (n 2) 347–362.

[109] See also art. 64(2) and art. 84(8)   [110] Art. 55(1)(a).   [111] Art. 66.

[112] Art. 67(1)(a) and (d).   [113] Art. 67(1)(c).   [114] Art. 67.   [115] Art. 63.

also prosecute heads of state or heads of government.[116] The immunities for criminal prosecution for state representatives before *national* courts were discussed in Chapter 6 where we saw that personal immunity/immunity *ratione personae* offers extensive protection from criminal jurisdiction to certain high-ranking state representatives. It was also noted, however, that the ICJ in the *Arrest Warrant* case stated that a high-ranking state representative can be prosecuted before international criminal courts, where they have jurisdiction. In 2004, in a decision concerning the immunity of Charles Taylor, who was indicted while he was the head of state of Liberia, the Appeals Chamber of the SCSL relied on the ICJ *Arrest Warrant* case in holding that 'the principle seems now established that the sovereign equality of states does not prevent a Head of State from being prosecuted before an international criminal tribunal or court'.[117] And in the *Bashir* case concerning the criminal prosecution of the incumbent head of state of Sudan, the Pre-Trial Chamber of the ICC in 2011 concluded that neither sitting nor former heads of state can invoke immunity in opposition to prosecution by an international criminal court.[118]

If the decisions to deny immunity were based solely on the *international* rather than national character of the courts in question, they were misguided.[119] The reason why a state cannot invoke immunity before an international criminal court in relation to criminal prosecution of one of its officials or ex-officials is not due to the international character of the court but because it consented—in one form or another—to the court's jurisdiction.[120] After all, two states cannot adopt a treaty that alters the legal rights of a third state unless the third state gives its consent. So when determining if Charles Taylor was entitled to personal immunity from prosecution before the SCSL, the Court needed to ascertain whether Liberia had consented to the Court's jurisdiction.[121] In a similar vein, in the case against Bashir, the ICC needed to examine the extent to which Sudan had consented to the Court's jurisdiction. The ICC also seems to have corrected its practice.[122]

Consent to an international criminal court's jurisdiction may be both explicit and implicit. First, a state will be found to have explicitly given its consent if it has chosen to become a party to a treaty that establishes an international criminal court. Since

---

[116] See, inter alia, art. 27.

[117] *Prosecutor v Charles Ghankay Taylor*, Decision on Immunity from Jurisdiction, SCSL-2003-01-I (31 May 2004), paras 50–52.

[118] *Prosecutor v Omar Hassan Ahmad al-Bashir*, Corrigendum to the Decision Pursuant to Article 87(7) of the Rome Statute on the Failure by the Republic of Malawi to Comply with the Cooperation Requests Issued by the Court with Respect to the Arrest and Surrender of Omar Hassan Ahmad al-Bashir, ICC-02/05-01/09 (13 December 2011), paras 18, 34–36.

[119] The claim does, however, find support in the literature: see, inter alia, Cassese and others (n 2) 320–322.

[120] See also the overview in O'Keefe (n 3) 106–110.

[121] Since the Security Council did not adopt the Statute of the SCSL it would appear that the Court's indictment of Taylor constituted a violation of his personal immunity: see also O'Keefe (n 3) 523–524. It is worth noting, however, that Liberia gave its consent to the arrest and subsequent prosecution of Taylor when he left office.

[122] See also *Prosecutor v Omar Hassan Ahmad al-Bashir*, Decision on the Cooperation of the Democratic Republic of the Congo Regarding Omar al-Bashir's Arrest and Surrender to the Court, ICC-02/05-01/09 (9 April 2014), para. 26.

the Rome Statute is a treaty, state parties to the Statute have consented to the Court's exercise of jurisdiction and cannot therefore invoke immunity. Secondly, consent will also—implicitly—exist if an international criminal court has been established by the UN Security Council in accordance with its powers under Chapter VII of the UN Charter. Article 25 of the Charter stipulates that the members of the UN accept the decisions of the Security Council. The ICTY and the ICTR are examples of international courts set up by the Council. It is the implied consent of all member states to accept the decisions of the Security Council that explains why the ICC can exercise jurisdiction over a situation involving a state that is not a party to the Statute (e.g. Sudan) if it has been referred by the Security Council.[123]

15.4 National prosecution of international crimes

Despite the widespread attention garnered by the establishment of international courts, including the ICC, international crimes are primarily supposed to be prosecuted at the national level by the states themselves. In fact, the inherently subsidiary role of international prosecution is reflected in the principle of 'complementarity' mentioned in Section 15.3.2.2. For reasons of legitimacy, speed and overall logistics, and proximity to the place of the crime, domestic prosecutions are in most cases to be preferred over trials before international courts. In addition, unlike international prosecutions, national prosecution of international crimes is not limited to those core offences that derive their criminalization directly from customary international law.

There is a rich history of national prosecutions of individuals suspected of having committed international crimes, including one or more of the 'core crimes'. The majority of cases are connected to atrocities committed during the Second World War. A well-known example was the prosecution of former high-ranking Nazi Adolph Eichmann in Jerusalem, Israel, discussed in Chapter 5. More recently, national cases have been brought against individuals for crimes committed in the former Yugoslavia and Rwanda in the 1990s, including in Denmark where in 1998 a criminal court convicted a Bosnian national of war crimes committed in a Croatian detention camp.[124] In 2001, a Belgian court prosecuted a number of Rwandan nationals for crimes, including war crimes, committed in Rwanda in 1994,[125] and Sweden has twice prosecuted former Rwandan citizens for genocide. In the last such case, in May 2016 a Swedish court convicted a (now) Swedish national of participating in widespread massacres of Tutsis.[126] Domestic prosecutions of international crimes have also been conducted before a number of national courts with 'special jurisdiction' set up with international assistance, such as the criminal prosecution of former high-ranking members of the Khmer Rouge before the Extraordinary

---

[123] See Rome Statute art. 13(b). See also *Prosecutor v Omar Hassan Ahmad al-Bashir* (n 118) paras 29–30.
[124] UfR1995.838H.
[125] *Public Prosecutor v The 'Butare Four'*, Assize Court of Brussels, verdict of 8 June 2001.
[126] B 12882-14, 16 May 2016.

Chambers of the Courts of Cambodia (ECCC).[127] Other examples include the special courts set up under the District Court of Dili in East Timor by the UN Transitional Administration in East Timor (UNTAET),[128] the introduction of specialized sections for war crimes in Bosnia and Herzegovina,[129] an International Crimes Tribunal in Kosovo,[130] an International Crimes Division in the High Court of Uganda[131] and the Extraordinary African Chambers in Senegal, which in May 2016 convicted the former president of Chad, Hissène Habré, for crimes against humanity.[132]

The primary basis for prosecuting international crimes nationally is the many conventions that oblige states to criminalize and/or prosecute certain international crimes before their national courts. The purpose of these conventions is to prevent individuals suspected of the conduct in question from going unpunished. While the precise contents of the treaties differ, they generally oblige states to enact legislation that will enable them to assert prescriptive jurisdiction over certain offences on the basis of the principles of universal jurisdiction we visited in Chapter 5.

At times, national prosecution of international crimes is complicated by the existence of legal impediments particular to the state in question. Most states operate with *statutes of limitation* according to which prosecution for certain crimes may not be initiated after a specified period of time (e.g. 10 or 20 years) has elapsed. Restrictions on limiting the period during which international crimes can be prosecuted are found in treaty law.[133] Another domestic legal impediment is a *grant of amnesty* where national decision-makers have decided that conduct which was once criminal is no longer considered unlawful, with the consequence that the authorities are then barred from initiating criminal proceedings.[134] An amnesty for genocide would appear to be incompatible with article 1 of the 1948 Genocide Convention, according to which the state parties undertake to 'prevent and to punish' the crime of genocide. Amnesties may also violate a treaty-based obligation to prosecute or extradite (*aut dedere aut judicare*), especially if the grant of amnesty is not a result of a genuine wish to promote reconciliation in society.[135]

---

[127] Law on the Establishment of Extraordinary Chambers in the Courts of Cambodia (as amended on 27 October 2004), art. 2. See also Agreement between the United Nations and the Royal Government of Cambodia concerning the prosecution under Cambodian law of crimes committed during the period of Democratic Kampuchea, Phnom Penh, 6 June 2003 (ECCC Agreement), art. 1.

[128] See SC Res. 1272 (25 October 1999), UN Doc. S/RES/1271.   [129] See O'Keefe (n 3) 389–390.

[130] Ibid, 401–402.   [131] Ibid, 395.

[132] For an overview and discussion, see Sarah Williams, 'The Extraordinary African Chambers in the Senegalese Courts: An African Solution to an African Problem?' (2013) 11 *Journal of International Criminal Justice* 1139.

[133] See the Convention on the Non-Applicability of Statutory Limitations to War Crimes and Crimes Against Humanity (adopted 26 November 1968, entered into force 11 November 1970), 754 UNTS 73; International Convention for the Protection of All Persons from Enforced Disappearance (adopted 20 December 2006, entered into force 23 December 2010), 2716 UNTS 48088, art. 8(1) and the OECD Convention on Combating Bribery of Foreign Public Officials in International Business Transactions (adopted 17 December 1997, entered into force 15 February 1999), DAFFE/IME/BR(97)20. See also *Prosecutor v Anto Furundžija* (n 5) para. 157, and from the Inter-American Court of Human Rights, *Barrios Alto v Peru*, 14 March 2001, Series C, No 75 (2001) para. 41. See Cassese and others (n 2) 315.

[134] For a debate and overview, see John Duggard, 'Dealing with the Crimes of the Past Regime: Is Amnesty Still an Option?' (1999) 12 *Leiden Journal of International Law* 1001.

[135] See also ECtHR, *Ould Dah v France*, App. no. 13113/03, 17 March 2009, 17; Human Rights Committee, 'General Comment No. 20: Article 7: Compilation of General Comments and General Recommendations Adopted by Human Rights Treaty Bodies' (1994), UN Doc. HRI/GEN/1/Rev.1, para. 15; O'Keefe (n 3) 474–475.

Summary

International criminal law is a fairly recent addition to international law. It seeks to ensure that perpetrators of certain heinous acts are criminally liable for their acts either before national or before international criminal courts or tribunals. Prosecution of international crimes occurs either before international courts or before national courts. International courts consist of both ad hoc and permanent criminal courts—the ICC. International courts generally have jurisdiction over a number of core international crimes that are directly prescribed under customary international law: genocide, crimes against humanity, war crimes and aggression. The principles of liability and possible defences are well known to national lawyers. National prosecution of international crimes may relate to both the core international crimes as well as the offences listed in a number of conventions that generally oblige states to either prosecute or extradite individuals, located on their territory, who are suspected of committing the listed offences.

Recommended reading

The literature on international criminal law is growing rapidly. Major general works include Roger O'Keefe, *International Criminal Law* (Oxford University Press, 2015); Antonio Cassese and others, *Cassese's International Criminal Law* (3rd edn, Oxford University Press, 2013); William A. Schabas (ed.), *The Cambridge Companion to International Criminal Law* (Cambridge University Press, 2016); and Robert Cryer and others, *An Introduction to International Criminal Law and Procedure* (3rd edn, Cambridge University Press, 2014).

On the distinction between international and national criminal courts, see Astrid Kjeldgaard-Pedersen, 'What Defines an International Criminal Court? A Critical Assessment of "the Involvement of the International Community" as a Deciding Factor' (2015) 28 *Leiden Journal of International Law* 113.

For the ICC, see William Schabas, *An Introduction to the International Criminal Court* (4th edn, Cambridge University Press, 2011). On the principle of complementarity, see Jann K. Kleffner, *Complementarity in the Rome Statute and National Criminal Jurisdictions* (Oxford University Press, 2008). For an overview of the process that led to the agreement on the crime of aggression in the ICC, see Claus Kress and Leonie von Holtzendorff, 'The Kampala Compromise on the Crime of Aggression' (2010) 8 *Journal of International Criminal Justice* 1179. A debate about JCE is available in Jens David Ohlin, 'Joint Intentions to Commit International Crimes' (2011) 11 *Chicago Journal of International Law* 693, 706–709. On immunity and the ICC, see Dapo Akande, 'International Law Immunities and the International Criminal Court' (2004) 98 *American Journal of International Law* 407.

Questions for discussion

1. Conceptually, what is the difference between an 'international' and a 'national' criminal court?

2. Why are some international crimes referred to as 'core' crimes?

3. What does the principle of 'complementarity' in the Rome Statute mean?

4. The United States is not a party to the Rome Statute. What would it require for US servicemen to be prosecuted before the ICC?

5. What are the differences between the three forms of Joint Criminal Enterprise (JCE)? Why is the third form deemed to be controversial?

6. The power of the Security Council to refer a situation to the ICC Prosecutor includes a situation that involves nationals of a state that is not a party to the Rome Statute. Why does a Council referral not violate the consensual nature of the jurisdiction of the ICC?

Glossary

AD HOC Formed for a particular purpose.

AUT DEDERE AUT JUDICARE The principle that requires a state to either prosecute or extradite an individual to another state.

DE JURE As of right or law.

DELICTA JURIS GENTIUM Crimes against public international law.

DEROGATION The non-application of a rule.

ERGA OMNES OBLIGATIONS Obligations not merely owed to another state but to the international community as a whole.

EX AEQUO ET BONO A decision or judgment based on such general principles as a court find appropriate.

EX INJURIA JUS NON ORITUR A principle that legal rights cannot arise from wrongful conduct.

FORCE MAJEURE The occurrence of an irresistible or unforeseen force.

FORUM PROROGATUM A court's jurisdiction on the basis of consent after a case has been submitted.

GOOD FAITH A principle that stipulates that states must act honestly in the fulfilment of their international obligations.

IN ABSENTIA Trials conducted without the presence of the accused.

INTER ALIA Among other things.

INTER SE Between the parties.

JURE GESTIONIS State acts of a commercial character.

JURE IMPERII State acts of a sovereign or governmental nature.

JUS AD BELLUM The international legal regulation of the use of force.

JUS COGENS OBLIGATIONS Norms accepted and recognized by the international community of states as a whole as obligations from which no derogation is permitted.

JUS GENTIUM A law of people or nations, in the Middle Ages considered inferior to JUS NATURALE (see below).

JUS IN BELLO The international regulation of the conduct of hostilities.

JUS NATURALE Natural law meaning an all-embracing range of ideas about natural and social life in the universe.

LEX POSTERIOR A principle that stipulates that law which is later in time prevails.

LEX SPECIALIS A principle that stipulates that in a case of conflict between a norm of general and specific character, the latter prevails.

MALA CAPTUS, BENE DETENTUS A principle whereby a state can prosecute an individual even if he or she was brought before the court by irregular means.

NE BIS IN IDEM A principle that specifies that an individual should not be punished twice for the same offence. Also referred to as 'double jeopardy'.

NON-REFOULEMENT The obligation not to return an individual to a state where he or she is at risk of being subjected to ill-treatment.

NULLUM CRIMEN SINE LEGE The principle that no crime can be committed unless it was considered a crime at the time of its commission. Also referred to as the principle of legality.

OPINIO JURIS The belief that a practice is obligatory and a requirement in the formation of customary international law.

PACTA SUNT SERVANDA The fundamental rule that a treaty is binding on the parties.

PERSONA NON GRATA An unwelcome individual. Used in diplomatic relations to refer to an individual who is considered unwanted on the territory of the receiving state.

RATIONE MATERIAE By reason of the subject matter in question.

RATIONE PERSONAE By reason of the person.

REBUS SIC STANTIBUS A claim that an obligation has terminated due to a fundamental change in circumstances.

RES COMMUNIS Territory not open to acquisition by any states but instead available for the enjoyment of any member of the international community.

RES JUDICATA The principle that a decision is final and a matter already dealt with should not be reopened.

RESERVATION A caveat or an exception to acceptance of a treaty.

SUI GENERIS Falling outside the normal categories.

TERRA NULLIUS Territory that does not belong to any state or people. Also known as 'no man's land'. Unlike *RES COMMUNIS*, *TERRA NULLIUS* is open to occupation and acquisition.

TRAVAUX PRÉPARATOIRES Material preparatory to a treaty, often derived from a conference.

ULTRA VIRES Not authorized by a legal power.

UTI POSSIDETIS A principle that stipulates that borders and frontiers of emerging states conform to those of the 'old' state or territory.

Index